AF505104

EMPTY QUARTER

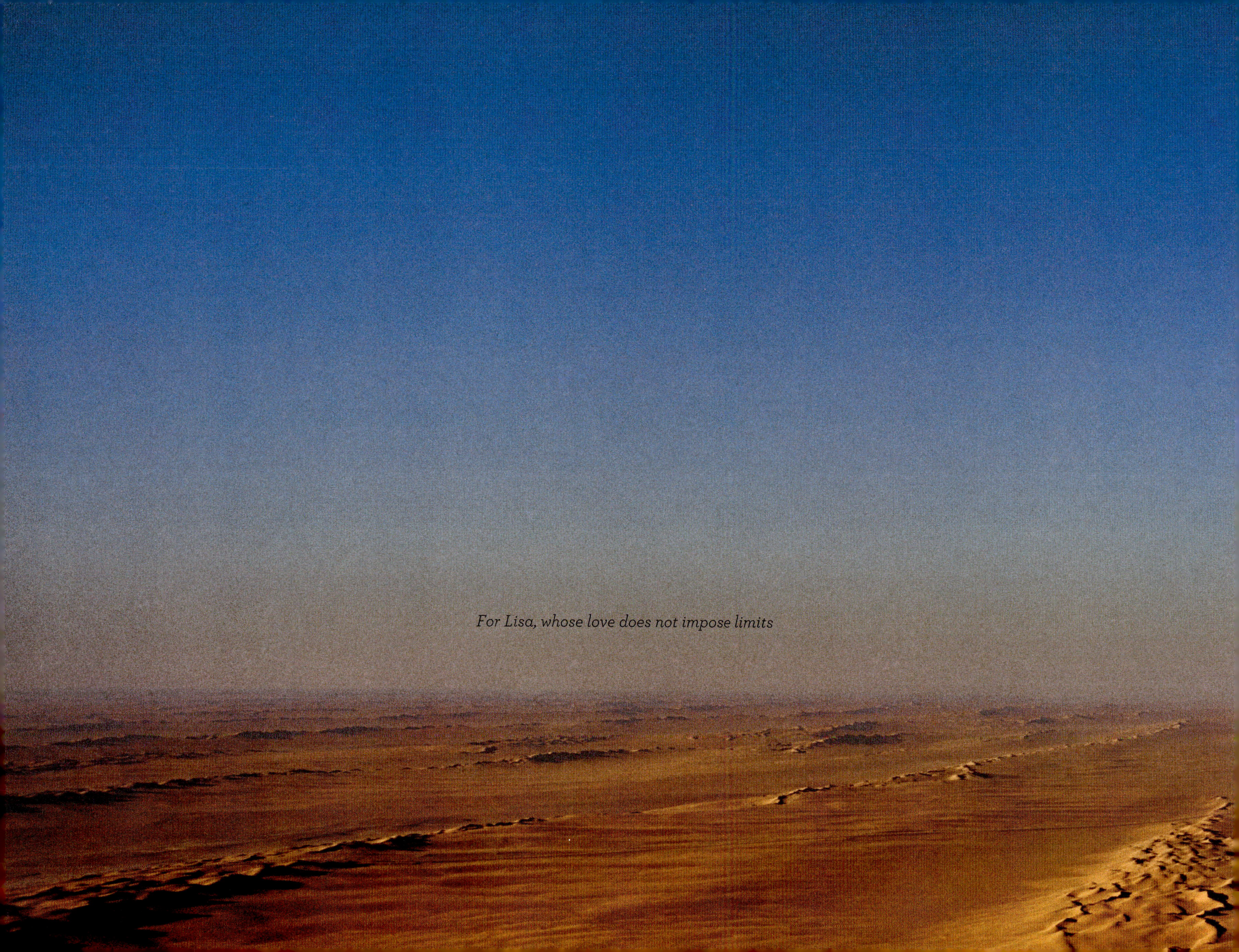

For Lisa, whose love does not impose limits

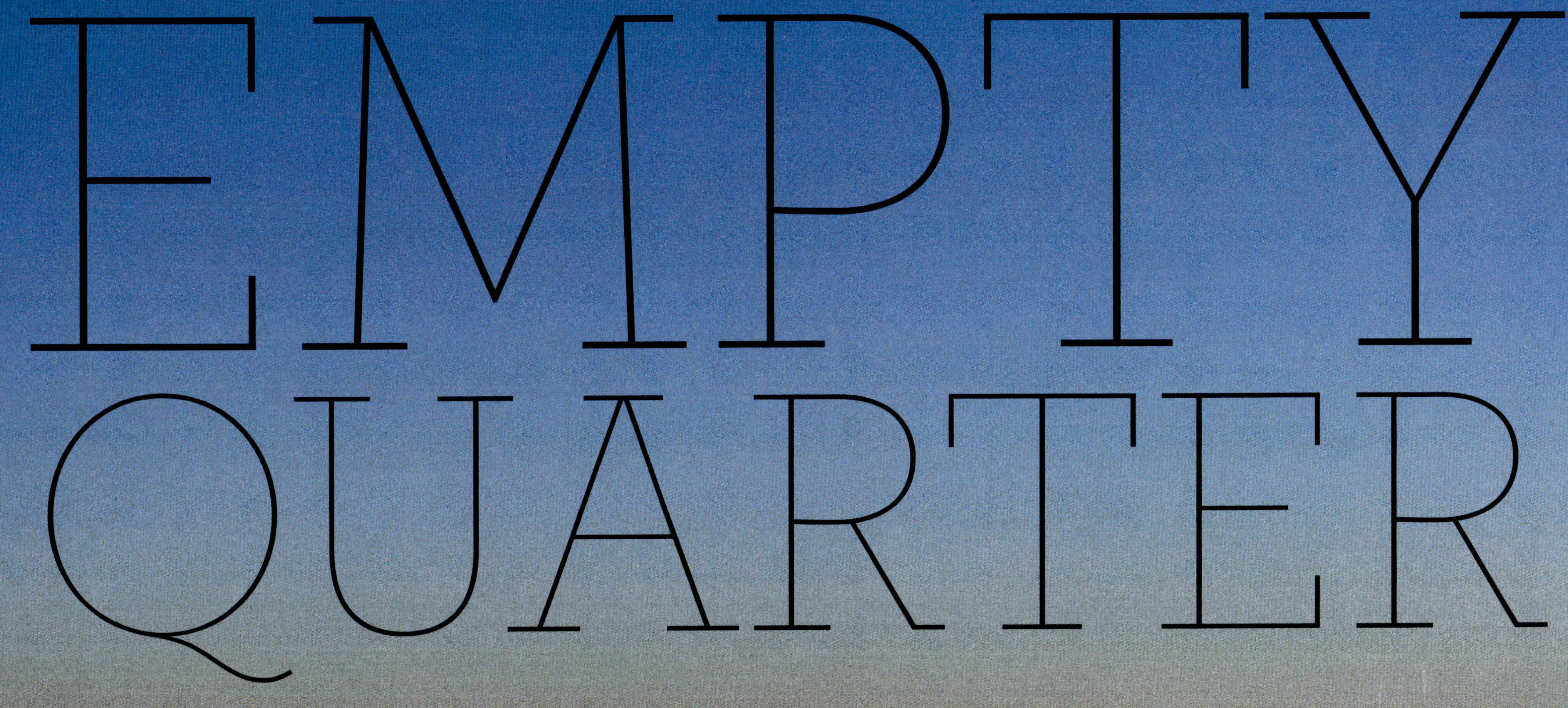

EMPTY QUARTER

A PHOTOGRAPHIC JOURNEY TO THE HEART OF THE ARABIAN DESERT

GEORGE STEINMETZ

ABRAMS, NEW YORK

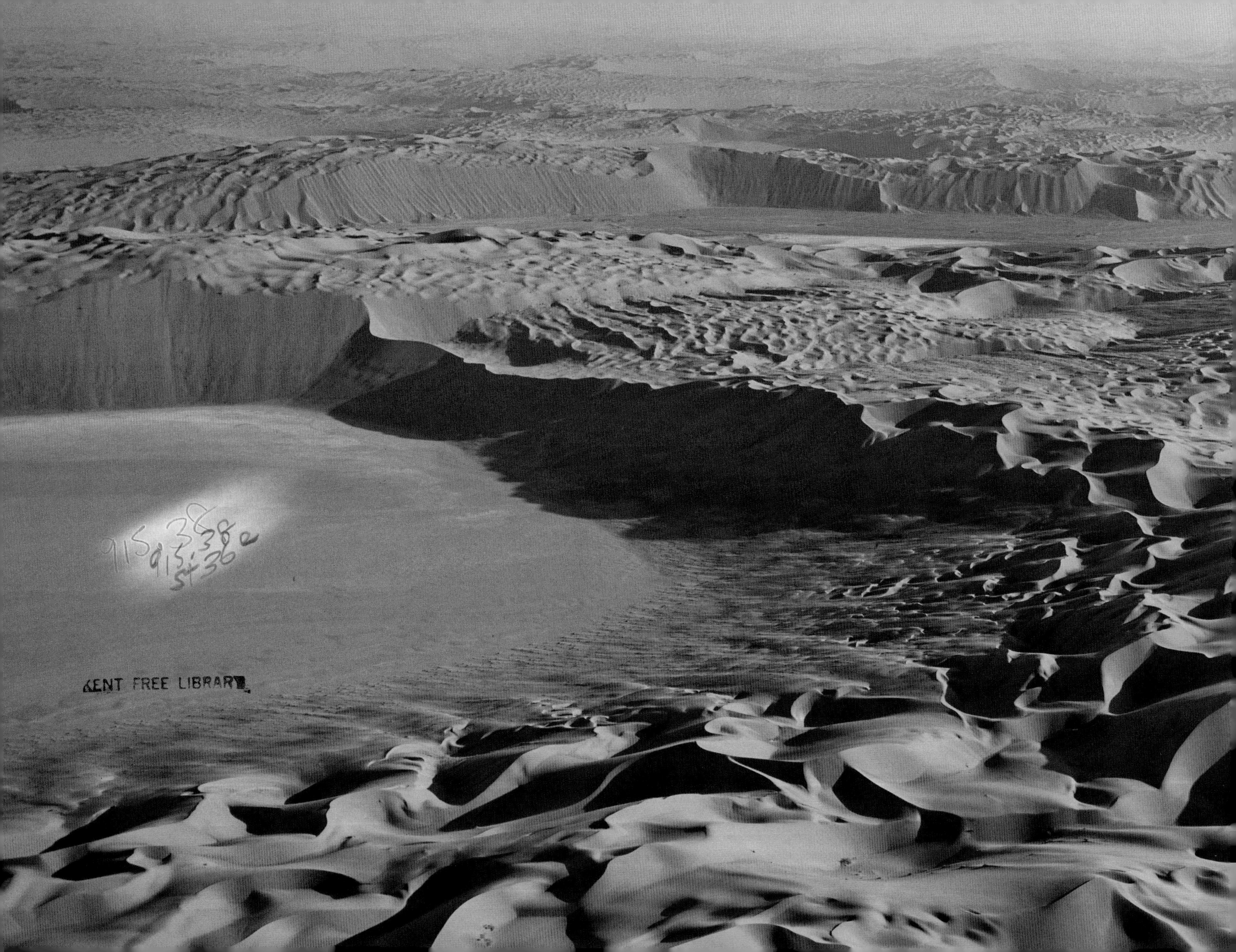
915.38
915.38 e
st 36

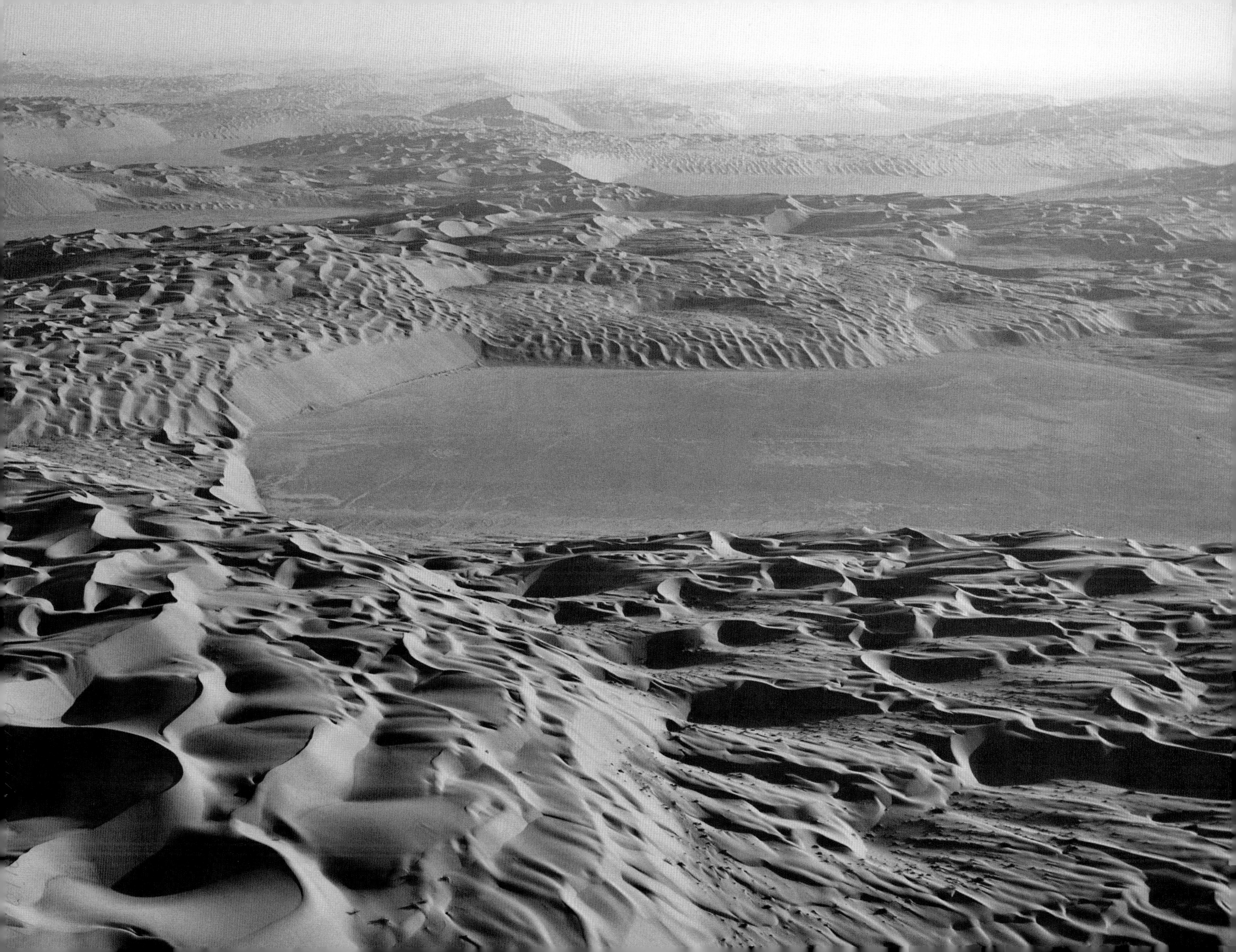

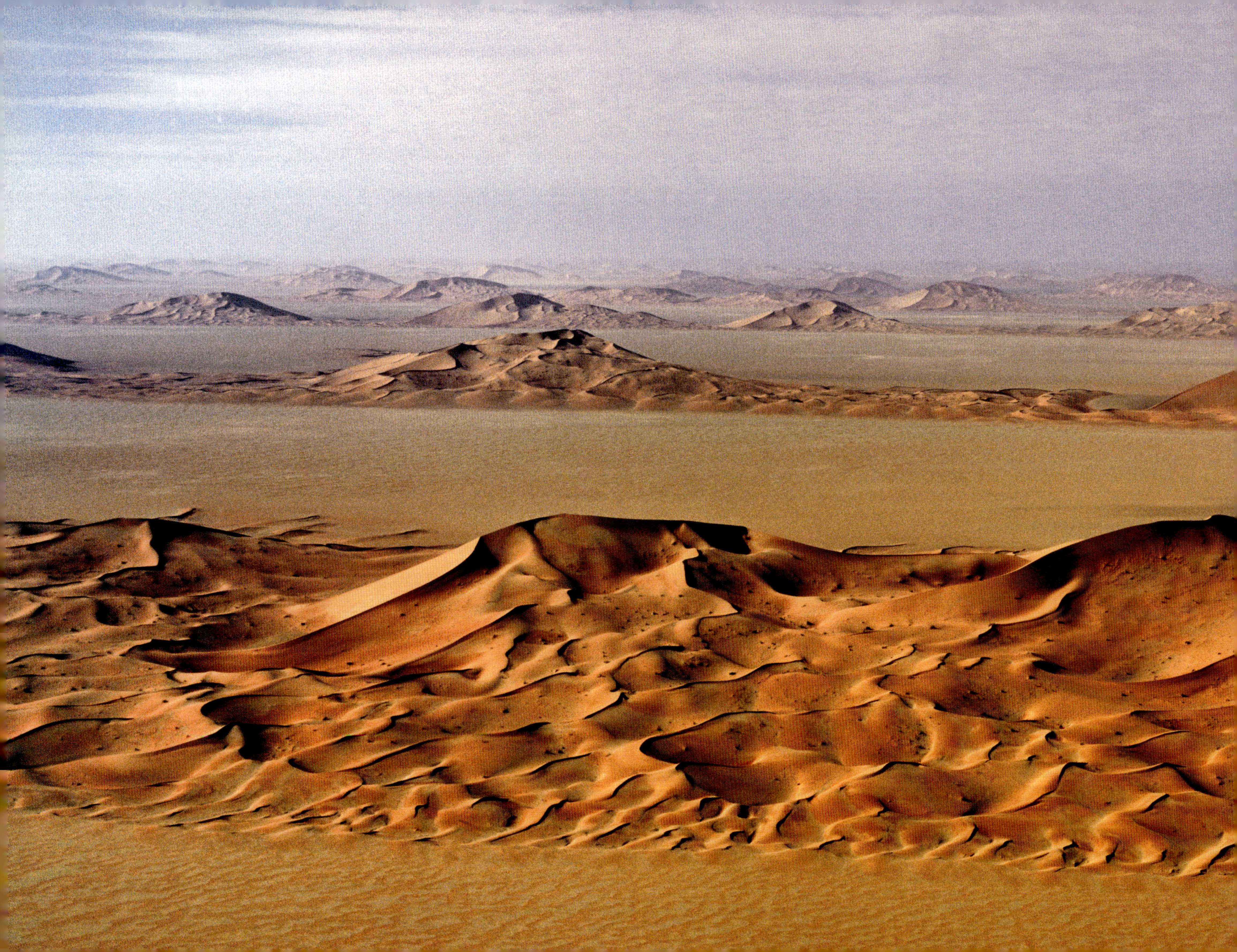

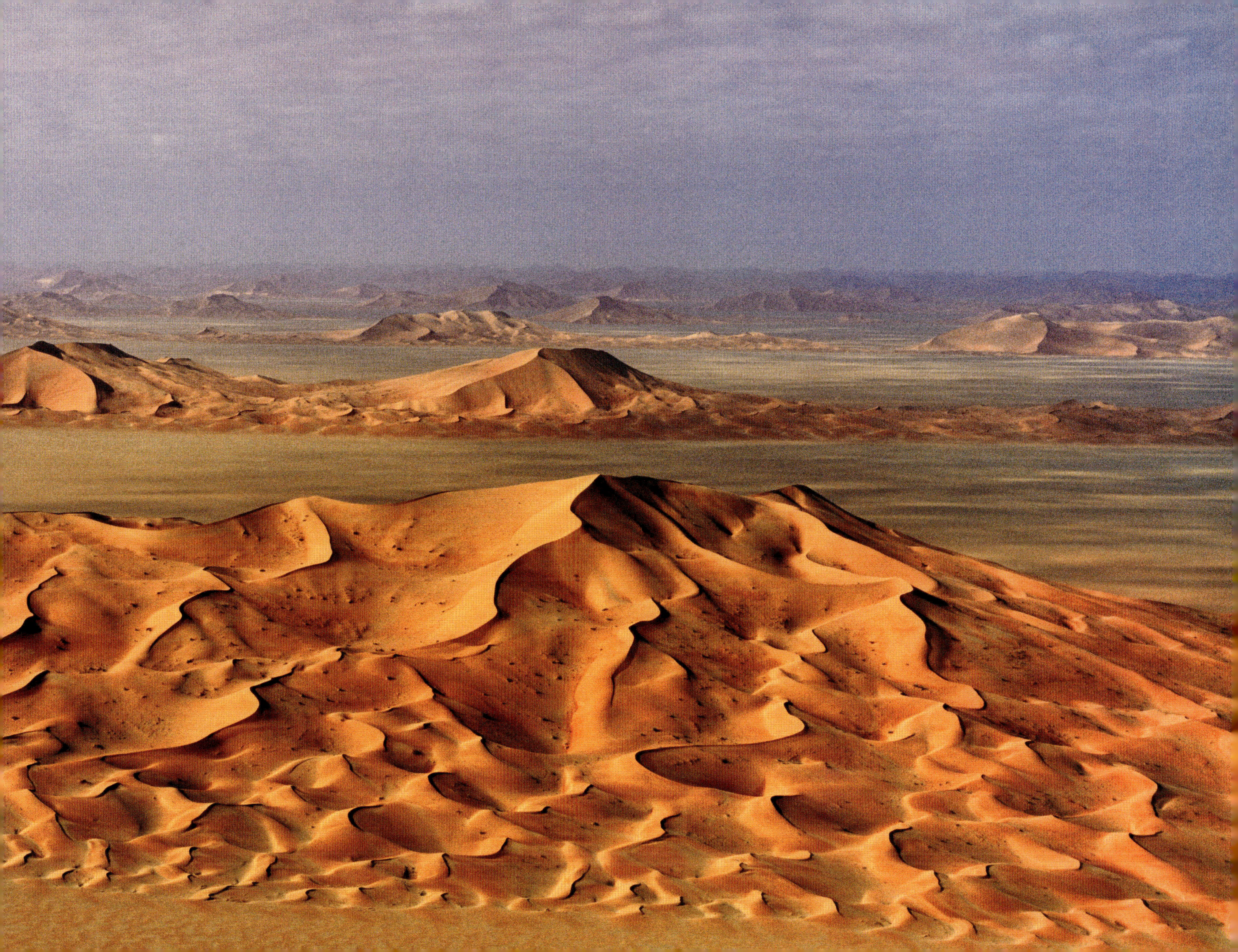

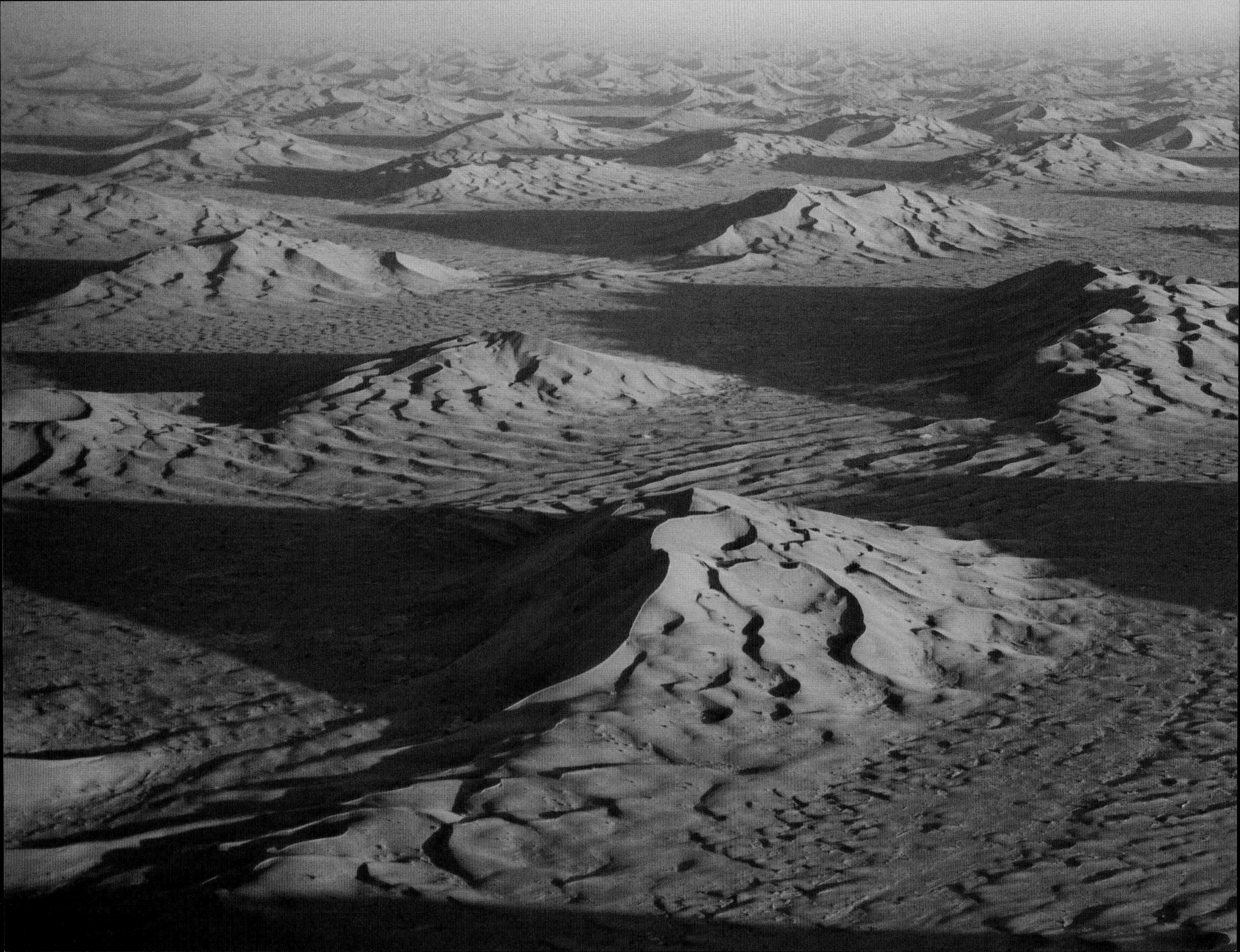

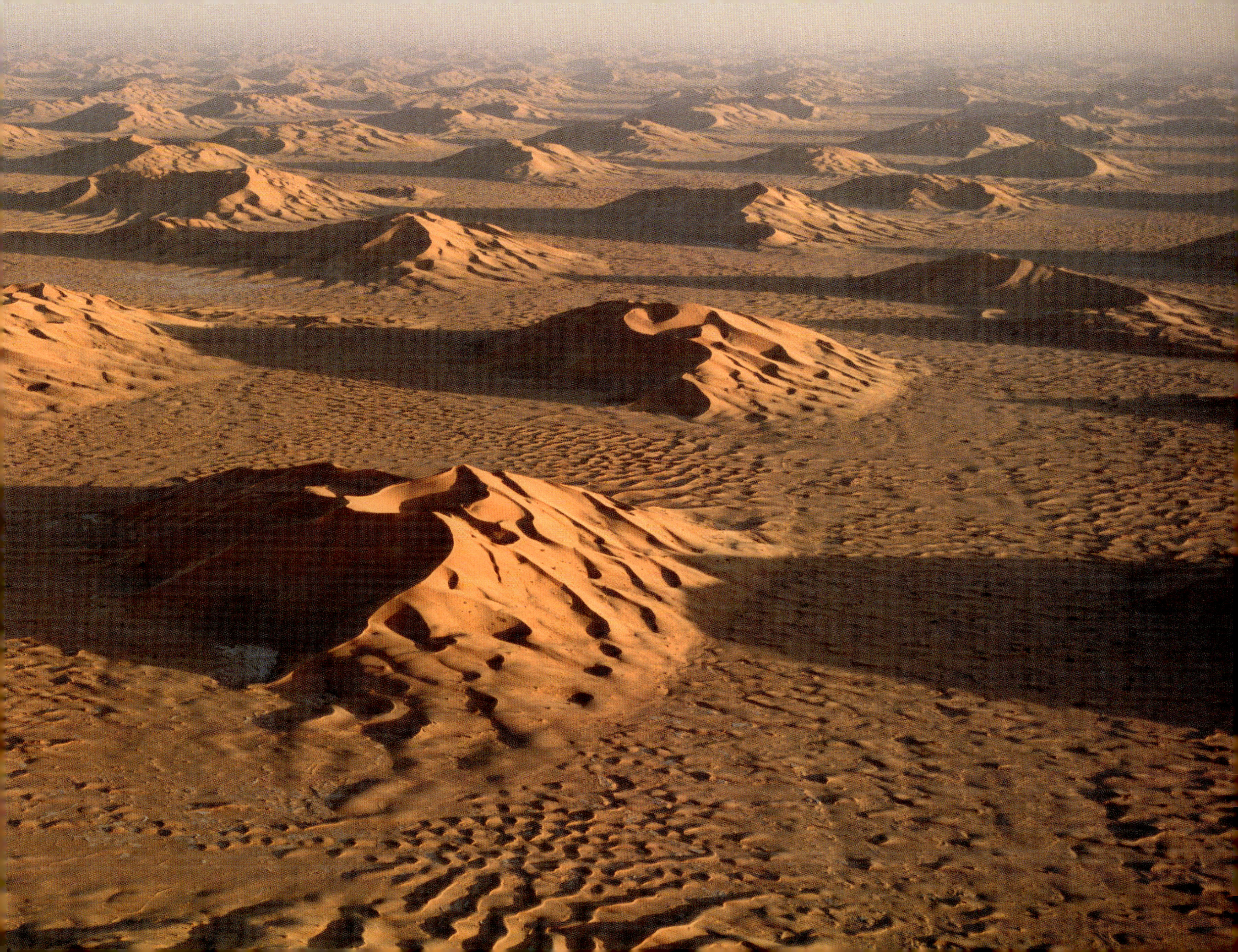

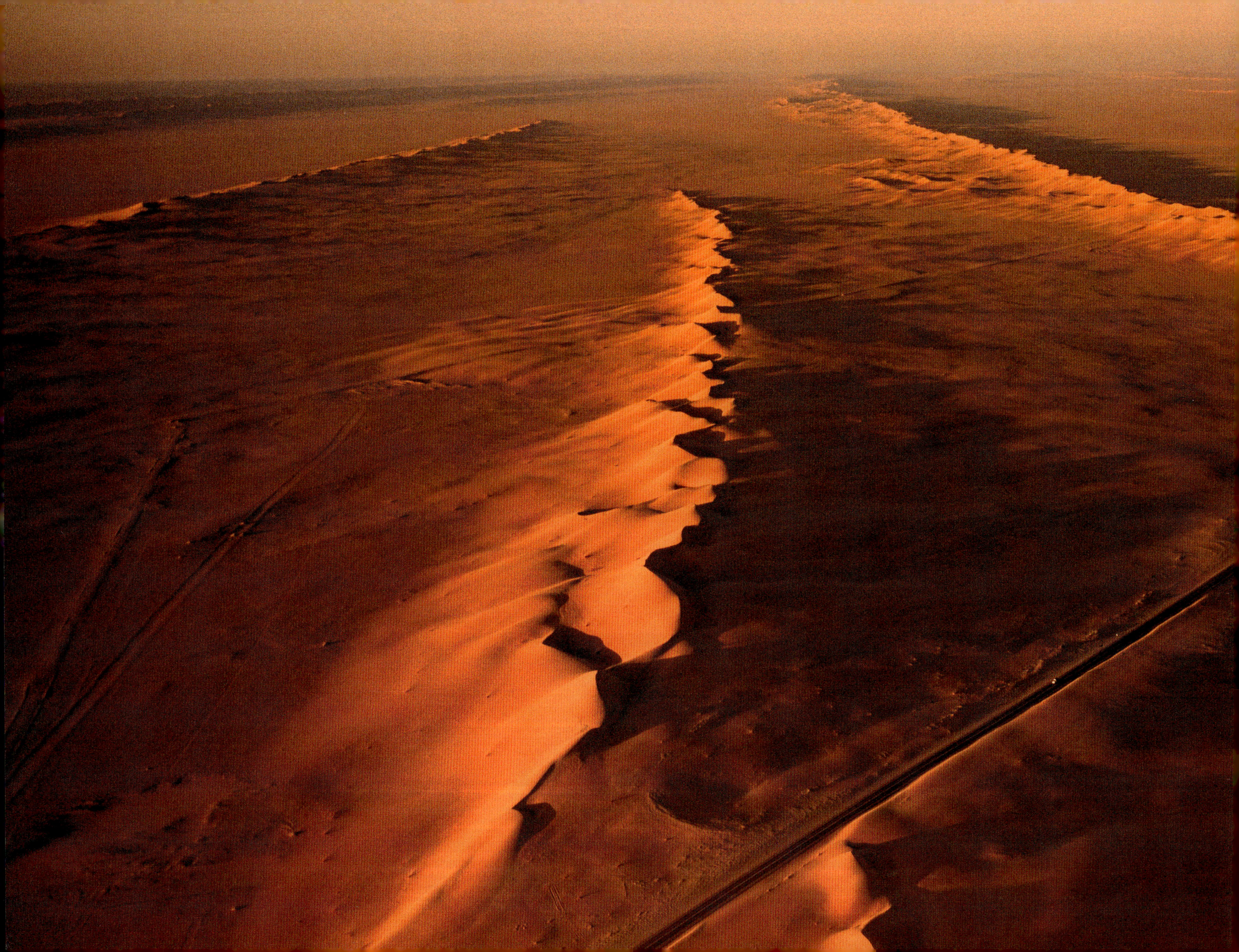

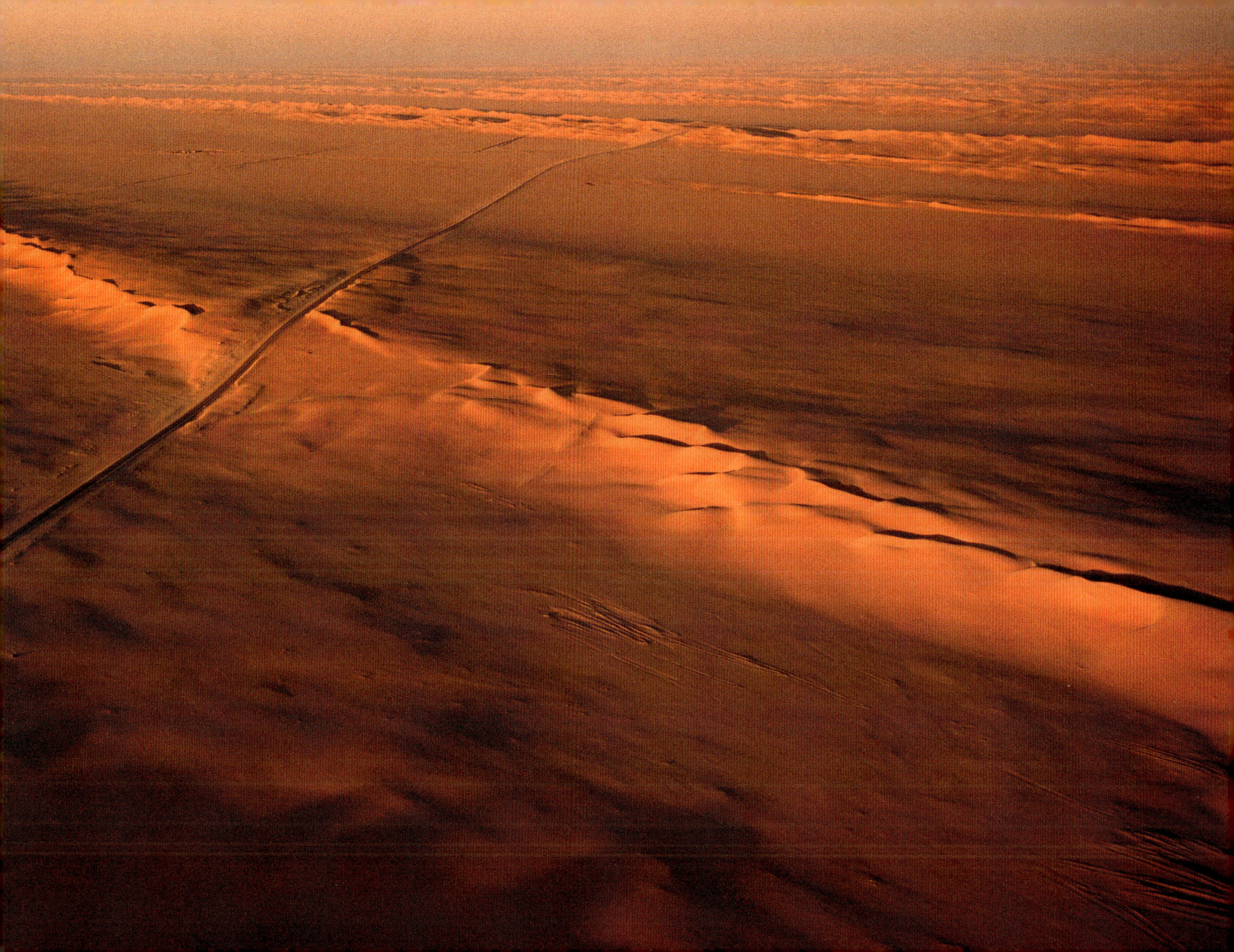

EXPLORATION

PRECEDING PAGES

PAGES 2–3:   Vein dunes, Shaqqat al Kharitah, Saudi Arabia
PAGES 4–5:   Complex barchan dunes, 'Uruq al Shaybah, Saudi Arabia
PAGES 6–7:   Star dune chains, 'Uruq al Mutaridah, Saudi Arabia
PAGES 8–9:   Star dunes, Ramlat Fasad, Oman
PAGES 10–11: Road to Sharurah, Shaqqat al Kharitah, Saudi Arabia

OPPOSITE: George Steinmetz flying his motorized paraglider over Shibam, Yemen

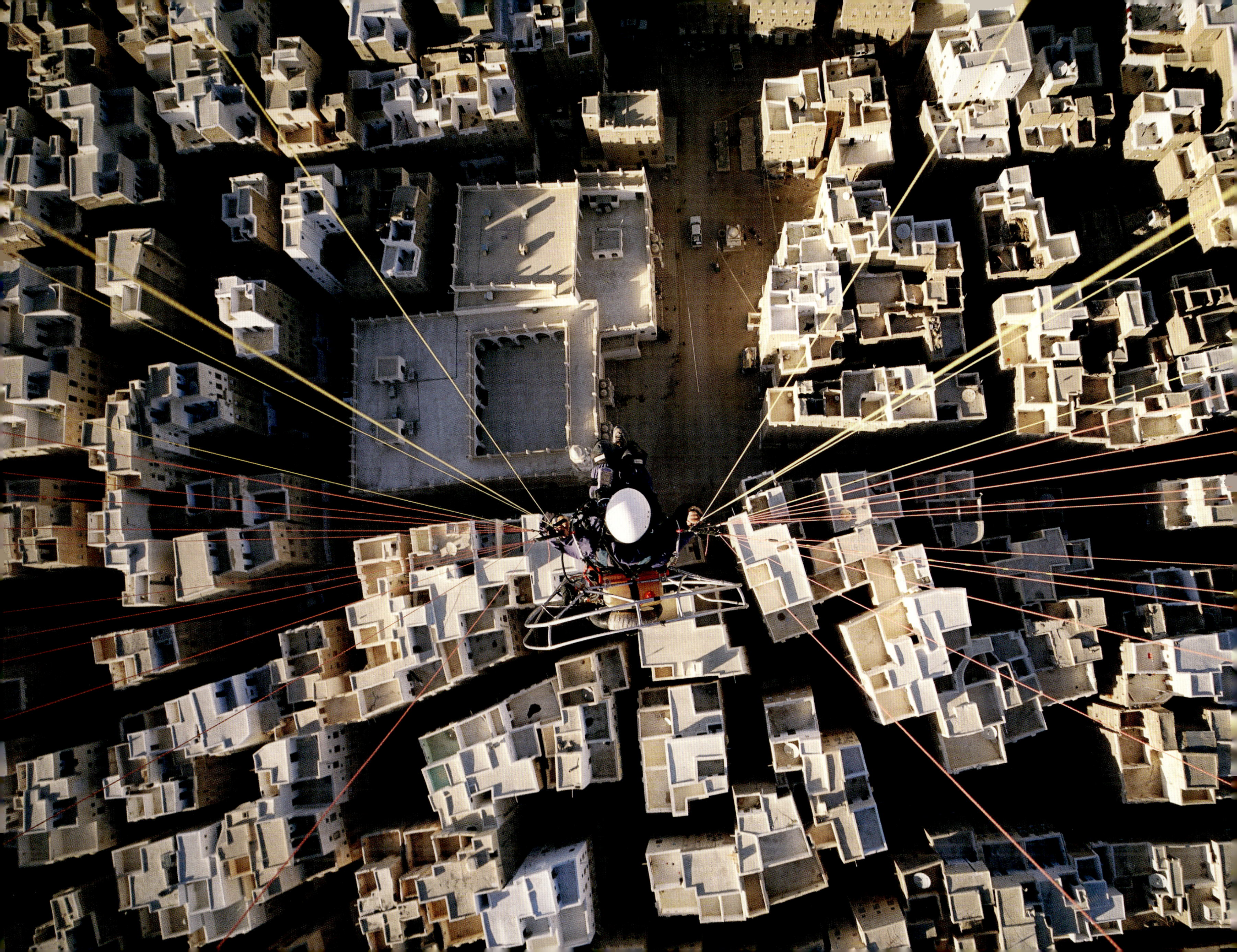

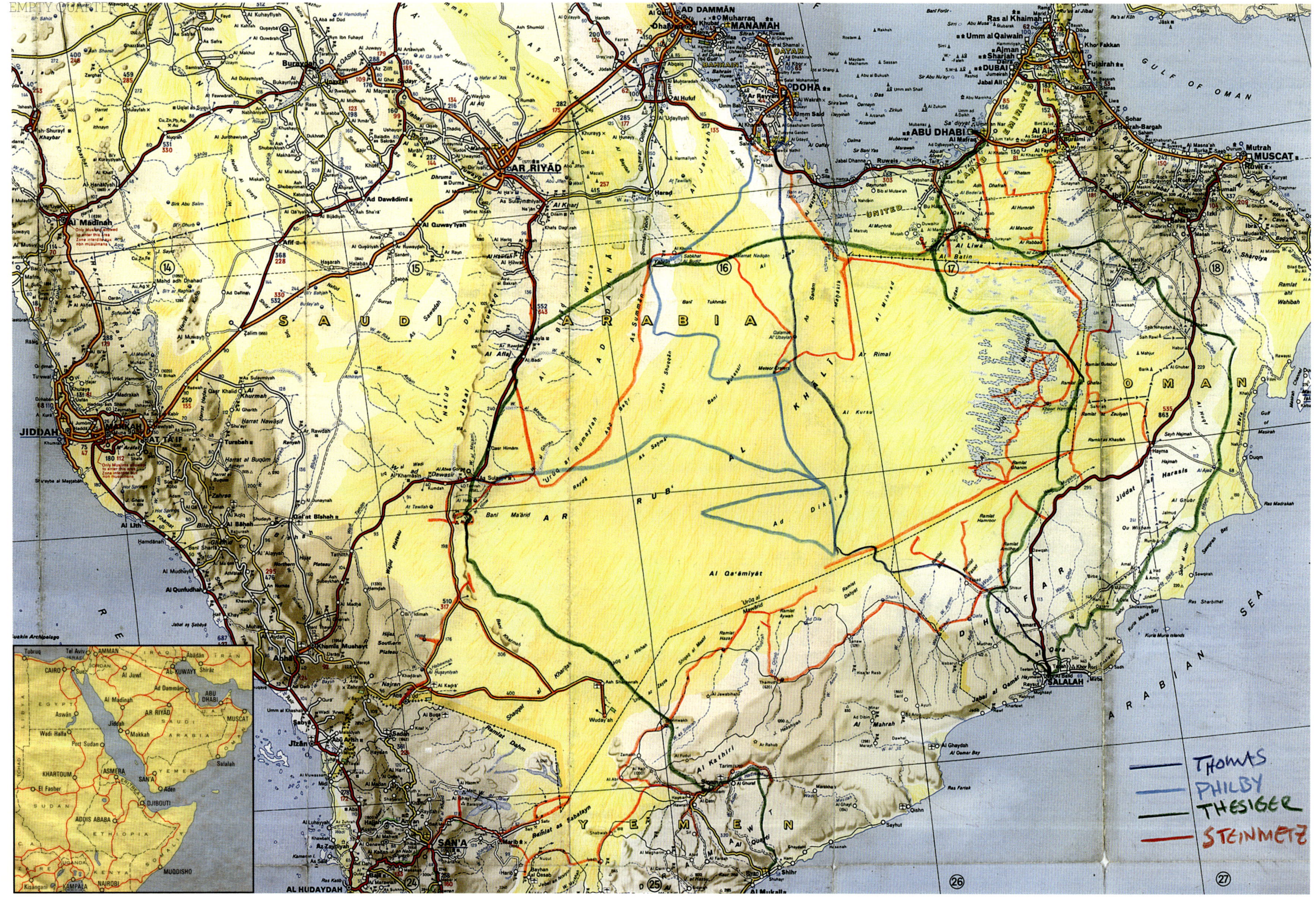

 George Steinmetz's Michelin field map with routes of his and others' explorations

"Insularity, bigotry, and intolerance are indigenous growths with a long pedigree. Hence an area equal to half the superficies of Europe had remained a blank on the maps."

Bertram Thomas, *Arabia Felix*

I first heard of the Empty Quarter in 1979 when, as a young man, I picked up a copy of *Arabian Sands,* Wilfred Thesiger's epic account of his two crossings in the 1940s of the world's most extreme desert. Studying a Michelin map of the area, I was intrigued by the big blank no-man's-land that separates Saudi Arabia, Oman, Yemen, and the United Arab Emirates. Despite its enormous size, that part of the map was mysteriously blank because so little of the Empty Quarter had been explored. This vast sea of sand, covering over 250,000 square miles, is bigger than France, Belgium, and Holland combined. It's also the hottest place on Earth, with summer temperatures over 142°F in the shade, and aside from the polar ice caps, one of the most forbidding environments on the planet.

The origin of the term "Empty Quarter" is almost as mysterious as the place itself. The name is a direct translation from the Arabic *Rub' al-Khali,* but where that expression comes from is not clear. Some say it's from a book by the Arabian seafarer Ibn Majid. Others say that the name came from early European explorers who probed the area over many centuries, or because its sands cover a quarter of the Arabian Peninsula.

By 1979, only a handful of foreign expeditions had ever crossed it. Thesiger wrote: "This cruel land can cast a spell which no temperate clime can match." As a young man eager to explore the world, I longed to one day be under its spell and fill the massive empty space on the map with my own experiences. I resolved to go there myself eventually.

It would take more than twenty years, but in 2001, the opportunity to explore the Empty Quarter finally presented itself. I had been working as a professional photographer for many years, primarily focusing on remote areas of the world. In the late 1990s, I had begun a project to photograph all of the world's deserts from the air. To accomplish this, I had learned how to fly a motorized paraglider, which allowed me to access remote landscapes, many of which had never been seen or photographed before. My project had already led me to the Sahara in Africa, the Gobi in China, and the Atacama in Chile. But after five years, I was finally ready for the big daddy of them all, what Thesiger had simply called "the sands."

I realized that half a century after Thesiger, the world of the Arab nomad would have largely disappeared, but the extreme nature of the Empty Quarter continued to intrigue me. With a motorized paraglider, I had a unique method of exploring the vast, remote landscape, but there would be significant obstacles to overcome. Some eighty percent of the Empty Quarter lies in Saudi Arabia. And while Saudi Arabia has changed drastically since the discovery of oil in 1938, it is still almost as difficult for anyone but a Muslim on a pilgrimage to visit the kingdom today as it was in 1946, when Thesiger set out on foot with four Bedouin and a string of camels. Saudi culture is wary of photography, and I would need a special permit to photograph anything beyond a rock or a sand dune. In addition, I was going to need permission to import and fly my experimental aircraft. The obstacles were daunting, to say the least, but I was determined to photograph one of the most forbidding landscapes in the world in a fresh way.

GETTING STARTED

Everything began to fall into place in 2001, when I read an article in the magazine *Saudi Aramco World* that Saudi Arabia was beginning to open up to foreign tourists. The person in charge of this effort was Prince Sultan bin Salman bin Abdul Aziz Al-Saud, the nephew of the current king. Prince Sultan was the first Arab in space, as a payload specialist on the space shuttle *Discovery*. I decided to try to make contact with the prince—I figured that as an astronaut he would be sympathetic to my desire to explore in flight and at the same time be able to push

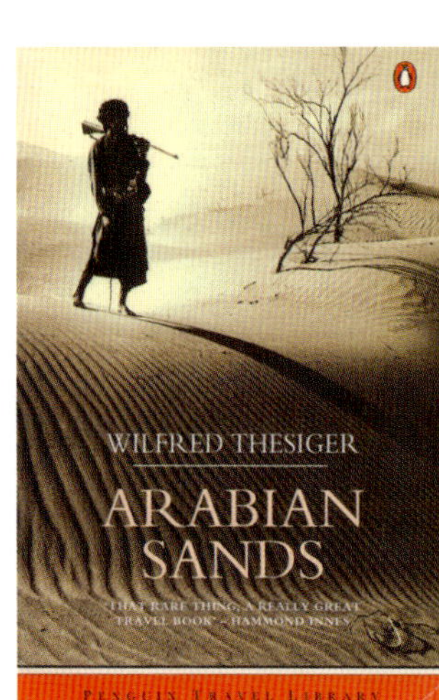

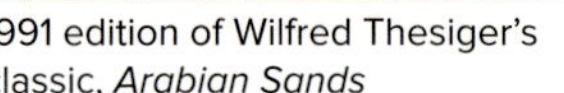

1991 edition of Wilfred Thesiger's classic, *Arabian Sands*

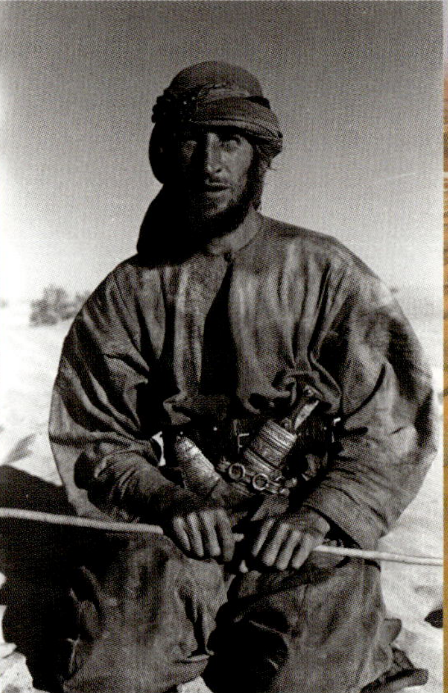

Thesiger, U.A.E., 1948

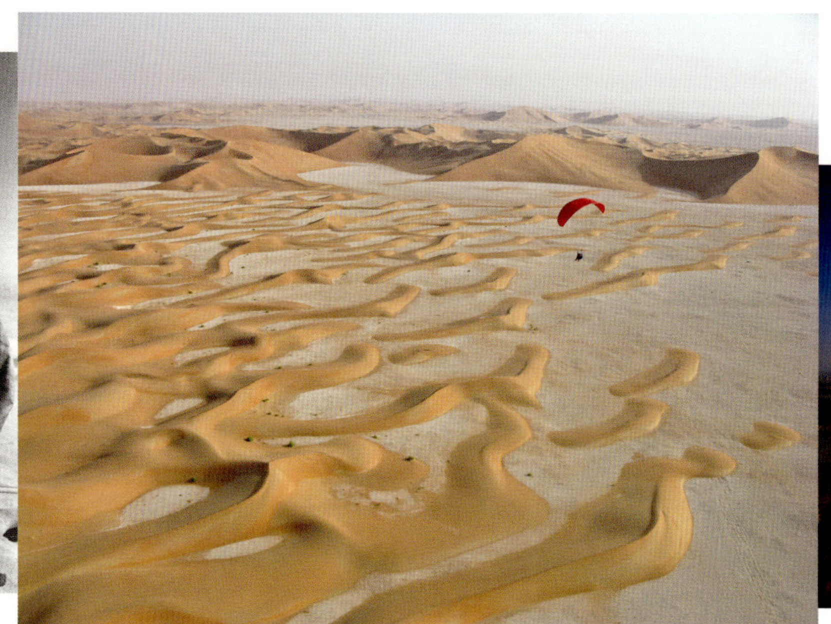

George Steinmetz in flight, Umm az-Zamul, U.A.E., 2008

my request through the royal bureaucracy. I thought that he might appreciate the fact that we both wanted to fly over the same patch of sand; he had flown in the fastest and heaviest aircraft ever invented, and I wanted to use the lightest and slowest. But before I could ask permission, I had to know what to ask for.

Trolling the Internet late one night, I found some old aerial photos of the Empty Quarter taken by a geologist in the 1950s. The images were utterly surreal, not unlike the surface of Mars, with dunes shaped like enormous orange-meringue cookies laid out on a limitless plain. But I had no idea where in the Empty Quarter the photos were taken. Internet searches led me to Ron Blom, a researcher at NASA's Jet Propulsion Lab, who had processed satellite imagery to find ancient caravan towns now buried under the sands. Ron's images covered the remotest section of the desert, where Saudi Arabia, Oman, and Yemen come together. The most bizarre dune formations were in the far east of Saudi Arabia, where chains of eight-hundred-foot-tall star dunes bunched up into the shape of an enormous eggcrate that could easily trap even the best team of cars and drivers. But we would need to get in fairly close to the area by car, since I wouldn't want to fly much farther than ten miles from a rescue vehicle with my frail little aircraft. The thought of getting stuck

in one of those deadly sand traps in 120°F heat was intimidating, so I started to search for maps to help navigate through this labyrinth of sand. Marianne Alireza, an American author who lived in California and was once married to a Saudi, had been leading small groups of tourists to Saudi Arabia and kindly lent me a set of old topographic maps of the Kingdom. Made by the U.S. Geological Survey in the 1960s to help discover oil reserves, they were incredibly detailed, but their accuracy was questionable, of course, given their age. Now, with some idea of where I wanted to go, it was time to go after financing.

I went to Hamburg in September 2001 to convince *GEO* magazine to pay for the trip, and while *GEO*'s editor, Peter-Matthias Gaede, was interested, he was also deeply skeptical that I could get Saudi permission for the expedition. Unfortunately, the timing of my trip to Germany coincided with the terrorist attacks in the United States, leading the magazine to conclude it would be extremely unlikely that I could get into Saudi Arabia. Yet during that strange and disorienting time in the immediate aftermath of 9/11, there was a tremendous outpouring of sympathy toward the United States. I sensed that this could be the perfect time to get permission from the Saudis to do what would, at any other time, be impossible.

I contacted Prince Sultan through Iyad Alzaru, an enterprising businessman who ran a travel agency in Riyadh. Iyad took on the challenge of getting the visas and permits for the trip. As the world learned that the majority of the 9/11 terrorists were from Saudi Arabia, my friends and family in the United States thought I was crazy to be going to Arabia. But I had been hoping to make this trip for twenty years. I was determined to go, and *GEO* agreed that if I could get in, they would pay for it. After months of email and countless noncommittal maybes, we got our visas and final permits just days before departure.

FIRST EXPLORATIONS OF THE EMPTY QUARTER

My trip would be crisscrossing the lost tracks of a handful of explorers who had made the first traverses in the 1930s and 1940s. Their methods had been perfectly in tune with their times—traveling by camel and sextant from well to well—but it would be physically impossible to replicate their feats today. I had exchanged camels and sextants for cars and GPS, but I would hear echoes of their epic struggles as I experienced my own.

The first recorded attempt by a Western explorer to cross the Empty Quarter was in the early 1930s. At that time, the

George Steinmetz in flight,
Wadi Mitan, Oman, 2004

'Uruq al Mutaridah, Saudi Arabia, 1950s

IN FORBIDDEN ARABIA

Mr Bertram Thomas's Story of a Great Exploration

PRELIMINARY EXPEDITIONS

BLOOD FEUDS AND PAGAN RITES IN QARA MOUNTAINS

A MIDNIGHT ADVENTURE

(WORLD COPYRIGHT RESERVED)

By BERTRAM THOMAS

Glasgow Herald, 1931

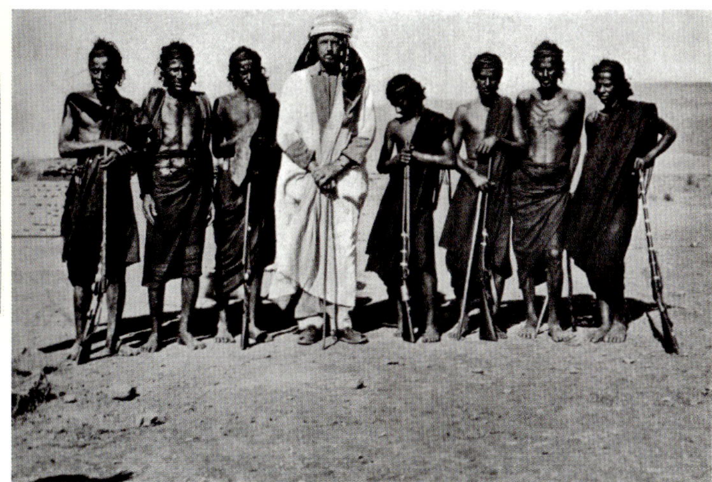

Bertram Thomas in the Empty Quarter, 1931

Poles, the source of the Amazon, and most other remote regions of the world had been mapped. The Empty Quarter was the last sizable *terra incognita.* Two British foreign officers, Bertram Thomas and Harry St. John Philby, were vying for the prize of crossing it first. Harry Philby's son, Kim Philby, grew up to become the infamous Soviet double agent.

Being a convert to Islam and a principal advisor to the Saudi king Ibn Saud, Philby had a tremendous advantage, but he was stymied due to fighting between Saudi and Yemeni border forces, and in 1931, the king refused to let him travel in the Empty Quarter. Thomas, who served as a Finance Minister and Wazir to the Sultan of Oman and was Philby's former deputy, chose a stealthier approach. His methods were appropriate for Arabia in the 1930s, a time before the discovery of oil, when potentates vied for territory across unmarked boundaries. Thomas wrote about his experiences in his book entitled *Arabia Felix:*

Then, too, I knew the mind of authority and so avoided the pitfall of seeking permission from my designs. Was not the lesson of Burton before me? The British official attitude, with which, let me add, I am in general sympathy, is, in view of the anarchy that normally prevails in Desert Arabia, inimical to exploration. The good official must avoid responsibility and commitments, and to learn of, and not forbid, and expedition implies tacit authorization. So my plans were conceived in darkness, my journeys heralded only by my disappearances paid for by myself and executed under my own auspices.
(Bertram Thomas, *Arabia Felix*, p. xxv)

Thomas traveled fast and quietly, with a party of thirteen camel-mounted Bedouin, including several guides, a personal servant, five baggage camels, a cinema camera, an electric flashlight, a sextant, and two aneroid barometers. He was fortunate to have chosen a wet year for the journey, so his camels encountered some grazing here and there, and his savvy guides led him on a route linking numerous hand-dug wells. The sole purpose of two of the camels was to provide Thomas with milk. To avoid illness, the milk was his principal diet, but it caused him to lose twenty pounds. He was careful to avoid hostile tribes and Bedouin loyal to King Ibn Saud, as Thomas had no permission to travel through the hundreds of miles of Saudi territory that lie between southern Oman and Qatar. Thomas also feared the Ikhwan, a radical religious militia that killed not only infidels but also Muslims not sharing their narrow Wahabist views.

Thomas's crossing was shrewdly planned during Ramadan, while most of the local Bedouin were fasting in their villages on the edge of the desert, and he was able to travel across 380 miles of sand without incident in twenty-six days. Throughout his Arabian travels, he collected insect and animal specimens and measured the heads of the tribal people he encountered, to further the then-popular science of racial identification by cranial measurement. When news of his triumph reached London, Thomas was a hero of the newspapers and lecture circuit, and soon had a handsome book contract.

When Philby heard the news, he felt terribly betrayed. He sent Thomas a congratulatory telegram and then shut himself indoors for a week, where he wrote to his wife:

Damn and blast Thomas … I have sworn a great oath not to go home until I have crossed the R.K. twice! And left nothing in it for future travelers.
(*Philby of Arabia*, p. 164)

The following winter Philby set out to do just that. With relative calm on the Yemeni frontier, King Ibn Saud provided him with fifteen men, thirty-two camels, and supplies for

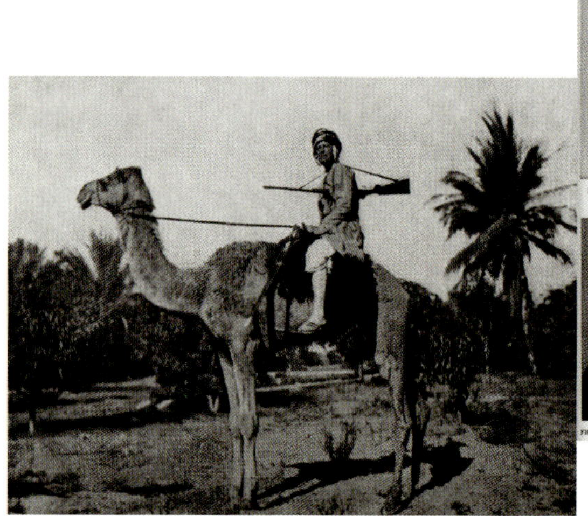

Thomas on his favorite mount, Khuwara, Oman, 1931

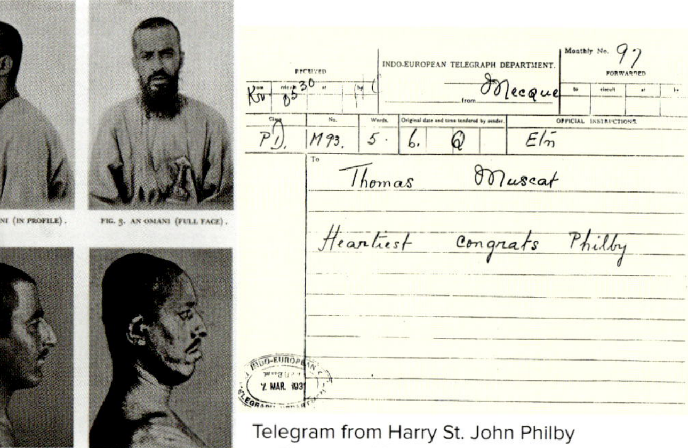

Cranial studies by Thomas, 1931

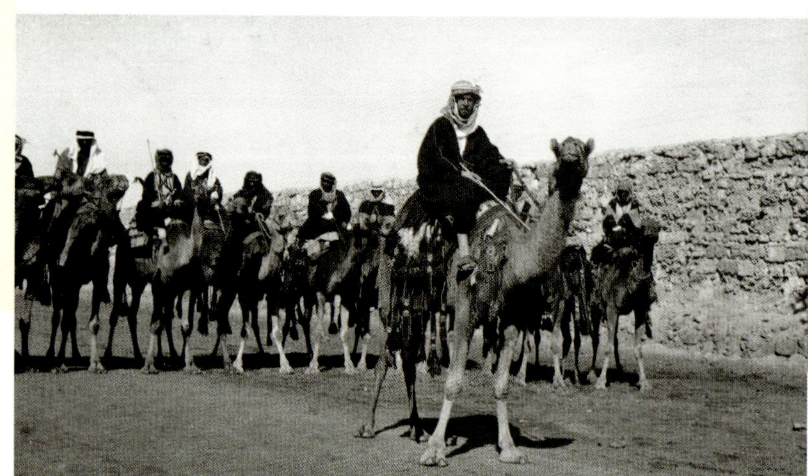

Telegram from Harry St. John Philby
to Thomas, 1931

Philby and escort, Jiddah, Saudi Arabia, 1917

seventy-five days. One of their first stops was the supposed ruin of the lost city of Ubar, which according to the Koran had been destroyed by a cataclysmic event after its king scoffed at a prophet of God. What Philby found instead was a pair of large meteorite impact craters half-buried in sand, and he transliterated the name in his reports as "Wabar," the name that has been used ever since. Surrounding the craters were low-impact walls that the Bedouin had assumed were remnants of an ancient castle, which were in turn surrounded by a scattering of "black pearls," later determined to be bits of molten rock resulting from the heat of impact.

I too wanted to visit the site, even though the largest meteoritic fragment, weighing over two tons, had already been hauled off to Riyadh in the 1960s. No one had ever been able to fly over the remote sight, and I hoped that a low-altitude survey might reveal something new.

Disappointed in his findings at Wabar, Philby continued on to the well at Shanna, which had been Thomas's jumping off point into the heart of the sands. But to proceed south would have risked encountering hostile Yemeni tribes, so after some backtracking he split his group, took the strongest men and camels, and set out west for Sulaiyil. They covered 375 miles in

nine days, without water for the camels, the last four of which were without food. It was the longest recorded trek anyone had made across the sands without water, and Philby emerged with bragging rights to a piece of the Empty Quarter.

WILFRED THESIGER

Wilfred Thesiger was not the first foreigner to cross the sands, but he wrote a better account of his travels than Thomas or Philby, and *Arabian Sands* soon became a classic. It is, as one reviewer describes it, "the book about Arabia to end all books about Arabia." What is so compelling about his journey is not so much what he did, but the way he carried it out—in close company with a small group of Bedouin. Embarking some fifteen years after Thomas and Philby, he was not looking to make his mark or establish any firsts. Indeed, Thesiger did not sit down to write *Arabian Sands* until ten years after his two crossings:

No, it is not the goal but the way there that matters, and the harder the way the more worth while the journey. … I felt instinctively that it was better to fail on Everest without oxygen than to attain the summit with its use. If climbers used oxygen, why should they not have their supplies dropped to them from aeroplanes, or landed by helicopter? … I would not myself have wished to cross the Empty Quarter in a car. Luckily this was impossible when I did my journeys, for to have done the journey on a camel when I could have done it in a car would have turned the venture into a stunt.
(Wilfred Thesiger, *Arabian Sands,* pp. 278–9)

Thesiger made his first crossing in the winter of 1946–47. He took the most difficult route, straight across the biggest dune chains that are each separated by the quicksands of the eastern Empty Quarter. He traveled by foot with four wild-looking Bedouin of the desert and a small string of camels. He deeply admired his Bedouin companions and treated them as equals, if not superiors, adopting their dress, sharing their food, and letting the sands sink into his soul. It was a dangerous and epic journey, where their very survival depended on their camels:

Twenty waterless days was the very limit that the camels would stand, traveling for long hours across heavy sands; and they would only do this if they found grazing. Should we find grazing? It is the continual problem, which faces the

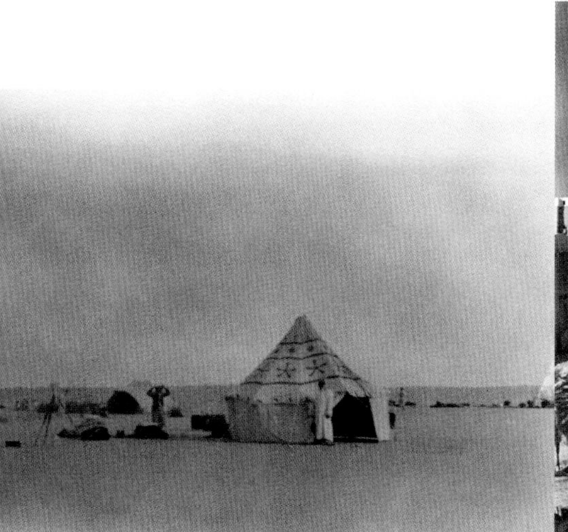

Philby's tent, Wadi Sahba,
Saudi Arabia, 1932

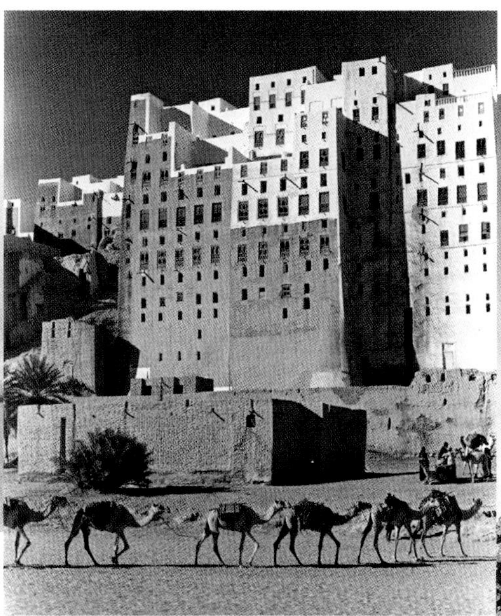

Shibam taken by Thesiger, Yemen, 1947

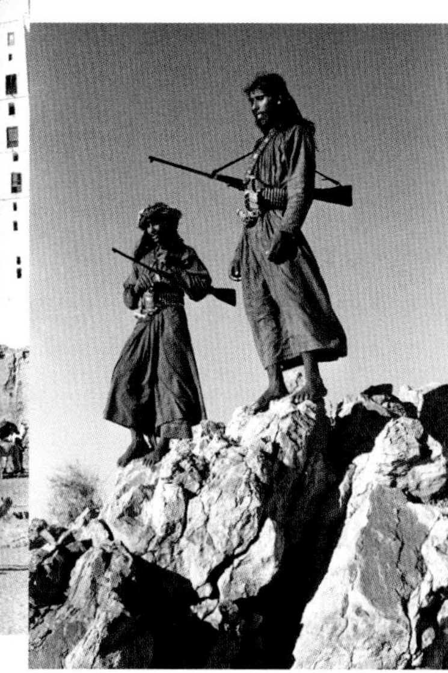

Thesiger's companions bin Kabina
and bin Ghabaisha, Oman, 1950

Thesiger's group, Saudi Arabia, 1948

*Bedu. If we did not find it, the camels would collapse and
that would be the end of us all. It is not hunger nor is it thirst
that frightens the Bedu; they maintain that riding they can
survive in cold weather for seven days without food or water.
It is the possible collapse of their camels which haunts them.
If this happens, death is certain. I asked al Auf again what he
thought; would we find grazing? "God knows," he answered.*
(ibid., p. 118)

They emerged two weeks later in the oasis of Liwa, in what
is now the United Arab Emirates. They were parched, hungry, and exhausted, and feared that they would be captured as
bandits emerging from the great empty. And as a Christian in
Arabia, Thesiger faced the same perils as Thomas: He too was
worried about encounters with the Ikhwan and had to travel like
a fugitive along the north and eastern borders of the sands on
his way back to Oman.

His second crossing was in the following year, through
the more gently rolling sands in the southwest of the Empty
Quarter, from the Wadi Hadramawt to Wadi Dawasir. Here
some thirty-five hostile Yemeni tribesmen pursued him, out to
kill the infidel and his four Bedouin companions, but they were
unable to catch them. When Thesiger's party arrived in Sulaiyil,
they were promptly arrested until King Ibn Saud, in consulta-
tion with Philby, telegraphed orders for their release:

*I was an intruder from an alien civilization, which they iden-
tified with Christianity. They knew that the Christian had
subjugated most of the Muslim world, and that contact with
their civilization had everywhere destroyed or profoundly
modified the beliefs, institutions, and culture they cherished.
Naturally they did not realize how little sympathy I had
with the innovations and inventions with which they asso-
ciated me, nor how much sympathy I had with the way of
life they sought to preserve.*
(ibid., p. 249)

Thesiger and his companions then made their way north
across a vast expanse of desolate dunes, once again arriving
hungry and exhausted in Liwa. But this time they became the
honored guests of Sheikh Zayed bin Sultan Al-Nahyan, the
founder and first president of the modern state of the United
Arab Emirates, who was impressed by Thesiger's pluck and
comportment.

Thesiger made other explorations, but he is best remem-
bered for the two crossings of the Empty Quarter. Unlike the
famous T. E. Lawrence, whom locals today perceive as something of a costumed opportunist, Thesiger is the legendary
foreigner who still garners respect for his achievements. For
him the journey and the camaraderie of the Bedouin were more
than adequate rewards. He was prescient enough to realize that
he was seeing the end of an era and wanted to document this
vanishing world, as oil wealth and the rush to modernity were
already beginning to change Arabia forever.

Certainly countless Arabs before him had crossed the
Empty Quarter, or perished trying, but only foreigners
like Thomas, Philby, and Thesiger left written accounts. I
found records of only a handful of crossings of the Empty
Quarter since Thesiger: One was in May 1994, by a group
promoting the endurance of the Hummer, the civilian version of the U.S. military's Humvee. Among that group was
geologist Jeffrey Wynn of the U.S. Geological Survey, who
endured temperatures of 142°F in the shade and nighttime
lows of around 100°F. In the process of mapping the Wabar
site, Wynn discovered a third crater and dated the meteorite
impact to 1863.

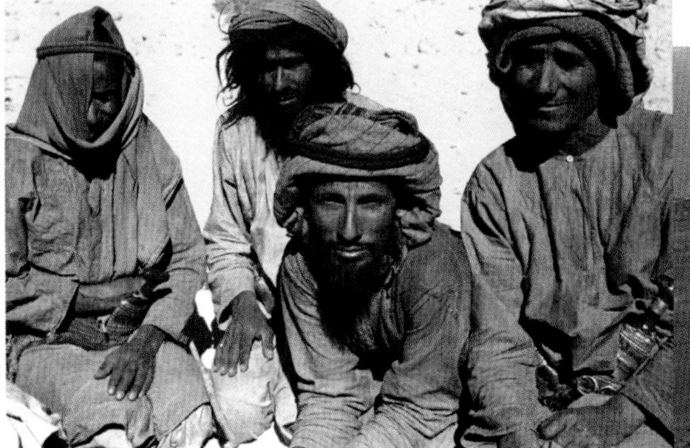
Thesiger's companions, Oman, 1946

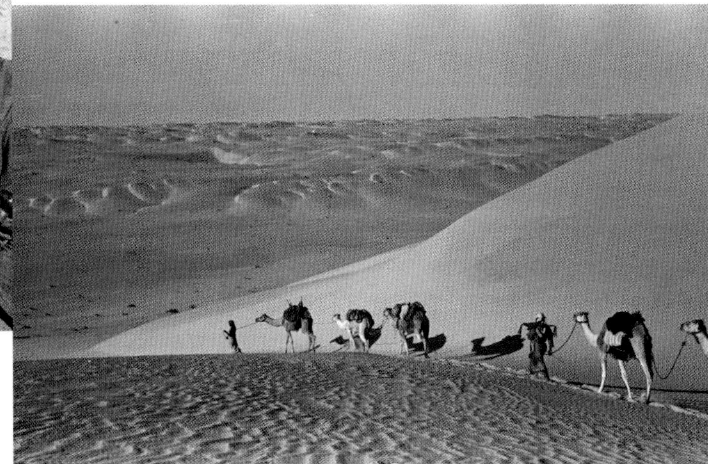
Thesiger's group, Saudi Arabia, 1948

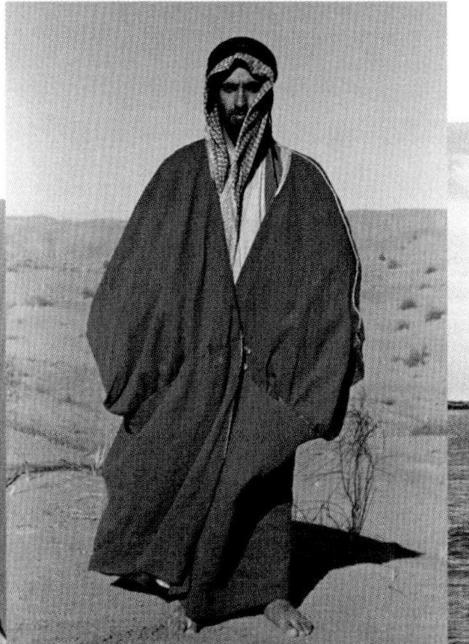
Sheikh Zayed bin Sultan Al-Nahyan, U.A.E., 1949

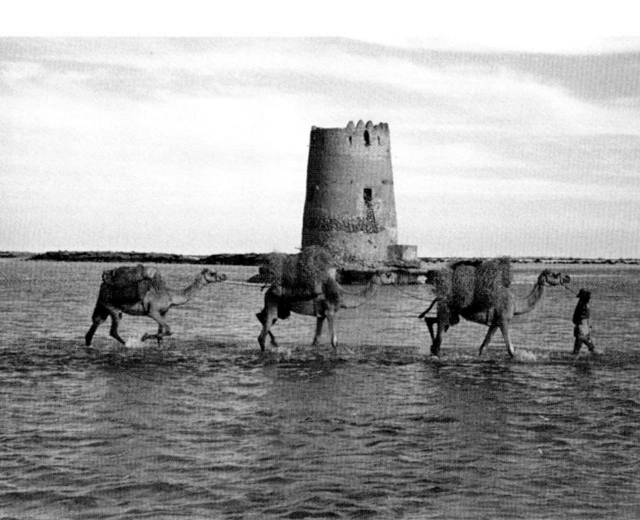
Thesiger's group approaching Abu Dhabi, 1949

There was another crossing of the eastern sands by three Canadian adventurers and four Omani Bedouin in 1999, using camels with vehicle support to retrace part of Thesiger's first crossing in 1946. But the people who traveled in the desert the most and know it best were those with an economic interest: geological teams hired by Saudi Aramco to find oil reserves under the sands. But their findings are, for the most part, closely held corporate secrets. They, like the native Bedouin, left no accessible record.

The age of exploration by camel ended many decades ago; even Thesiger in the late forties realized that he was one of the last outsiders to see a vanishing world. Without many months of training, I doubt that camels today are tough enough to go 350 miles in soft sand without food or water, as they are now used for meat, milk, and the occasional ride but not for long-distance travel. It would also be difficult to find a twenty-first-century Bedu up to the task. In addition, the wells that used to supply the nomadic Bedouin are mostly filled with sand or lost to disuse. It was time to try to explore the sands in a different way, and I knew that my motorized paraglider could open up new ways to view and document the desert.

PRACTICALITIES

The early explorers had had different agendas than I did. They were interested in acquiring bragging rights, finding specimens of flora and fauna, mapping watercourses, analyzing meteorite craters, measuring the depth and quality of wellwater, or even recording the shape and size of natives' heads. I wasn't particularly interested in any of these, but I did share a love of the desert and a desire to test myself against it. It's my guess that that challenge was what also drove them to go out there, and the rest was little more than rationalization. But while these early explorers were great leaders, linguists, and amateur naturalists, they didn't have much visual sophistication. Even Thesiger, who took extraordinarily good photos under difficult conditions, limited his efforts to documentation of his friends and personal experiences and took very few of the landscape.

I was fascinated with the idea of exploring and photographing the desert, especially from the air. I wasn't out there for the thrill of flying a crazy aircraft high above the sand. More times than I care to remember, I found myself subjugating abject fear for the sake of a picture or even the chance of a picture. I simply wanted to create a visual record of what I guessed would be one of the most astoundingly beautiful places on Earth that few had ever seen. And captured from above, especially at the low altitudes I prefer, I hoped that the extreme physicality of the place could be laid out like a three-dimensional map on a human scale. In this extreme environment, 4x4 cars and motorized paragliders were the way to do it, to get above the ant-like perspective that one has while driving across the dunes. With my little aircraft I would also be able to map out a car route through this labyrinth of dunes and quicksand. My motorized paraglider is a foot-launched aircraft that needs an area only slightly larger than a basketball court to take off and land, and it fits neatly into the back of a 4x4 car. It weighs only seventy pounds and can carry ten liters of fuel, which is enough for about two hours of flying at thirty miles per hour. With a pair of motorized paragliders and a few cars, I figured there would be a chance to see one of the most extreme places on Earth in a way that the early explorers could never have imagined.

But crossing such a vast area of remote terrain with no possibility of rescue is dangerous and intimidating. If we got stuck out there, the high temperatures would reduce air density to the point where even helicopters could not land with enough fuel

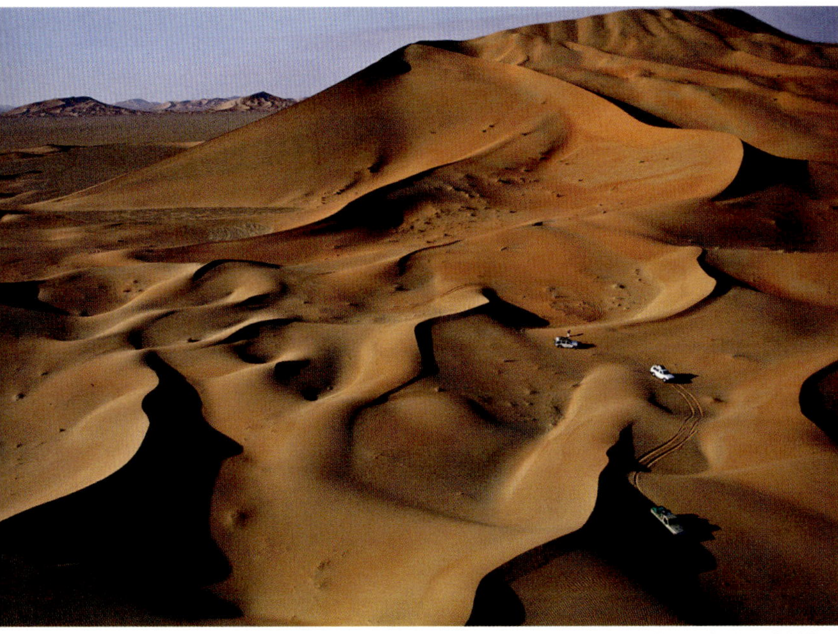
George Steinmetz's group crossing 'Uruq al Mutaridah, Saudi Arabia, 2002

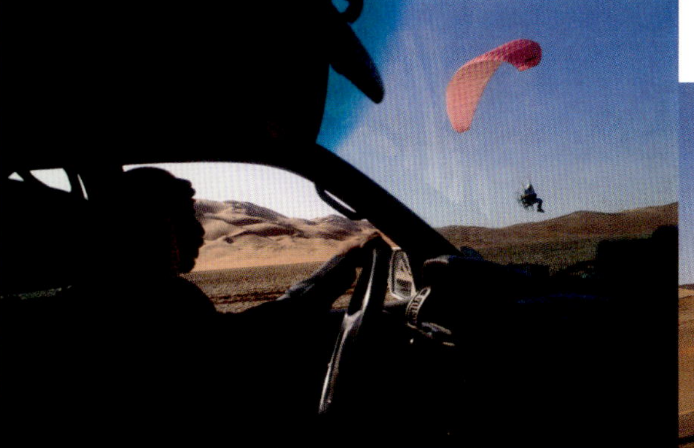
George Steinmetz flying beside Ali Al-Mari, Saudi Arabia, 2004

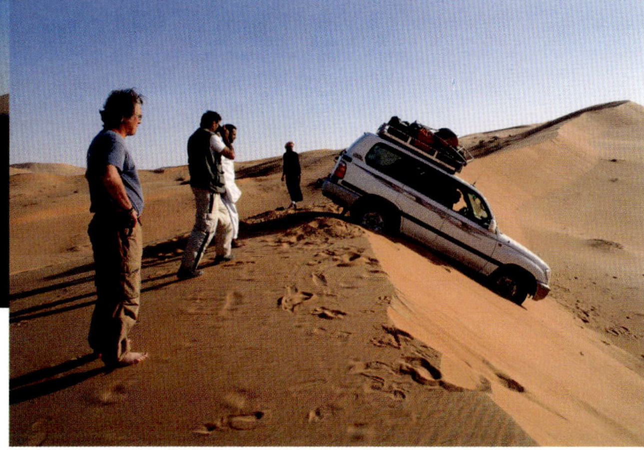
Donovan Webster (far left) watching as a car crests a dune, Saudi Arabia, 2004

for the return trip. The most interesting and perilous section of the Empty Quarter is the easternmost section, with slip-faces of sand many hundreds of feet on all sides that descend onto salt flats called *sabkhas*. This dune-sabkha-dune pattern repeats itself every few miles and continues for hundreds more to form one of the most stunningly beautiful and surreal death traps on Earth. One mistake on a slip-face and your vehicle could roll and tumble out of control. Once at the bottom of these sand traps it can be nearly impossible to climb back out. And getting across the sabkha bottom presents an entirely different problem. These crusty flats are only a thin layer of sand covering what is essentially a lake bottom of salty mud. It can be flat and firm for many miles, allowing cruising speeds of sixty miles per hour, and then suddenly the surface gives way into a deep layer of greasy mud. The sound of tires spattering mud requires a quick and deftly executed U-turn out of a quagmire that is real quicksand, not a Hollywood fantasy.

Just as the early explorers depended on their camels for their lives, so we depended on Toyota Land Cruisers and Nissan Patrols. A simple mechanical failure or deferred maintenance could prove fatal, so we needed multiple cars in perfect condition, with lots of spare parts, tires, and tools. I settled on three cars as a minimum, because it seemed highly unlikely that all three would break down at once. We would need two passenger cars and one pickup; the pickup would be used for two-hundred-liter drums of fuel, fifty-liter bottles of water, plus firewood, shovels, sand-ladders, and other useful items. When we approached sketchy terrain, we would have our best driver and guide go first, so that the others could pull his car out in case it got stuck. Fuel was another major concern, as there are no towns or gas stations in the Empty Quarter, so we had to carry all fuel with us. Yet, to keep from sinking into the sand and sabkha, we would have to travel as lightly as possible and organize our trips into segments lasting only a few days at a time.

It seemed like the best strategy was to keep to the perimeter of the Empty Quarter. I suspected that the most interesting things might be on the edge of the sands, where there could be towns, Bedouin camps, archaeological sites, dune patterns and vegetation, or transitions into different terrain. Yet, the essence of the Empty Quarter for me is lifelessness, and so I made a rule to limit my travels to the first town I encountered on the edge of the sands.

For flight safety I contacted my friend Alain Arnoux, a world champion of motorized paragliding who had been with me on many desert expeditions before. *GEO* assigned their top expedition man, Uwe George, to travel with us and write our story, as he had headed up dozens of explorations all over the Sahara. Iyad Alzaru put me in touch with a most unusual man, Colonel Mohammed Banounah of the Saudi National Guard, who had trained as a commando at Fort Benning in Georgia. He would help Iyad organize vehicles and ground personnel for the trip. He spoke perfect English and had a passion for the desert, having led many groups out into its lesser-known regions. But even he had never ventured into the Empty Quarter. It seemed like nobody who could be reached by telephone had the deep-desert experience we needed, except for our second driver, Ali Al-Mari, who came from Yabrin on the edge of the sands. But with some old maps and Ron's satellite photos, I hoped we might be able to go where few had ever been before.

Getting permits to fly in seldom-visited parts of the Arab world is an opaque process. Assiduously worded letters are sent to a carefully selected individual, and weeks can go by without response. Things generally come together at the last minute

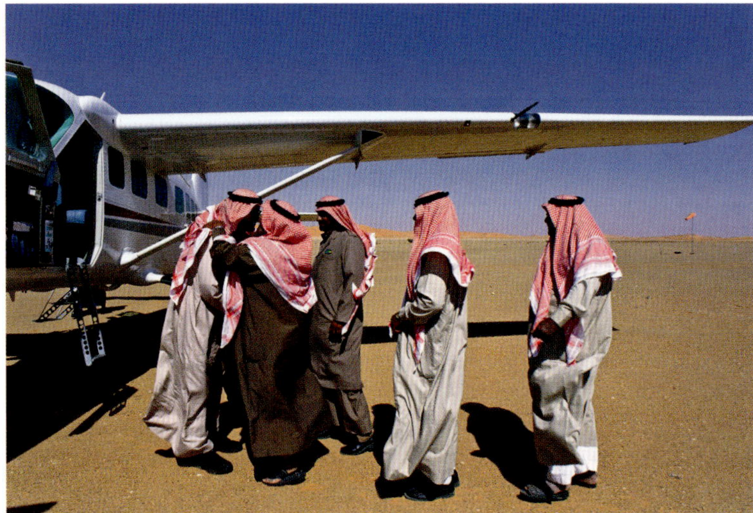

Prince Sultan upon arrival in Bani Ma'arid, Saudi Arabia, 2002

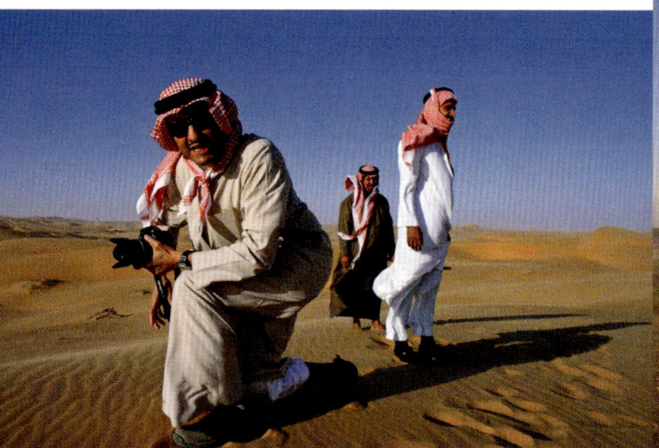

Prince Sultan photographing oryx,
Bani Ma'arid, Saudi Arabia, 2002

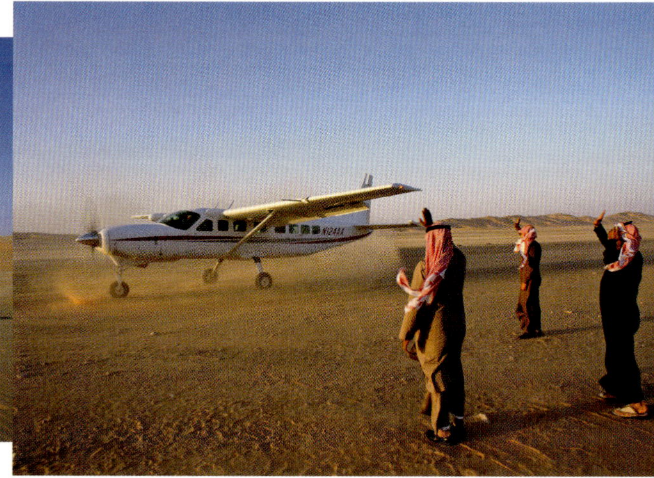

Prince Sultan departing Bani Ma'arid, Saudi Arabia, 2002

or drag on beyond the narrow window of acceptably cool, clear midwinter flying conditions, and trips have to be cancelled or postponed to the following year. I was not interested in geopolitics or terrorism; rather, my mission was to document the strange beauty of one of the harshest and least-known corners of our globe. Perhaps that is why I was lucky to be granted permission on my first try, in 2001. Geography is not threatening to most people, and a request such as mine can appeal to national pride.

RENDEZVOUS WITH AN ASTRONAUT-PRINCE

We all met in Riyadh on January 19, 2002. After a few days of procuring supplies and checking the cars, we headed south into the desert. One of our first stops was the newly created wildlife reserve at 'Uruq Bani Ma'arid. Here we had a rendezvous with Prince Sultan, who had chartered a small plane to meet with us out in the desert for the day. It was a rather surreal experience, waiting at an unmarked dirt airstrip to meet the member of the Saudi Royal Family who had obtained the permits that made our trip possible. The rangers at Bani Ma'arid, who lived

in wind-battered mobile homes with small dunes of sand on the shag carpet inside their doors, had spent days preparing for his arrival. After the chartered plane touched down on the airstrip, the rangers pressed noses with His Royal Highness, as is the Bedouin custom, and then we three foreigners shook his hand. We were then whisked off in a fleet of new Nissan 4x4s to a pair of large canvas tents where an enormous feast awaited us. Two sheep had been roasted whole and were laid upon a pile of garnished saffron rice in the center of enormous platters. We all sat around them on traditional carpets, tearing the cooked flesh apart with our right hands, like civilized vultures devouring a mound of exquisitely prepared carrion. Over tiny cups of coffee he told us of his 169 hours (111 circles of earth covering 2.9 million miles) in space aboard the *Discovery*, where he observed the official end of Ramadan with the onset of a new moon and had difficulty orienting his prayers toward Mecca in the zero-gravity environment. But Prince Sultan was on a whirlwind visit, and soon after lunch wildlife expert Eric Bedin took us out onto the reserve, where from the top of a dune we sighted the prized herd of elusive oryx that he had been tracking with the aid of radio collars. Before he left, I asked Prince

Sultan if he would like to be a passenger in one of our motorized paragliders (Alain is one of the few people in the world who can carry a passenger on his paraglider). But Prince Sultan politely declined, and when I chided him that I thought it was less dangerous than the space shuttle, he smiled politely but said he didn't have the time if they were to get back to Riyadh before dark. Alain and I were both slightly relieved, as it was a windy day and a botched take-off with our royal host would have been a bit awkward, to say the least.

From Bani Ma'arid we continued south and passed through one of our first goals, the extraordinary sequence of 'Uruq or "vein" dunes that are perhaps the longest dunes in the world. On Ron's satellite images we followed individual ridges for over three hundred miles, and between them were corridors of hard sand and sediment that are actually the bottoms of dry lakes dating back to wetter times seven thousand to nine thousand years ago. Along these paleo-shores, scientists (especially Hal McClure, as noted in *Saudi Aramco World* 5–6/1989) have found freshwater shells and even the teeth of a hippopotamus. We stopped to camp for the night in the bottom of a dune corridor, and I took off with my paraglider at sunrise.

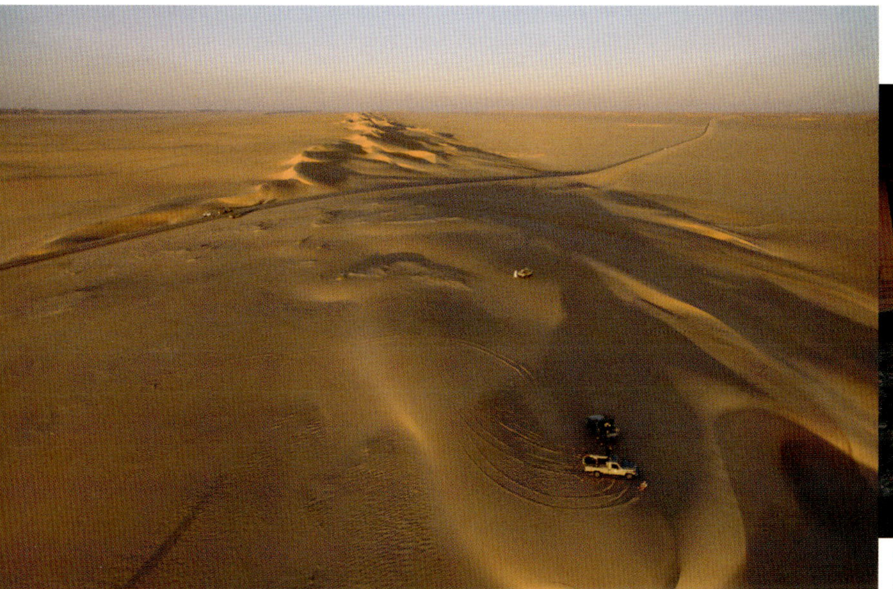
Saudi military patrol waiting for George Steinmetz
to land near Yemeni border, 2002

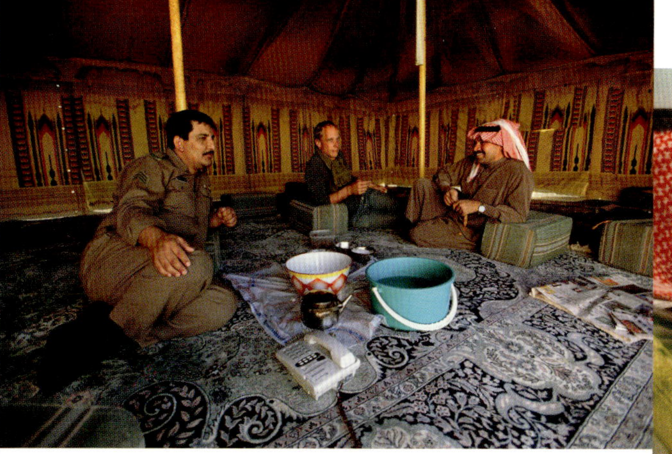
George Steinmetz having breakfast at Saudi border
post after landing near Yemen, 2002

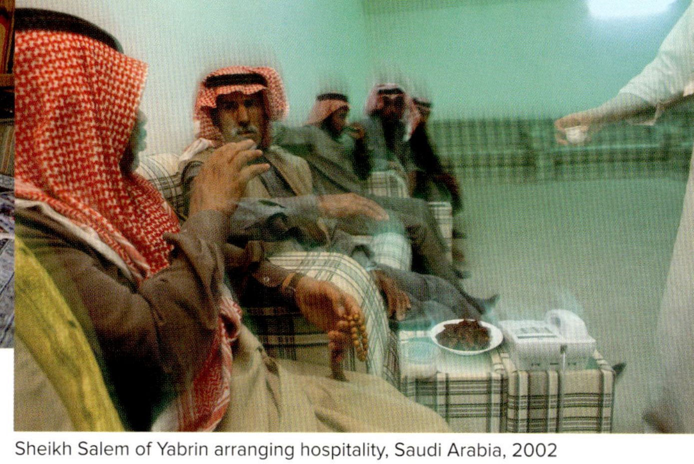
Sheikh Salem of Yabrin arranging hospitality, Saudi Arabia, 2002

It was a beautiful scene below me, a dune scape that looked like sandy waves in a frozen sea. After I had been in flight for about an hour, I noticed a pair of cars moving very fast through the sand and tried to maneuver myself into a position where I could get an oblique view of their dust cloud. But whichever way I moved they turned to come directly toward me. As they got closer, I realized that they were Saudi military pickups with heavy machine guns mounted in back. I urgently called Alain and Banounah on the radio, since they had been loosely shadowing me from the road. I didn't know what to do—if I tried to outrun the military I could make the situation worse, but if they got close they could easily shoot me down. I was a big, pink target drone. So I kept my altitude and loitered nervously until Banounah could catch up to them and show the travel papers that Prince Sultan had arranged for us. After that I landed adjacent to their cars in the sand and apologized for causing an emergency. I hadn't realized we were so close to the Yemeni border and that there was an army presence in the area.

After an effusive round of apologies, we were invited back to their camp that guarded this section of the frontier and offered small cups of coffee and omelets with flat bread. Meanwhile, the officer in charge made phone calls to his superiors from his large carpeted tent in the sand. An hour later we parted as friends with a memorable adventure in common.

THE PERILS OF HOSPITALITY

It's an unsettling experience to turn off a paved road and head out into the world's largest sea of sand with nothing but a GPS point 350 miles away, but that is what we had come to do and it was the only way to discover things few people have seen. If you succeed you're a hero, if you fail you're an idiot, and sometimes it seems there is very little besides dumb luck that separates the two. *Inshallah*, as the Arabs would say—it is God's will.

It took us two full days of driving through gently rolling white dunes to reach Yabrin, our driver Ali Al-Mari's home village, and he swelled with pride that we were making the commitment to visit there. It is one of the oldest settlements deep in the sands, and the closest reliable fuel supply to Wabar. It is a small, very close-knit community, and with Ali as our host, anything seemed possible. As we were taken from tent to tent, it seemed that everyone we met in Yabrin had the tribal last name of Al-Mari. The

following afternoon we were invited out on an afternoon falcon hunt with Ali's cousin. Mohammed Hamad Al-Mari launched the $4,000 bird into the air from his gloved hand stretched out the open window of his Toyota Land Cruiser and then sped after the raptor as it attacked a pigeon on the fly and ripped it to pieces.

As we sat around the fire that night in a carpeted tent, the men of Ali's extended family grilled me about the events of 9/11 and America's support of Israel, and then we ran into some serious trouble. The sheikh of Yabrin, Salem Faisal Al-Jaber Al-Muradhaf, had just learned that foreigners were in town, and we were told that it would be a great insult if we didn't partake in his hospitality. We were summoned to his home late that evening, which was the largest in Yabrin. He invited us in to his reception hall—a large, windowless room lined on all four walls with low foam cushions, with a telephone placed in the center of the carpet. We declined, explaining apologetically that we had just eaten dinner and needed to leave at sunrise on a twelve-hour drive through unmarked sand to the meteor crater at Wabar, the Ubar site that had been visited by Philby. But he was upset. As the sheikh of the area, his hospitality was a matter of honor to him, and our refusing his invitation would have

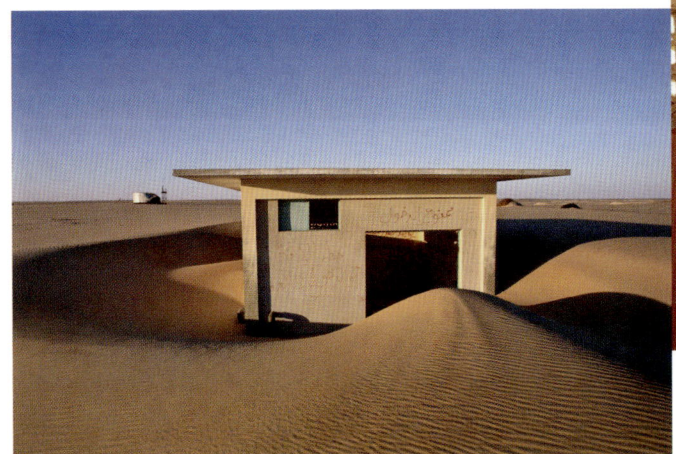

Abandoned nuclear weather station, Ubaylah, Saudi Arabia, 2002

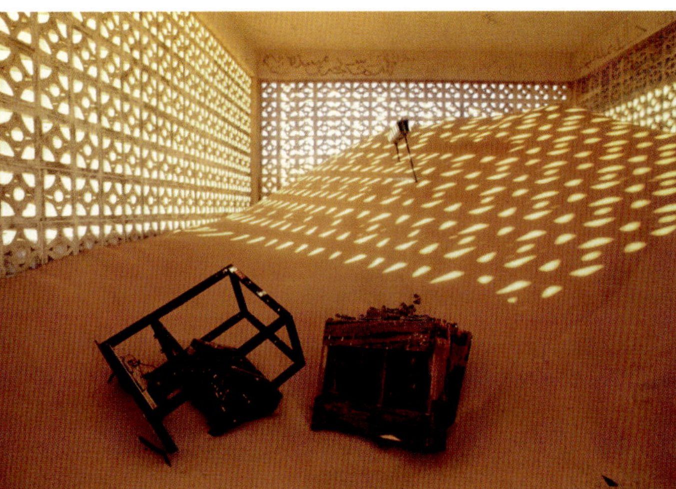

Radioactive equipment, Ubaylah, Saudi Arabia, 2002

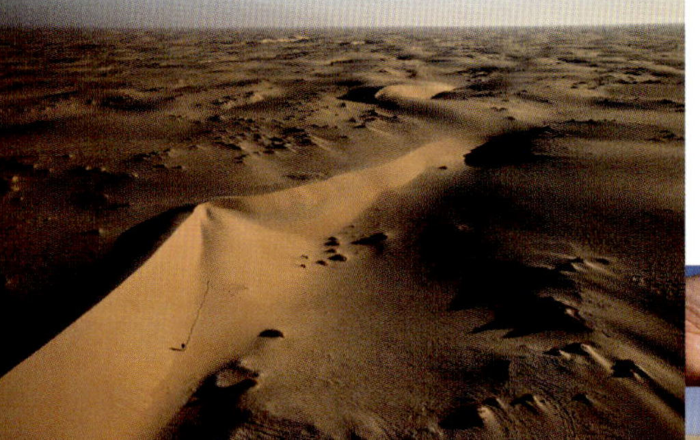

"Philby A" meteor crater, Wabar, Saudi Arabia, 2002

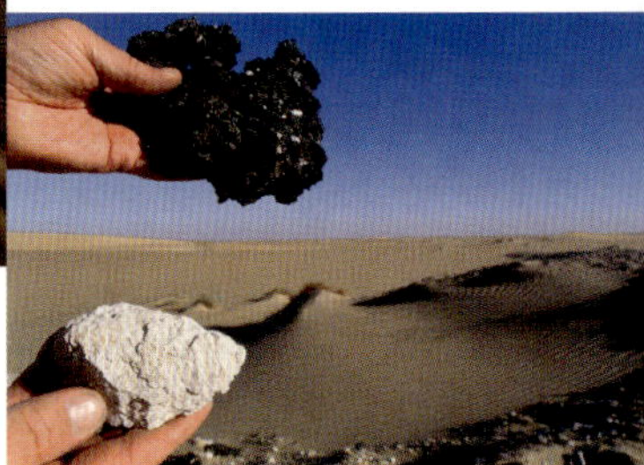

Meteoritic debris and fused sand, Wabar, Saudi Arabia, 2002

created a political problem for Ali. We were unsure as to what to do, until Sheikh Salem abruptly commanded us to come for breakfast before sunrise the next morning.

We felt strange showing up at the sheikh's house in the inky light before dawn and waking up his son to let us in. A little after sunrise we were ushered into his home, and in the center of the carpeted floor was an enormous platter of garnished rice with a whole roasted sheep in its center. We felt terribly guilty, thinking of how his wife and family must have suffered, staying up all night to slaughter the animal and prepare this meal. We also felt a bit piggish driving out of there at 8 A.M., our bellies swollen with meat and greasy rice. But an aerial photo of the meteorite crater had never been taken, and I had promised one to geologist Jeff Wynn, who had mapped out the Wabar site. I was sorry I could not linger with Sheikh Salem, but I was not willing to sacrifice a once-in-a-lifetime opportunity.

WABAR

We raced through the unmarked dunes, trying to reach the remote site before darkness, but it was tough going and we became mired in the fine sand repeatedly. We stopped at an abandoned oil camp of Ubaylah just before sunset. Jeff Wynn had given me the coordinates of this place where he had happened upon an abandoned nuclear-powered weather station. Jeff had warned me of its invisible dangers, telling me how his Geiger counter had gone off the scale as he abandoned his approach. I spent only a few minutes taking pictures inside the small sand-drowned building before making a hasty retreat. We then headed north in the gathering darkness through an immense field of crescent-shaped barchan dunes, following the arrow of our GPS units toward the meteorite impact site. We almost rolled our cars a few times that night as we unwittingly plunged down slip-faces in the dark but arrived safely at our destination around ten. We camped a few hundred meters away so as not to disturb the site, and I took off at sunrise to survey the area.

I didn't know what I might find. Wynn had warned me not to expect too much, because the craters had become almost totally filled with sand in the seventy years since Philby had visited the site. Often I've discovered things from the sky that even the most seasoned guides and scientists had overlooked. Flying low and slow above the long shadows in the early morning, patterns

that are completely invisible on the ground pop out like colored dots in a test for colorblindness. But here my optimism was dashed much like Philby's had been, for below were two shallow depressions filled almost to the rim with light beige sand. The great "Atlantis of the Sands," as Bertram Thomas named it, wasn't even a hole in the ground. We explored the area on foot as well, but there was little here to be found.

ORANGE SNAKES

After our morning at Wabar we headed cross-country, striking out again through virgin terrain, this time for the big Saudi oil facility at Shaybah. Iyad had lent me a satellite phone in case we had a problem, but when we tested it, I found that all the credit had expired. But there really was nobody to call for a rescue anyway. We had to be careful, and I felt a strange sort of kinship with Thesiger; in today's desert, our lives depended on camels of Japanese steel to carry us across with our water and food. There was no track or route marker, so we trusted symbols on an old map that were probably placed with little ground correlation. Late that afternoon, we discovered some

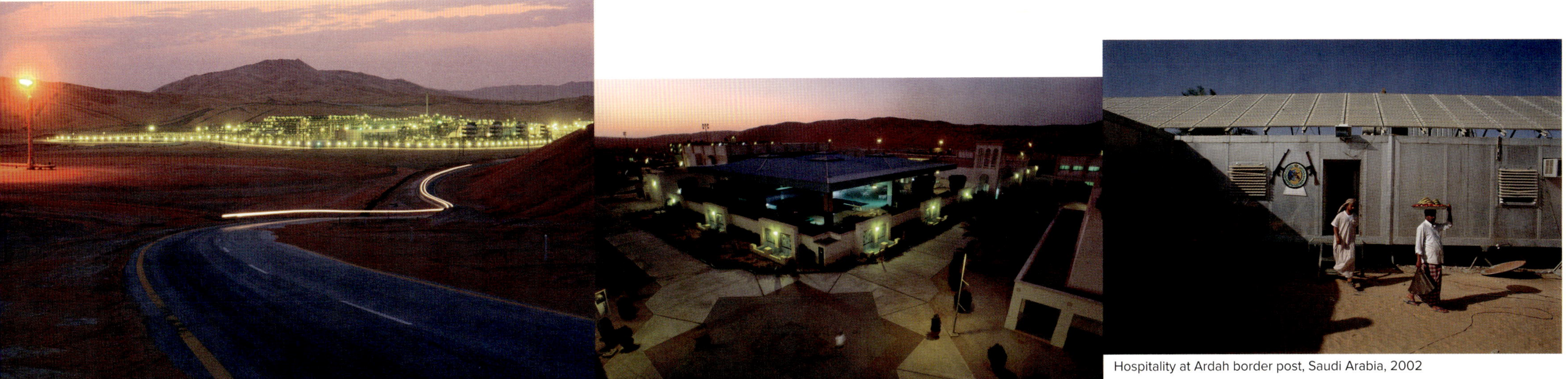

Gas-oil separation plant, Shaybah, Saudi Arabia, 2004

Swimming pool at the residential complex, Shaybah, Saudi Arabia, 2002

Hospitality at Ardah border post, Saudi Arabia, 2002

vehicle tracks and followed them onto what turned out to be a heavily used sandy track running north. We followed them until we saw a small convoy of vehicles loaded with families heading in our direction. We stopped to find out where they were coming from, and through Banounah were told it was an unmarked route from the Arabian Gulf to a military post on the Yemeni border. Greatly relieved that there was a safe way out of the sands, I made a gesture with my fist to indicate it was a good, fast route, only to have Banounah and the families recoil in shock. My innocent hand movement signified to them a desire to have sex, and I saw the eyes of a young wife grow wide as she stared at me through her veil from the car window. But my unwitting insult soon dissolved into a hearty round of awkward laughter. That gesture became our camp joke for the rest of the trip. After saying our good-byes, we drove on into the night again, losing the track and getting stuck in a sandstorm as we halted near midnight at the foot of a one-hundred-foot-tall barchan dune. After sunrise the following day we crested the top of a high dune and caught sight of the first paved road in a week. A few hours later, our three dusty cars rolled into Shaybah with all fuel tanks empty.

It was strange to find ourselves in a modern air-conditioned oil facility with laundry service, a cafeteria, American-style hotel rooms, and a shaded oversize swimming pool. With great effort, our writer, Uwe George, was able to catch a ride on a small survey plane flying a low-level grid over the massive dunes in the easternmost part of the Empty Quarter. Uwe, who has seen more of the Sahara than anyone, was absolutely stunned. "It's fantastic, fantastic! The most amazing dunes I've ever seen! One place looked like rows of snakes! Orange snakes!" He also described an artesian spring shooting many meters up into the sky before turning into a river in the sands. In the northern section around Shaybah, the complex barchan dunes were bunched up and looked very much like an eggcrate, but further south the sabkhas opened up into corridors (*shug* in Arabic) that spread out until they morphed into a grid of massive orange star dunes. At this point in the journey, Uwe had most of what he needed for the magazine and wanted to meet with Saudi Aramco geologists, so he decided to leave for Dhahran on the Saudi Aramco jet the following day. I was sad to see him go, but Uwe had left us with an incredible tip. Unfortunately, the location of the spring and snake dunes he had found were

over 150 miles to the south of us through the largest and most dangerous eggcrate dunes of the Empty Quarter. The next morning I ended a paraglider flight near a Saudi border post on the edge of the oil field, and we were invited into a tent for tea. Colonel to colonel, Banounah explained our mission and asked about the condition of the road south. Miraculously, we were offered a military escort through the eggcrate dunes to the Omani frontier.

At dawn the next morning we entered what seemed like another planet. The oil company had bulldozed ramps of sand through the eggcrate dunes until the sabkha opened up into long corridors, or shugs, that were bounded by huge ridges of orange sand. The dunes rose steeply, over eight hundred feet, on both sides but the shug was flat and dry, and we were able to drive at near highway speeds. We turned south when we came to one of the small concrete markers that delineate Saudi Arabia from Oman, and a couple of hours later arrived at the Saudi border post of Ardah, a small collection of aging, wind-battered mobile homes discarded by oil exploration crews.

(continued on page 28)

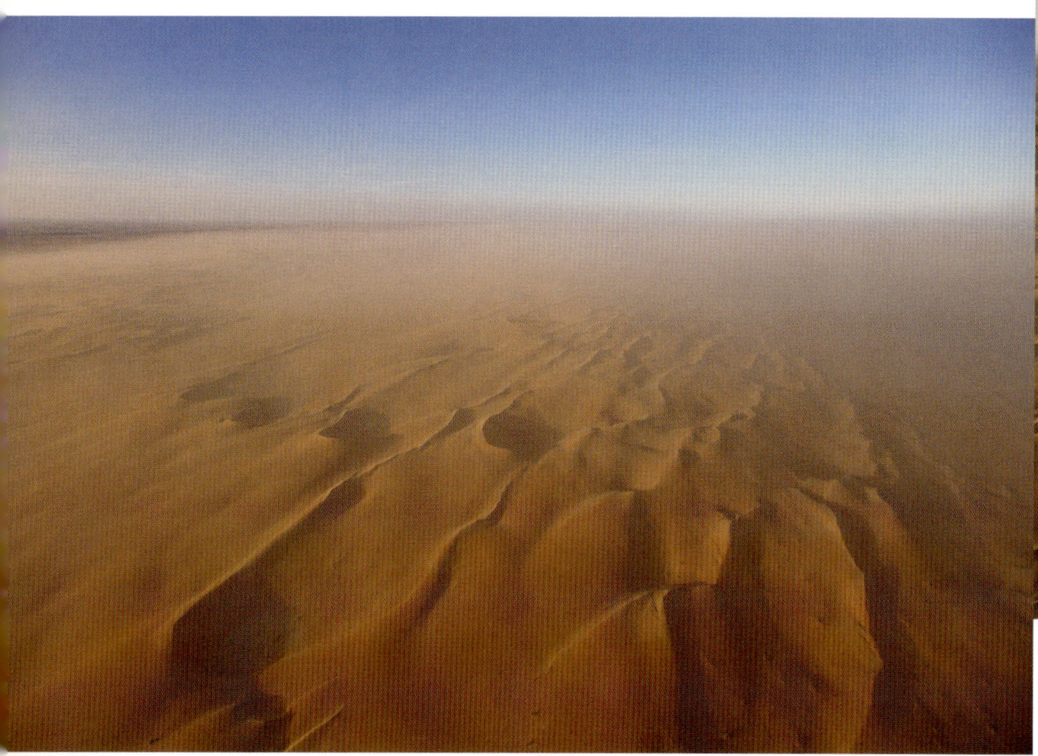
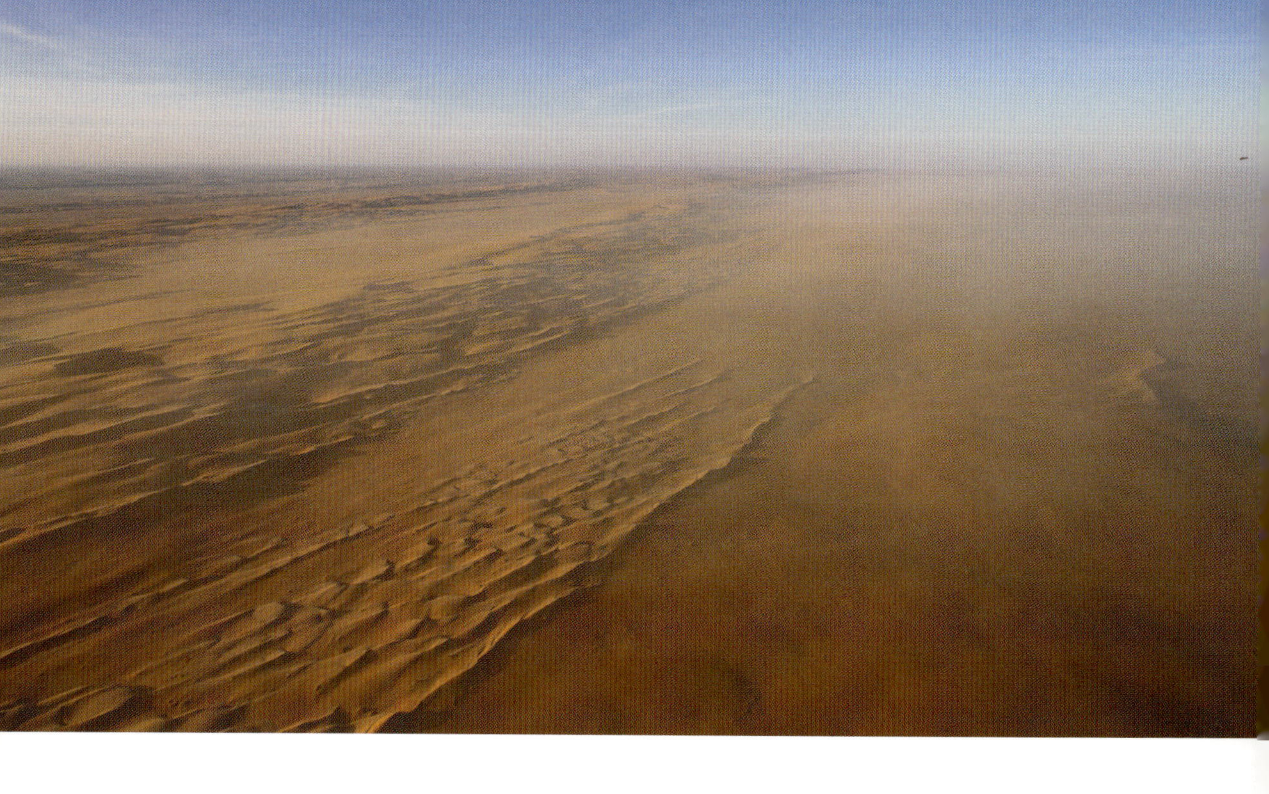

Approaching sandstorm, Yemeni–Saudi Arabian border, 2004

"Looking a few thousand feet below, I soon realized that this fog was not static at all, but was moving fast in my direction. I puzzled over this for a few minutes before I realized that what I was watching was a fast-moving wedge of cold air sweeping underneath me like an avalanche. I'd been caught in a sandstorm before, and I felt a panic rise up inside me. I looked back toward camp where I had taken off a half hour earlier, and knew that in a sandstorm I would never make it back."

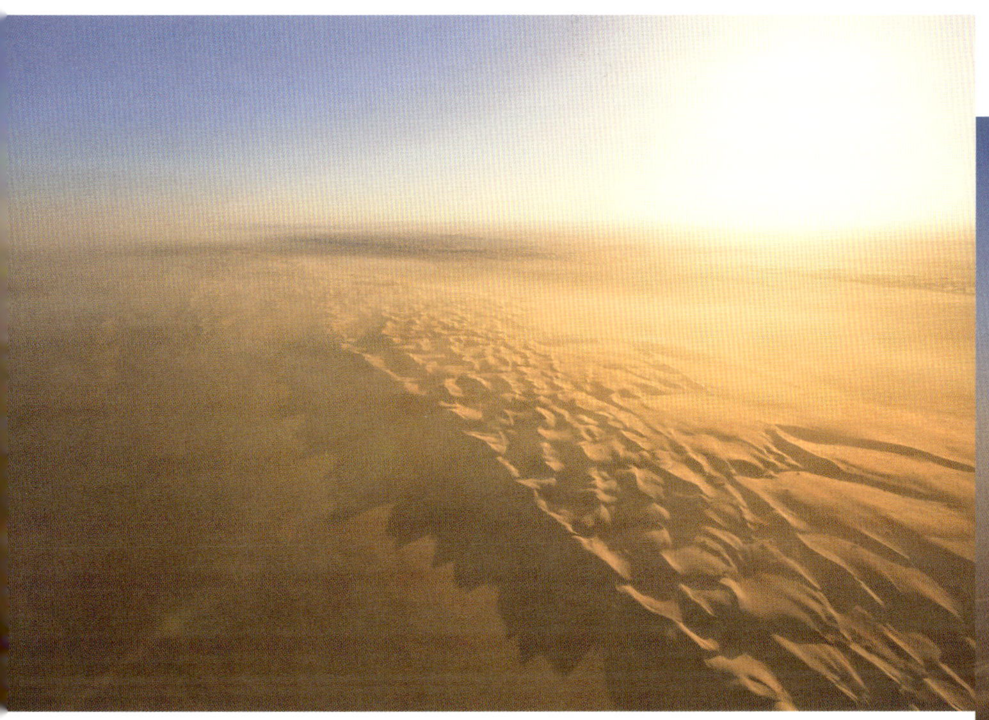
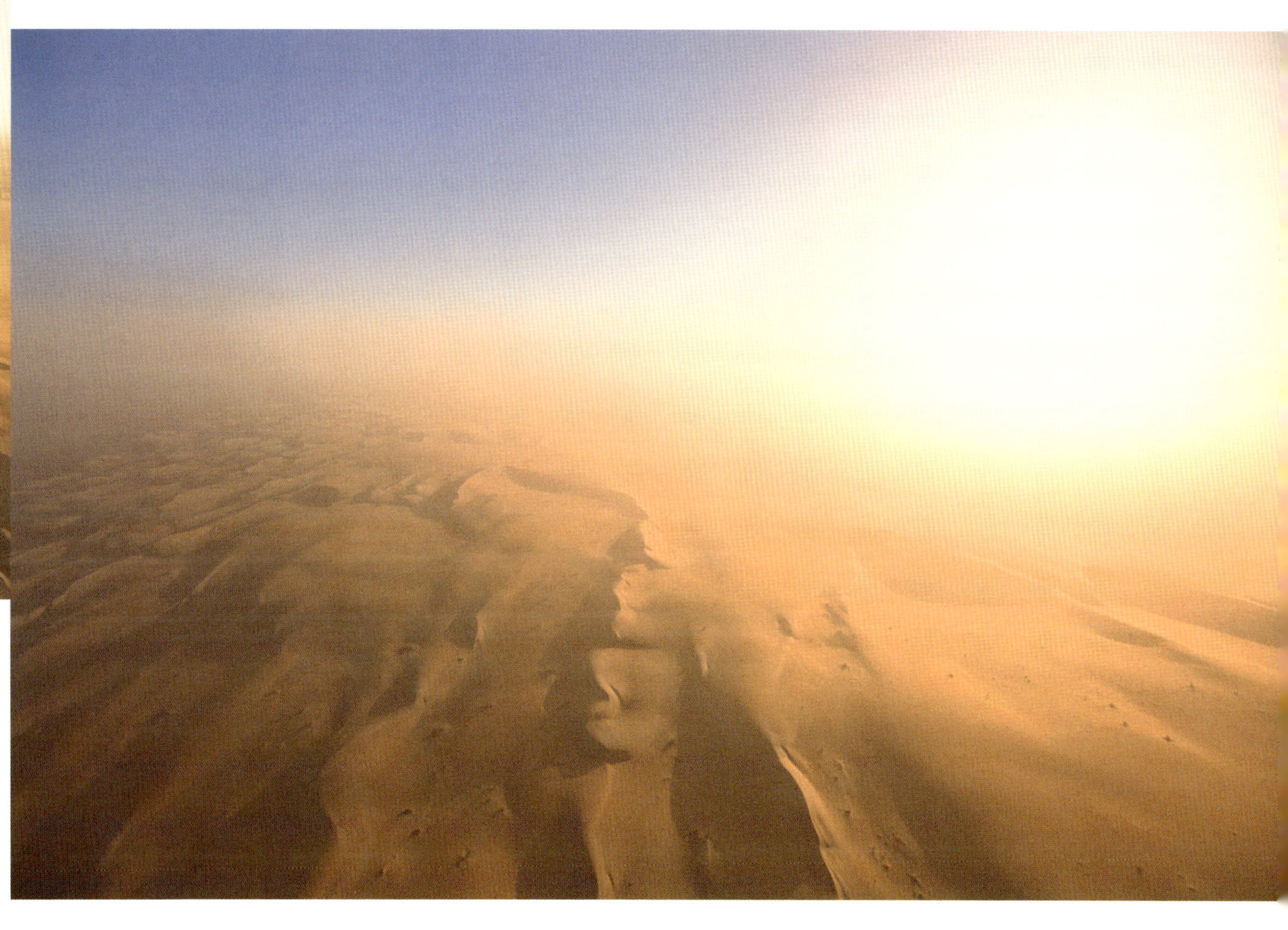

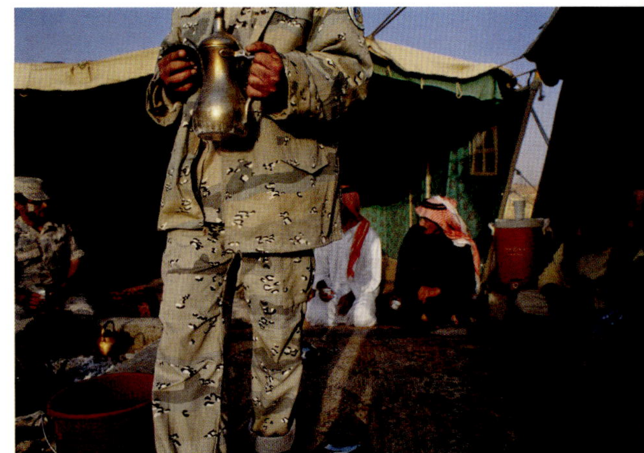

Traditional coffee service at border post,
Markaz Dar Balutan, Saudi Arabia, 2004

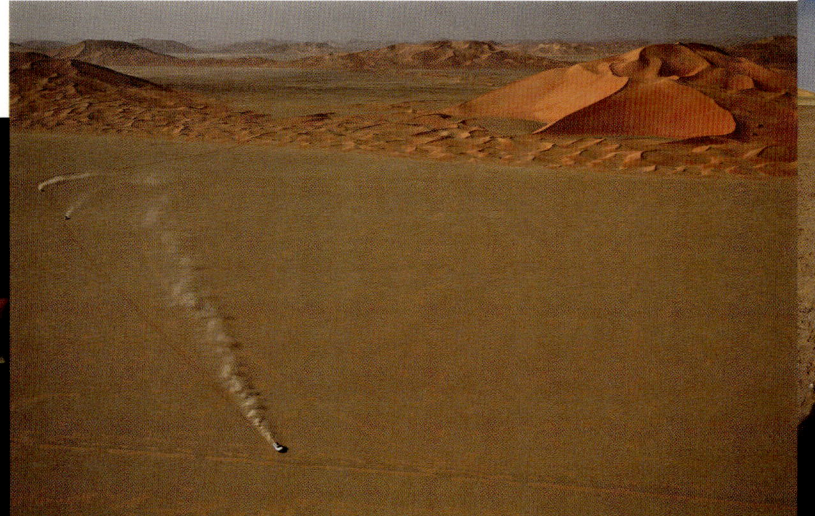

George Steinmetz's team chasing after him in high winds,
'Uruq al Mutaridah, Saudi Arabia, 2002

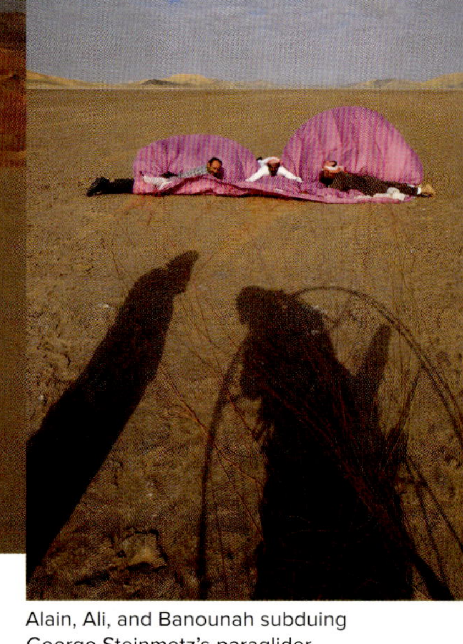

Alain, Ali, and Banounah subduing
George Steinmetz's paraglider,
'Uruq al Mutaridah, Saudi Arabia, 2002

(continued from page 25)

It was a bleak place, and they were thrilled to have visitors. The border guards insisted that we stay for lunch, which we could not refuse without deeply offending our hosts. By now we had grown accustomed to these obligatory pit stops. The trick was to accept and bow out quickly without getting stuck in a "time trap," as Uwe called them. The fact was we would not have been there without their kindness, so it was the least we could do. We asked them if they had many visitors. "Oh yes," they replied. "There were some Canadians who came across by camel three years ago…"

They gave us 360 liters of fuel, and a few hours later a four-foot-wide platter of rice emerged with yet another roasted sheep on top of it. We asked about the big dune country to the west, where Uwe had found the snake dunes and artesian fountain, and while they claimed no knowledge of the place, they offered one of their own to accompany us. We accepted their offer of a guide, as it seemed more likely they would come looking for us if one of their own failed to show up two days later. We set off into the unknown a few hours before sunset and drove through the virgin dunes as fast as we could until darkness fell. I became increasingly worried that we would get stuck as we followed the glowing arrows of our handheld GPS units, with our old topographic maps illuminated by headlamps, and the high beams of the cars lighting up the walls of dunes that surrounded us. We felt like five blind men in a labyrinth, and by ten o'clock that night were stuck in sand up to our axles and totally exhausted, with about twenty miles separating us from Uwe's field of snakes. While Ali, Alain, and I dug the lead car out of the sand, Banounah heated up a cooked chicken that had been wrapped in tin foil by our hosts back at Ardah. A sandstorm came up, which made eating particularly miserable as we had no tents and the cars were too filled with equipment to serve as a dining room. Alain was so exhausted he skipped eating and lay down on a dune, pulling his fleece jacket over his head to protect it from the blowing sand, and promptly fell asleep, undisturbed by the sand swirling around him.

I woke up Alain with a cup of hot espresso at 5 A.M., since I was determined to get an aerial photo of Uwe's snake dunes at sunrise. In the murky light before dawn we were able to find our way out of the dune pocket and broke free into a long shug that separated the dunes. The wind was strong, and with a hole in the clouds rapidly approaching the rising sun, Alain and I hauled my flight gear out of the back of the car, and fifteen minutes later I was flying over what seemed like an earthly analogy to Mars. It was one of the most beautiful flights I've ever experienced and was all the more sweet for the Herculean effort we had made to get here, a place that no one, except Uwe and the jaded members of his flight crew, had ever seen before.

I went up a few thousand feet to get an overview of these chains of star dunes and realized that the strong winds were blowing exactly parallel to the dunes, and the star dunes appeared to be caused by back-eddies that had found their equilibrium. It was a spectacular sight, but the wind was so strong at two thousand feet that I was going backward across the ground while flying into the wind at an airspeed of thirty miles per hour. It's very unsettling flying with negative ground speed, but as soon as I touched the ground, Alain grabbed my parachute lines and the whole team jumped on my paraglider to keep me from being blown across the salt flats. After the euphoria died down and the gear was packed up, we faced the daunting challenge of reaching Uwe's mysterious fountain in the sand. It was sixty miles south of us, but the three-hundred-foot-tall dune chains ran east-west. According to our old geological maps, there were twenty-five lines of dunes between the spring and us. Since leaving Ardah, we had driven in nothing but soft sand and playa mud and were using up our fuel at an alarming rate. We had to be very careful that our loop route didn't turn into

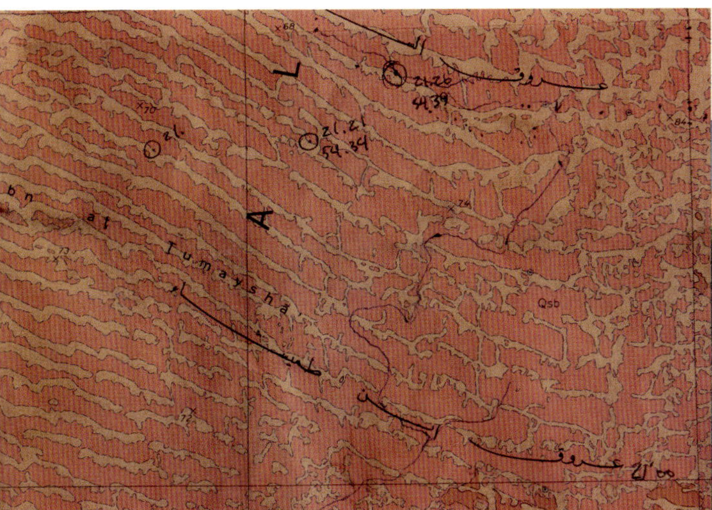

George Steinmetz's route through dune chains
of 'Uruq al Mutaridah, Saudi Arabia, 2002

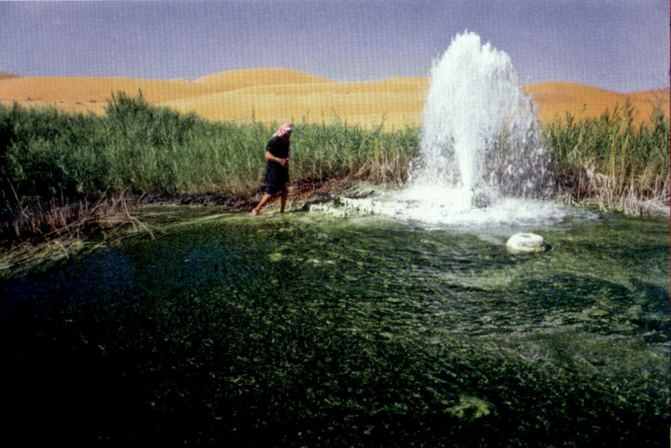

Uwe's geyser, 'Uruq al Mutaridah, Saudi Arabia, 2002

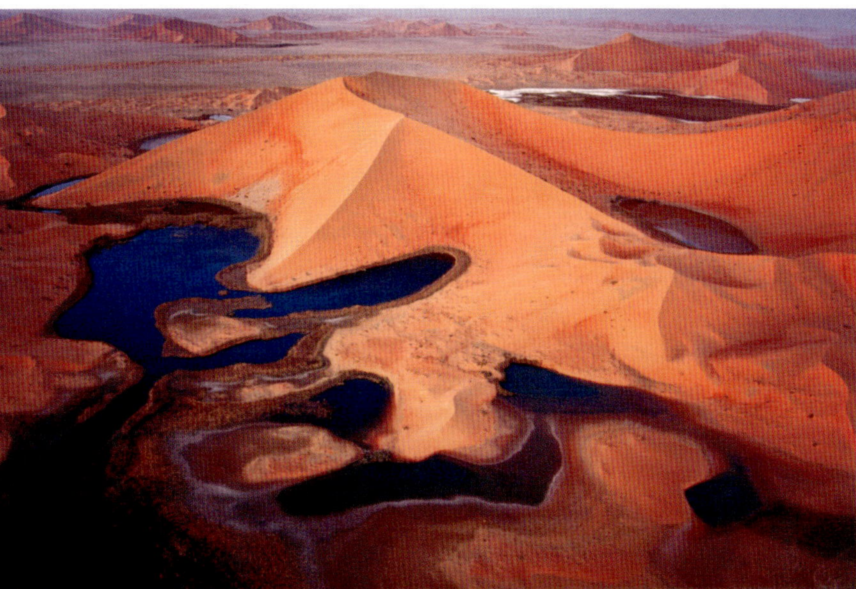

Freshwater springs of Khawr Hamidan, Saudi Arabia, 2002

a dead end without enough fuel to double back. But our maps had proved incredibly accurate in the dark the night before, in spite of the fact that they were over forty years old. It appeared that the larger dune forms here were completely static, and now we decided to bet on it. Alain plotted the shortest zigzag course through the cordons of dunes, making GPS waypoints where the dune chains looked the thinnest, and we were off. It was a most surreal environment out there, especially on only a few hours' sleep in 110°F heat. I felt as if I was hallucinating as we drove through the desert with music blaring from my iPod. Within a few hours the dunes started to thin out, and we were able to find breaks in the dune chains instead of having to cut through them. And then we started to cross the tracks of other vehicles, presumably left decades before when the area was last explored for oil. Eventually the tracks all converged in the direction of Uwe's fountain, which we discovered to be an old abandoned wellhead spewing hot sulfurous water up into the sky.

As we headed back toward Ardah, I rifled through my collection of maps, looking for something else to explore, and spotted a water hole named Khawr Hamidan on my old Michelin map. We knew we were getting close as the ground changed from brown to white, presumably from the alkaline salts left by evaporating spring water. When Banounah and Ali stopped to refuel

from the two-hundred-liter drums in the pickup, I decided to take a sunset flight. Just as the sun disappeared I glimpsed the oasis of Khawr Hamidan, and with Alain, Ali, and Banounah in ground pursuit, I headed directly for it. I arrived in the gloomy light of dusk at the most amazing site—a meandering necklace of clear freshwater lakes wrapping around an enormous orange dune. I took a few photos in the failing light and then landed in the headlights of our three cars. I was torn, as I wanted to stay in this most unusual place, but our time was up.

We had experienced one of the most extraordinary landscapes on our planet, and I was haunted by my decision to leave. Had we really seen the best of the Empty Quarter, or were we merely scratching the surface? But I was no longer living the bachelor life of Thesiger. My wife, daughter, and newborn twins were waiting for me at home, and I needed to get back. I vowed to myself I would return if I could ever find a way.

THE SECOND CROSSING

It wasn't until two years later that I returned to the Empty Quarter on an expedition for *National Geographic*. My proposal was to pick up where we had left off two years before, in the mega-dunes of the eastern sands, and continue across the

border into Oman and Yemen. I wanted to explore more of the extraordinary dunescapes that we had found in the last days of my previous trip and was hoping to find more Bedouin culture alive on the southern edge of the sands.

Here in Oman lay the real ruins of the lost city of Ubar, which was the beginning of a chain of ancient oasis towns that were stopping points for camel caravans carrying frankincense all the way to Palestine. Some two thousand years before, the Sabeans controlled the southern part of the Empty Quarter. They and their legendary Queen of Sheba had profited off the incense trade, and Mahram Bilqis, rumored to be her Temple of the Moon, was being excavated that winter by an international team of archaeologists. Another Sabean trading center, Shibam, was a rare example of living archaeology; a walled city comprised of eight-story mud buildings known as the medieval Manhattan of the desert. The magazine asked my friend Donovan Webster to write the story, as we had collaborated on stories about the Sahara and Gobi deserts in the past with Alain, who agreed to help with flight safety once again.

My biggest obstacle this time was getting permission to cross the border from Saudi Arabia into Oman. While the two countries have cordial relations, there is no official border crossing. Indeed, there was no one on either side with

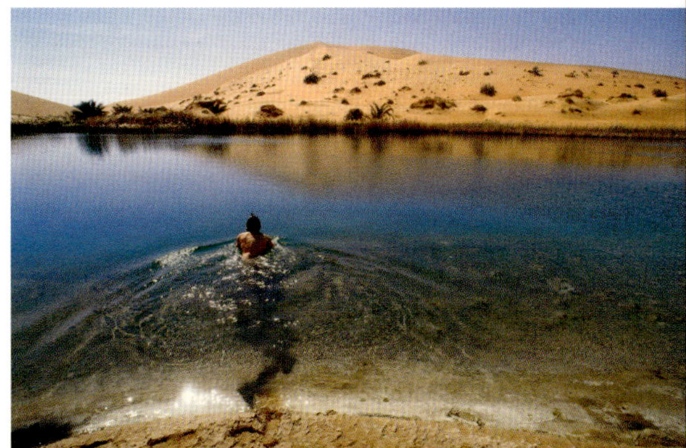

Donovan Webster swimming in
Khawr Hamidan, Saudi Arabia, 2004

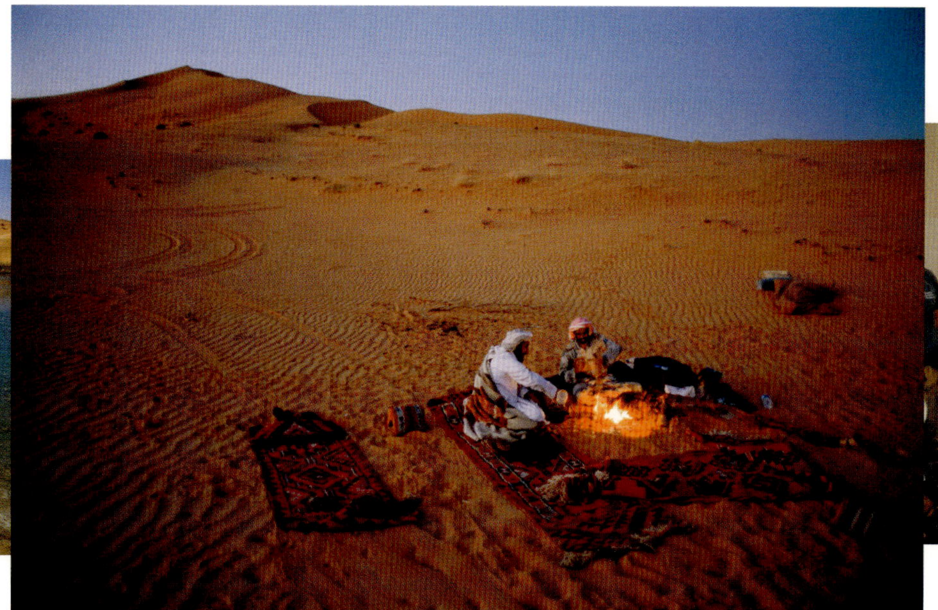

George Steinmetz's camp at sunrise, 'Uruq al Mutaridah, Saudi Arabia, 2004

Saudi and Omani military, border
post near Mugshin, Oman, 2004

a passport stamp because there simply is no land traffic. I inquired through the Omani embassy, but after months of waiting, they still couldn't process such an unusual request and advised us to fly to Muscat. Juris Zarins, the archaeologist who had spearheaded the discovery of the real city of Ubar, gave me the phone number of a senior advisor to the sultan of Oman. After many phone calls and emails, we were given the latitude and longitude of a point out in the desert where we could meet representatives of the Omani military at noon on the day I had selected: February 4, 2004. I couldn't help but think of Bertram Thomas, who had galloped through hundreds of miles of Saudi Arabia without a permit. He couldn't have imagined faxing ahead passports and vehicle insurance documents, but that was long before the discovery of billions of dollars of oil under the sands, the demarcation of desert borders, and the emergence of al-Qaeda.

We arrived in Riyadh in late January 2004 and were in Shaybah a few days later. But the atmosphere in Saudi Arabia was dramatically different from just two years before. The United States had invaded Iraq the previous winter, and there had been numerous terrorist bombings in Saudi Arabia. Prince Sultan had organized a military escort for our entire time in the remote Saudi part of the Empty Quarter, and when we got to

Shaybah we found a much-heightened sense of security, and it was impossible to get permission to fly over some of the same areas I had access to only two years before.

So we fueled up and headed straight to the miraculous lakes of Khawr Hamidan. We spent a day there, this time leaving time to explore. One of the lakes was fresh enough to drink, but we saw no signs of wildlife or Bedu visitation. After a morning flight, Don and I left our crew and took a swim; it was a sublime experience. But trips like this are only to be savored for brief moments, as we had a lot of desert to explore before our appointment on the Omani border. We spent a handful of days driving over a thousand miles in the sands. It was a tour of the most surreal dune forms in the world, with sheefs of satellite images of dunes to choose from and old maps as our guide. Five days later, our team of three cars left the last border post in Saudi Arabia and headed across the no-man's-land into Oman.

CROSSING INTO OMAN

The mysterious latitude and longitude coordinates given to us by the Omani military turned out to be a tidy government-built settlement occupied by a few families of settled Bedouin who were adjusting to the sedentary life of a small suburban

subdivision. We entered a gate onto paved streets with check-ered curbs, streetlights, rows of identical air-conditioned homes, a mosque, and a government center. Inside was our reception committee, dressed in their fresh white robes and ceremonial canes, who had driven from Mugshin, the regional capital, to meet us. They had brought a huge amount of fresh fruit, dates, and a wide variety of foods that lay carefully arranged on a carpet covered with a thin plastic sheet. The Saudi and Omani military men had never met, although they had lived for years in camps less than a dozen miles apart. The Omani government was worried about our safety, and our new escort of elite commandos had two desert-camouflaged Land Cruisers with light machine guns mounted on the dashboards. After a long lunch of pleasantries and thank-yous, we said good-bye to our Saudi entourage and made our way out to the dreaded *Umm as Samim,* or Mother of Poisons. It's the largest basin in the Empty Quarter and covered with nine-hundred square miles of quicksand. Thesiger was the first European to see it and made a short traverse, with his companions and their camels becoming mired in the greasy mud as they broke through the brittle surface. It has a reputation as a foul and evil place, but what we found was an area that had been abandoned after being intensively explored for oil, with a bulldozed

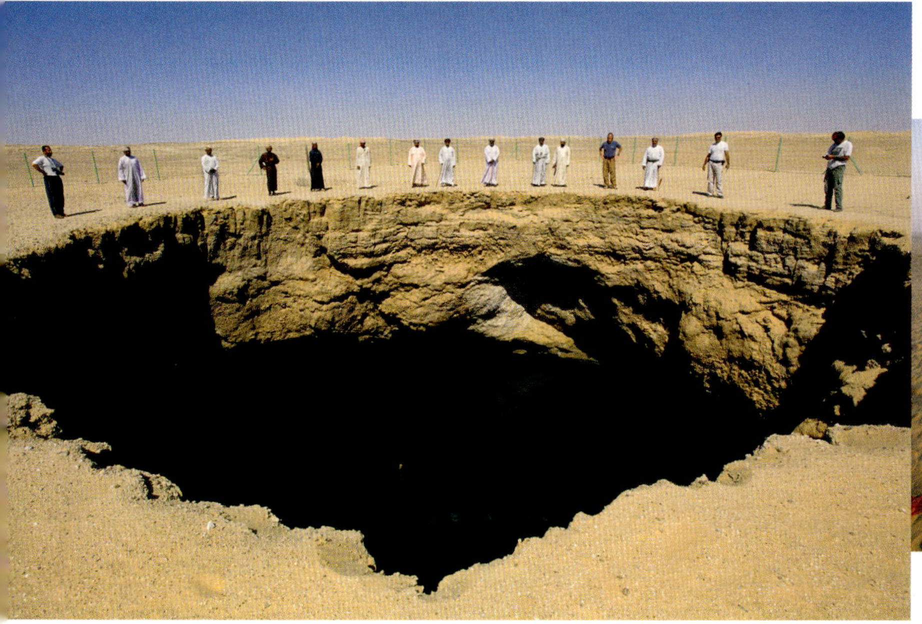

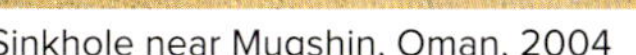

Sinkhole near Mugshin, Oman, 2004

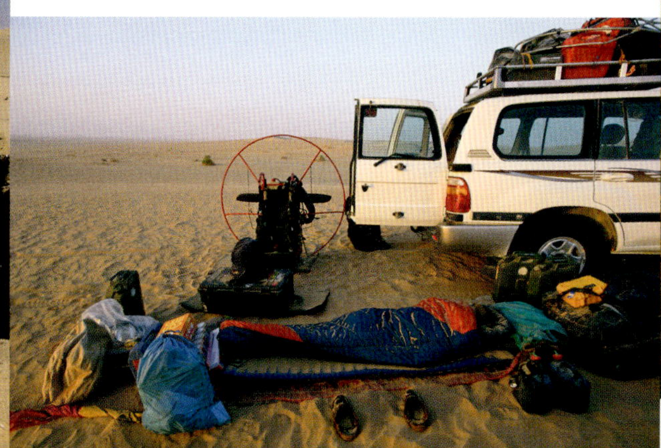

Alain Arnoux sleeping through a morning sandstorm,
Ramlat Amilhayt, Oman, 2004

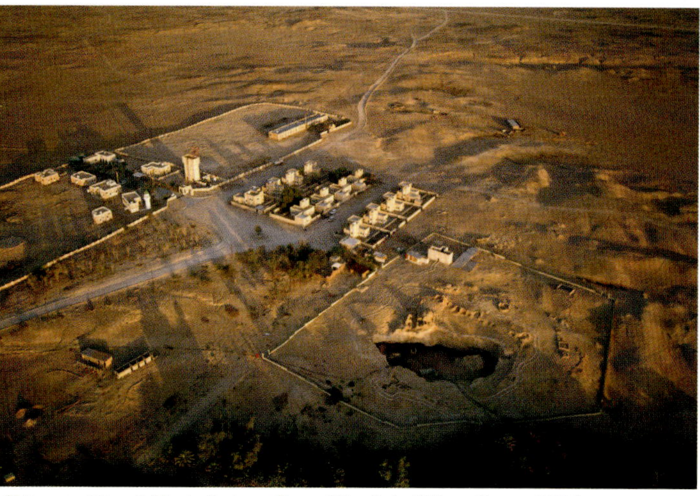

Shisur and the sinkhole that swallowed the fort of Ubar, Oman, 2004

track marked with empty two-hundred-liter oil drums. When Don tried to leave the track, we all gained renewed respect for Thesiger as we spent hours extracting our flight car.

Our next stop was Juris's discovery of the ancient caravan settlement of Ubar, which over the centuries had morphed into the modern Omani settlement of Shisur. The frankincense trade had started in the mountains of Oman, an area once known as Ubar, which separated the Empty Quarter from the coast. The historical references to Ubar were actually not to a town, but to a region where local tribes would scrape the bark of gnarled trees for the sap of *Boswellia sacra*. It was then transported, presumably by donkey, down trails through the stony desert to one of the caravan towns of Ubar, which acted as a gathering point and caravanserai. There it was loaded onto camels for the winter caravans that plied routes around and across the sands all the way to Rome and Persia, where it was worth its weight in gold. Frankincense was used primarily for cremations and religious ceremonies, much as in Byzantine rites today, and the trade flourished from around 2800 BCE to 300 CE. The caravan trade was extremely lucrative, with a route designed to avoid bandits, pirates, and toll takers, much like the drug traffic today, and shifted with climatic and political situations. Each town along the way benefited by supplying water, fodder, food, and some

level of protection to passing frankincense caravans. Most likely, Shisur was a center for the desert route that was used in the winter, while other shipment points on the coast grew wealthy from maritime routes that took advantage of seasonal monsoon trade winds. Ron Blom had analyzed the satellite images for traces of caravan tracks that led from the coastal mountains out along the edges of the sands. Although the Landsat satellite data only recorded one pixel for an area the size of two basketball courts, Ron was able to follow four-thousand-year-old tracks with the invisible spectra of reflected light that could readily distinguish the tracks from the surrounding terrain. The trails converged on modern Shisur, which bore little resemblance to T. E. Lawrence's imagined Atlantis of the Sands. Shisur in 2004 was like every other resettlement center—a small suburban development of sterile, generic air-conditioned homes built by the Omani government. The only possible evidence of the ancient Ubar was a small stone building that was crumbling at the edge of a large sinkhole. Zarins and his multidisciplinary team had discovered remnants of eight towers connected by a wall that surrounded the ancient well, and this matches the Koranic description of a many-towered city. And so it appeared that just as the frankincense trade was declining, the mythical Ubar had simply sunk into the sands, or more precisely, fallen into the water source

that once supported it. Perhaps it was a cataclysmic earthquake or a disobedient king who finally precipitated its final moment, but Zarins suspected something more common: Sinkholes are usually the result of a dropping water table, and for thousands of years Arabia has been suffering from increased aridity and rampant, unsustainable irrigation. The fort at Shisur probably would have been rebuilt if it hadn't been for the adoption of Christianity as the state religion of the Roman Empire, which all but eliminated demand for frankincense by banning pagan cremation.

For a sense of completion, I made a flight over Shisur and was even more disappointed than I was with its misidentified cousin, Wabar. While the histories of Ubar and Wabar were fascinating, the ruins that I saw were little more than holes in the ground to the untrained eye, and we had little time to waste.

Our way west from there was along the frankincense route toward Yemen.

On the Omani side of the border most of the desert towns from former southern Arabian cultures had been converted into these newly built suburban settlements with water, electricity, schools, and even air-conditioning. As I sat in one resettlement center after another, under the ubiquitous oversize portraits of Oman's leader, Sultan Qaboos, I heard the same

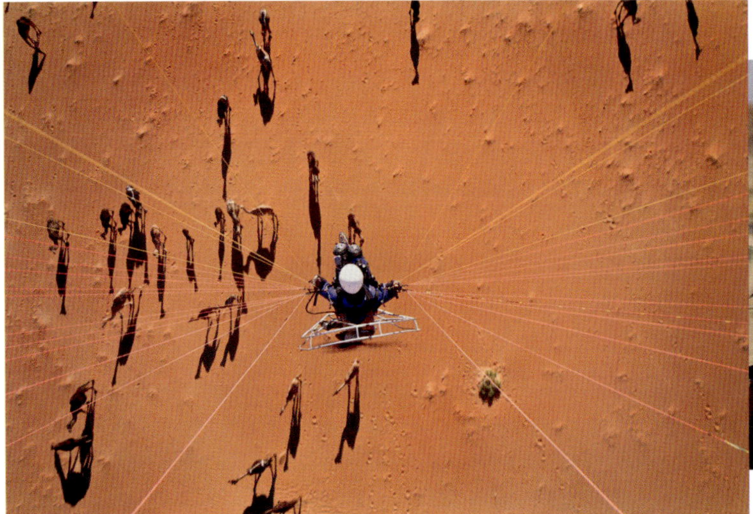

George Steinmetz in flight over camels, Wadi Mitan, Oman, 2004

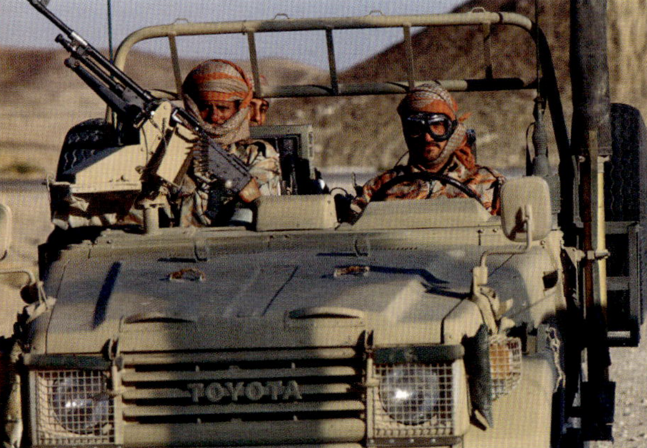

One of two military security cars assigned to
George Steinmetz, Wadi Mitan, Oman, 2004

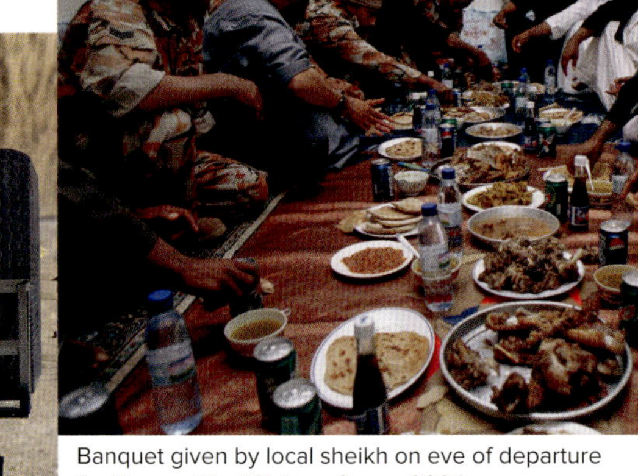

Banquet given by local sheikh on eve of departure
for Yemen, Wadi Shihan, Oman, 2004

story: The government gave the Bedouin a free place to live and basic commodities, so there was little incentive to struggle against the desert, and once the Bedouin children went away to school and discovered the outside world, they didn't return. The ancient caravan towns had been replaced by a chain of listless quasi-suburban settlements—Thesiger's Arabia had been erased.

But the Bedouin remained proud of their desert heritage, and we heard that there were still a few old-timers with stories to tell who might be found on the edge of the sands. The best place to find them was said to be in Wadi Mitan, near the corner where Saudi Arabia, Oman, and Yemen meet. We spent two days looking for them in that beautiful country of orange star dunes scattered across the alkali-stained plains, but there were few Bedouin to be found as it hadn't rained in many years.

But on an early morning flight I came across a small Bedouin camp just as a large herd of camels were being sent out to graze. I started taking photos from high above, looking straight down, with the long shadows of the camels projecting laterally across the multicolored sands. Suddenly Alain came on my flight radio telling me that the old Bedu who owned the camels was very upset and was threatening to shoot me down if I didn't stop disturbing his herd. I could see both his son

and the camels on the ground showing no signs of distress, and thought it highly unlikely that anyone would be foolish enough to shoot at me with a heavily armed military escort in plain view. So I kept flying to get just the right perspective on this rare situation. My guess turned out to be right, and he never did shoot, and I got one of the best pictures of the entire trip.

Two days later, on February 12, we crossed into Yemen at the border post of Wadi Shihan. Yemen has fantastic ancient cities comprised of high-rise mud buildings and a population that has not felt the rush of oil money, so we hoped to find more Bedouin still living on the fringes of the sands. But first we had to leave our military escort, interpreter, drivers, and vehicles behind and meet a team from Yemen that I had organized to meet us on the other side of the border. We had been putting in eighteen-hour days for twenty days in a row, and I sensed that our team of drivers from Riyadh was at the end of their rope. Fortunately, they weren't threatening to kill me like they had Philby, but they were definitely ready for a change of pace and scenery. A few weeks later I would learn that in their haste to return to Riyadh, they had rolled one of their cars while speeding around a curve near the Yemeni border; they were lucky no one was badly injured.

CAUGHT IN A SANDSTORM

As we continued southwest we detoured to explore the seldom-visited edge of the sands in Yemen. The best, unexplored patterns on Ron's satellite photos were in Ramlat Hazar, near the Saudi border. It took us a couple of days to get out there with our three cars, and on an early morning flight I spotted a most unusual sight—a rare ground fog enveloping the dunes some ten miles north in what appeared to be Saudi Arabia. There was a large patch of chaotic and untracked dunes below me in the no-man's-land of the militarized border, and I was reluctant to stray across into Saudi territory. Looking a few thousand feet below, I soon realized that this fog was not static at all, but was moving fast in my direction. I puzzled over this for a few minutes before I realized that what I was watching was a fast moving wedge of cold air sweeping underneath me like an avalanche. I'd been caught in a sandstorm before, and I felt a panic rise up inside me. I looked back toward camp where I had taken off a half hour earlier, and knew that in a sandstorm I would never make it back. I urgently called Alain on my flight radio. He had been blissfully unaware, relaxing with a coffee around the campfire before I called. I gave him my approximate GPS coordinates and let my glider descend into the storm for an emergency landing. By the time I got down to a few hundred feet, the ground was lost

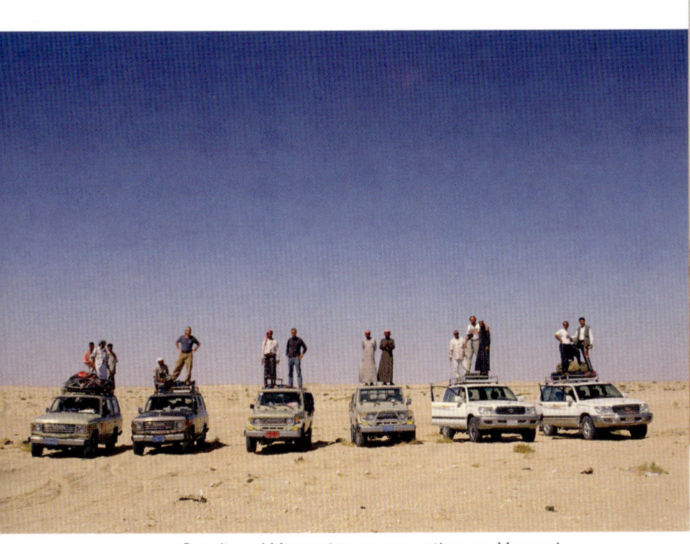

Saudi and Yemeni teams meeting on Yemeni-
Omani border, Wadi Shihan, 2004

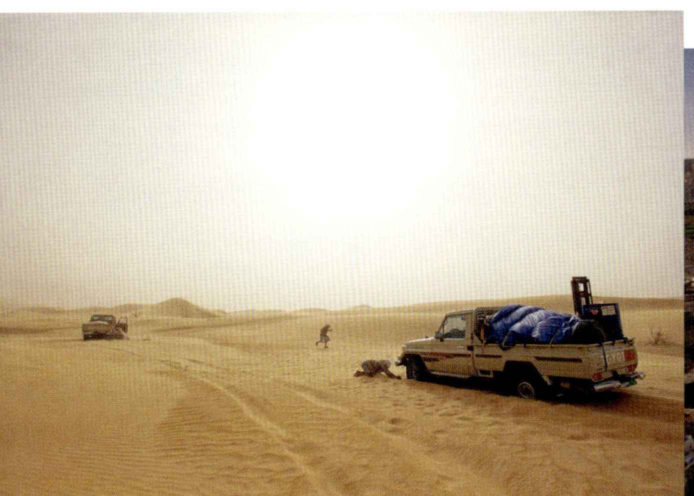

Escaping sandstorm, Ramlat Hazar, Yemen, 2004

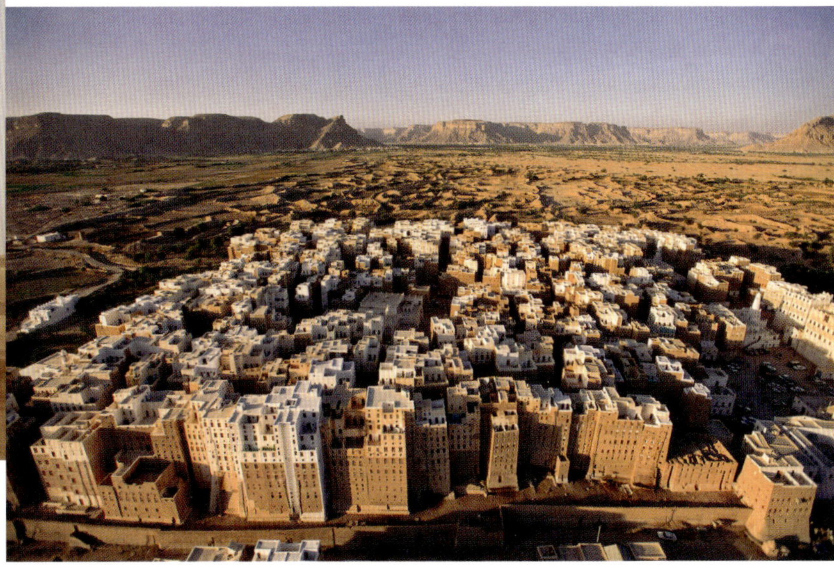

Shibam, Wadi Hadramawt, Yemen, 2004

in a swirling brown haze of sand, and I started to get tossed around by accelerating gusts of the storm front. I had once made the mistake of panicking in a similar situation and knew that I had to get on the ground as fast as possible before the winds strengthened. When I got down to about a hundred feet, I could make out the dunes and saw that I was actually moving backward while heading into the wind. As I approached the ground I got a break and the wind slackened for a moment. I killed the motor and I was able to hold my position as I touched the ground. I spun around to put my back to the wind and face toward the paraglider, which now tried to carry me across Yemen like a spinnaker in a gale. I dug my heels into the sand and left a pair of long trenches in the ground as I wound the brake lines of the paraglider around my hands to collapse the surface of the wing. After coming to a stop, I balled up the paraglider and radioed my new position to Alain, who was trying to find me by car. He showed up in about twenty minutes, but I couldn't see him until he was about fifty feet away. We greeted each other with a bear hug. The sandstorm followed us for two days as we headed south, and didn't stop until we reached the green Hadramawt Valley.

We spent a week exploring the Hadramawt, which is a long chain of ancient agricultural towns bordered by sheer one-thousand-foot-tall red-rock cliffs. The cliffs give rise to springs that have nurtured local agriculture for centuries. Here was living history, in the form of ancient walled cities that had flourished during the frankincense trade thousands of years before. A second frankincense route had developed along the coast that made its way up into the Hadramawt Valley. The most spectacular city along that route was Shibam, the so-called "medieval Manhattan," with eight-story buildings made of sun-baked mud and palm wood. The women in the Hadramawt are famous for their tall straw hats, which, combined with their long black gloves and cloaks, gave them the appearances of witches. Each community in the Hadramawt has a different style of hat, which is used to keep them cool in the blazing hot sun while they work in the fields.

We continued west along the edge of the sands that extend into the Ramlat Sabatayn, following the frankincense route. Our next stop was Shabwa, which two thousand years ago was the capital of the Hadramawt when it was rich from the incense trade. From the air I could easily see over ten square miles of fields and an irrigation system that had once supplied passing caravans with fodder, but now the area was largely abandoned, and the city nothing but a crumbled ruin.

We continued our tour of the frankincense trail in the equally unspectacular ruins of Bayhan, and then moved on toward Marib via an old smuggler's route and camped along the edge of the dunes. I took off from here at sunrise and followed the smuggler's track as it threaded its way between the sands and the foothills of the Yemeni highlands. Sixteen months earlier, a U.S.-operated predator drone had fired a hellfire missile here and incinerated a car carrying six suspected al-Qaeda operatives on this same route. I was unaware of the exact location of this strike until after I had flown right over it, but I had noticed that those on the ground greeted me less than enthusiastically. Half an hour later, I arrived over the archaeological site of Mahram Bilqis, the supposed temple of the Queen of Sheba. The temple was being excavated by an archaeological team led by Merilyn Phillips Hodgson, the sister of the adventurer Wendell Phillips who had been the first to excavate the site back in the early 1950s. Phillips, who did his fieldwork while carrying a holstered Colt 38 revolver on his hip, is assumed to have been part of the inspiration for the fictional Indiana Jones. Phillips was a charming and well-connected young oilman and explorer, and in 1950 he convinced the chairman of Chrysler to give him eighteen Dodge Power Wagons to aid his multiyear excavations of ancient South Arabian sites. The Queen of Sheba's temple had been the greatest archaeological find on

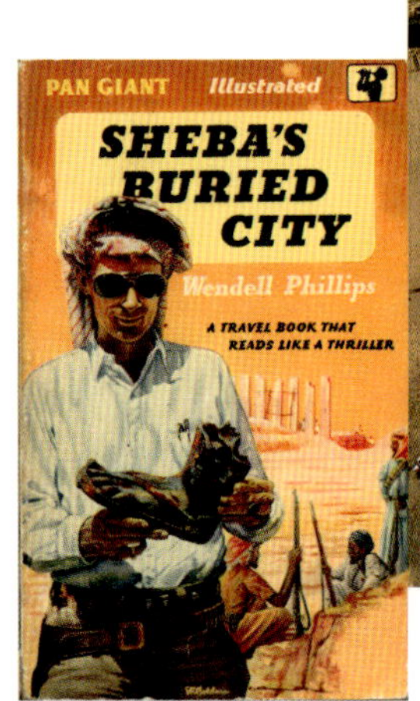

1958 edition of Wendell
Phillips's *Sheba's Buried City*

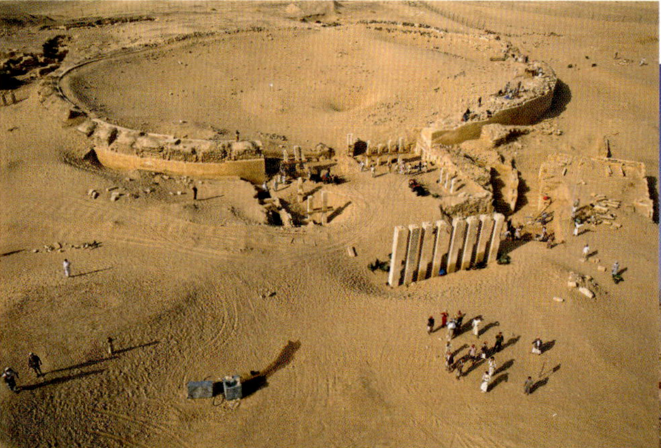

Archaeologists gazing up at George Steinmetz
from Mahram Bilqis, Marib, Yemen, 2004

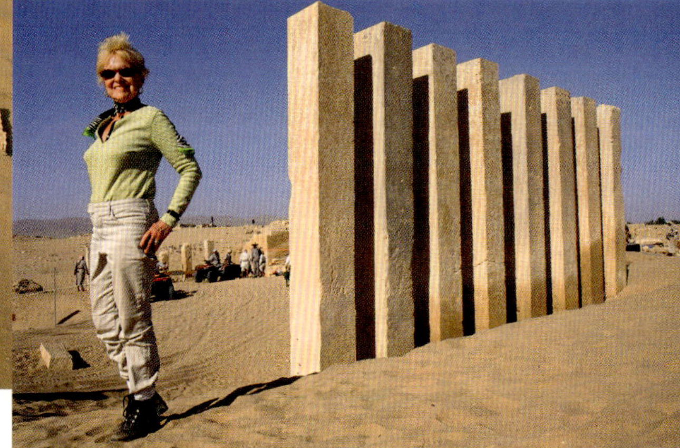

Merilyn Phillips Hodgson at pillars of Mahram Bilqis, Marib, Yemen, 2004

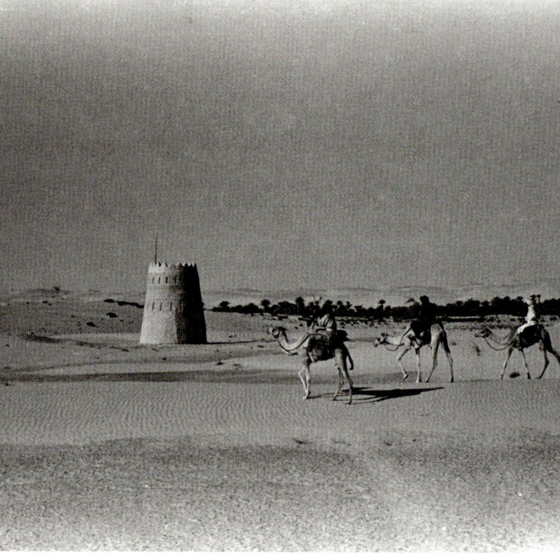

Thesiger's group passing fort, Liwa, U.A.E., 1948

the entire Arabian Peninsula, but it became buried in blowing sand after Phillips was forced to abandon the dig due to tribal suspicion and security concerns. As I approached Merilyn's team from the air, her military guard had a 50-caliber machine gun trained on me—apparently the security situation had not improved much. But Merilyn calmed them down, and I was able to take a few rare aerial photos of the spectacular site. I landed right in front of the eight limestone pillars that mark the entry to the 3,500-year-old temple. We shook hands heartily, as it was quite a dramatic arrival, and she introduced me to her crew. They had been digging there for about a month, with a team of international archaeologists and eighty Yemeni laborers moving 1,120 buckets of sand per hour. The site they revealed to me was unlike anything I had seen in Arabia, with its lifelike, three-dimensional sculptures of people and horses, both carved in stone and cast in bronze.

We stayed in Marib for a few days to document their impressive findings, but the town was a thicket of suspicion, and every male in this part of Yemen seemed to carry a Kalashnikov over his shoulder and a curved knife in his belt. Two clans near the excavation site had an active blood feud going, and the government had stationed armored personnel carriers in front of their homes to keep them from killing each other. We met with the governor of the province, Abdullah Al-Nase, who kindly gave me a police escort to fly over the ancient necropolis of Alam al-Abyad. But a few days later we were put under house arrest by the military on suspicion of spying. After a night under armed guard in the police station, we were allowed to stay in a hotel, where we were separately taken aside for questioning. We didn't have any official papers granting us permission to fly in Yemen, and now the governor was unable to help us. The officer in charge of the area kept demanding that I turn over my film. I had more than 250 rolls of exposed film by that point in the trip, so I refused, which made him all the more suspicious. I made numerous calls by satellite phone to my wife in New York and my editor in Washington, the U.S. Embassy in Sanaa, and a media advisor to the president of Yemen. After a few days we were released and were greatly relieved to find ourselves on the next flight out of the country.

THE UNITED ARAB EMIRATES

I returned to the Empty Quarter for one last trip in the spring of 2008. I felt my obsession would not be complete without a look at all the countries that shared the sands, and I had yet to see the U.A.E. At the time oil prices were at an all-time high, and the Emirates were awash in oil money. I couldn't find a magazine to pay for the trip, but my wife, who is an editor at the *Wall Street Journal*, convinced me to go to the U.A.E. with or without funding to capture the definitive story of the Empty Quarter. Ultimately, I paid for the trip out of my own pocket and asked my friend François Lagarde to join me to look after my safety and to have a little fun flying. We took a page out of Bertram Thomas's playbook and entered the country discretely. Without special permits, we were lucky to clear airport customs with our big, dirty bags of flight equipment. When we got into Abu Dhabi, we couldn't find a hotel for under $300 per night, so after a day assembling our paragliding motors in the parking lot, we just had one night in an air-conditioned room before heading out to the desert, where we spent two and a half weeks living out of the back of a rented Mitsubishi Pajero. We felt like a pair

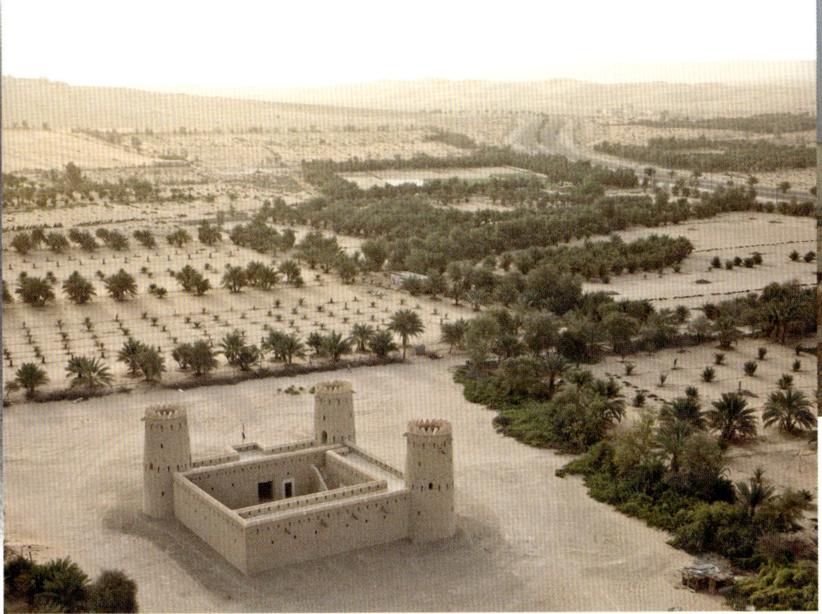
Restored fort of Jabbanah and modern irrigation, Liwa, U.A.E., 2008

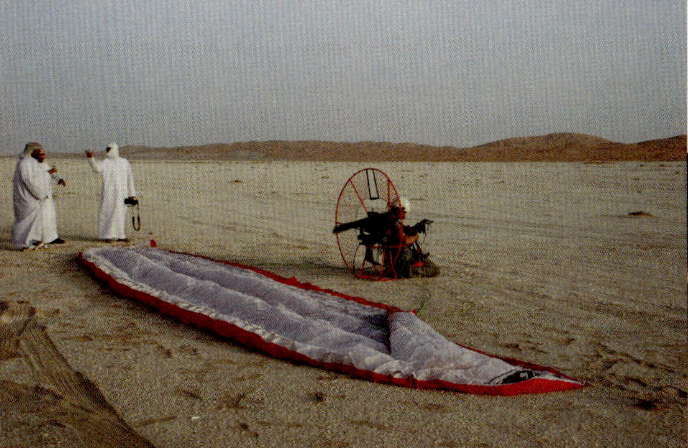
François Lagarde preparing for a flight, Umm az-Zamul, U.A.E., 2008

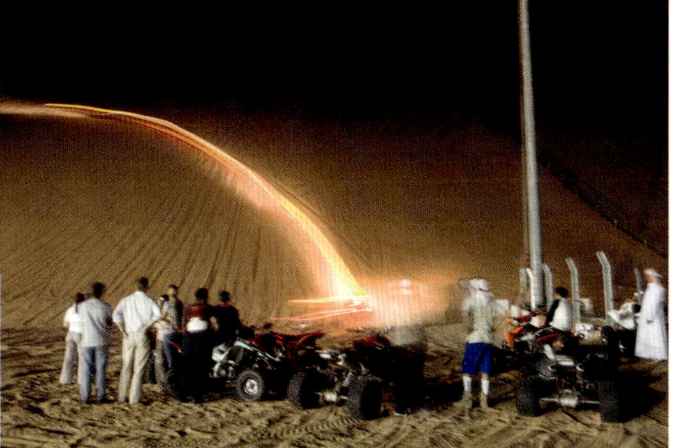
Sheikh roaring up dune in his California-built dune buggy, Moreeb, U.A.E., 2008

of foreign Bedouin sharing a Japanese camel. It was a real no-budget safari, with cold camps in the sand wherever we stopped for the night.

It was strange how asphalt and power lines had carved up the desert, and every night some kind of glow was visible on the horizon. The U.A.E. is a very thin strip of land, and most of the country is within a two-hour drive from the coast. Liwa, which had been a chain of sparse settlements at the end of the world for Thesiger on both of his crossings, was now a thoroughly modernized and heavily irrigated agricultural center with a network of deep wells.

Sheikh Zayed bin Sultan Al-Nahyan, the young leader who had taken in Thesiger after his second crossing, had built an enormous palace atop one of Liwa's largest dunes and irrigated the many acres around it into an enormous, golf-course-size lawn. There was even a huge, highway-size earthwork ramp leading up to it so that a car wouldn't have to zigzag up the hill.

While it would have been an interesting stunt to fly over the late Zayed's winter palace for a few pictures, I would certainly have been tracked down and arrested, and if the current ruler, Zayed's son Sheikh Khalifa bin Zayed Al-Nahyan, were there, I stood a good chance of being shot down. So we went further south to the end of the road at Moreeb, just eighteen miles north of the Saudi Arabian border near Shaybah. The Moreeb dune is the tallest in the Emirates, with a slip-face rising over five hundred feet at a forty-five-degree angle; getting up that slope requires extremely light but powerful vehicles. It had been turned into something of a weekend adventure park for wealthy Emiratis to come out and test their dune-climbing abilities in high-powered quad-bikes and dune buggies.

While camped there late one night, we were awakened by the lights and roar of a souped-up Southern California–built dune buggy piloted by a wealthy young sheikh with an entourage of young Western guests. The young sheikh popped wheelies while he roared up the face of the dune in the glare of parking lot lights and fog lamps. It was an amazing petro-feuled spectacle, but for me it was a sign that the serenity and majesty of this exquisite wilderness was coming to an end.

The following day one of these dune-climbers, Khalfan Al-Meharibi, invited us for lunch at his home in Liwa and took us for a tour of his family's date orchard. The aquifers in Liwa are rapidly drying up, and areas that once had water only five to ten feet underground now required wells over 250 feet deep, and the water was increasingly loaded with mineralized salts. In terms of population, the Empty Quarter of the Emirates was not so empty any more, and its meager resources were rapidly dwindling.

Thomas and Philby had noted that they made their crossings in particularly wet years, but it appears that the aridity of the desert is increasing, especially when compared to the monsoonal rains that once helped the ancient southern Arabian civilizations prosper. On my own transits through the sands, it was not uncommon to drive fifty miles without seeing a living plant.

I felt a bit like Thesiger, who at the end of his travels had felt disillusioned and lamented how the Arab world he knew and loved so well was disappearing before his eyes. While I had once assumed that the world's largest sand sea was impervious to outside influences due to its insular politics and by its sheer size and remoteness, now I am not so sure.

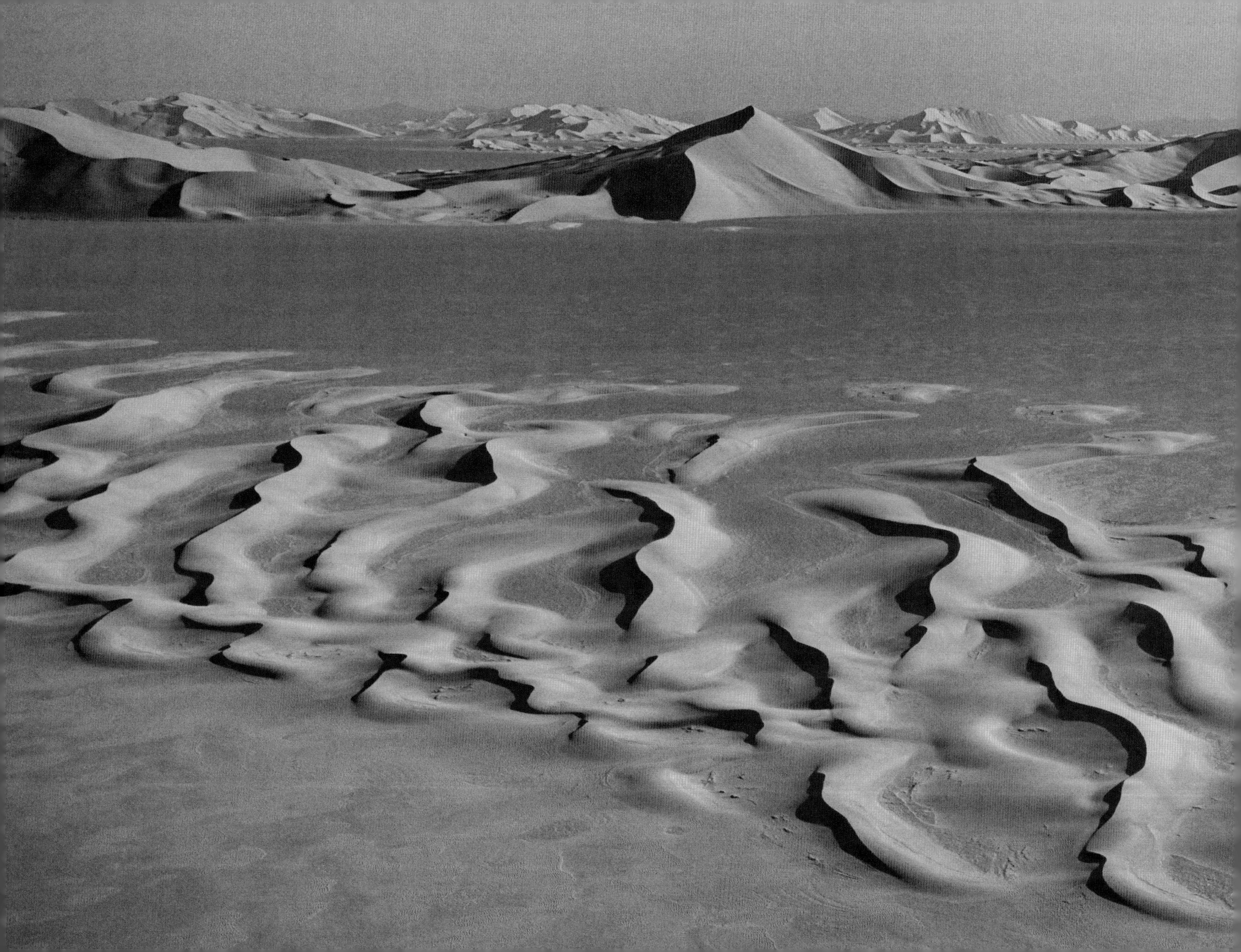

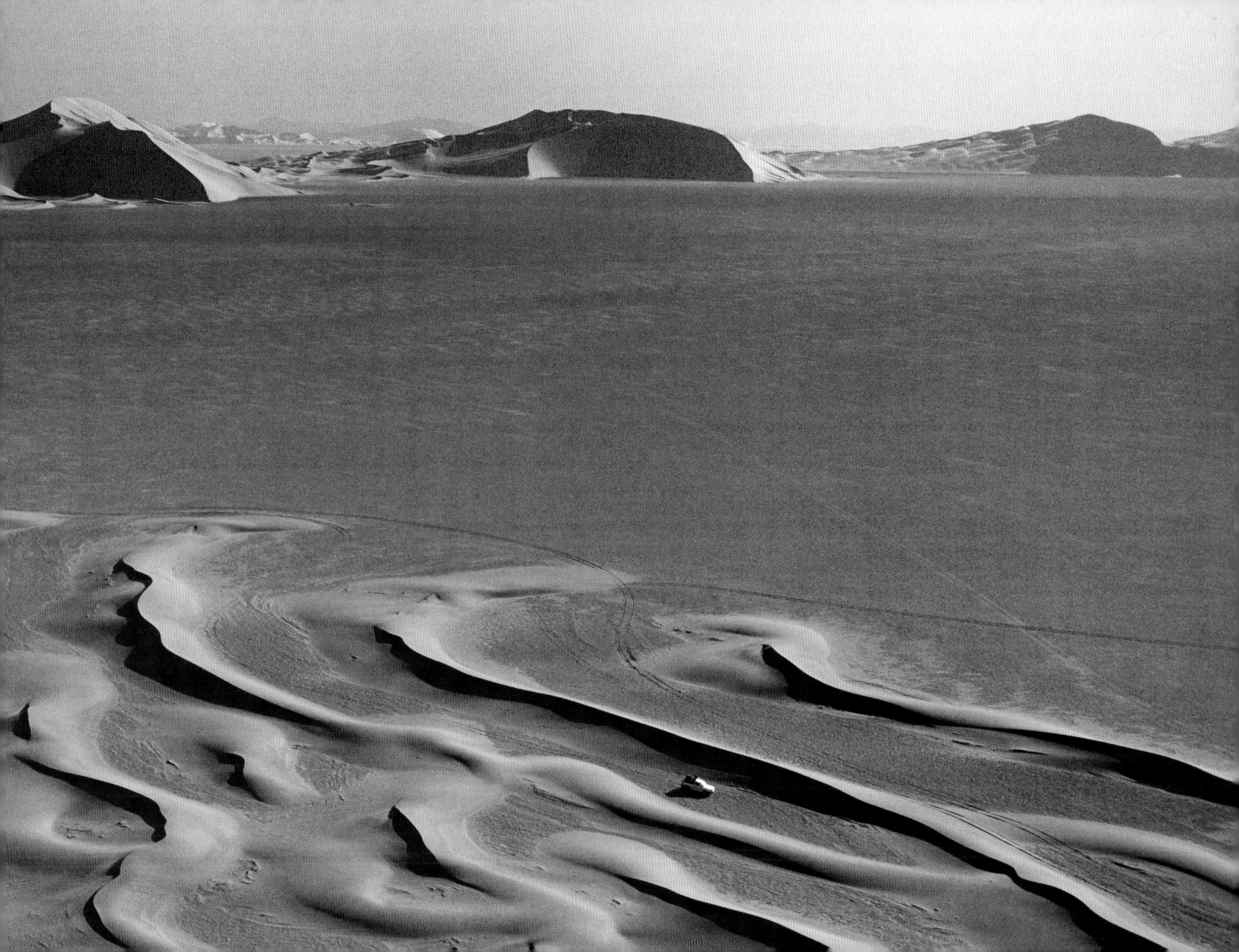

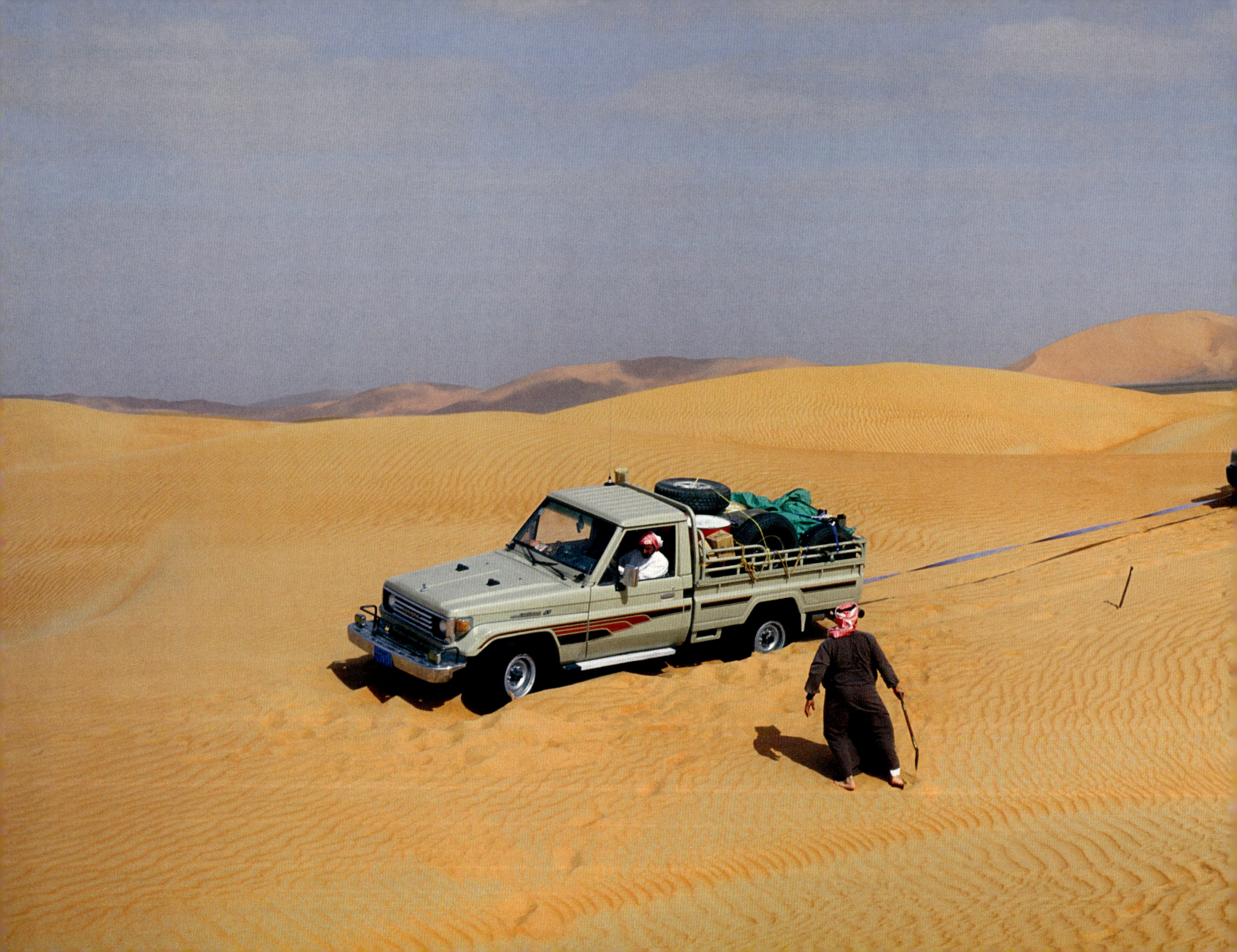

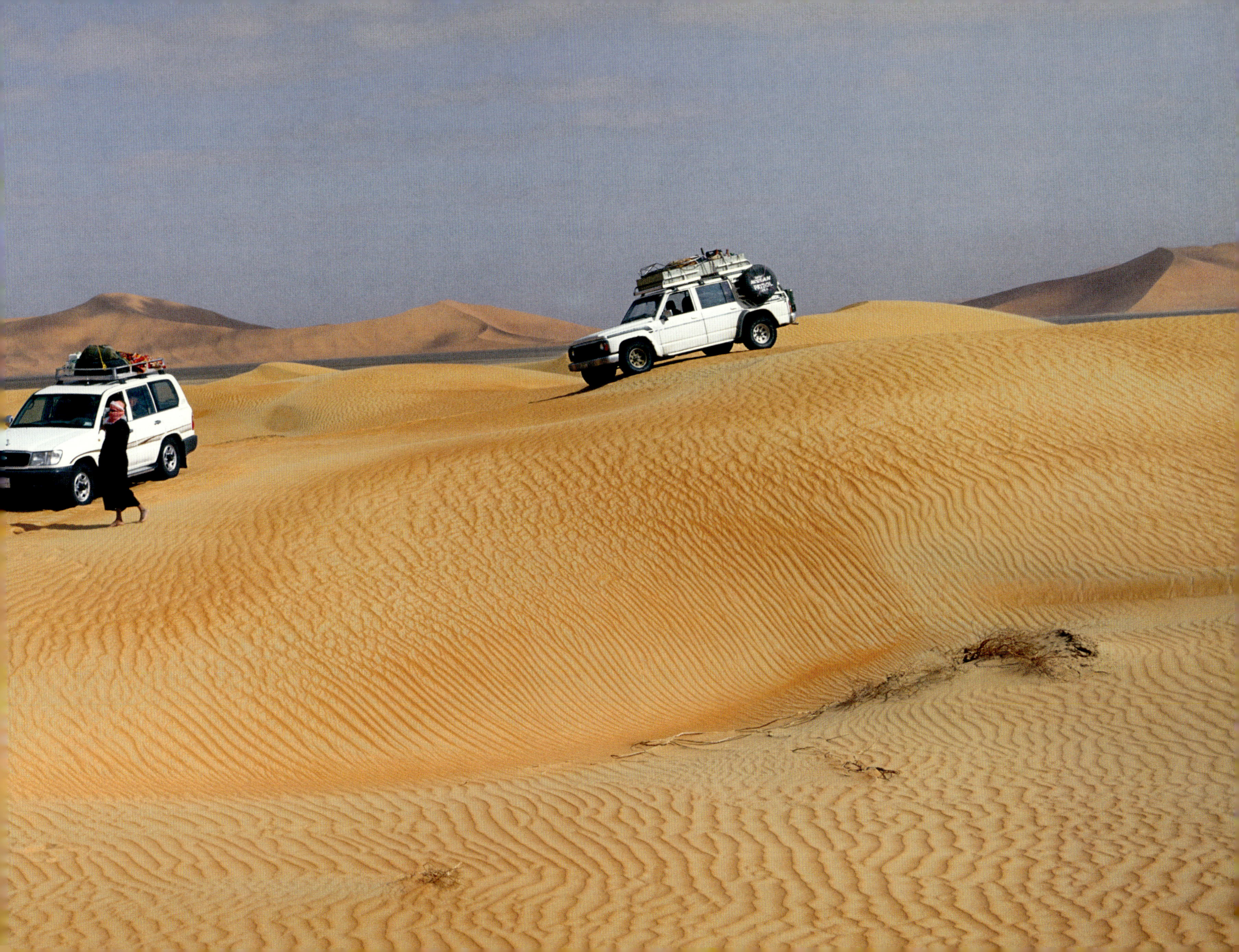

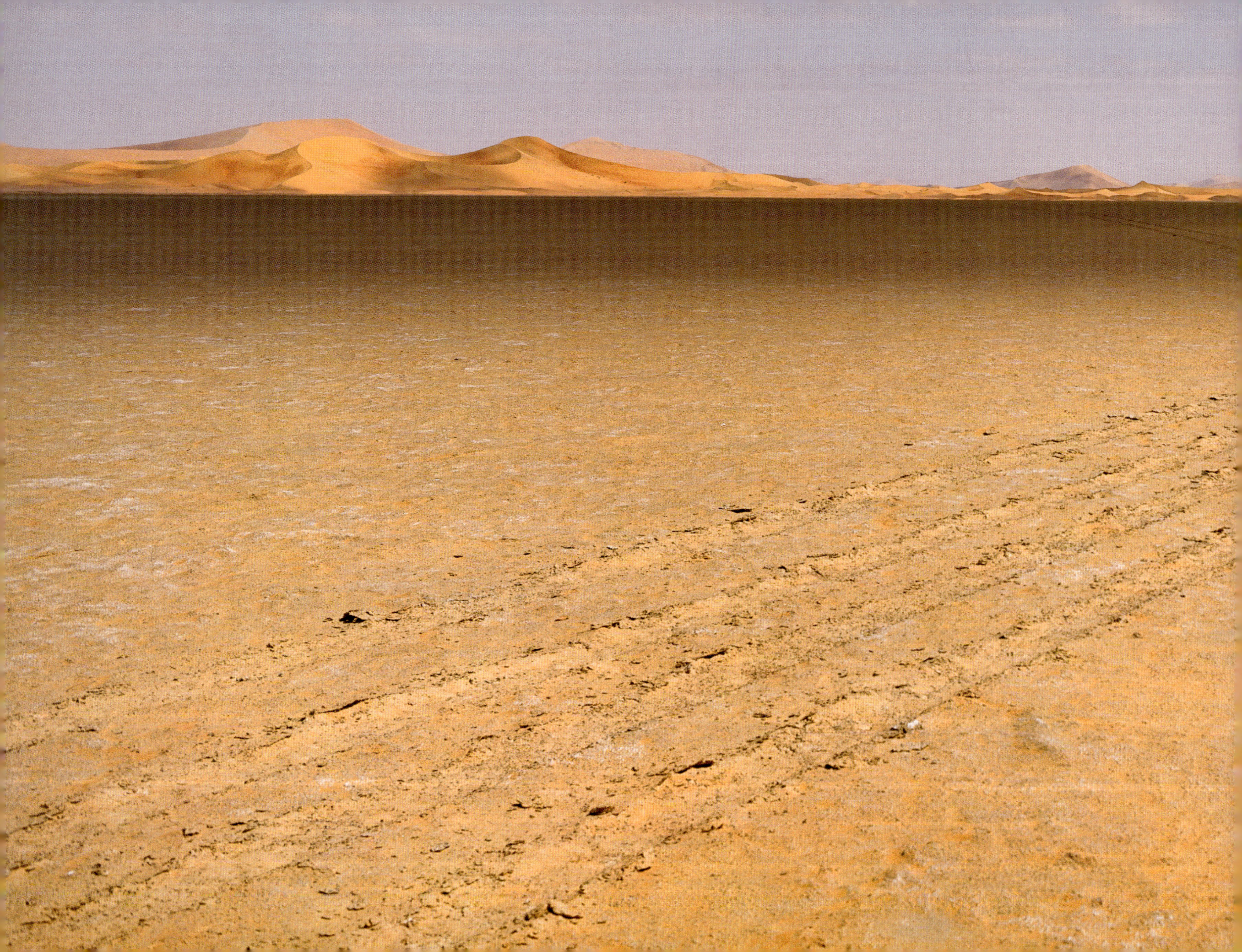

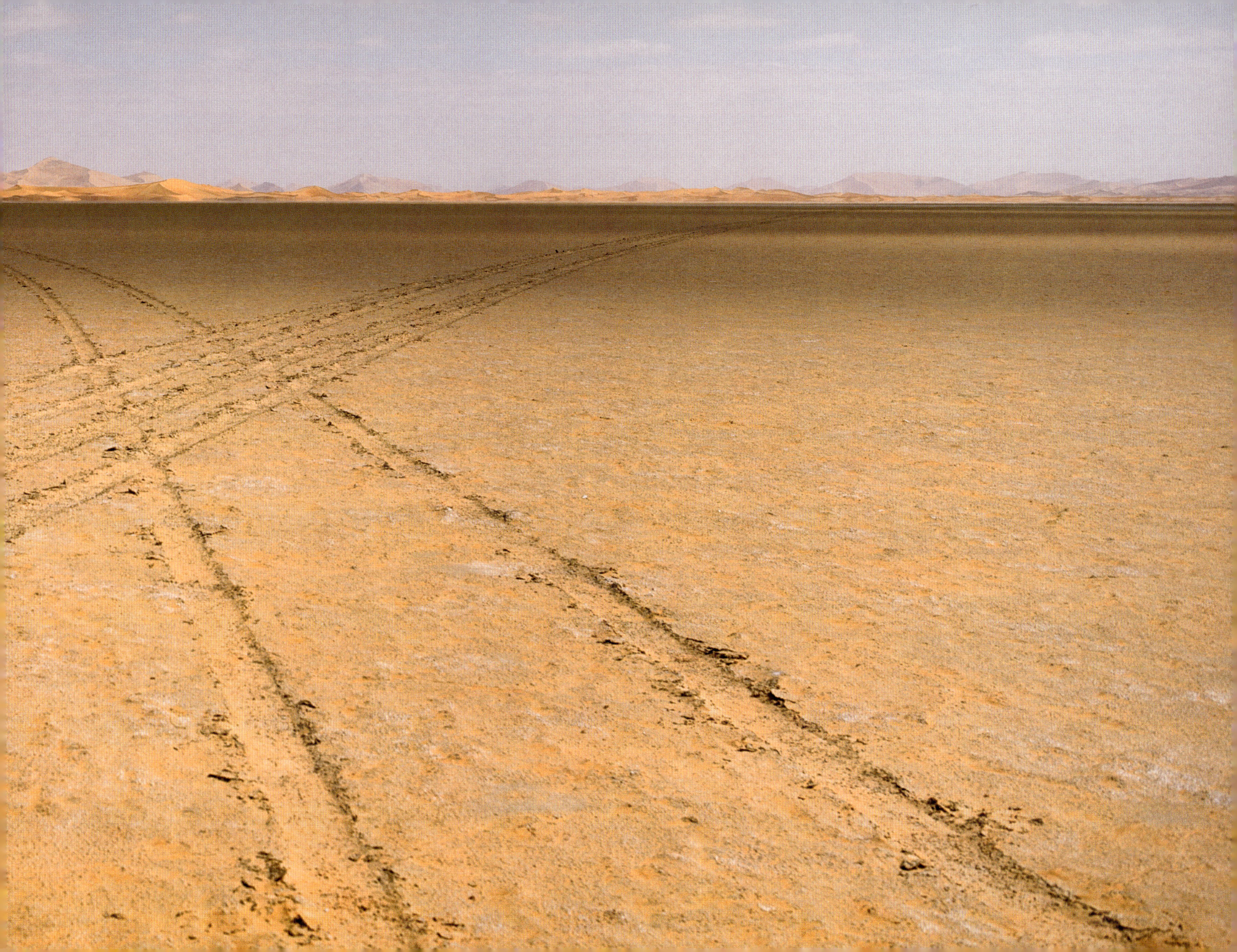

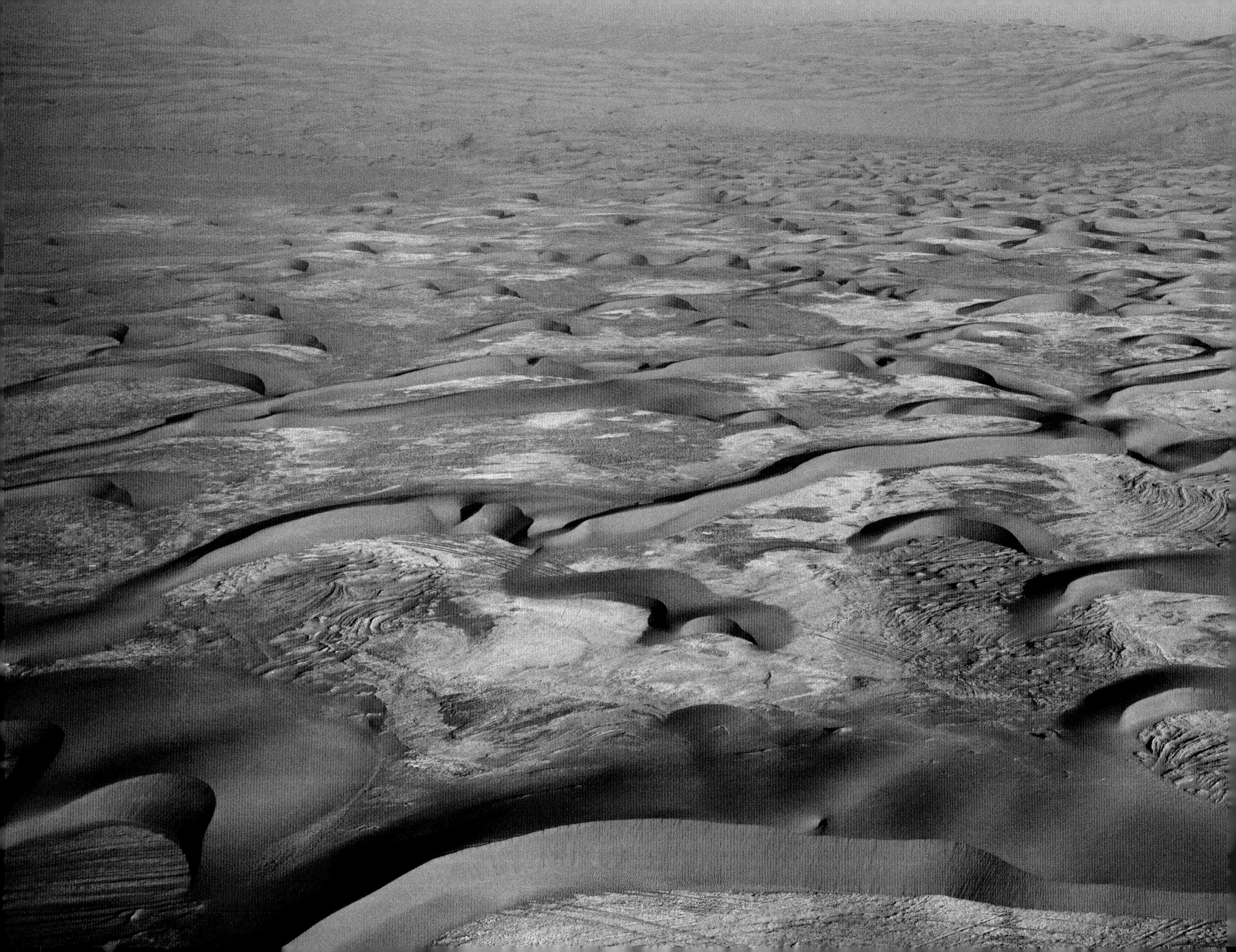

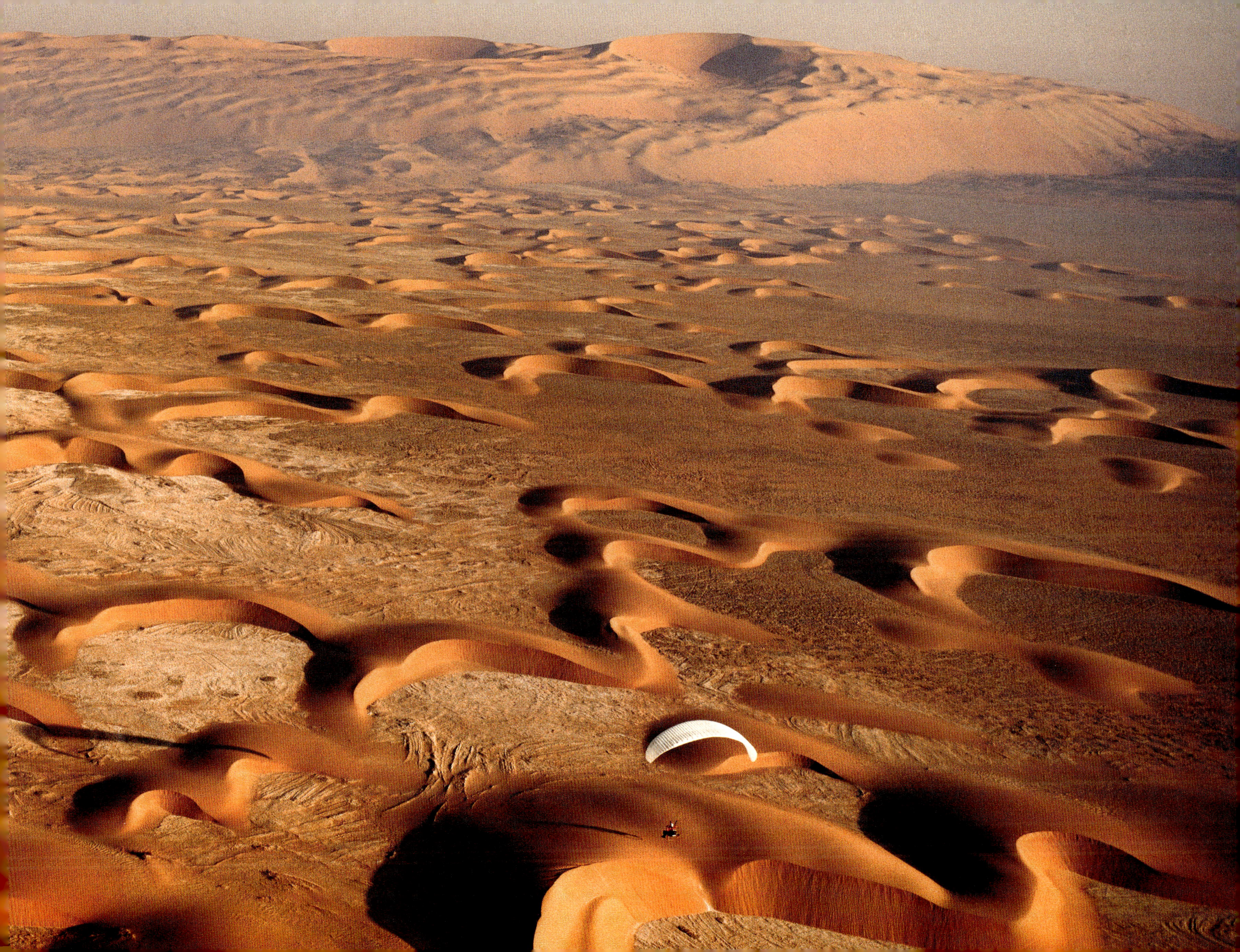

THE HEART OF RUB' AL-KHALI

"No, it is not the goal but the way there that matters,
and the harder the way, the more worthwhile the journey."

Wilfred Thesiger, *Arabian Sands*

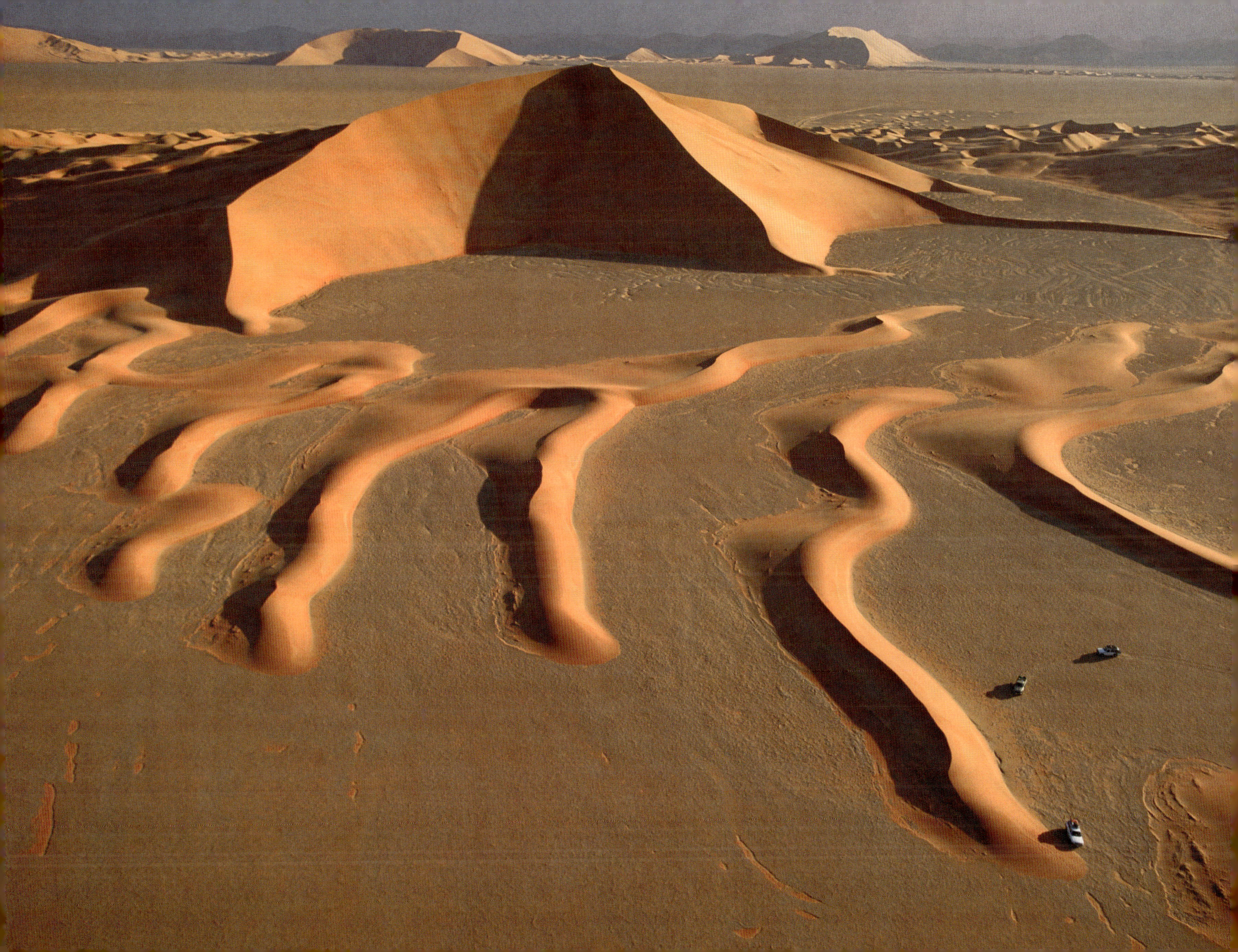

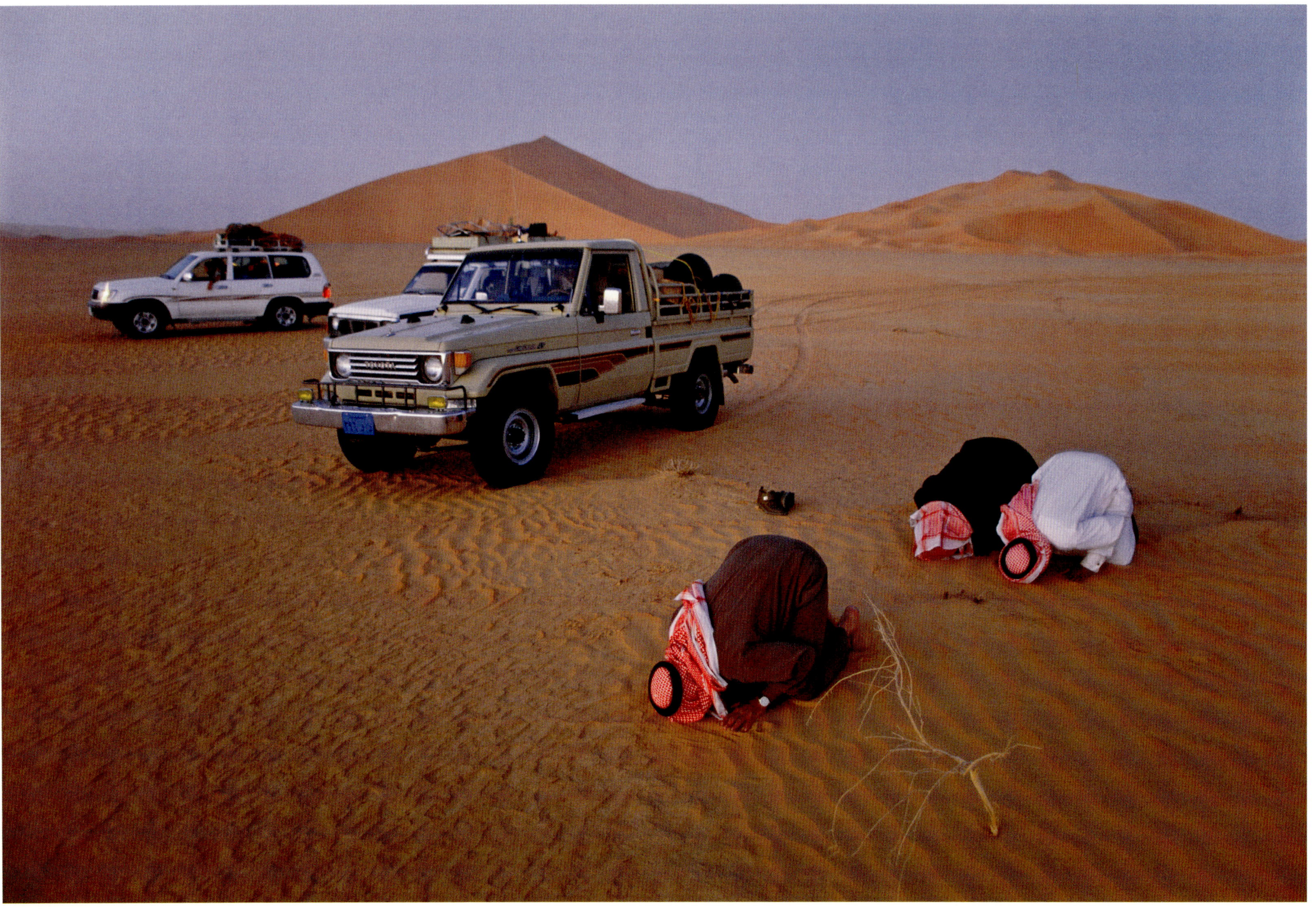

     Evening prayers, 'Uruq al Mutaridah, Saudi Arabia

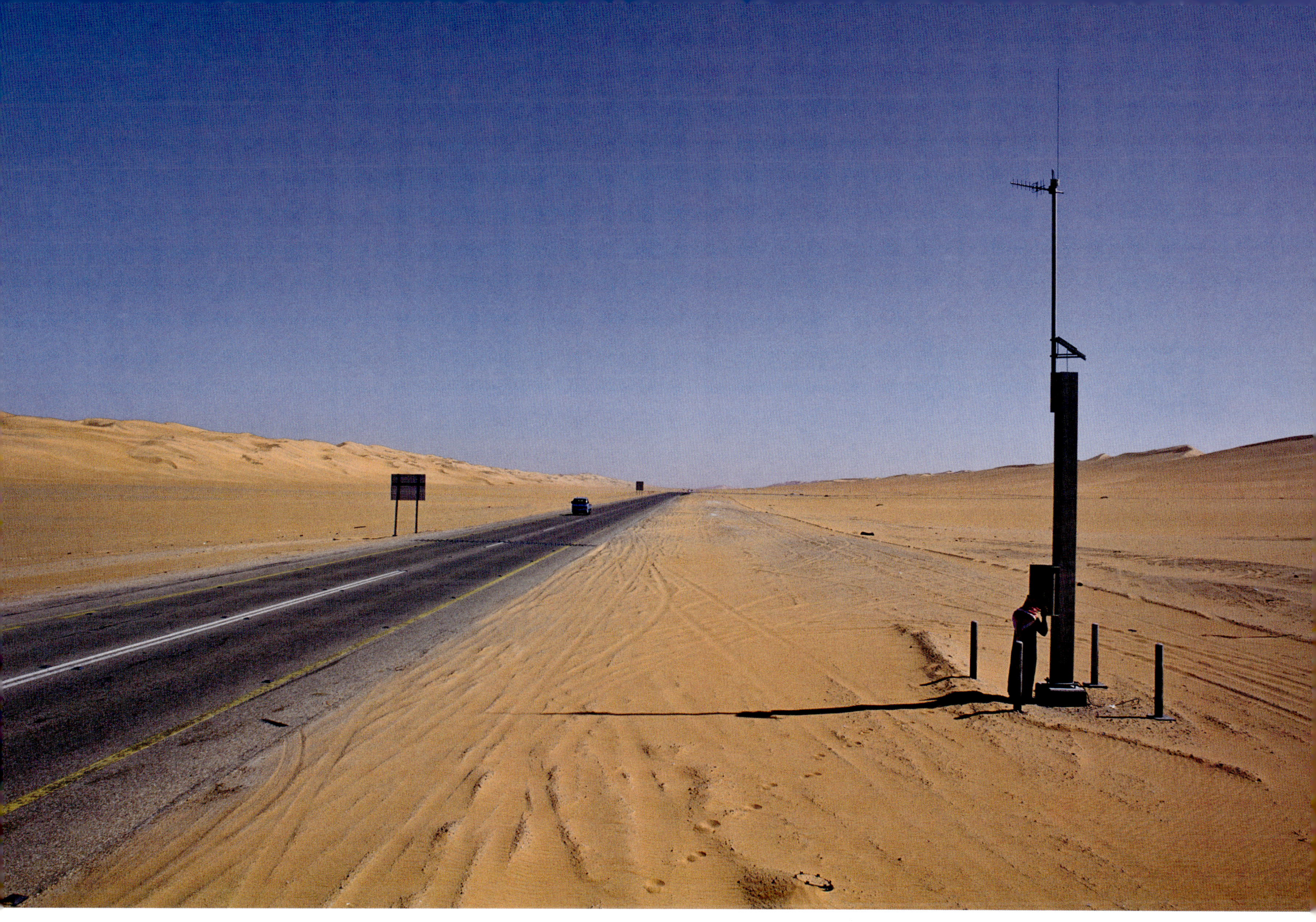

Microwave telephone near Sharurah, Saudi Arabia

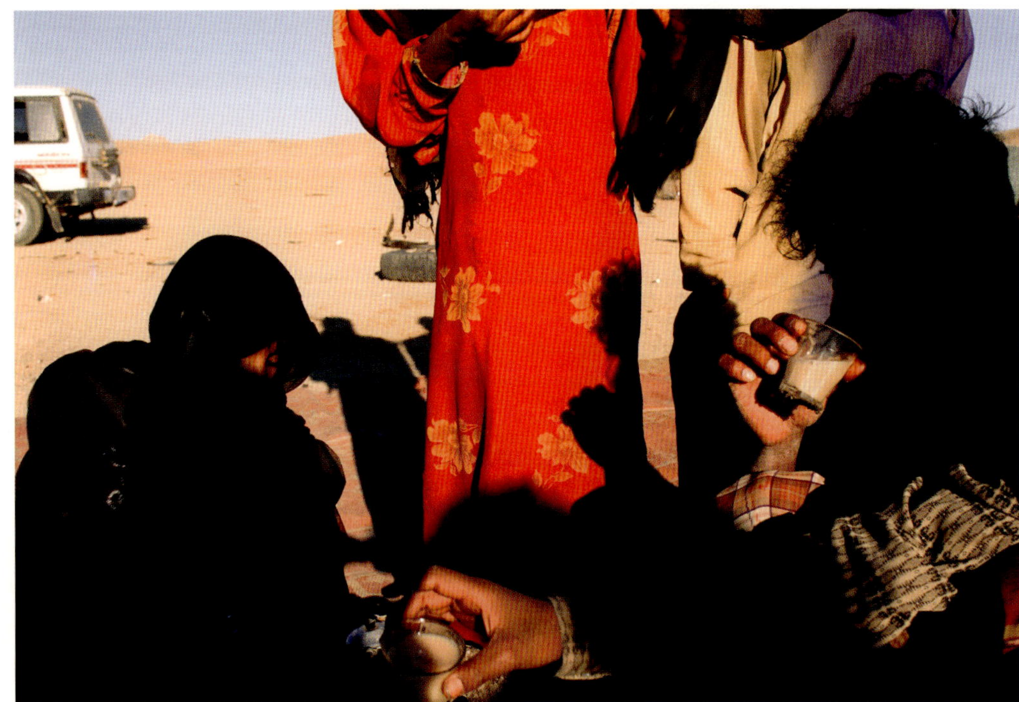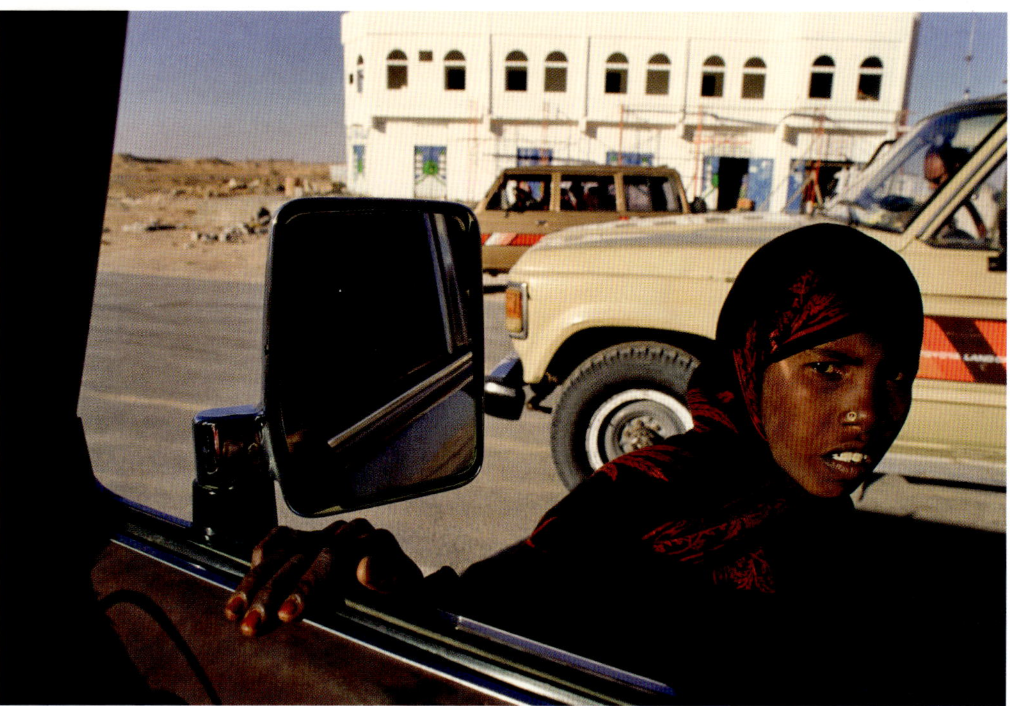

ABOVE LEFT: Morning tea in Bedouin camp near Sanaw, Yemen
ABOVE RIGHT: Alms for the poor, Sharurah, Saudi Arabia

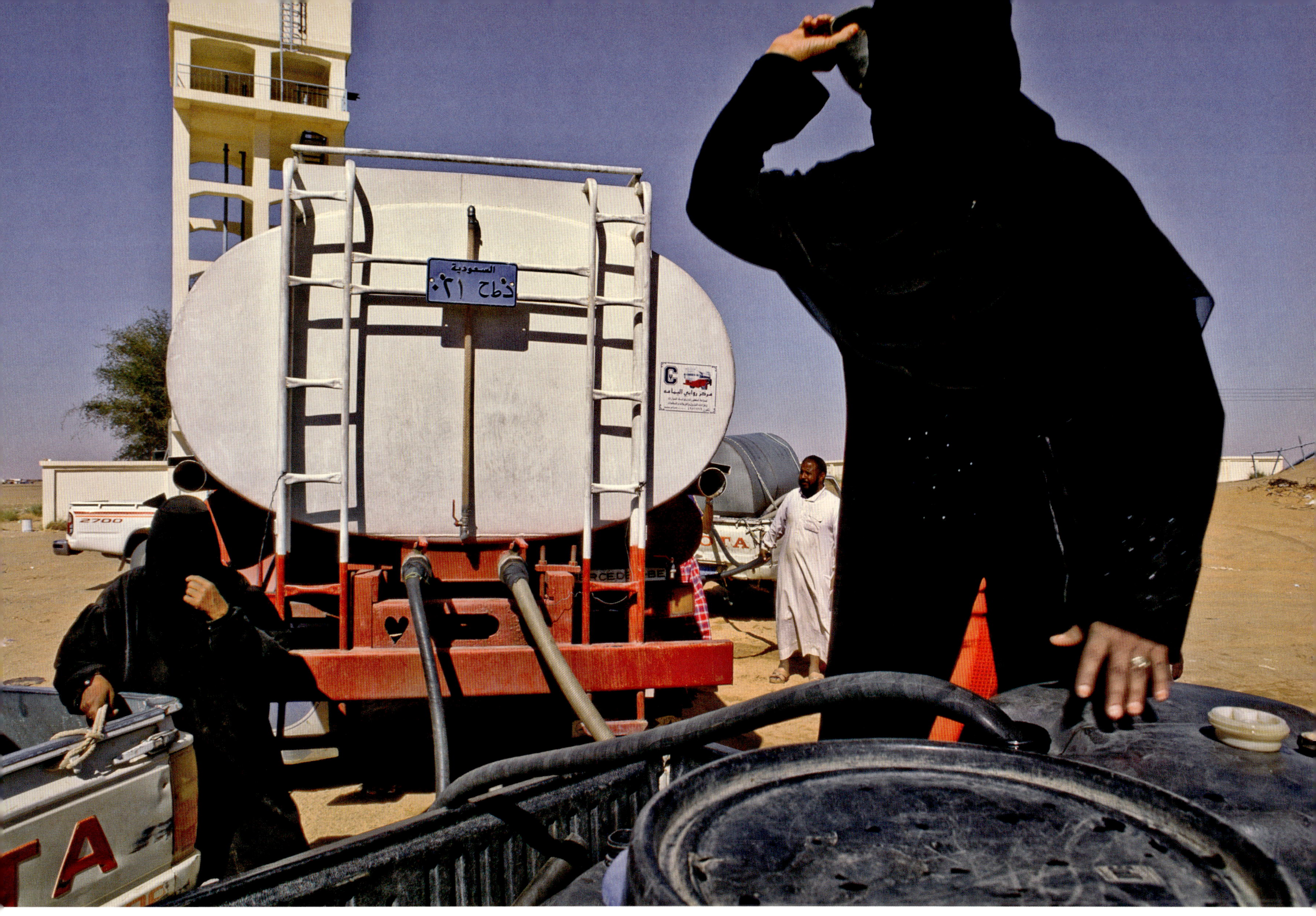

Bedouin throwing a shoe at a foreigner, Wuday'ah, Saudi Arabia

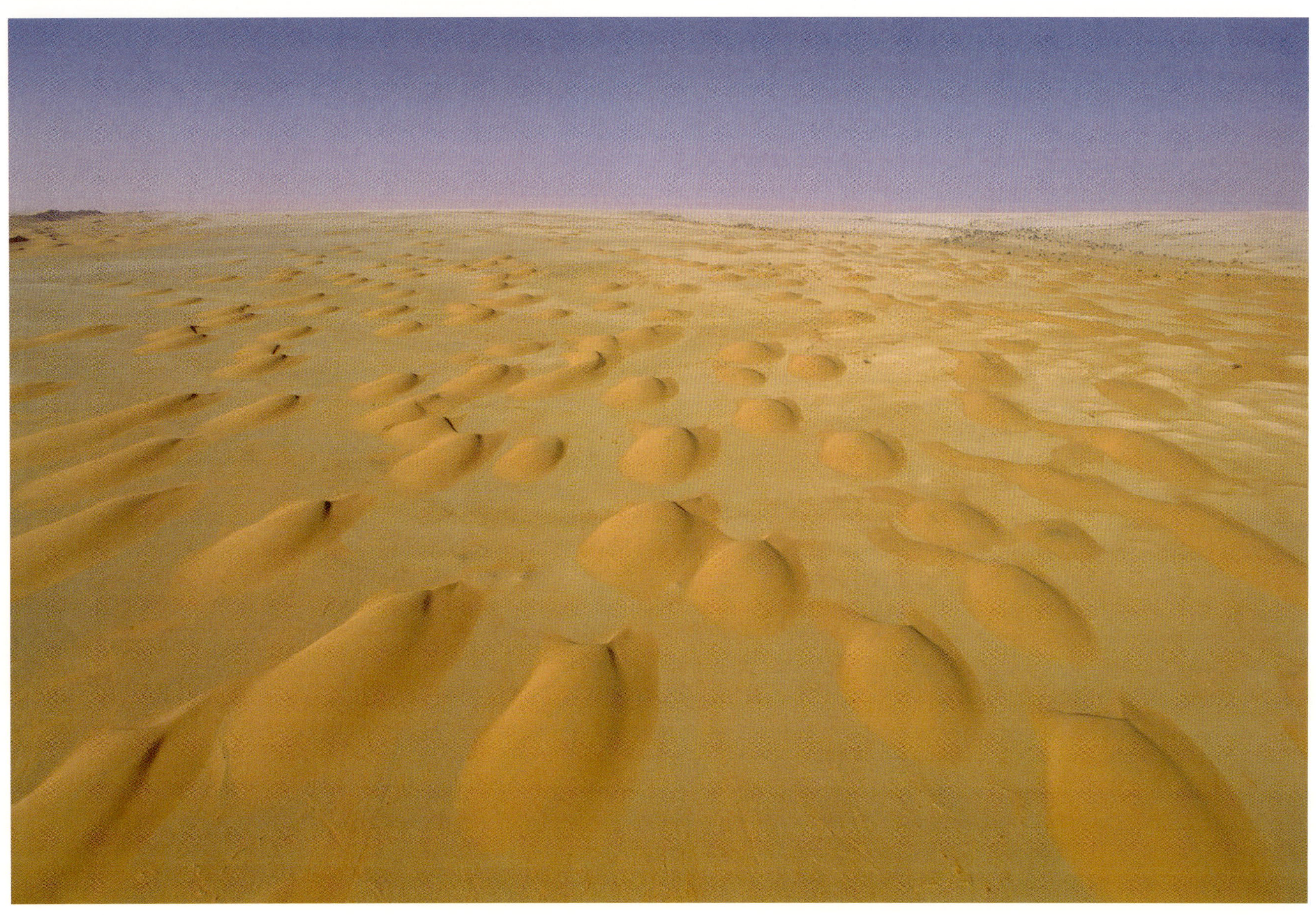

ABOVE: Blown-out barchan dunes, 'Uruq Bani Ma'arid, Saudi Arabia
OPPOSITE: Rheem gazelles, Umm az-Zamul, U.A.E.

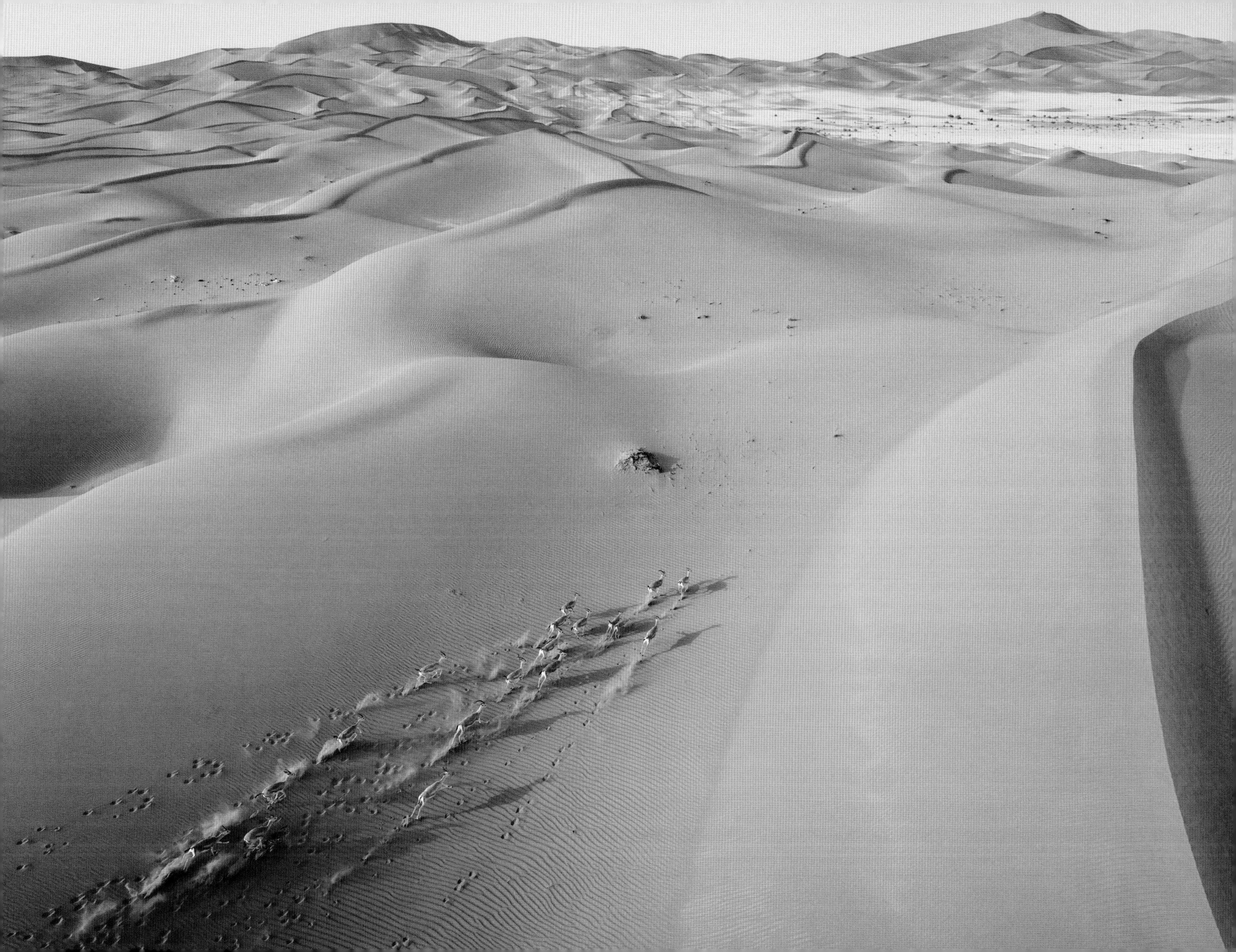

The first time I saw them was twenty years ago, on a jet traveling from Muscat to Cairo. From thirty-five thousand feet up I saw hundreds of circular green lily pads pop into view, set in stark contrast against the surface of a beige, lifeless plain. How could there be so much water out in the middle of the Saudi Arabian desert, and why would anyone irrigate in circles? I filed them away in my long-term list of global curiosities to visit some day. Before leaving for my first trip to the Empty Quarter, I scoured the Internet and came across these desert lily pads once again in a space-shuttle image. It depicted these emerald-green irrigation circles on the edge of the sands near Wadi Dawasir that were the result of a center-pivot irrigation, which tapped into subterranean aquifers of fossil water. The systems are relatively simple, with a well at the center of the circle and a pump distributing water through a thousand feet of rotating pipe and sprinklers.

It seemed like a great opportunity for pictures, and when I started my first circuit around the Empty Quarter, I made a point to visit them. As we drove out to the site, the Egyptian agricultural engineer who ran the operation explained that the first wells were drilled at Wadi Dawasir in 1983, and that his area now had over 155 square miles of desert in production.

With a little fertilizer, they were able to grow wheat, alfalfa, onions, potatoes, and tomatoes during the winter months. But naturally it took a huge amount of water—as much as twenty-eight gallons per square foot. The fields have to be irrigated year-round, even during the summer when it is too hot for the crops, just to maintain fertility by pushing down the salts that are always migrating to the surface with evaporation. In fifteen years the ground water pressure had decreased from the initial geyser-like artesian flow. It now had to be pumped from five hundred feet below ground, and he estimated that within five more years the pumping would no longer be economically feasible.

A week or so later, as we followed the chain of green lily pads out into the desert, we narrowly missed driving directly into a huge conical pit some hundred feet in diameter. From the edge we gazed into what looked like the center of a draining hourglass of sand. The local farm workers didn't know what it was beyond a great way to dispose of trash, and anything tossed into it was soon sucked down through the bottom of the "hourglass." But its proximity to the round alfalfa fields left little doubt: The conical pit was the top of a massive sinkhole filling the void created by huge losses of groundwater that had been pumped for irrigation. This was the same phenomenon that had caused the lost city of Ubar to sink into the sands.

While the sands of the Empty Quarter are two million years old, it hasn't always been a desert. According to Aramco geologist Hal McClure, in two periods, between five and ten thousand and seventeen and thirty-seven thousand years ago, the climate was so much wetter here that the dunes of the Rub' al-Khali were separated by ephemeral lakes that supported hippopotami and water buffalo and Neolithic peoples who hunted here with stone tools.

Some fifty miles farther out into the desert we stumbled across the stone circles of what appeared to be an ancient pastoral campsite from those wetter times. While we weren't in a position to excavate, *GEO* writer Uwe George, who had extensive experience with similar-looking Saharan sites, guessed it to be many thousands of years old. It would have to be, as there is no way you could support even a small flock of the hardiest animals on the barren sands of the Empty Quarter. I wondered what people thousands of years in the future would think when they come across the abandoned skeletons of center pivot irrigation equipment from the Late Petroleum Era. Would this be a wetter place again, and would they need a permit to excavate it?

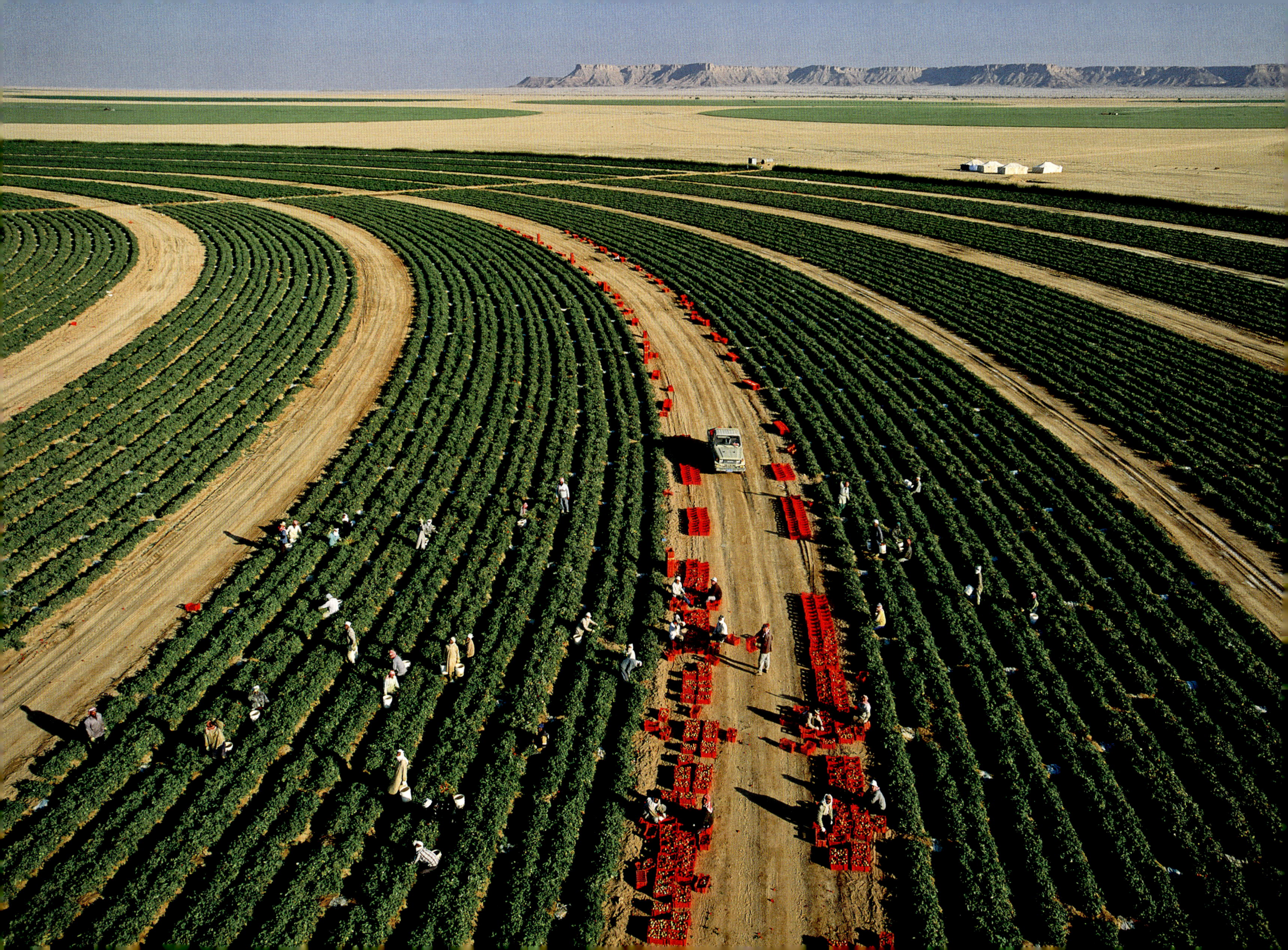

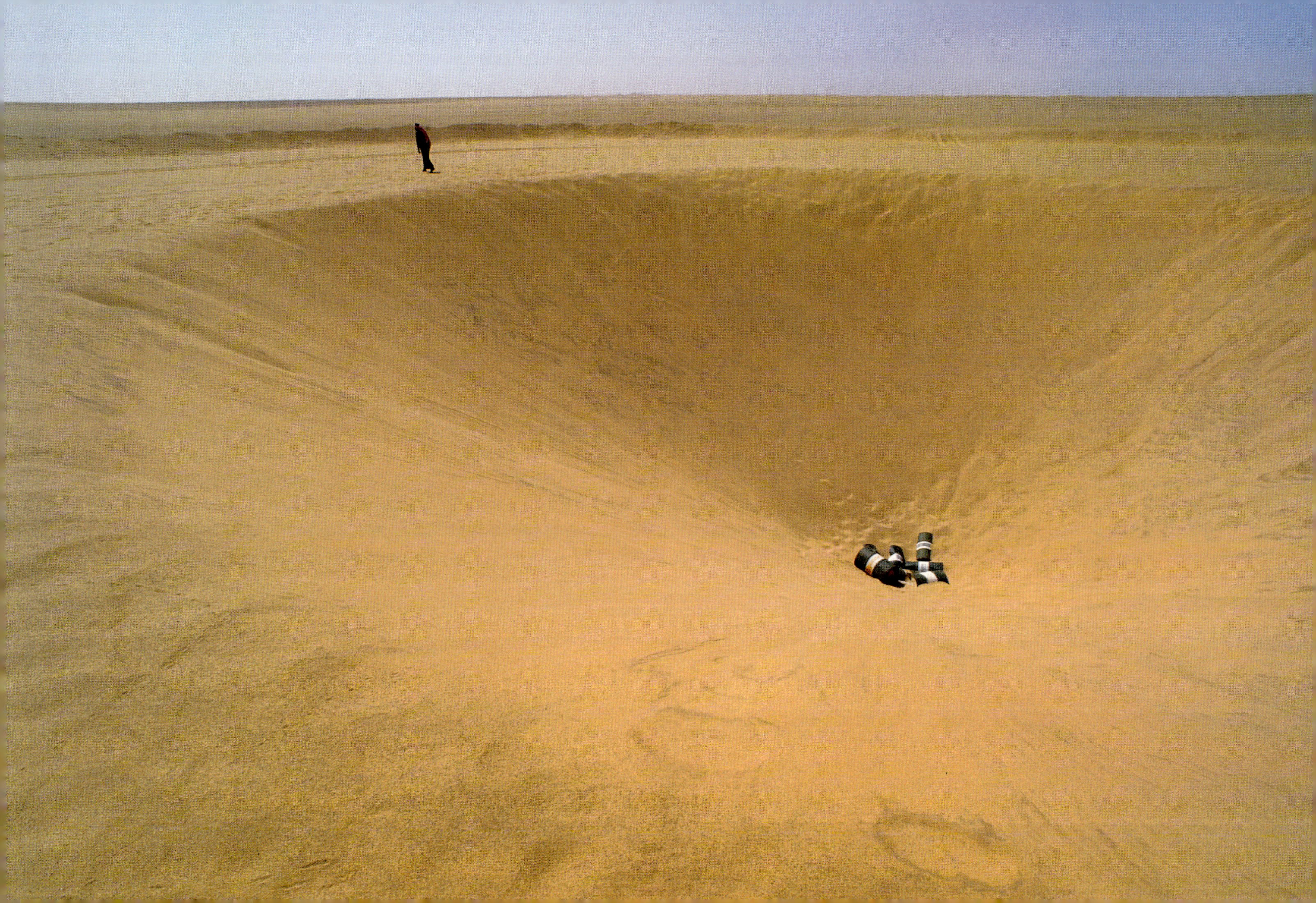

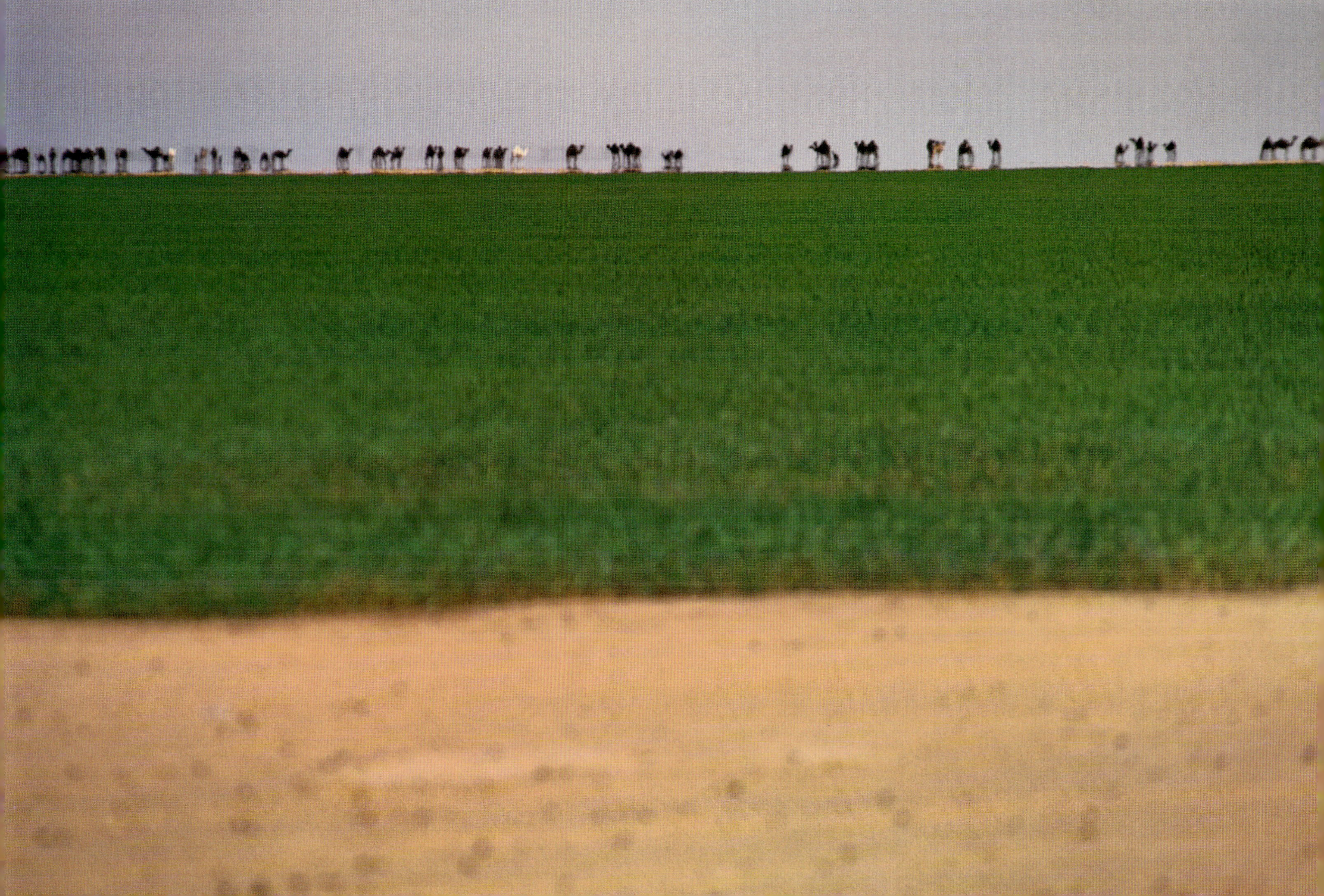

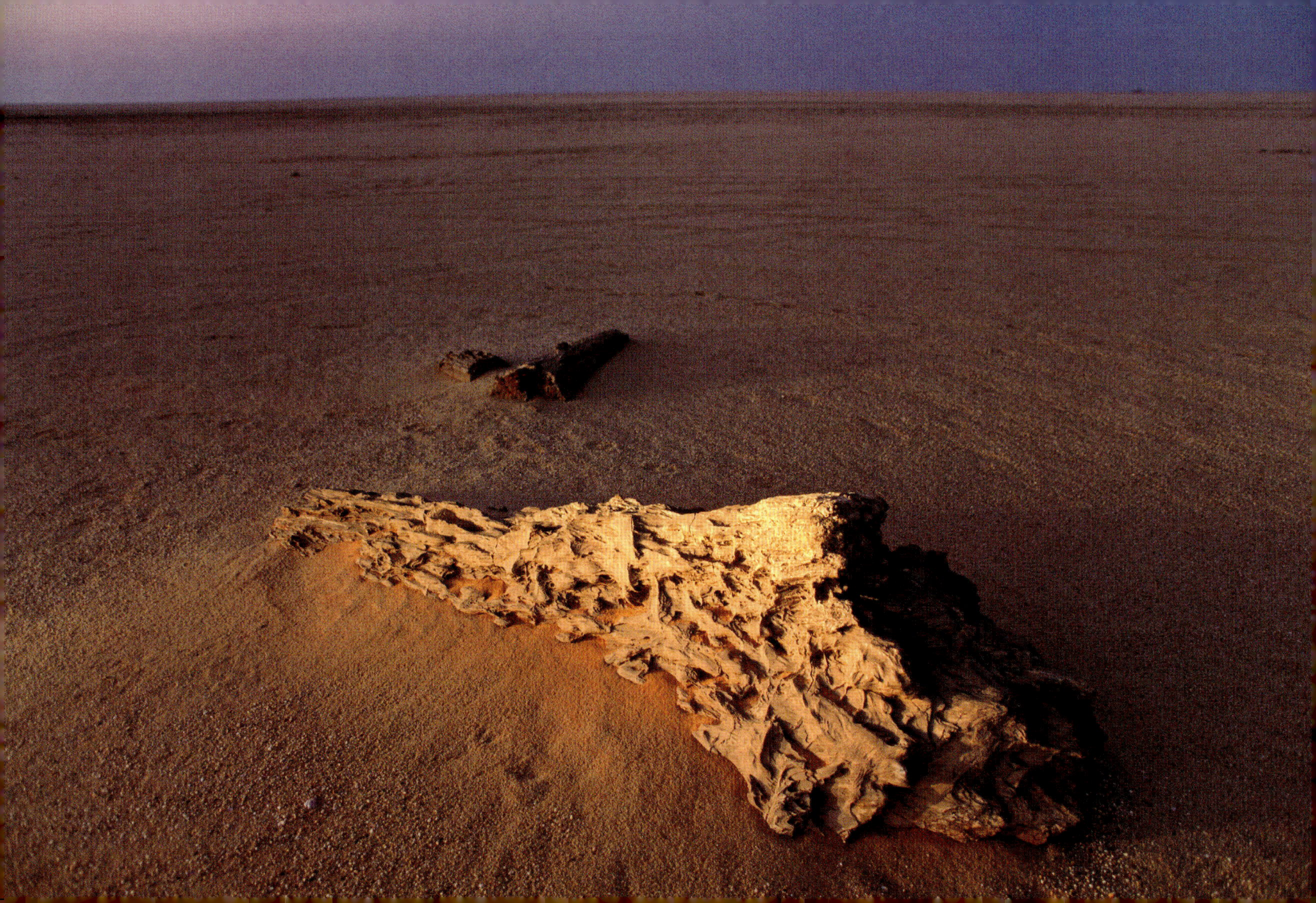

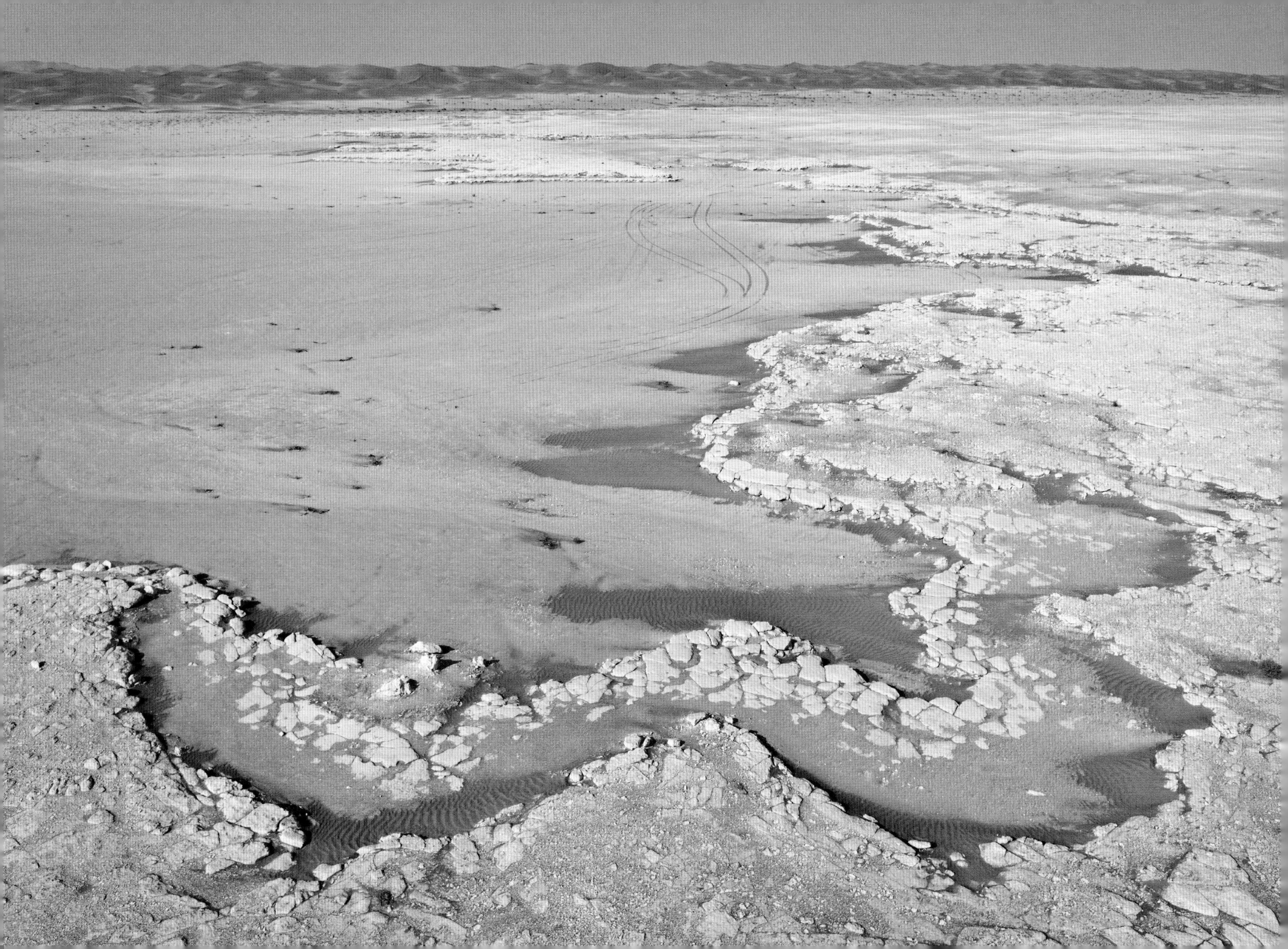

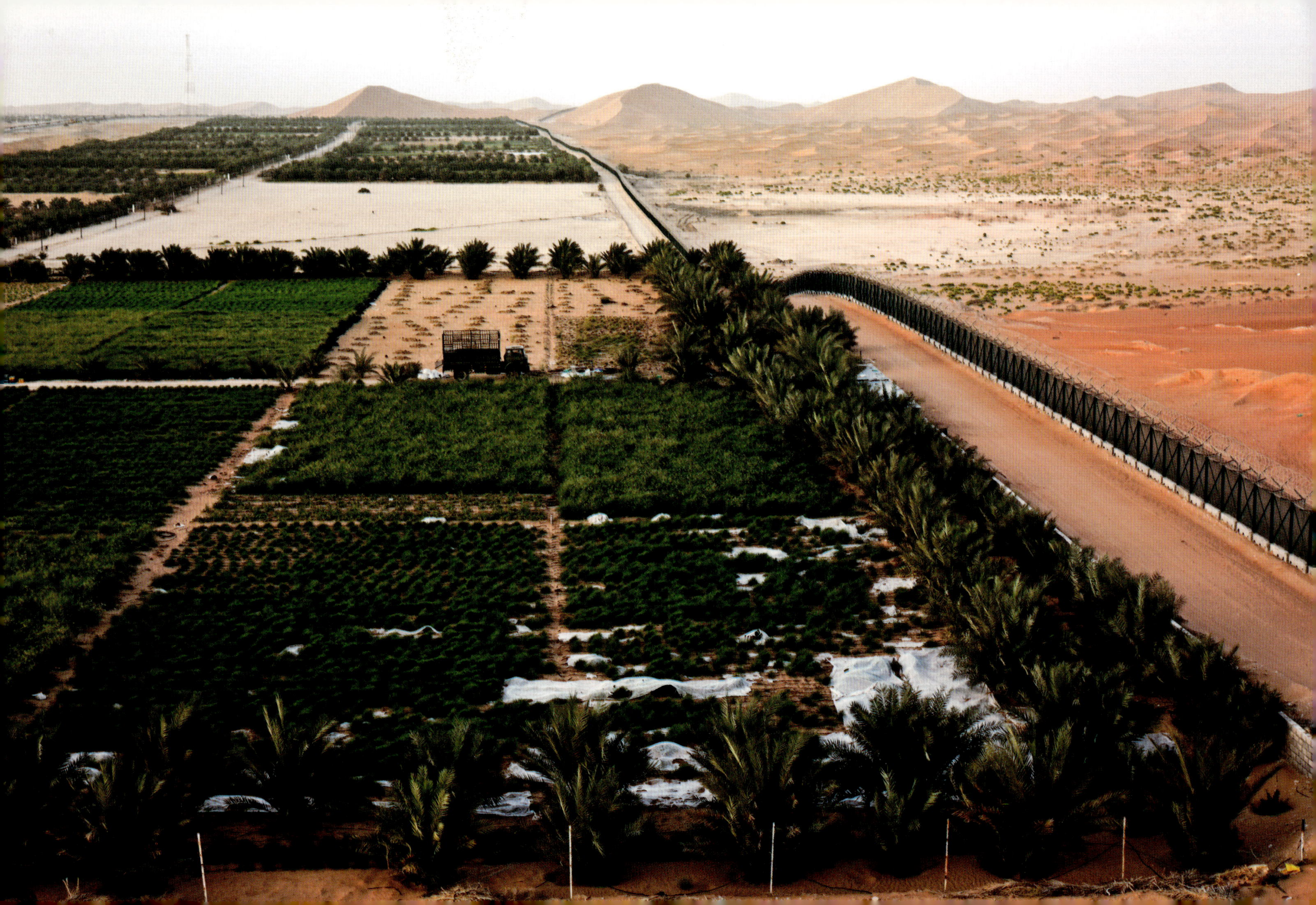

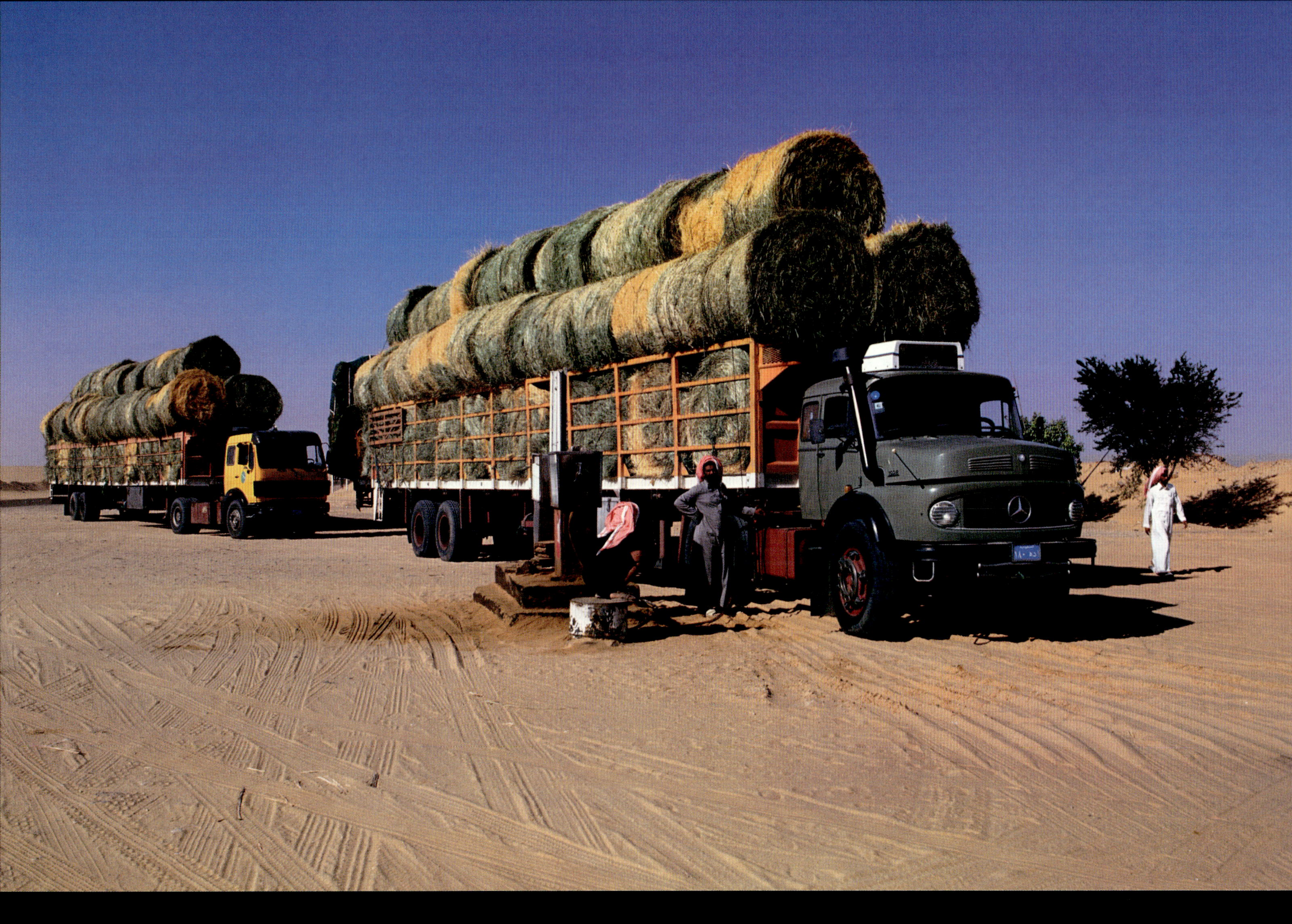

ABOVE: Alfalfa from desert irrigation project, Qaryat al-Fau, Saudi Arabia

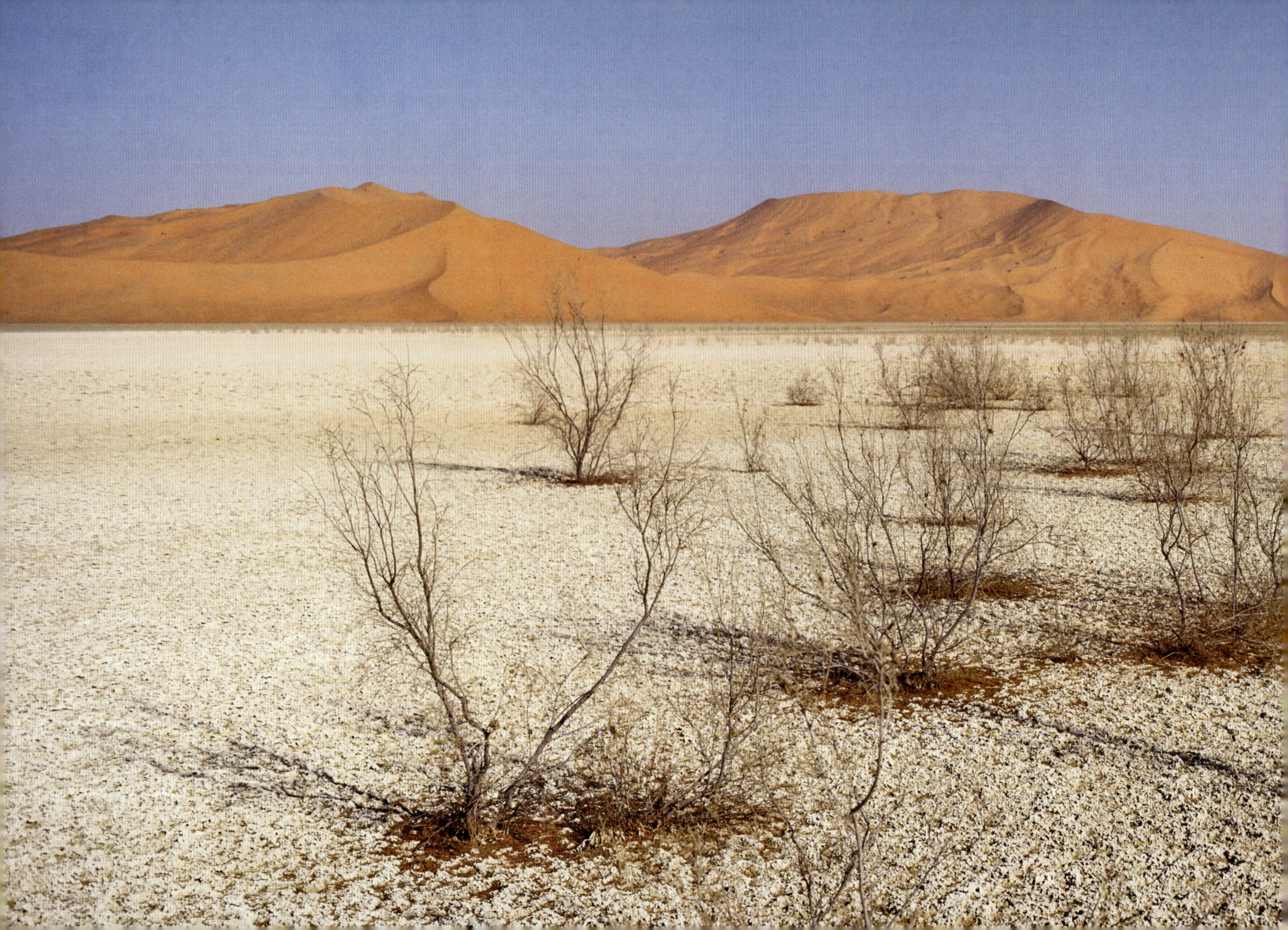

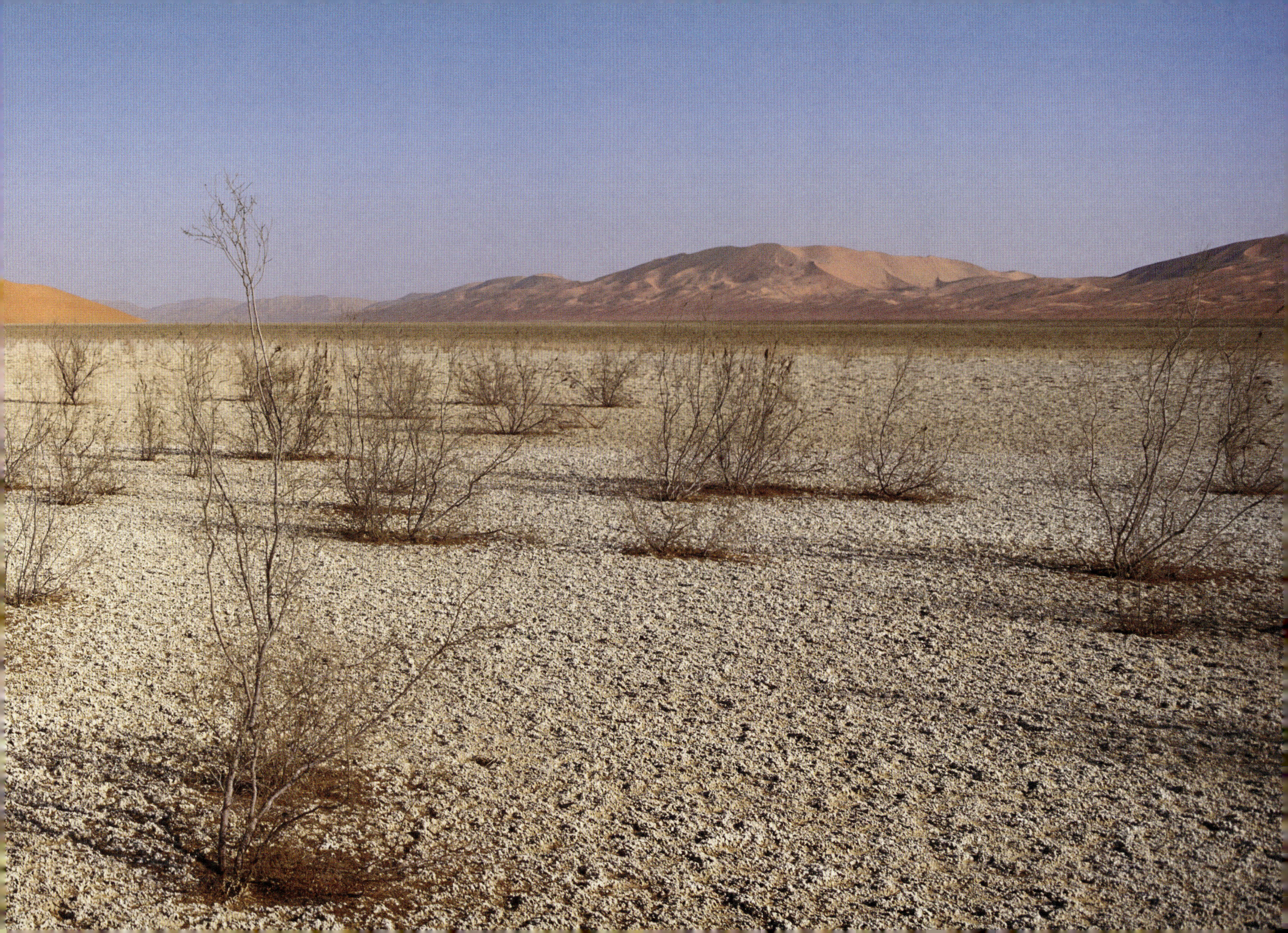

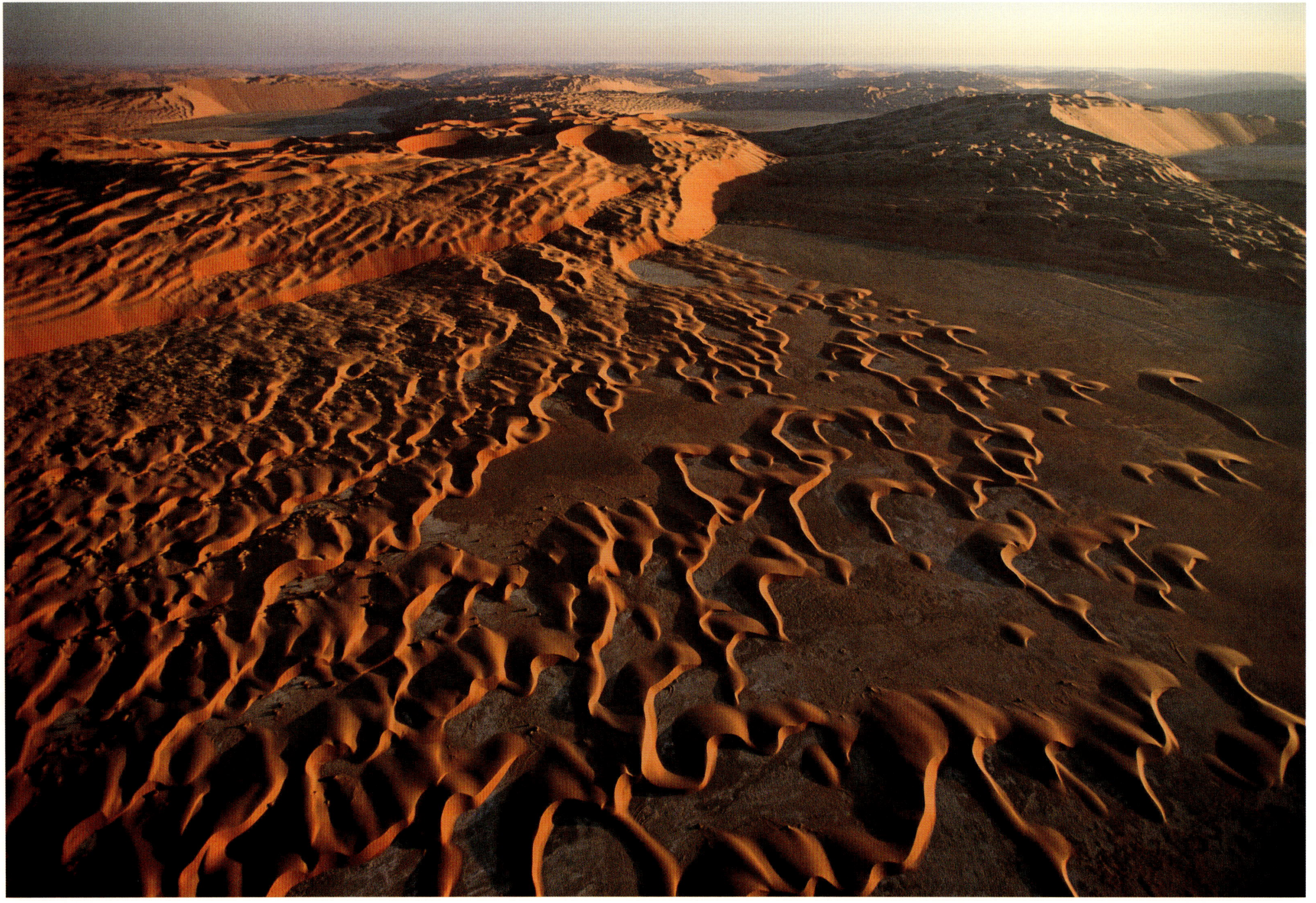

ABOVE: Barchan dunes, Shaybah, Saudi Arabia
OPPOSITE: Expedition car at the base of a star dune, Khawr Hamidan, Saudi Arabia

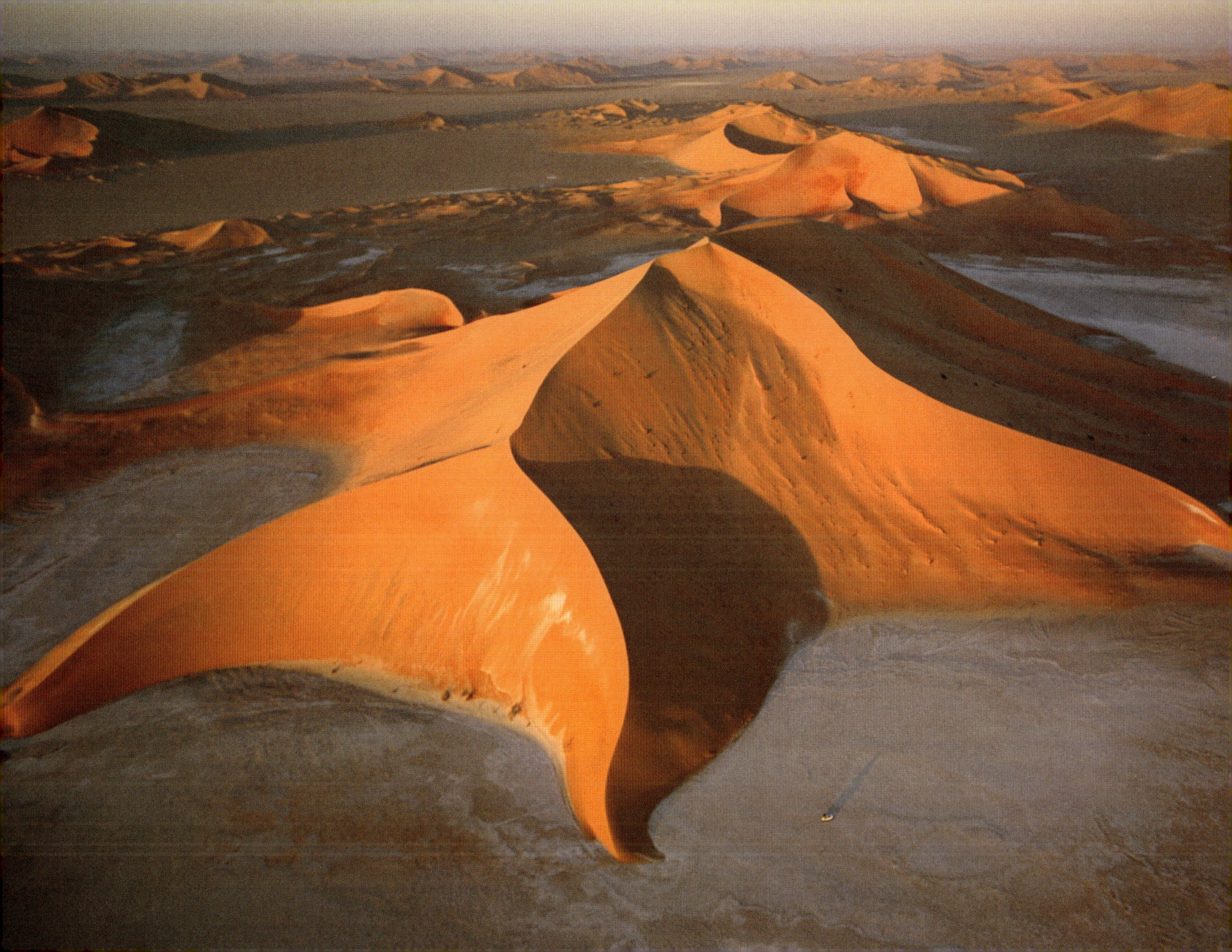

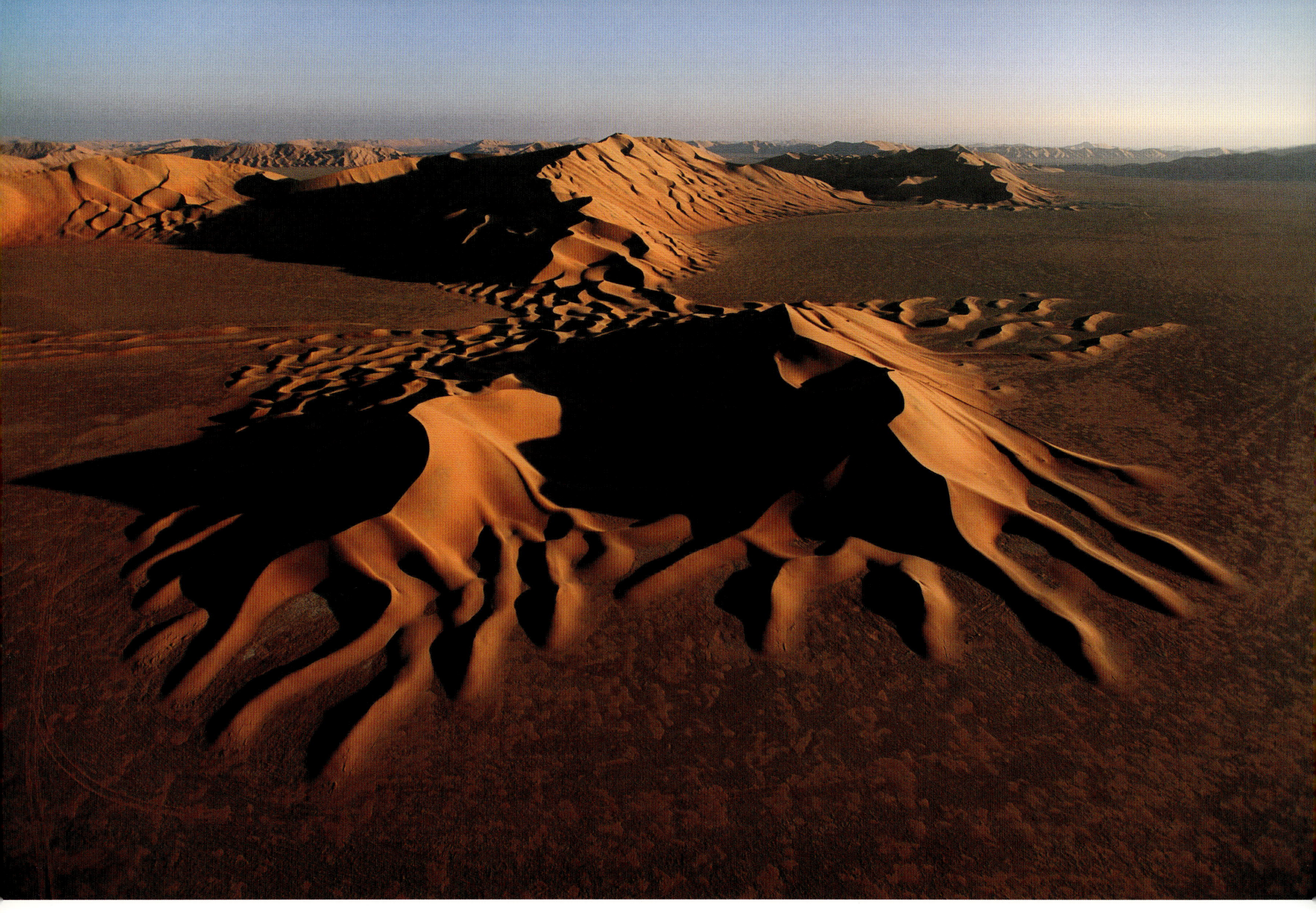

    Star dunes, Ramlat Mitan, Oman

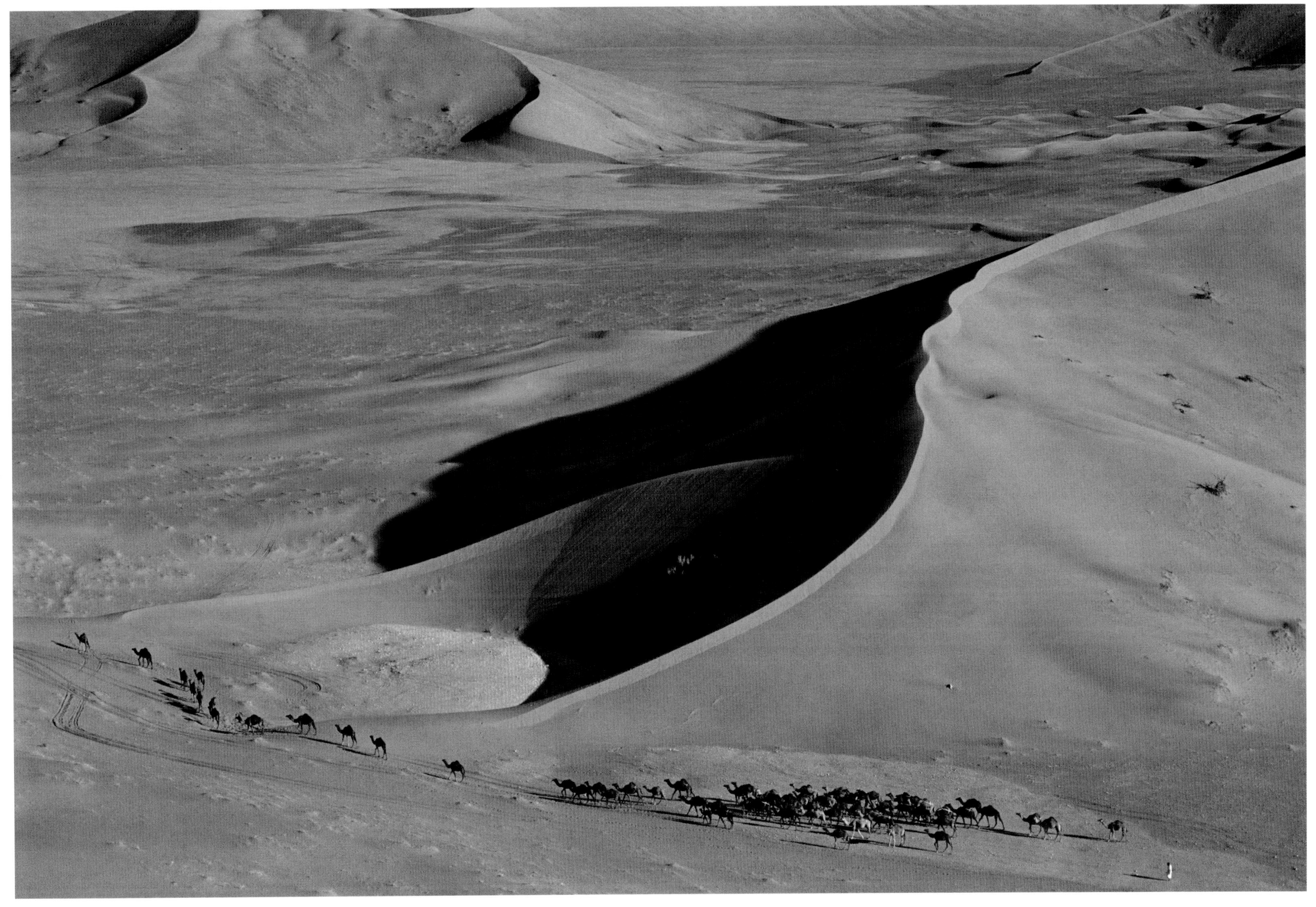

Camels look for grazing, Wadi Mitan, Oman

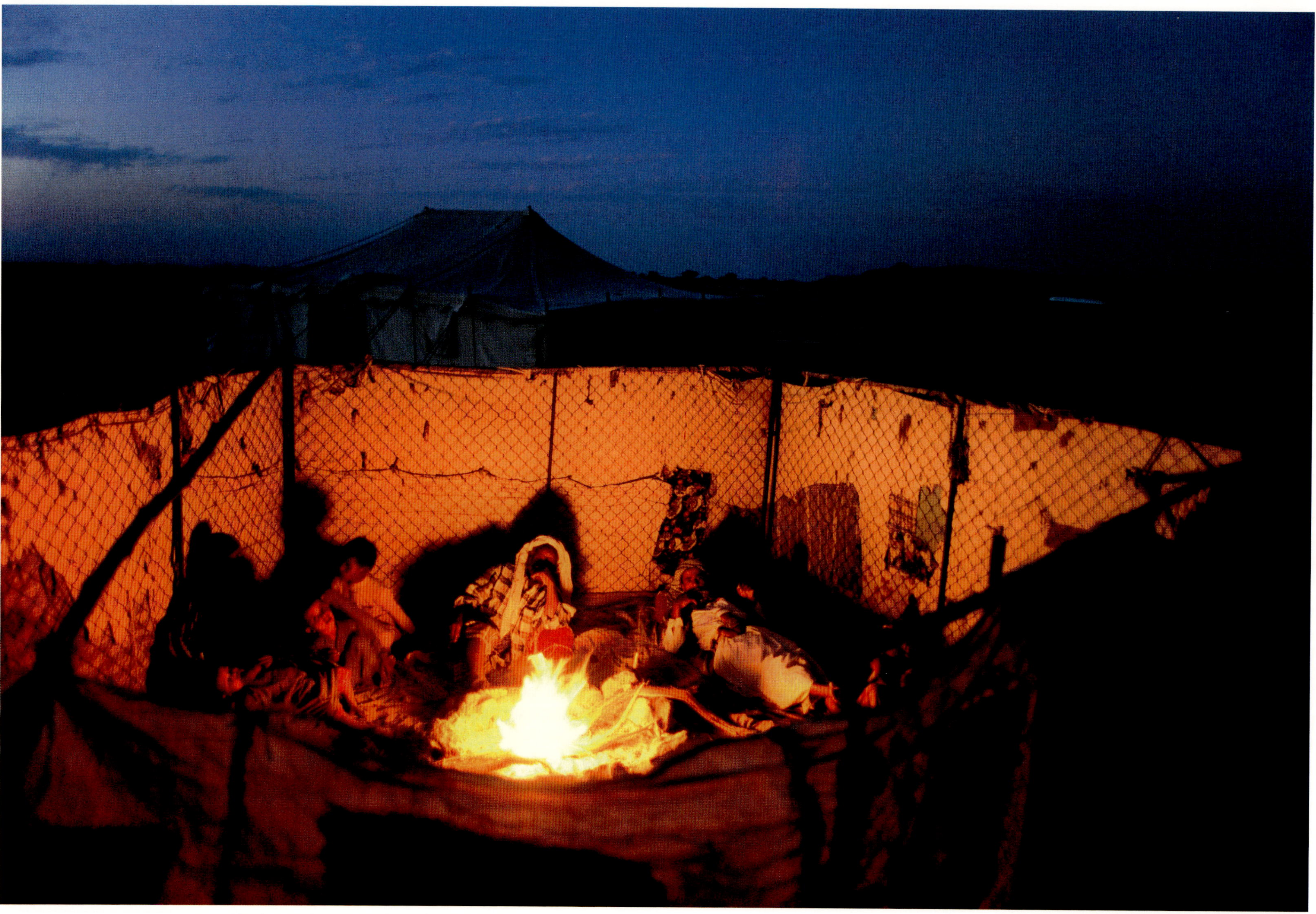

   Bedouin camp, Shabwa, Yemen

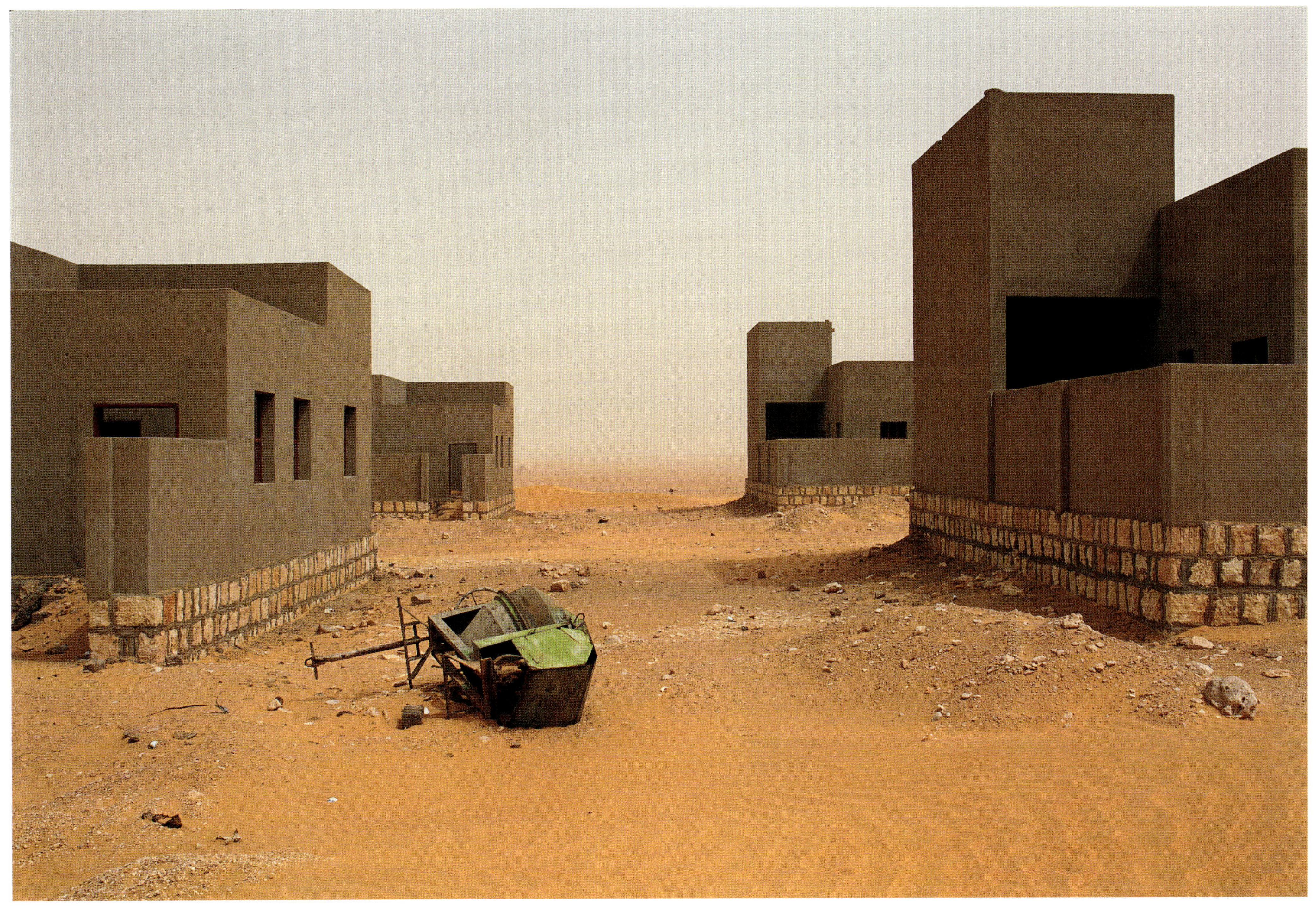

Deserted Bedouin resettlement camp, Hazar, Yemen

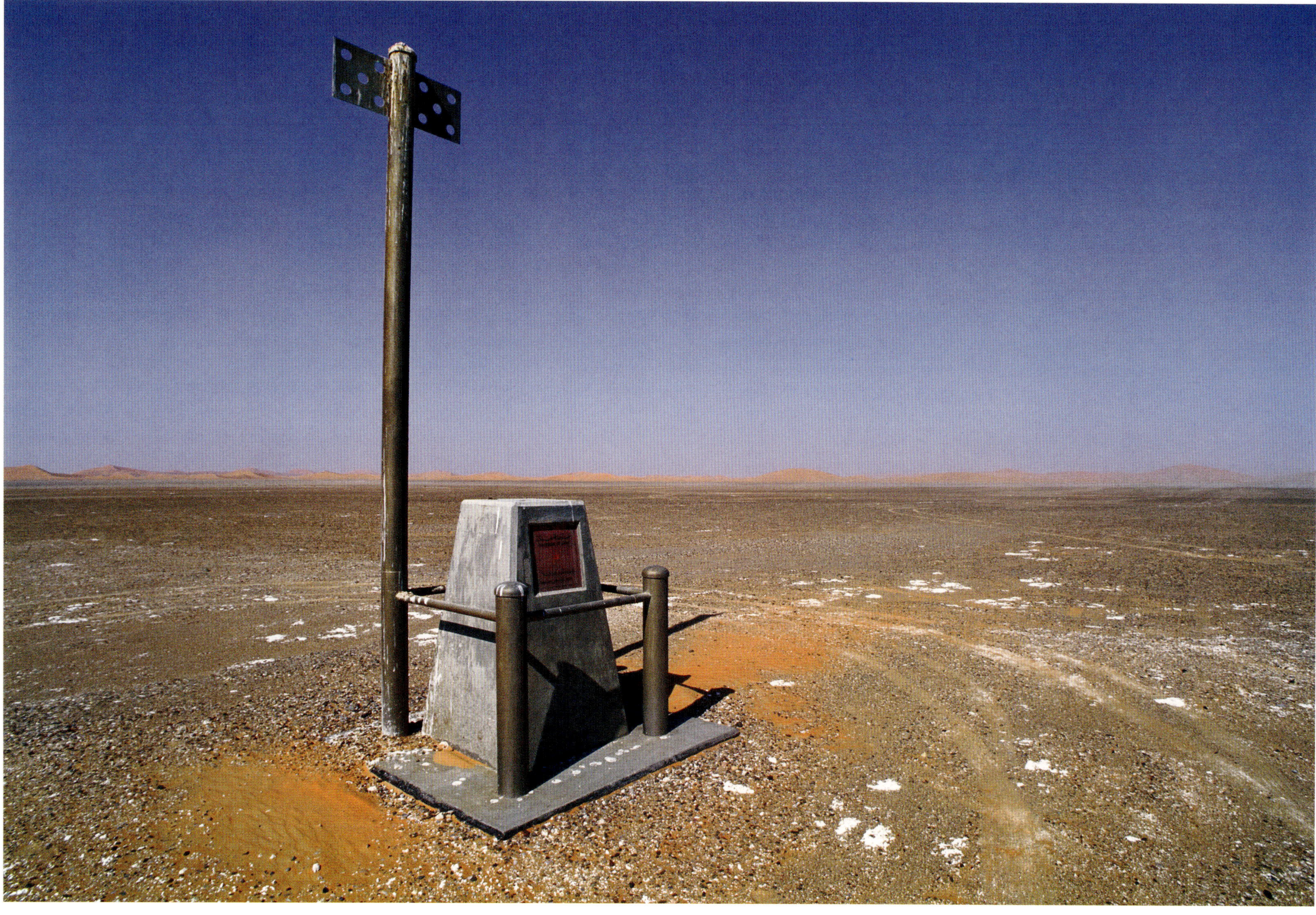

   Saudi-Omani border marker, near Ardah, Saudi Arabia

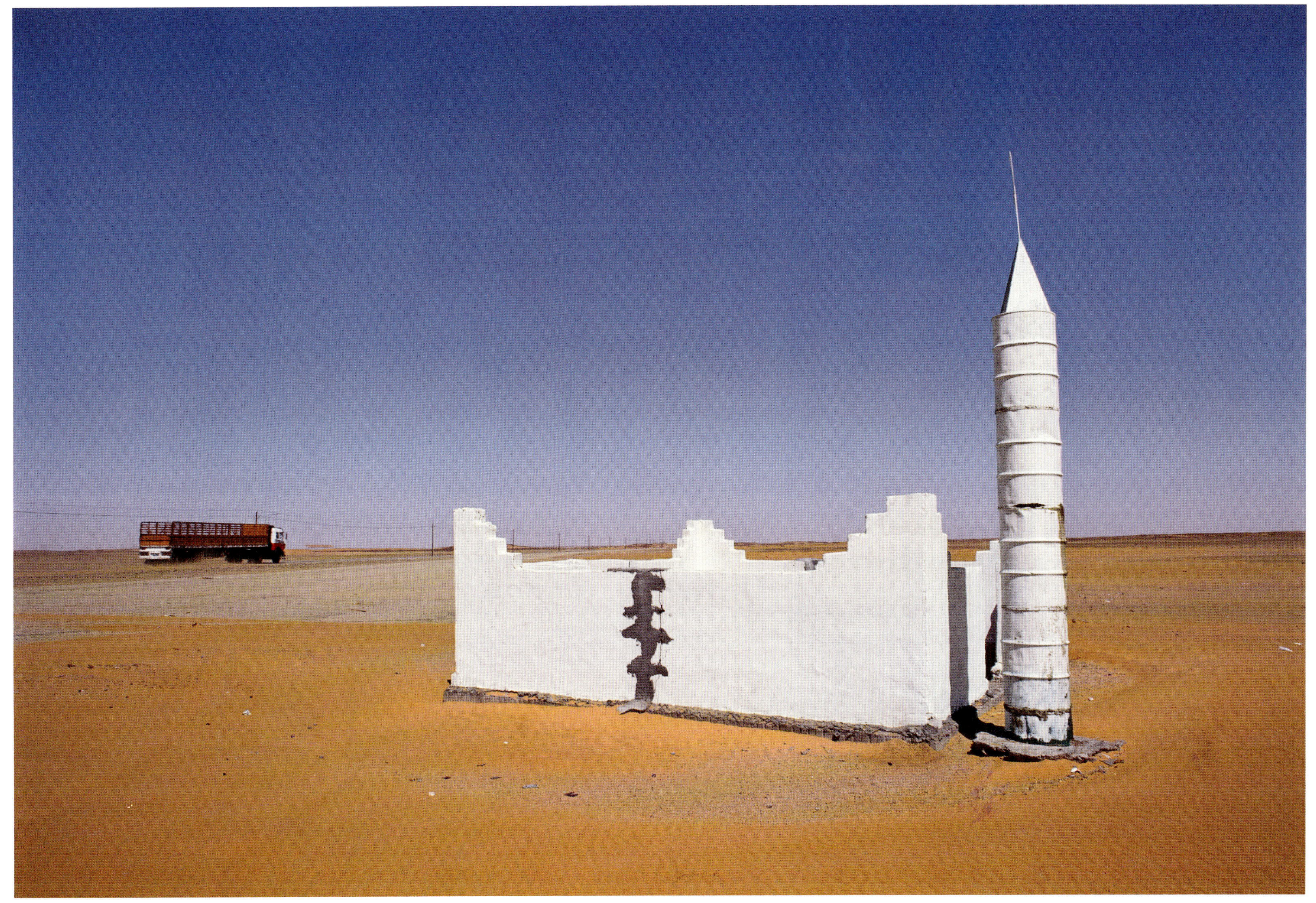

Roadside mosque, Wuday'ah, Saudi Arabia

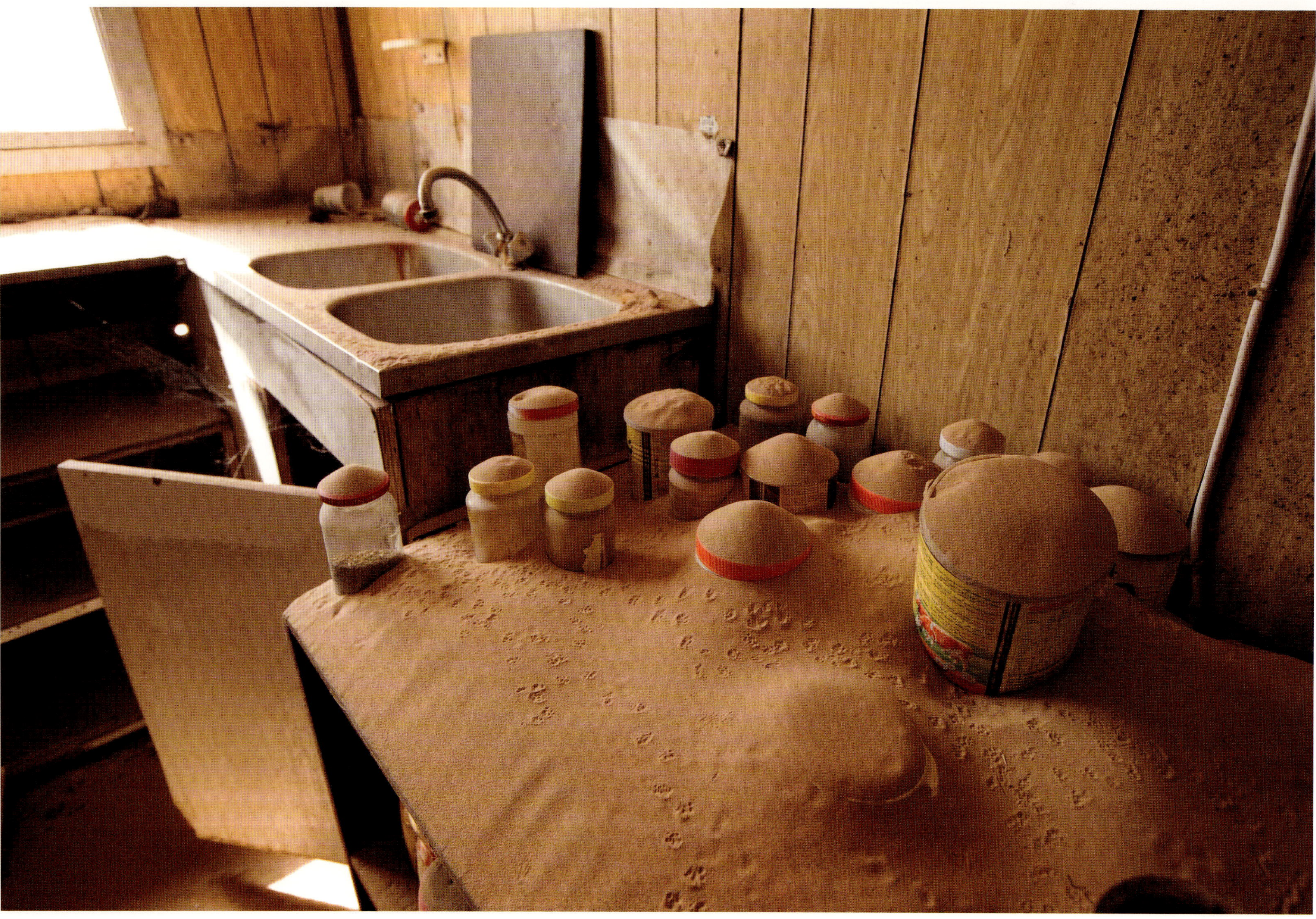

   ABOVE AND OPPOSITE: Abandoned construction camp, Umm Hisin, U.A.E.

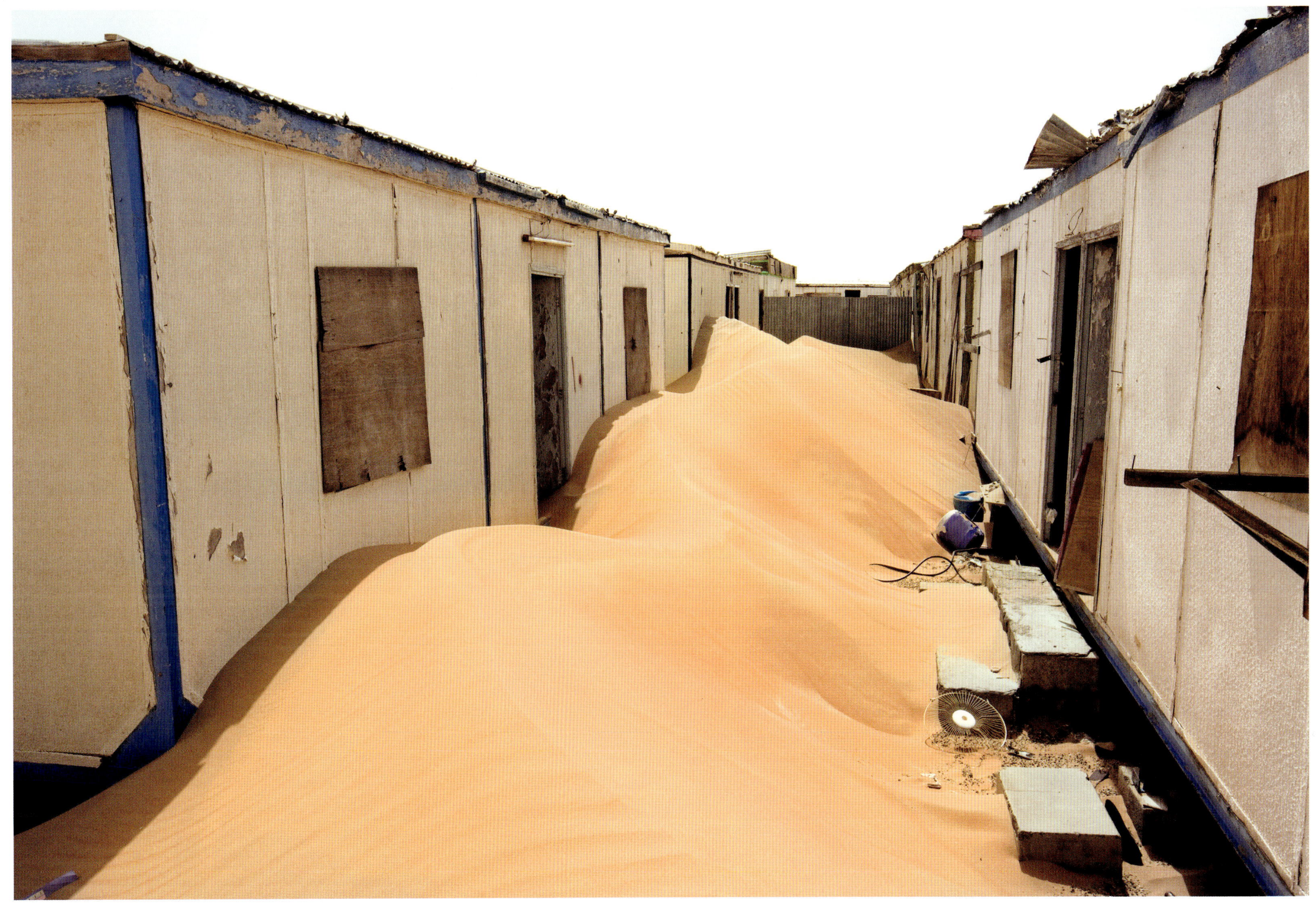

"In the deserts of southern Arabia there is no rhythm
of the seasons, no rise and fall of sap, but empty
wastes where only the changing temperature marks
the passage of the year. It is a bitter, desiccated
land which knows nothing of gentleness or ease.
Yet men have lived there since earliest times."

Wilfred Thesiger, *Arabian Sands*

          OPPOSITE: Sunrise and rare fog, Shaybah, Saudi Arabia

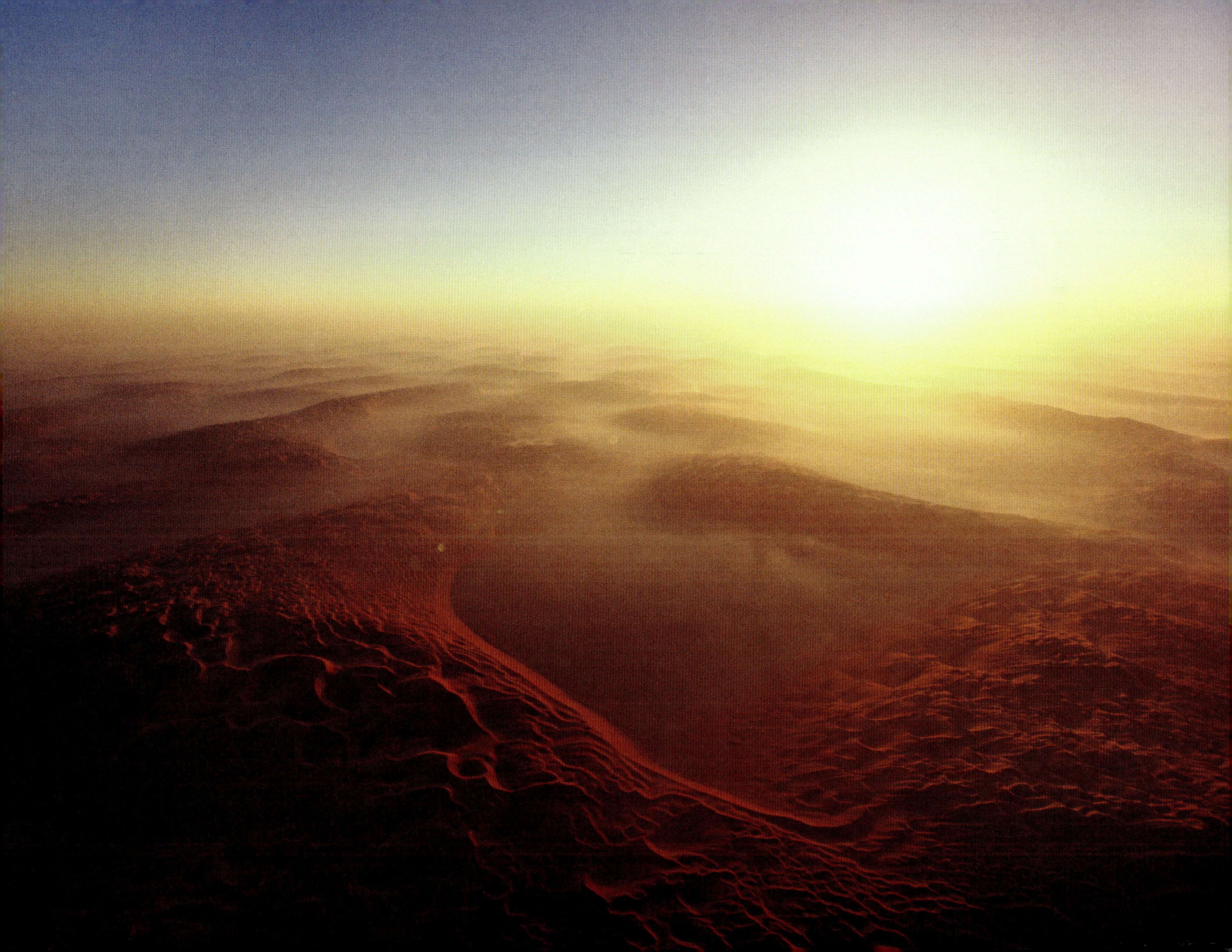

OIL

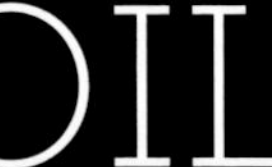

Rolling into Saudi Arabia's newest oil field, Shaybah, was a surreal experience. Most of the workers fly in on the Saudi Aramco jet from Dhahran, and heavy equipment is trucked in on the one two-lane road through the dunes. But we had been deep in the desert looking for meteorites and drove in cross-country from the southwest. There are no roads or facilities of any kind out that way, and we had to forge our way through a hundred and fifty miles of virgin dunes using forty-year-old maps, our GPS, and a lot of faith in our 4x4 cars. We caught sight of the oil field haul road from the crest of a dune a little after sunrise, and greatly relieved, sped toward it as though it were an asphalt lifeline that might disappear at any moment. Soon we were roaring down the pavement at eighty miles per hour for two hours without seeing a single person or checkpoint. The farther east we went, the larger and more beautiful the dunes became. We were entering the largest dune complex in the Empty Quarter, one that takes on the shape of an eggcrate with huge spikes of brick-orange sand standing over five hundred feet tall.

I had spent months trying to gain access to Shaybah and its multibillion dollar facilities, for this was one of the world's most spectacularly situated oil fields and the only civilian route into the big dunes. After all, what would a photo expedition depicting Saudi Arabia look like without pictures of oil production? We drove past wells, pipelines, and a massive gas oil separation plant without hindrance, and by the time we reached Shaybah's head office I felt like I had just walked in the back door of an enormous bank and wandered into the vault. We waited at the front gate for an hour while calls were made to check our permission, and then the barrier swung wide open. For me and my pilot-friend Alain Arnoux, Shaybah was a visual gold mine. This was Saudi Aramco's showcase oil field, which had been completed just four years earlier.

The field was discovered in 1968, but because of its remote location and the nature of its oil reservoir, it wasn't considered economic before advances in horizontal drilling led to construction that was finished in 1998. It remains the largest oil field completed anywhere in the world during the last twenty years. The logistics of building the giant oil facility here are impressive, as the field is 250 miles from the nearest highway. Even the sand used for construction had to be hauled in, as Empty Quarter sand is not suitable for making cement. In three years Saudi Aramco, the world's largest oil company, put in 250 miles of paved road, drilled one hundred wells, laid a four-hundred-mile pipeline to the coast at Abqaiq, and built a jet airport and a housing facility for seven hundred men. The field has a daily production capacity of 750,000 barrels of Arabian light sweet crude that is pure enough to be used as diesel fuel with little refining. Total reserves are estimated at nineteen billion barrels.

We were generously given free run of their facilities, which included a sprawling residential complex, the private jet airfield, a network of well-paved roads through one of the world's most spectacular dune scapes, and an unlimited free supply of fuel. Best of all, they had an emergency response room with a huge mosaic of high-resolution satellite images laid out on a table so that we could plan our paraglider flights after inspecting every sand dune that overlaid the three-hundred-square-mile oil field. They even had a buffet-style cafeteria; private motel-style rooms with phones, TVs, and showers; and a huge covered swimming pool that is chilled in the summer months to keep the water refreshing. We hadn't seen a toilet for ten days, let alone a change of clothes, so to us this seemed like paradise.

We were a bit of a curiosity, having driven in with our own cars and two experimental aircraft. Shaybah is a mature field so there wasn't a lot of activity going on, but there was one new well about to be put on line, and they had to burn its output for a few minutes to prevent impurities from flowing into their network. The result would be a huge flame and plume of black smoke that could be seen from ten miles away—the kind of thing that makes an oil field actually look like an oil field. The field manager told me that the Norwegian oil minister was making an official visit that week with a large delegation that included press, and he simply couldn't flare the well then as it wouldn't give the right impression to the foreign dignitaries. But he told me that if I was to come back the next week—when nobody else was looking—I could photograph it. We had a date and a week later I had my picture. ▣

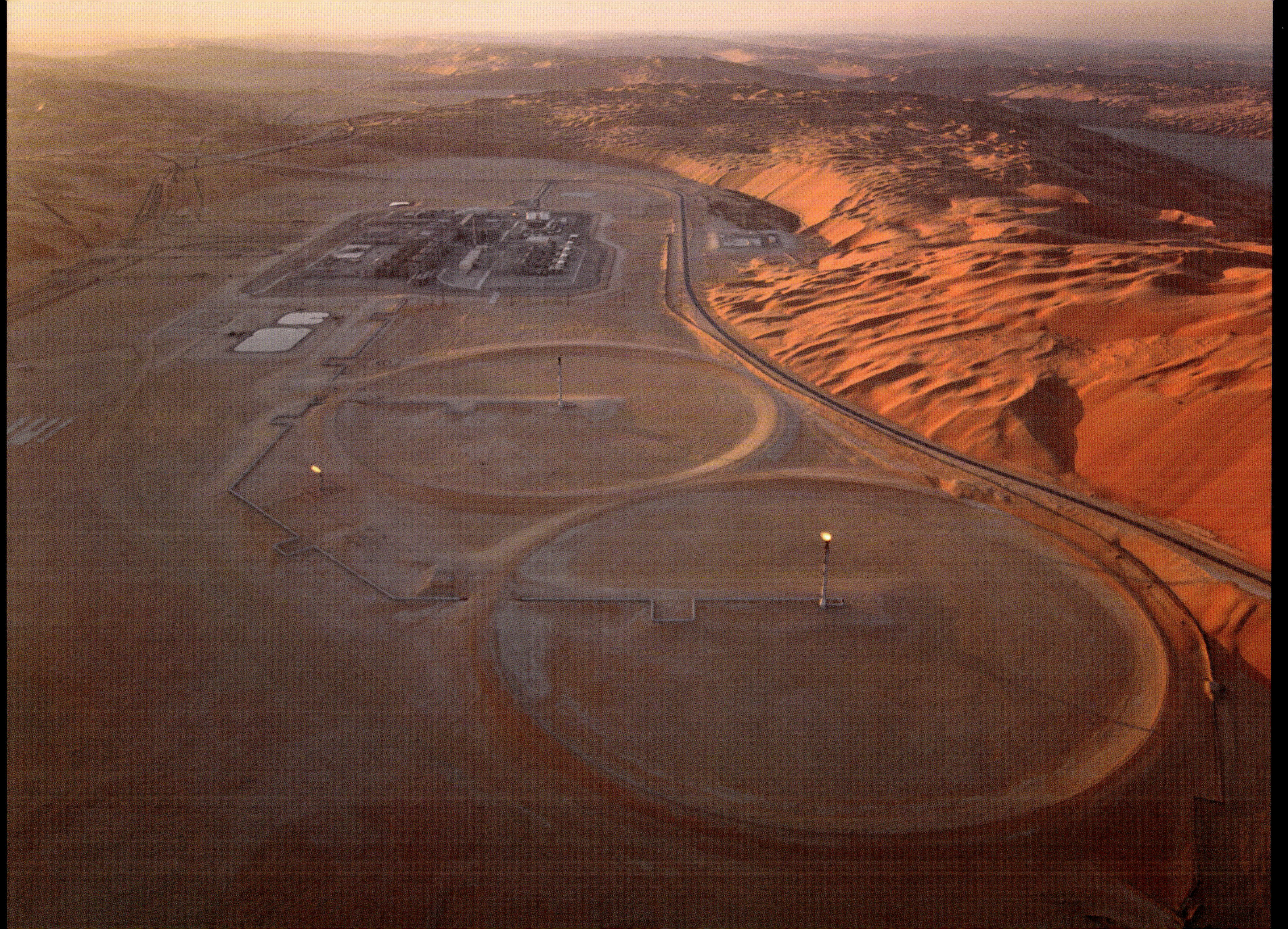

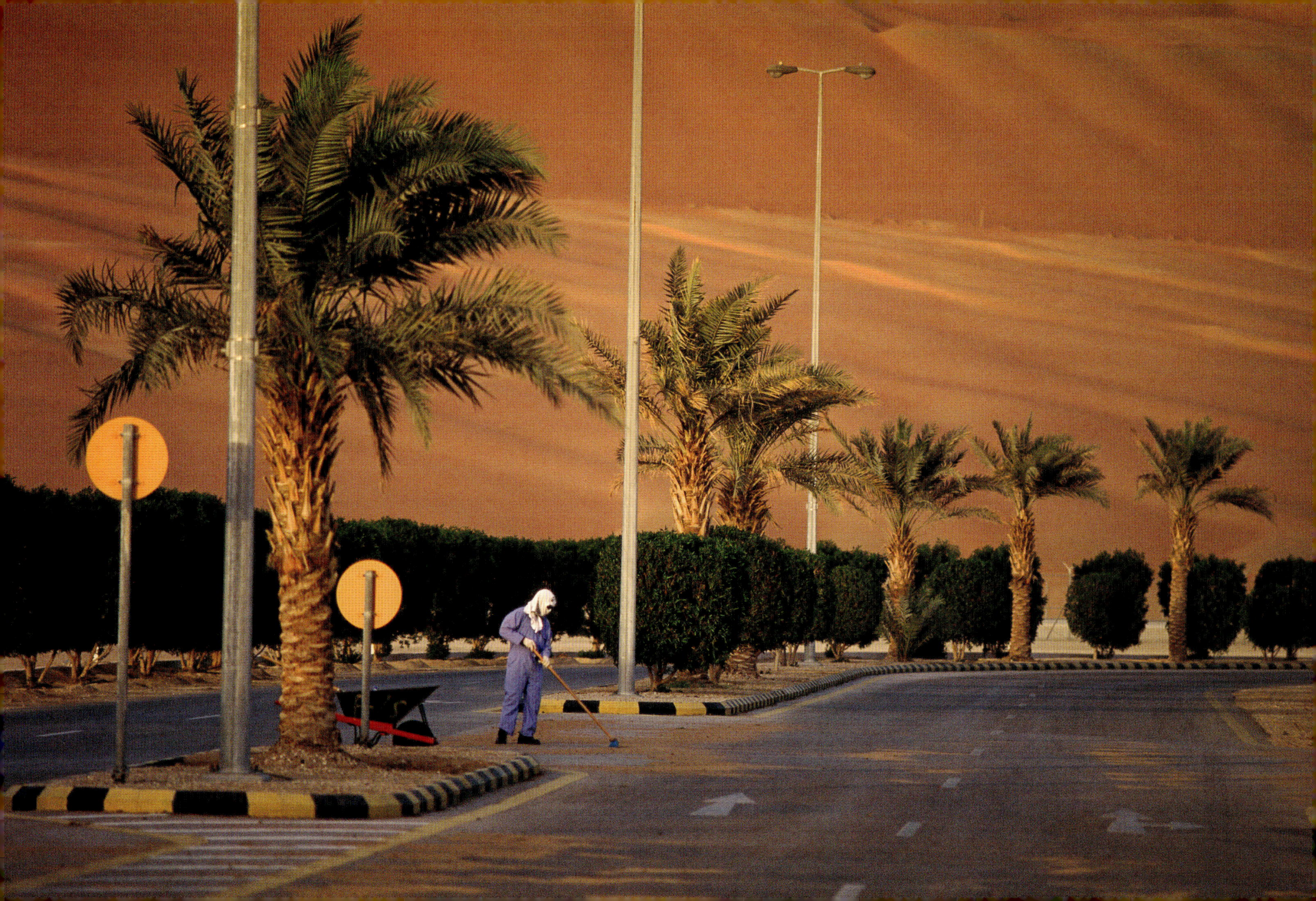

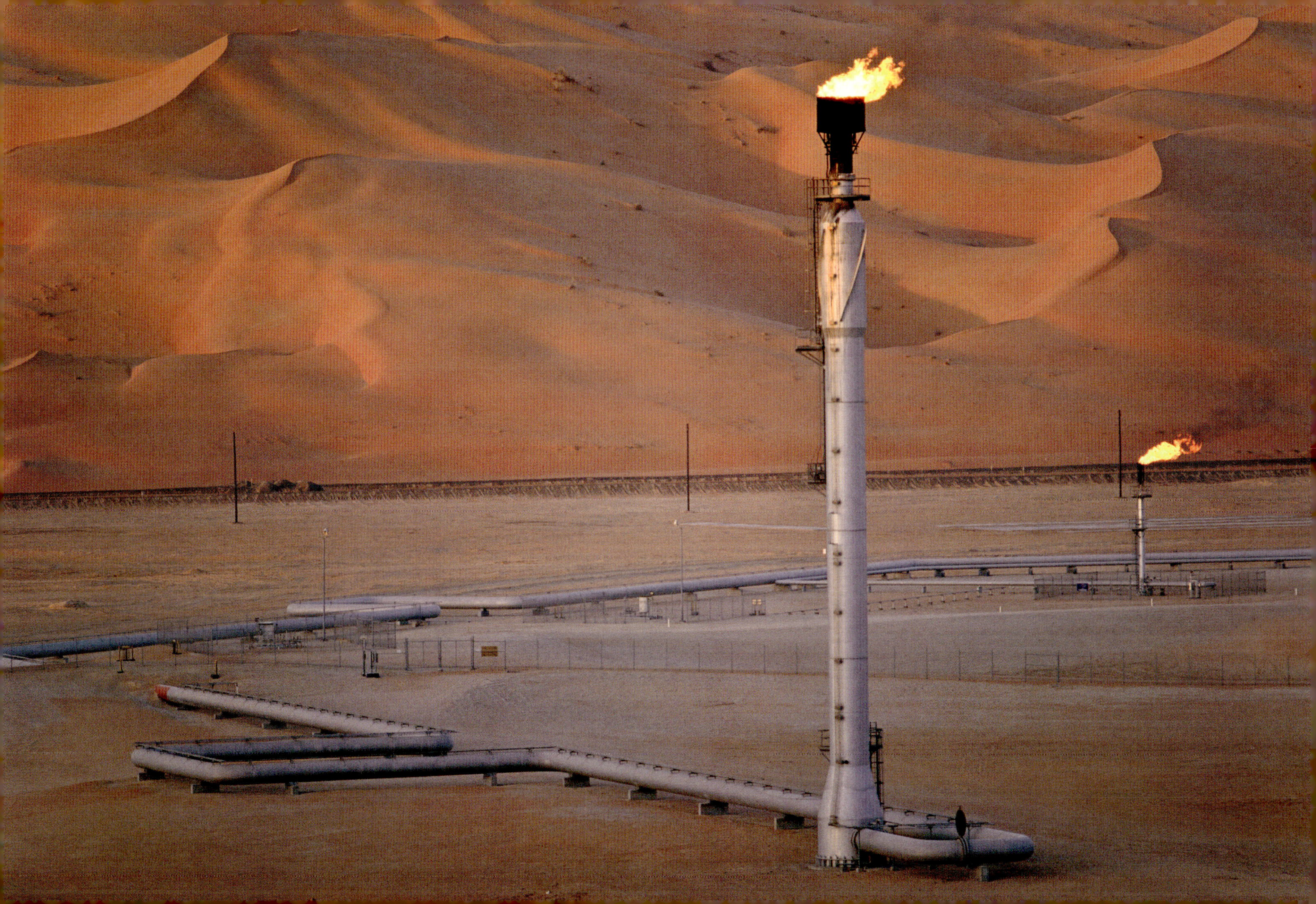

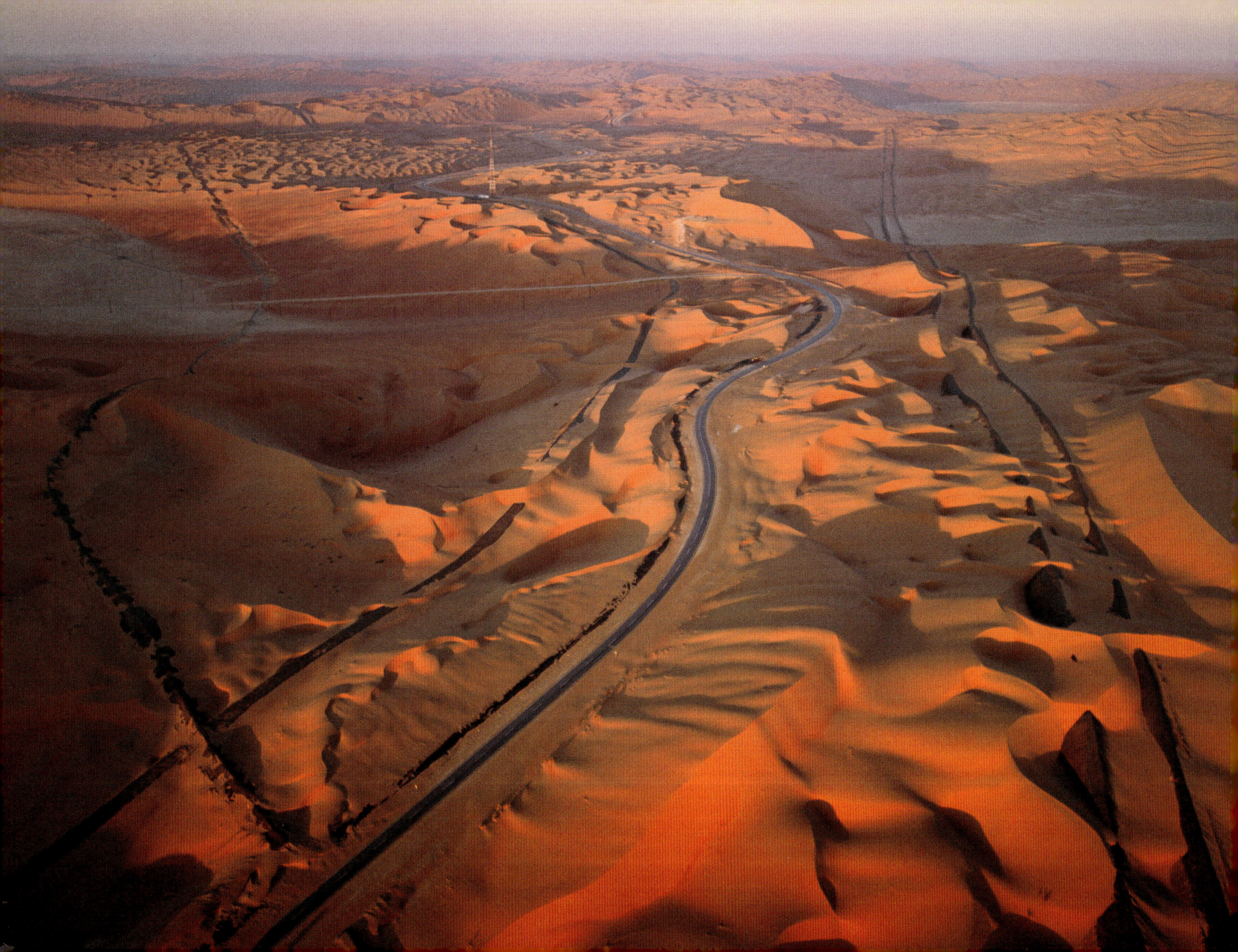

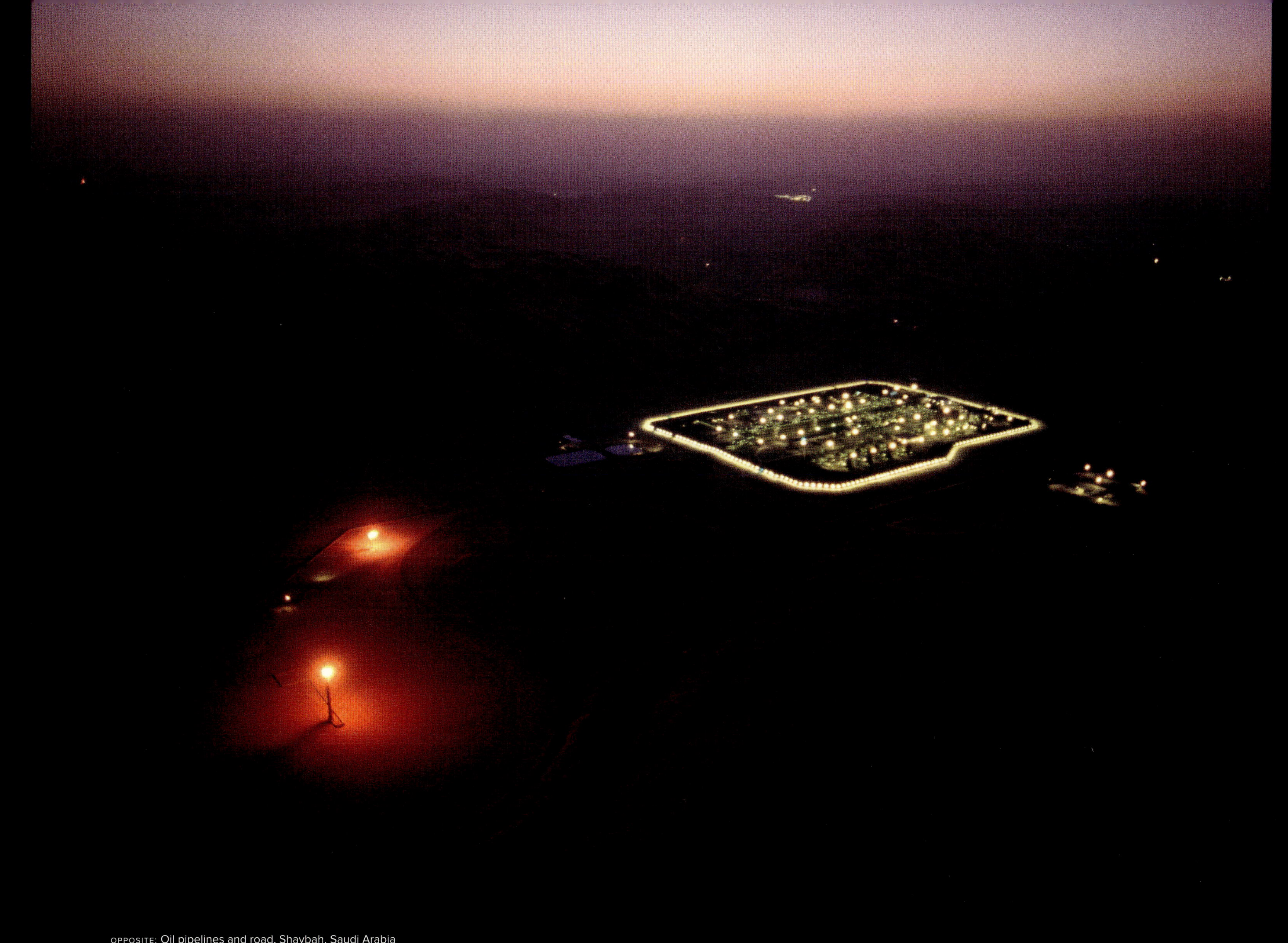

OPPOSITE: Oil pipelines and road, Shaybah, Saudi Arabia
ABOVE: Gas-oil separation plant, Shaybah, Saudi Arabia

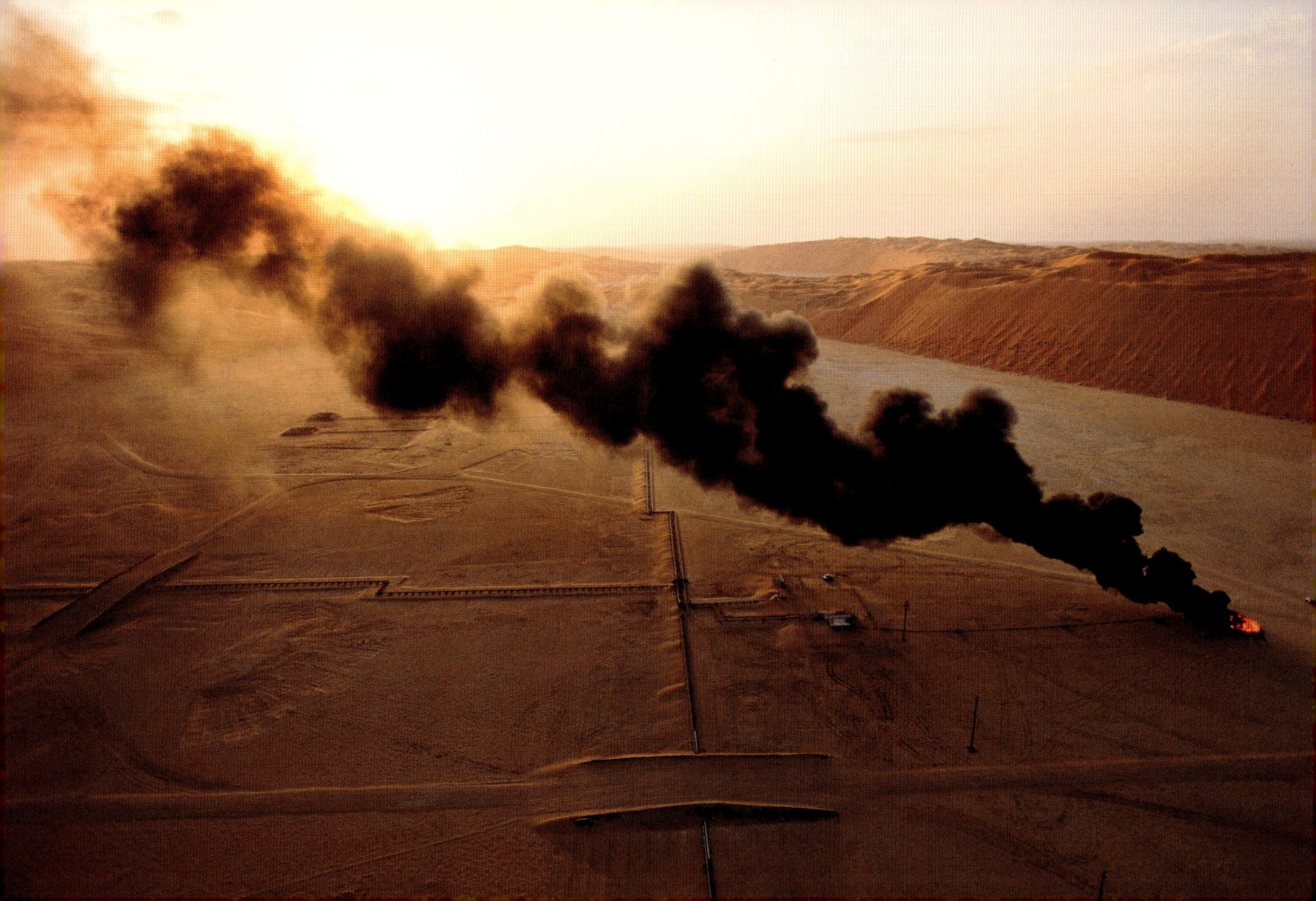

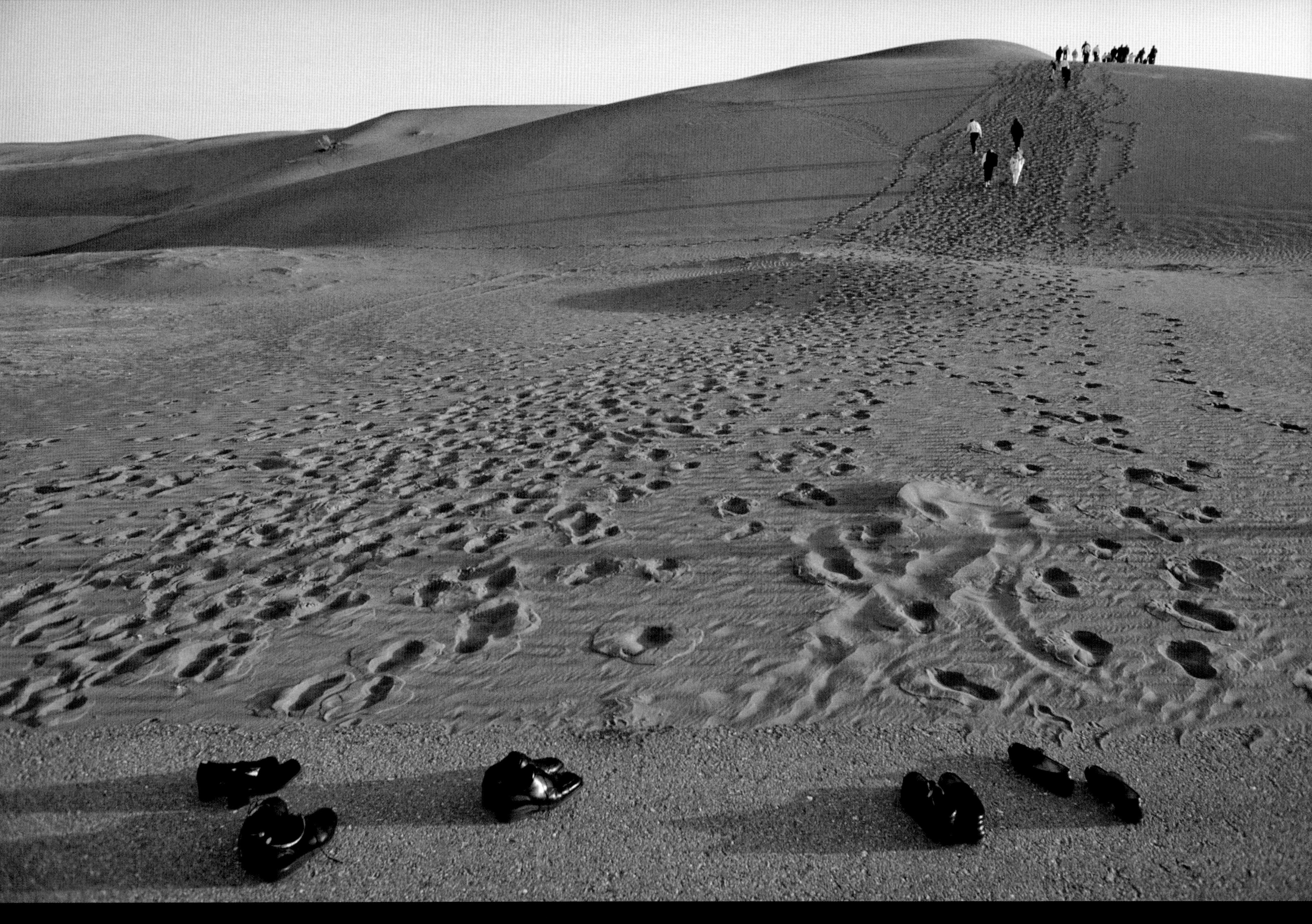

ABOVE: Norwegian oil minister with entourage climbing a dune at sunset, Shaybah, Saudi Arabia
OVERLEAF: Junction near airport, Shaybah, Saudi Arabia

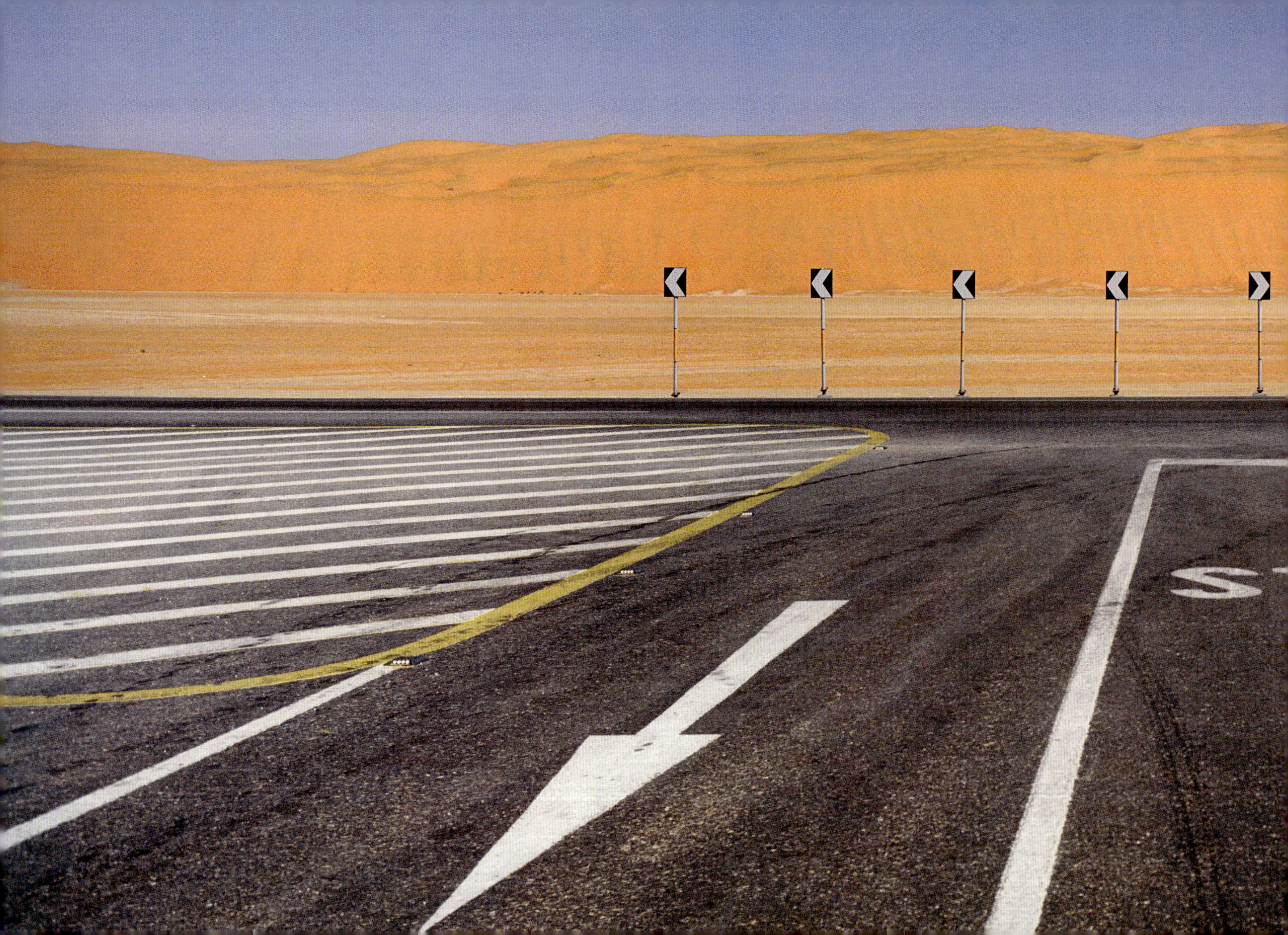
S

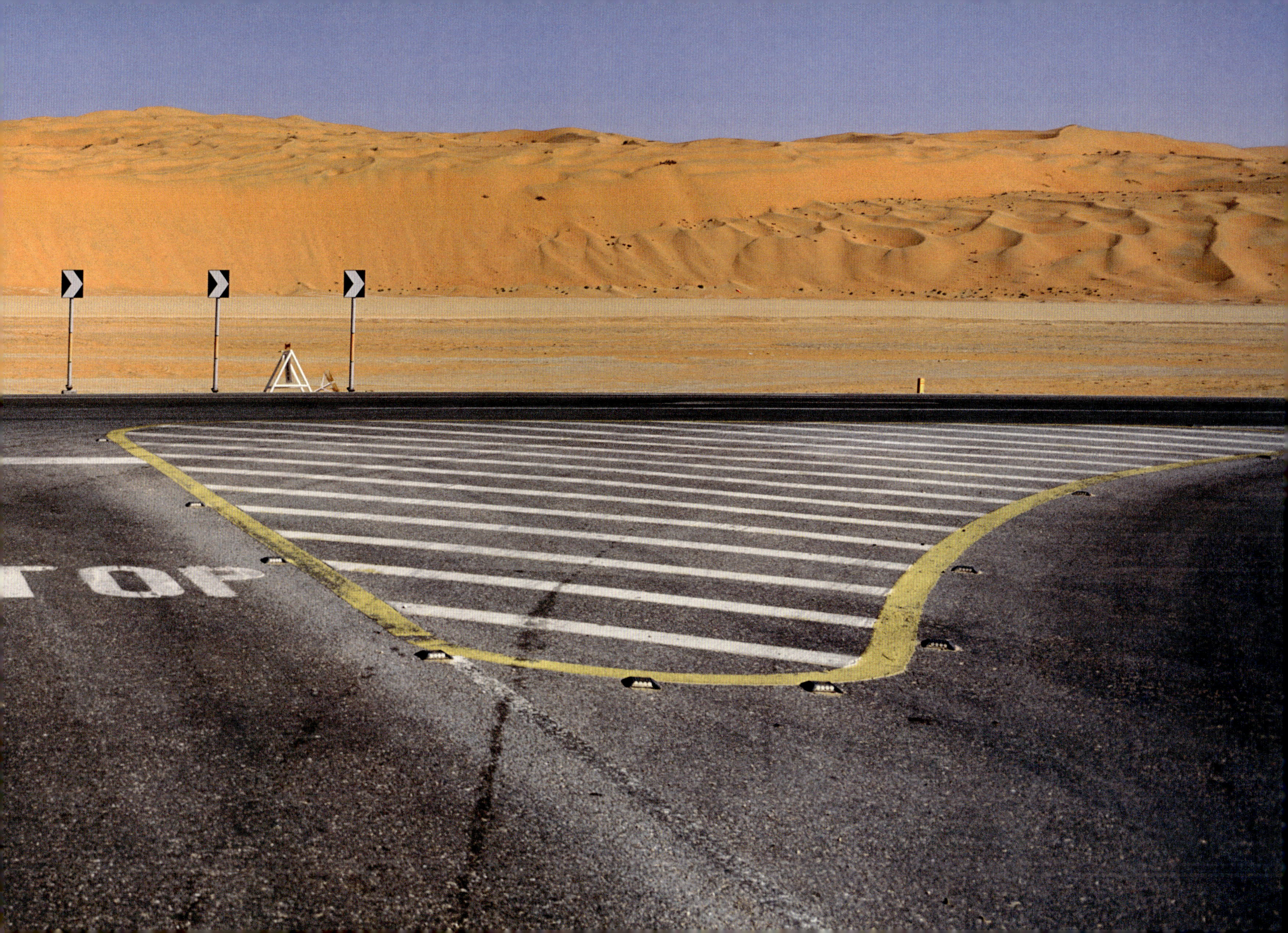
TOP

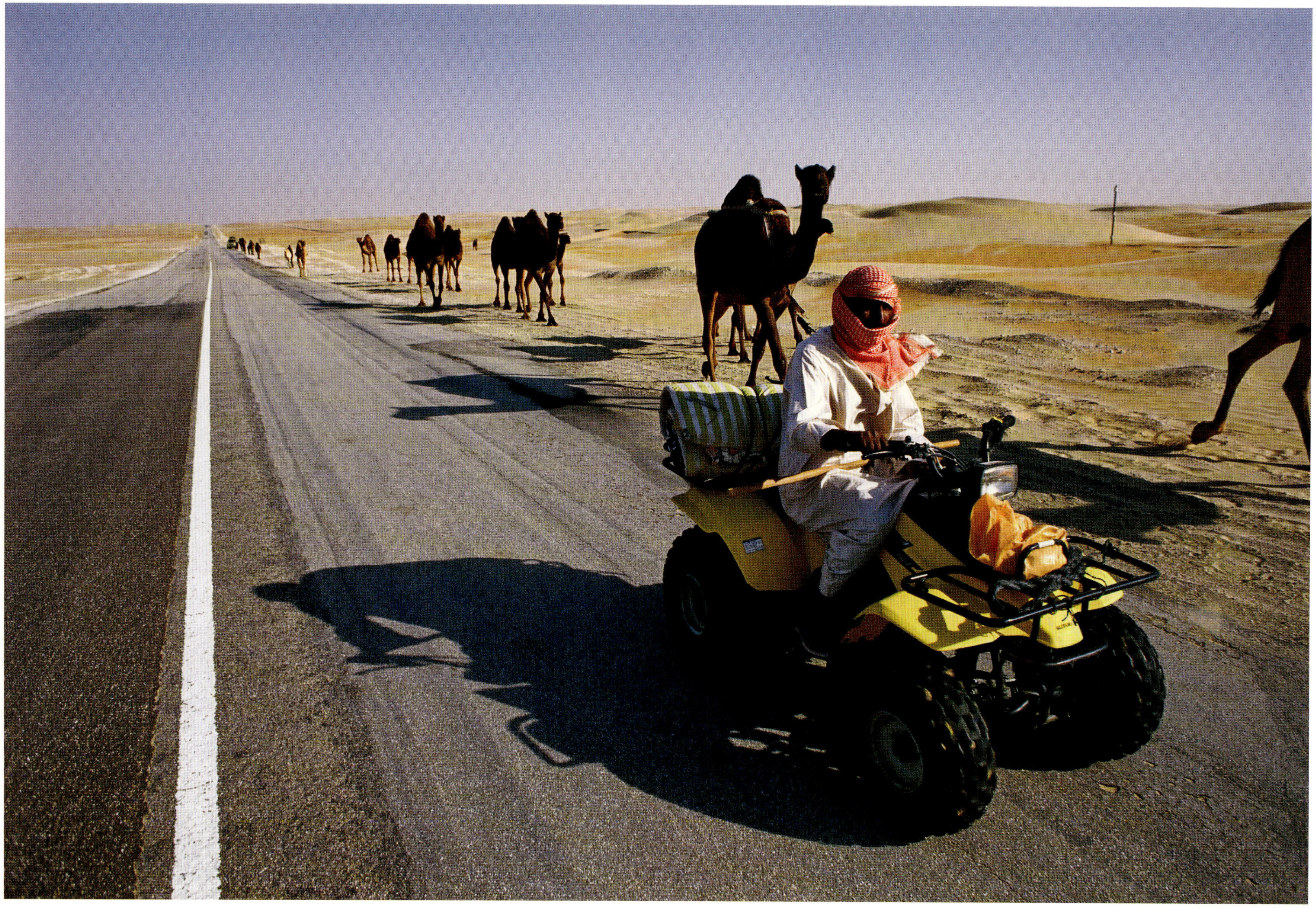

    Bedouin on road to Shaybah, Saudi Arabia

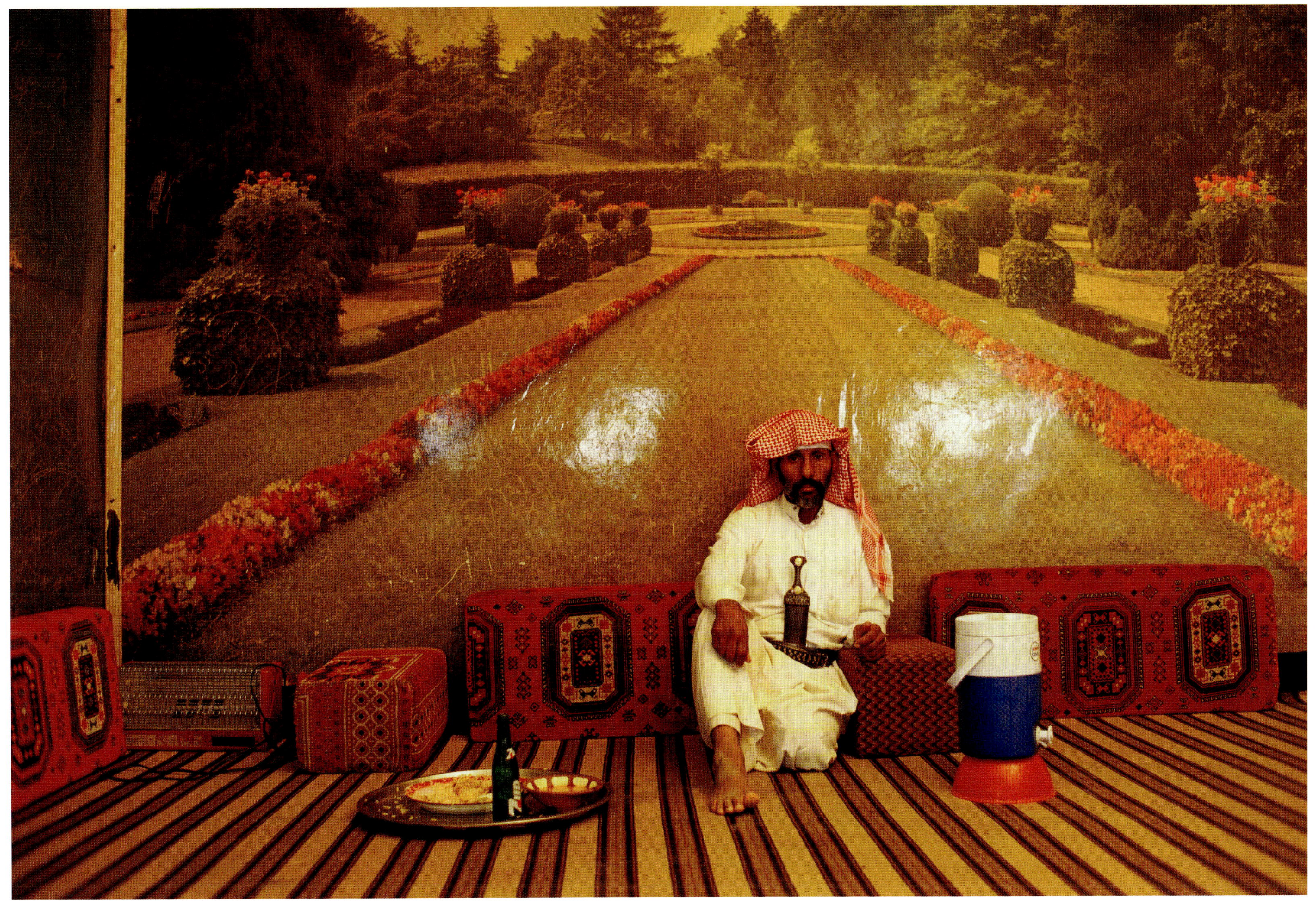

Roadside restaurant, Qaryat al-Fau, Saudi Arabia

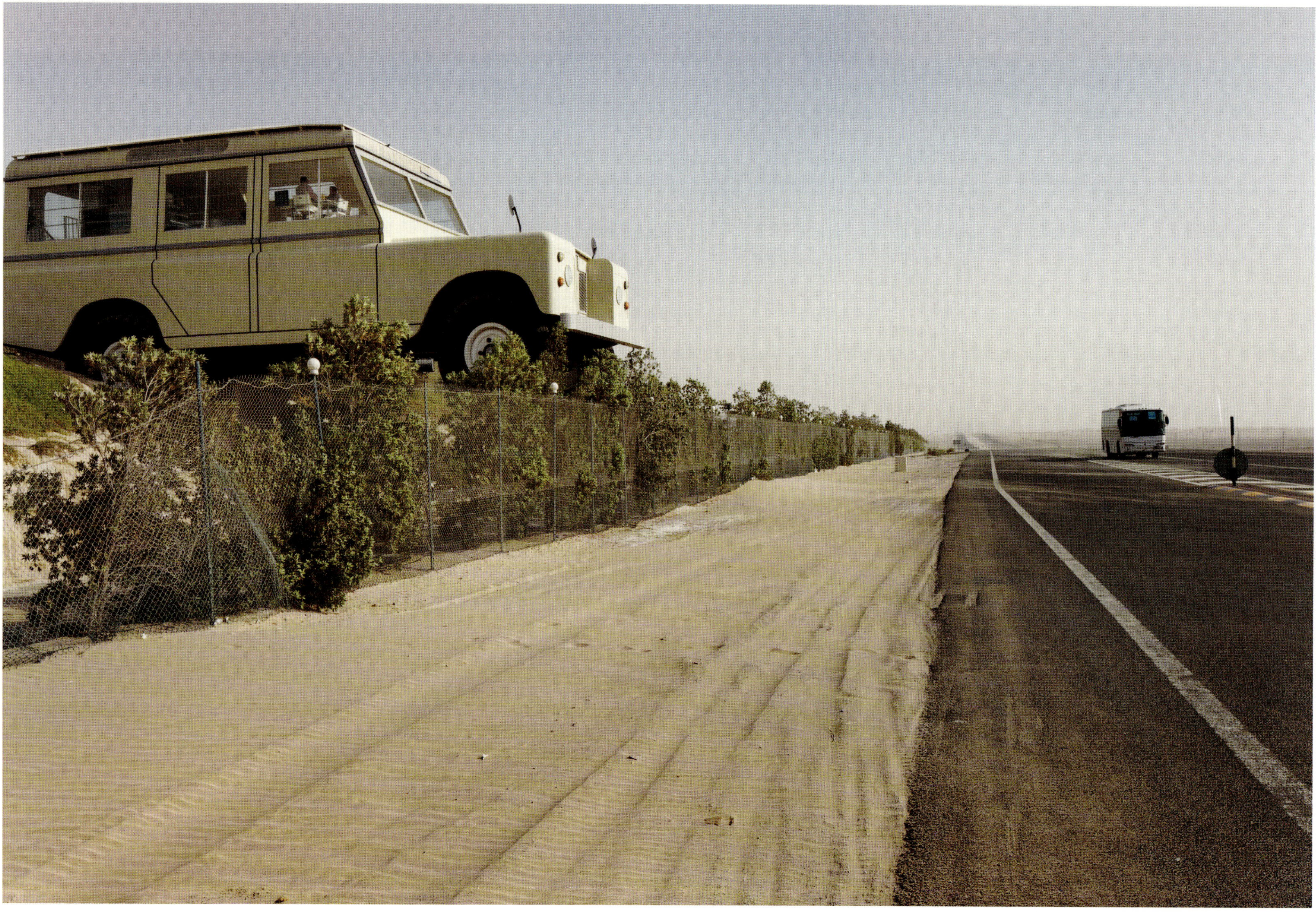

   Restaurant at the Emirates National Car Museum, Abu Dhabi, U.A.E.

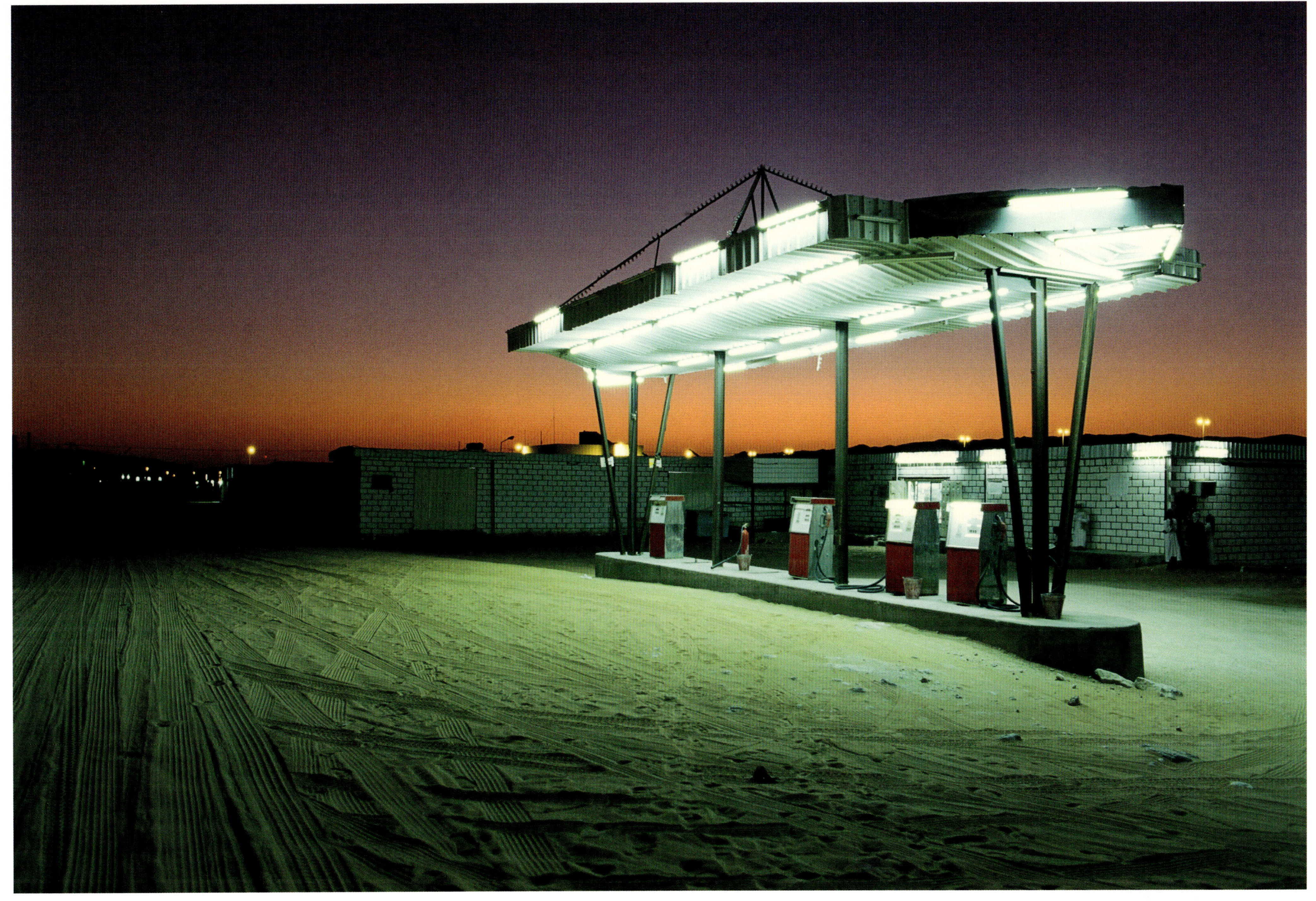

Fuel station, Kharkheer, Saudi Arabia

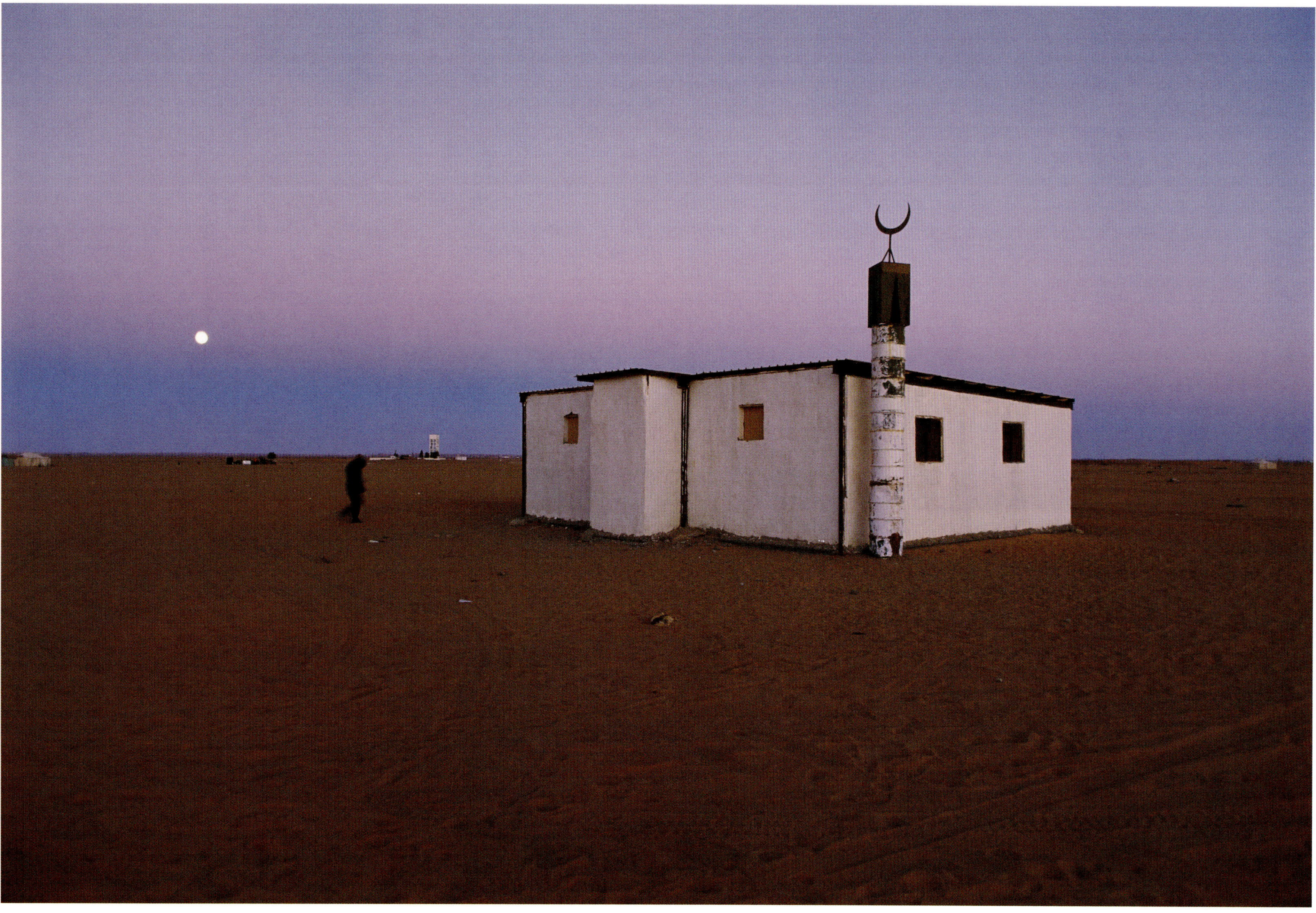

   Mosque in Bedouin camp, Wuday'ah, Saudi Arabia

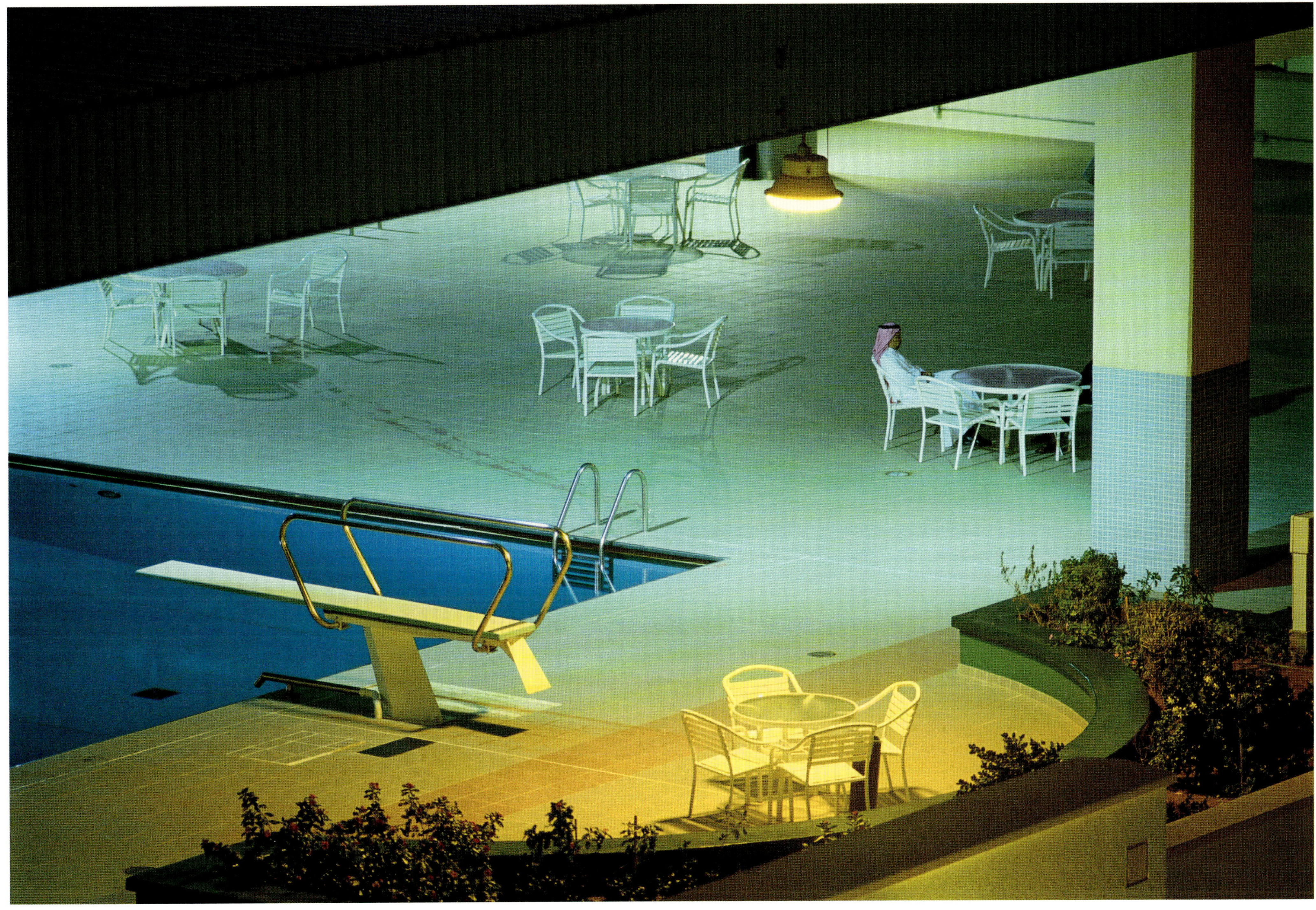

Chilled-water swimming pool in Saudi Aramco complex, Shaybah, Saudi Arabia

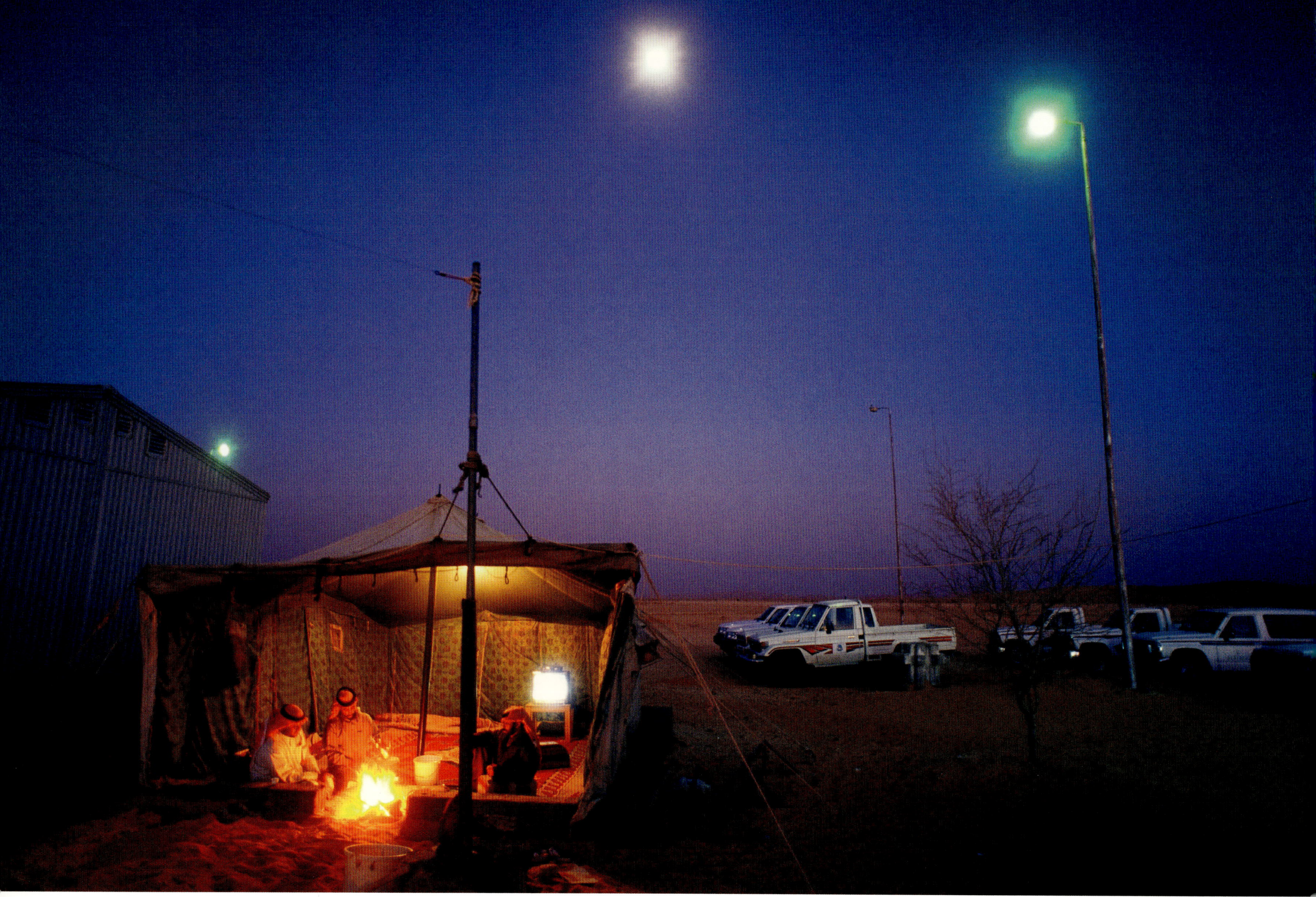

    Wildlife ranger camp, Bani Ma'arid, Saudi Arabia

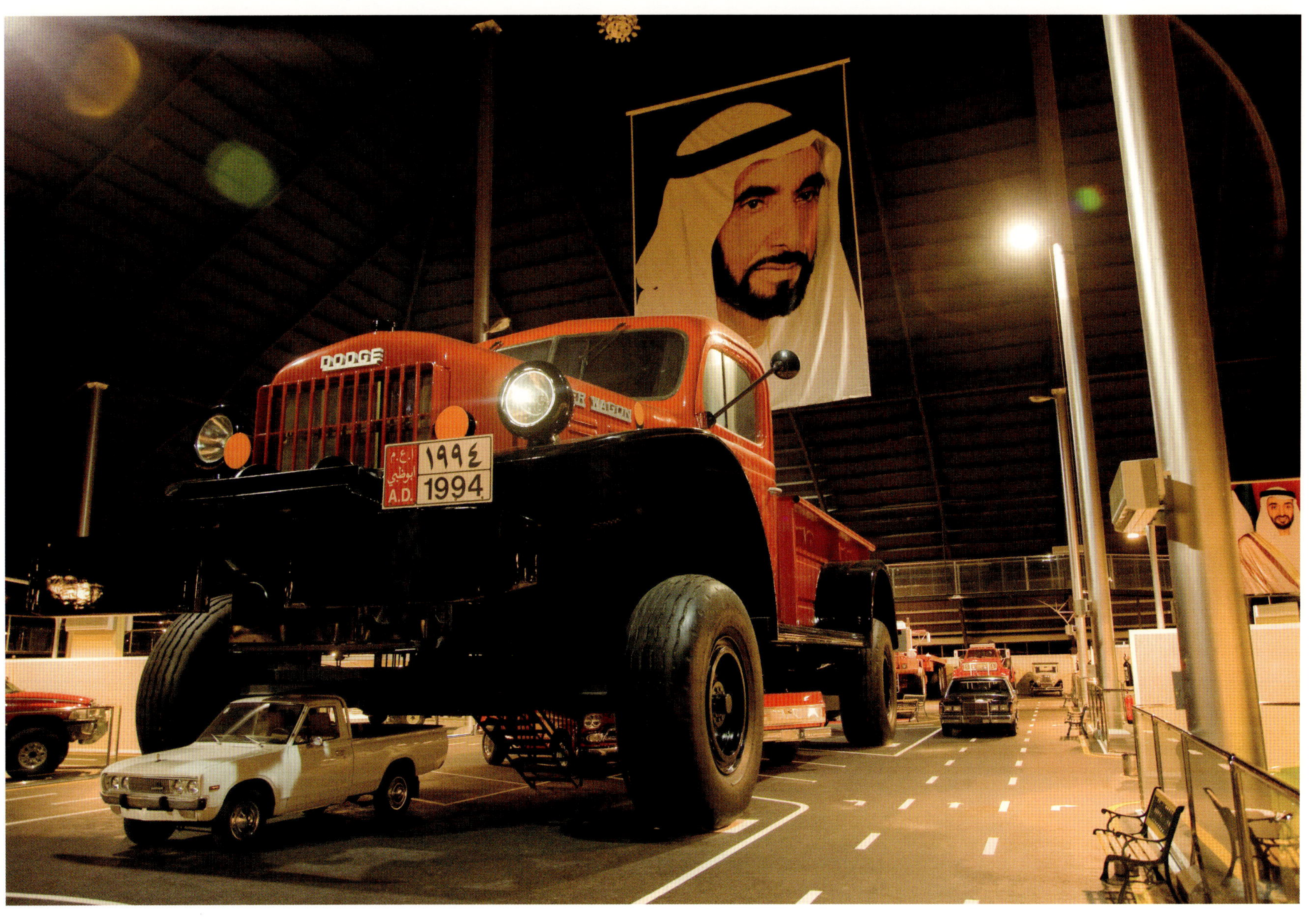

World's largest car, Emirates National Car Museum, Abu Dhabi, U.A.E.

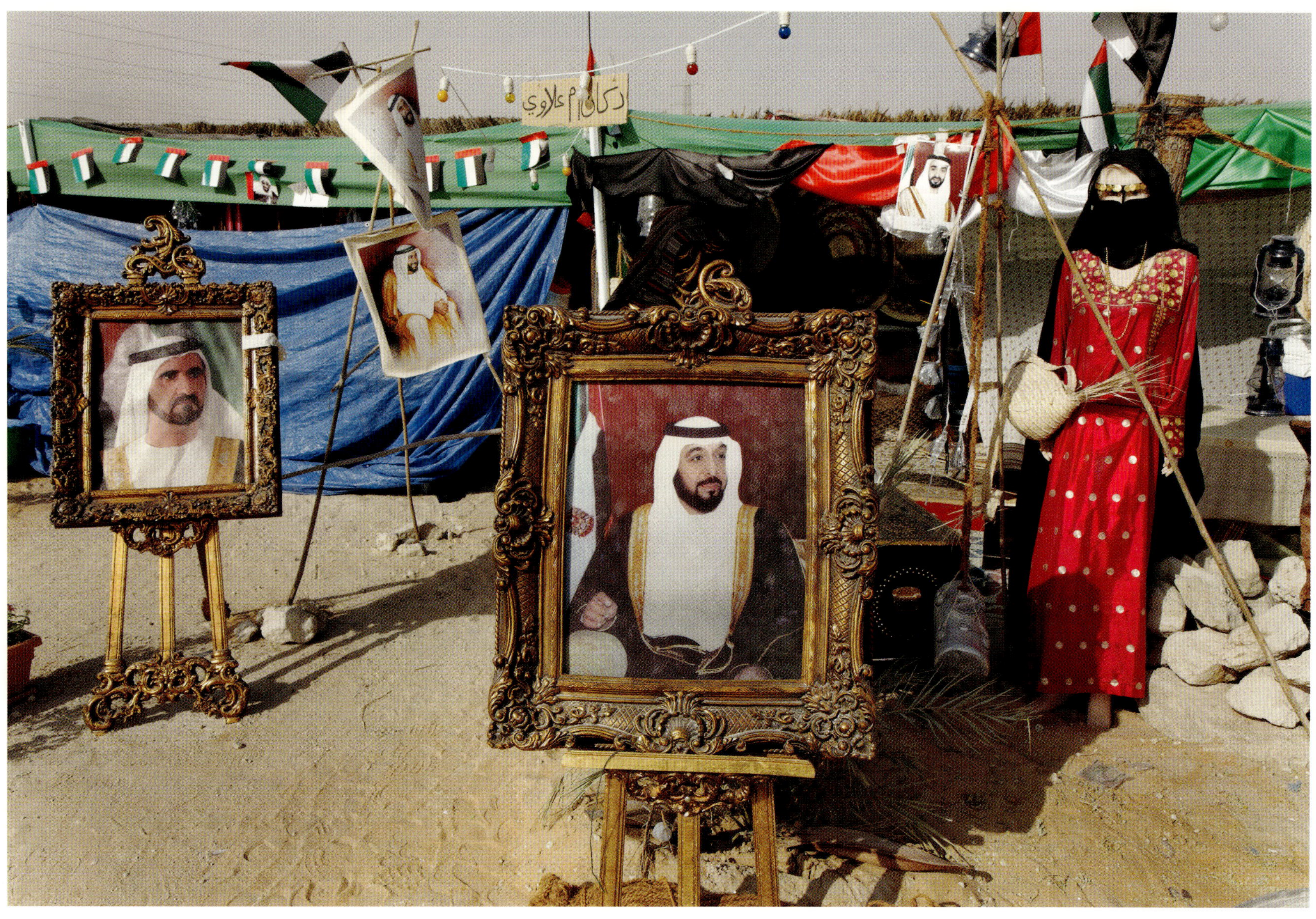

     Bedouin shop, Madinat Zayed, U.A.E.

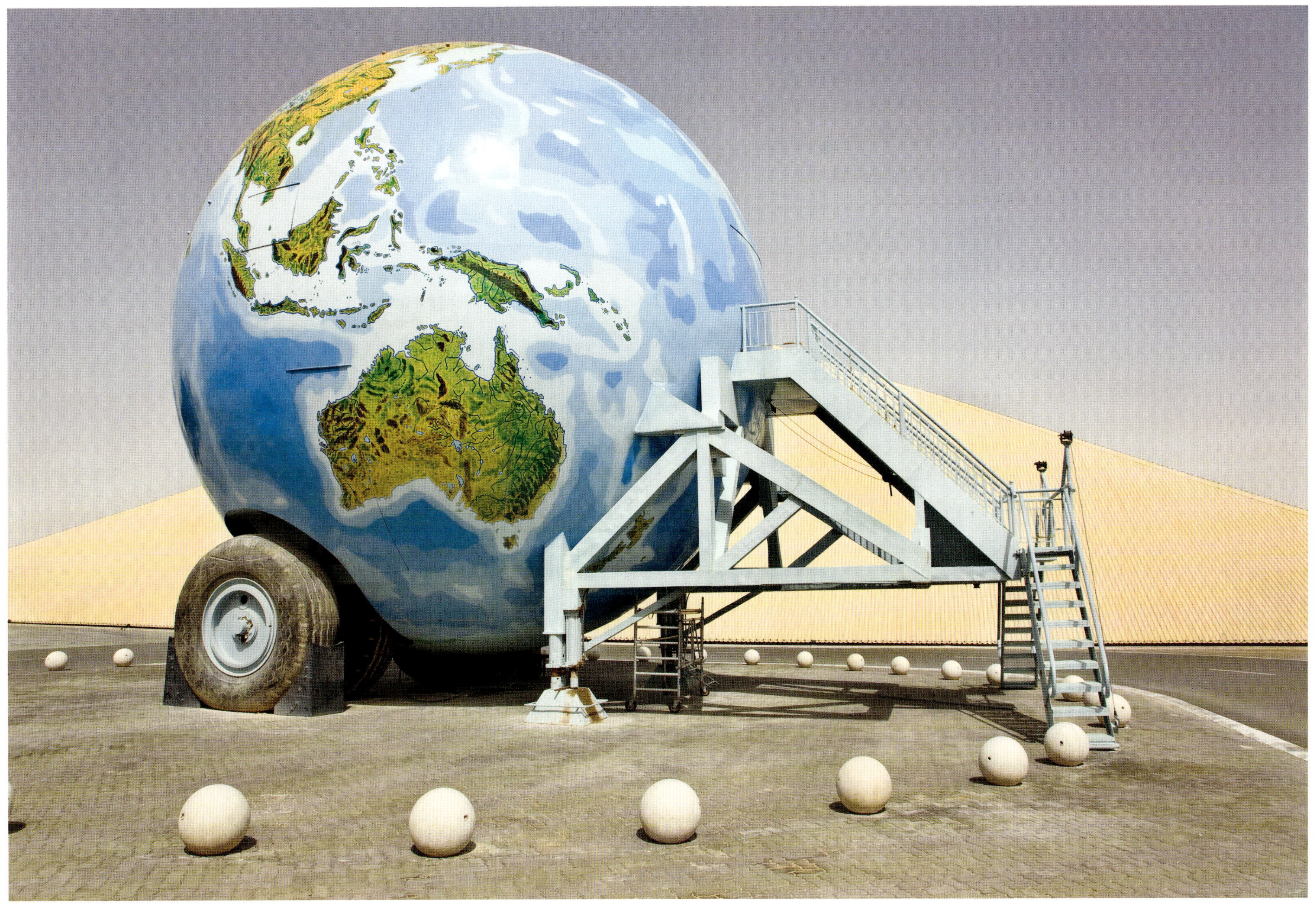

Mobile home, Emirates National Car Museum, Abu Dhabi, U.A.E.

"No man can live this life and emerge unchanged.
He will carry, however faint, the imprint of
the desert, the brand which marks the nomad;
and he will have within him the yearning
to return, weak or insistent according to his
nature. For this cruel land can cast a spell
which no temperate clime can match."

Wilfred Thesiger, *Arabian Sands*

          OPPOSITE: Smuggler's route from Marib to Timna, Yemen

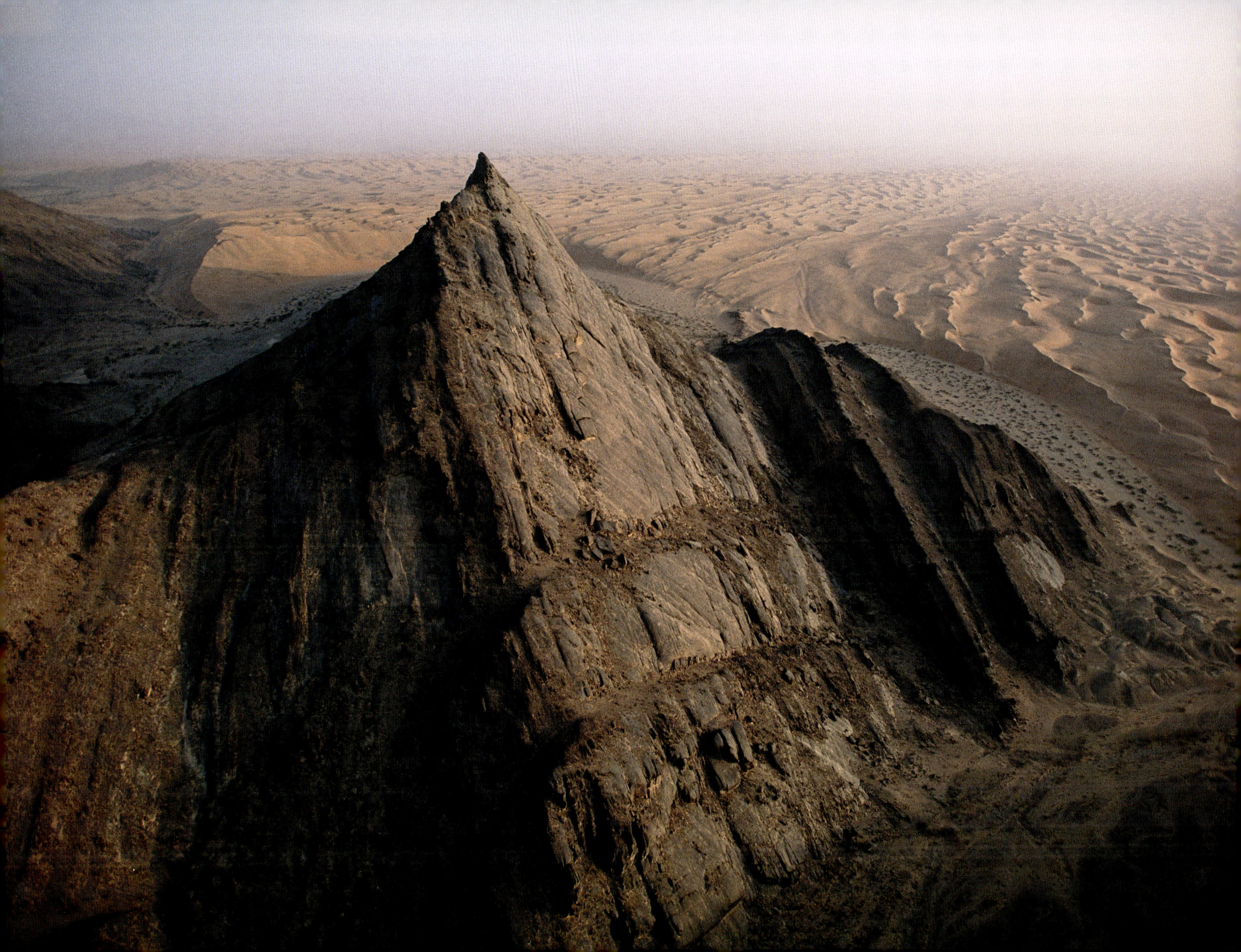

SHEBA

I spotted the ruins of an oval temple from a thousand feet up. Known as Mahram Bilqis, it was said to be the Queen of Sheba's Temple of the Moon, and was now being excavated for the second time in fifteen hundred years. As I circled overhead I could see the bewilderment on many upturned faces, as a motorized paraglider is an oddity in the deserts of Yemen. Soon I recognized the shock of blonde hair on the head of Merilyn Phillips Hodgson, the leader of the archaeological team, and as she looked up I waved. I took a few photos of the site before coming in for a landing on the sandy ground right in front of the eight pillars that formed the temple's entry. My dramatic arrival created quite a diversion from the sweaty tedium of excavation, and I was quickly introduced to the entire team. But then their head of security took me gently aside and informed me that I had waved at just the right moment, as his men might have shot me down with their 50-caliber machine guns had Merilyn not called them off.

Merilyn had come here to complete the archaeological work begun by her late brother, Wendell Phillips, who was the first person to excavate this site fifty years earlier. Wendell was a charismatic explorer and oilman who carried a bone-handled Colt 38 revolver on his hip during fieldwork and is rumored to have been an inspiration for the fictional character Indiana Jones. In 1952 his team removed the windblown sand that had covered Mahram Bilqis for centuries, revealing beautifully hewn stonework, inscriptions in ancient Sabean characters, and a wealth of finely detailed stone and bronze statuary. It was one of the greatest archeological finds on the Arabian Peninsula, with a level of cultural sophistication unexpected from this little-known period of Middle Eastern history.

The Sabeans ruled this corner of Arabia during the pre-Islamic era, from the eighth century BCE to 275 CE. In its time, Saba, or Sheba as it is more popularly known, was one of the most advanced civilizations in Arabia with its capital, Marib, "the Paris of the ancient world." Its wealth was due in part to its location on the frankincense trade route as well as its advanced irrigation system. Caravans used their aromatic cargo to pay for goods and services along the way, and the city of Marib, the route's greatest desert oasis, was a prime benefactor. The agronomic foundation of Marib was its dam, which was one of the ancient world's greatest engineering achievements and lasted more than a thousand years. First constructed in the seventh century BCE, the dam supported some twenty-five thousand acres of agriculture year round, and at one point it spanned 2,150 feet between sluices of finely fitted stonework. The rise of Sabean wealth ended with the demise of the frankincense trade in the third century CE, as the expansion of Christianity discouraged pagan rites and the use of incense. With decreased caravan revenue and deferred maintenance, the dam silted up and was destroyed in a torrential flood in the sixth century.

Over the course of twelve centuries many powers vied for control of Marib, with invasions by various south Arabian kingdoms as well as Ethiopian and Roman legions. When Wendell Phillips conducted his excavations, he found that most of the finely made stone and bronze statues had been ripped from their foundations by looters and marauding zealots bent on destruction, leaving only a small number of whole exquisite pieces mixed in with a scattering of broken hands and feet. Mahram Bilqis is littered with burned bits of frankincense and animal bones, the detritus left over from centuries of ritual animal sacrifice. But what made this site so sacred for so long remains a mystery. The site was reconstructed many times by subsequent invaders, and the Phillipses discovered that the areas between the inner and outer temple walls had become filled with cultural debris spanning a period of two thousand years, from 1500 BCE to 500 CE. Some walls of the temple were constructed using recycled materials such as a carved funerary headstone that was discovered by Merilyn's team.

The frankincense trade took many routes through south Arabia. It began as the scrapings of tree sap in the mountains of Oman and Yemen and ended in the markets of Mesopotamia, Persia, and Rome, where it was worth more than its weight in gold. In its time it was a bit like the current trade in illicit narcotics, with caravans of smugglers choosing shifting paths to the

 OPPOSITE: Mahram Bilqis during excavation, Marib, Yemen

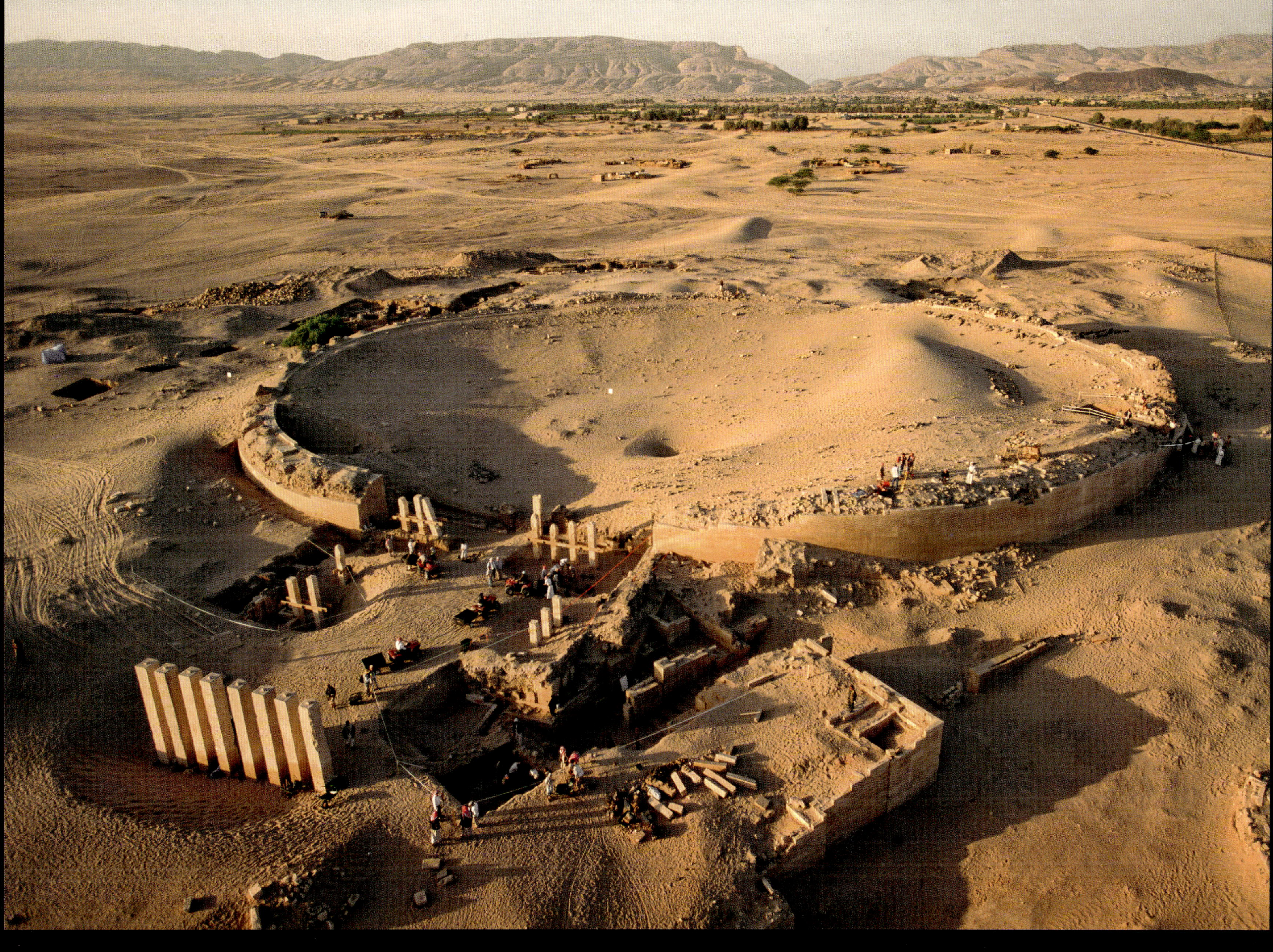

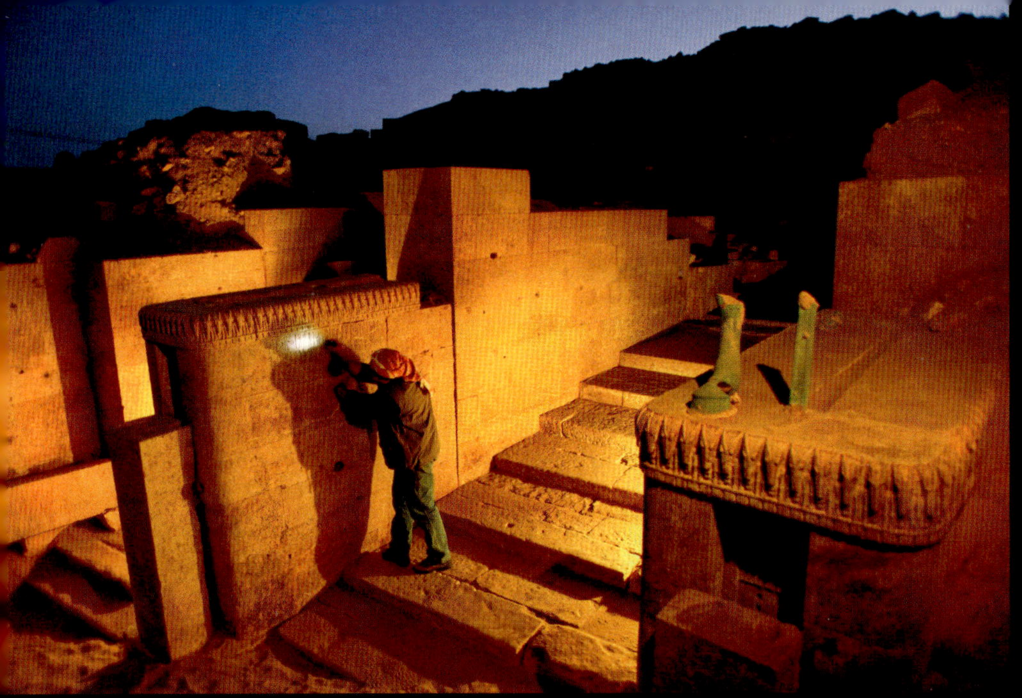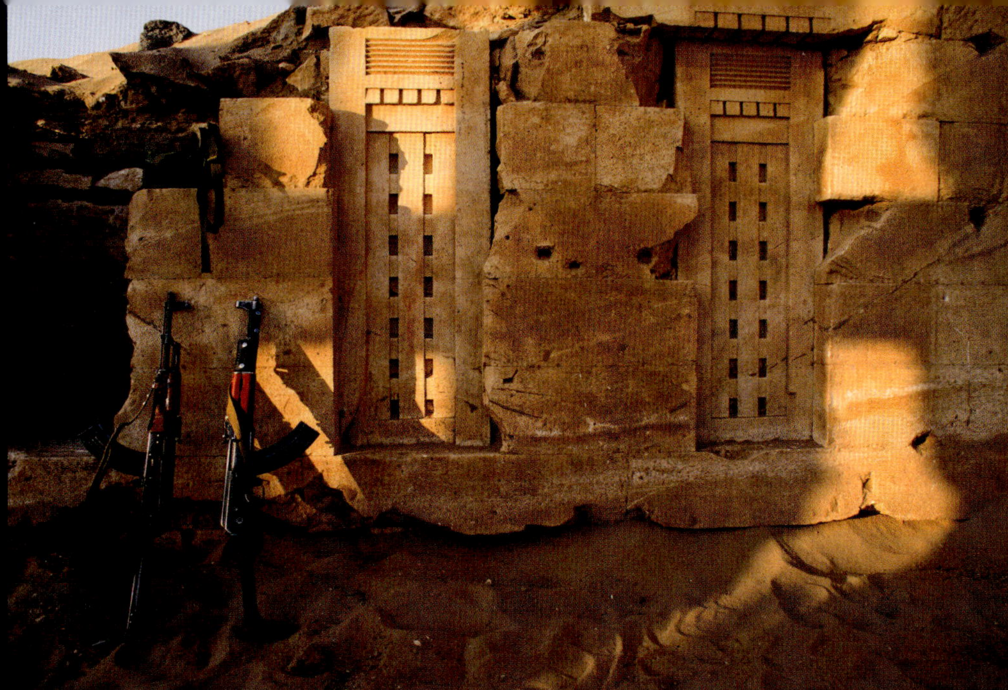

greatest profit. From Marib the trail forked around the Empty Quarter, with one branch leading up the inland side of the Red Sea coast to Petra and Palestine, while the eastern branch led north toward Qaryat al-Fau in present-day Saudi Arabia and then on to Mesopotamia.

Qaryat al-Fau is now abandoned, but it was recently excavated by a Saudi team led by Professor A. R. al-Ansary from the University of Riyadh, revealing a temple, fortified marketplace, residential quarter, cemetery, and a canal system. The town flourished from the second century BCE to the fifth century CE, and like Marib, was littered with Mediterranean trade goods and finely made artifacts in bronze and glass. It was known as

the kingdom of Kinda, and they were prosperous enough to have minted their own silver and bronze coins, complete with human faces and writings. On a visit here I made a flight up over the top of the escarpment that lies just beyond al-Fau, where I saw mysterious lines of stones with small triangular forms on their tails, like stone kites. Dr. al-Ansary thinks that these stone "kites" might have been used for astrological purposes, while others speculate that they could have been used to channel desert gazelle and ostrich for hunting. No one knows who built them or their meaning, but in that cool winter morning when I flew over them, I noticed that they all pointed toward the rising sun. 🔲

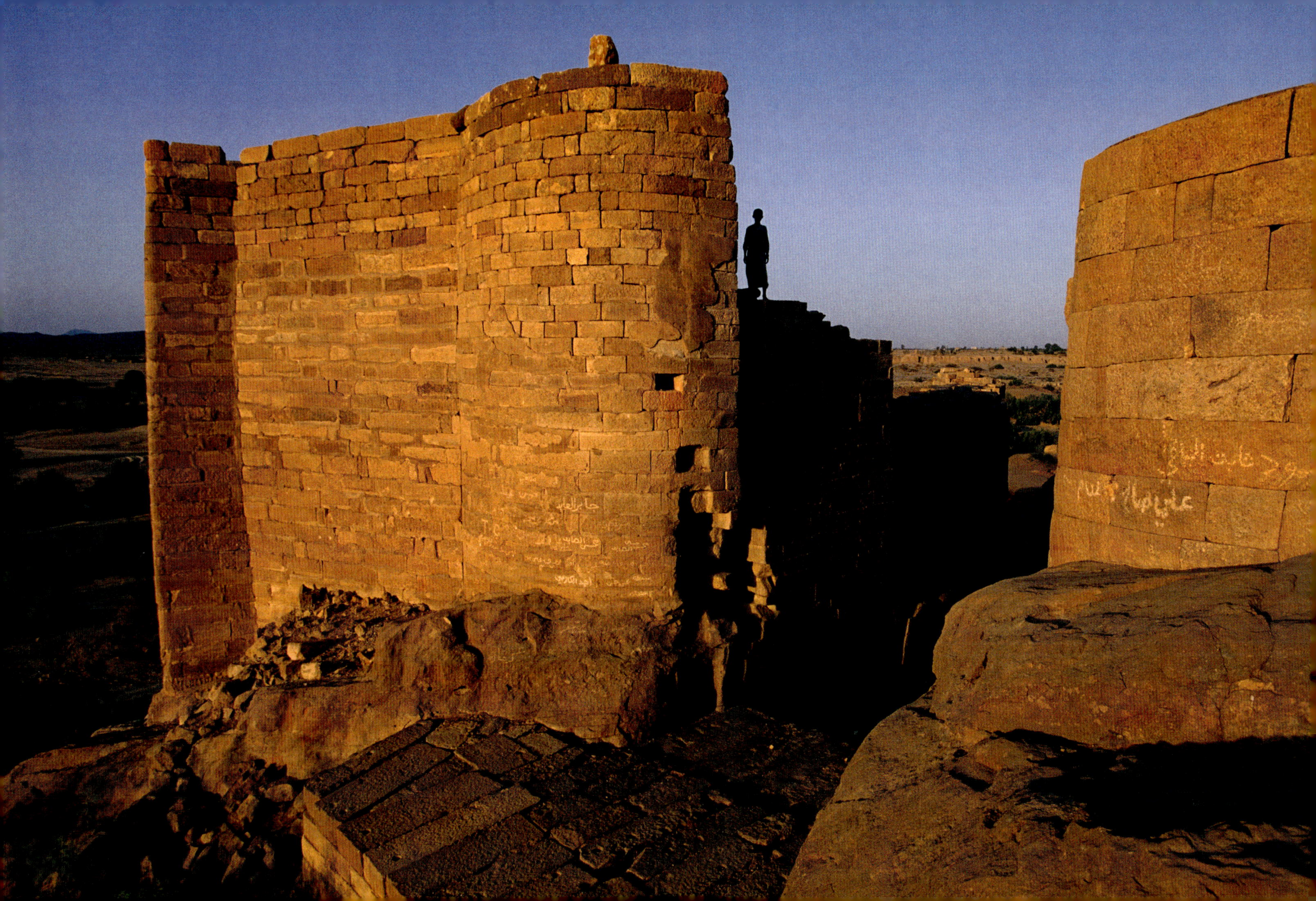

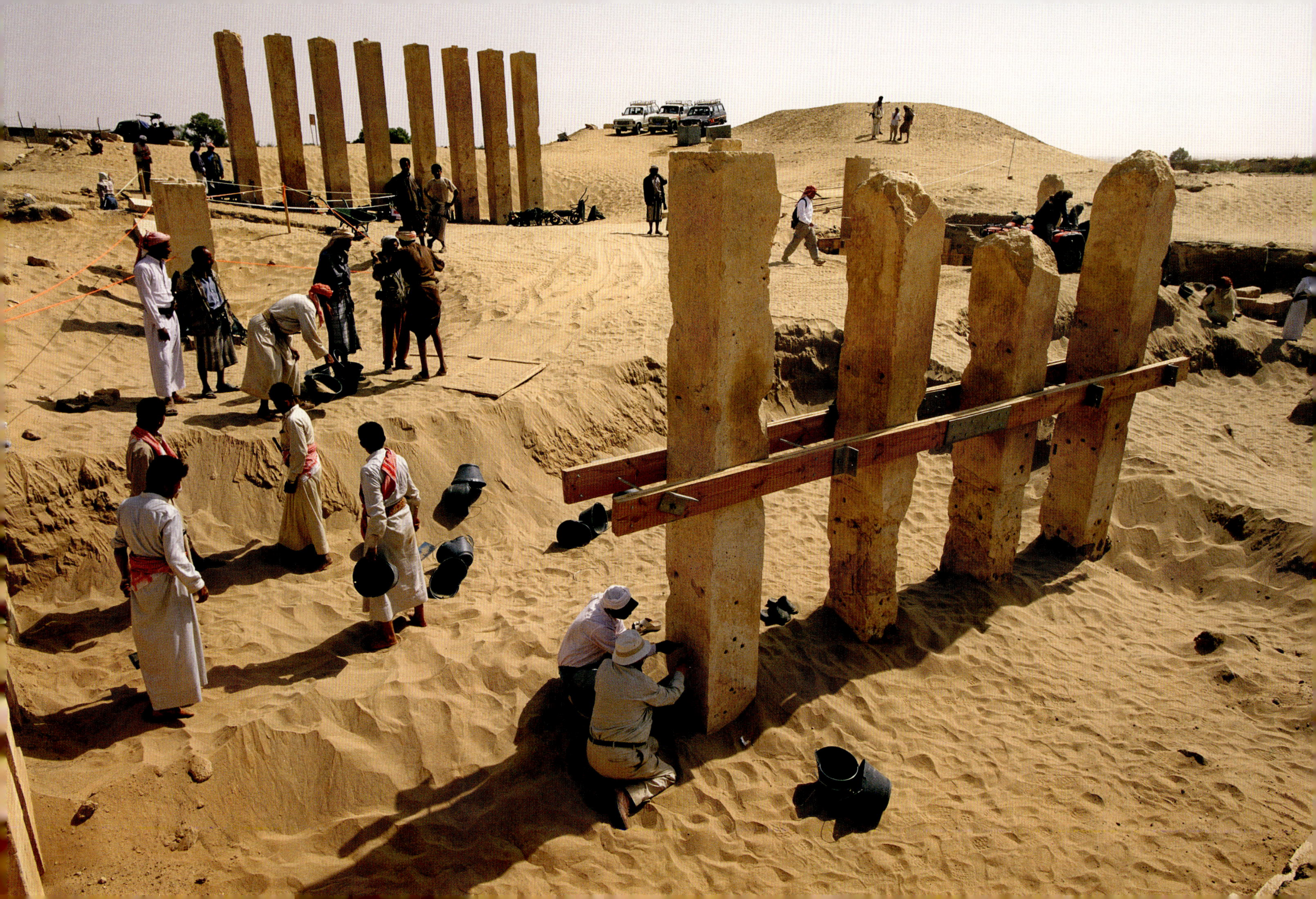

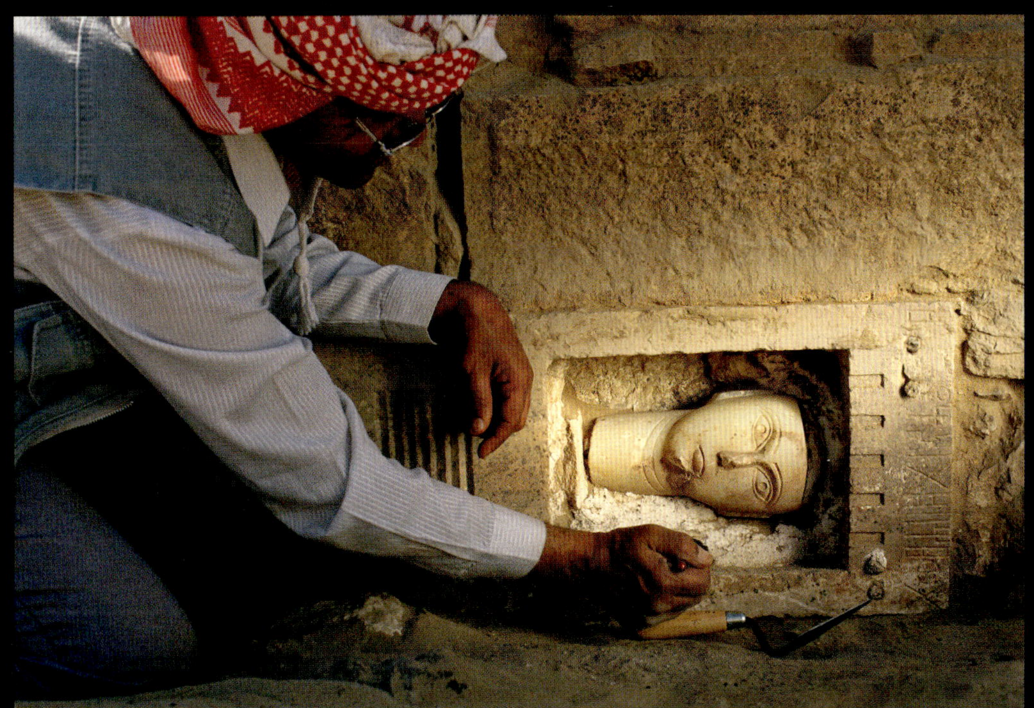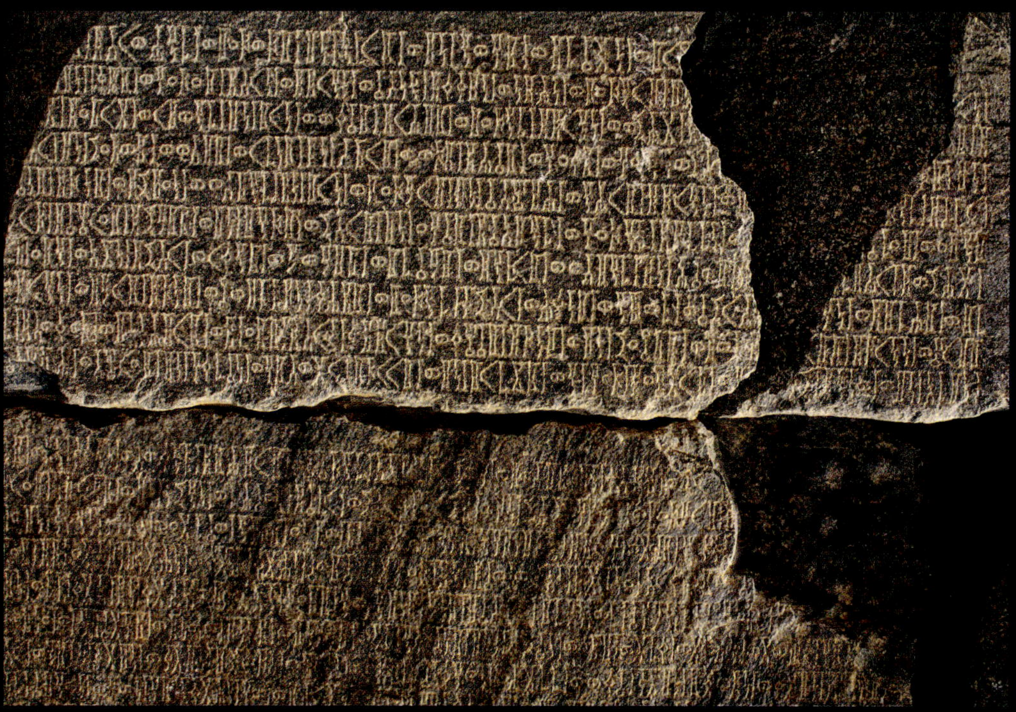

ABOVE LEFT: Abdu Ghaleb examining grave marker used in ancient wall of Mahram Bilqis, Marib, Yemen
ABOVE RIGHT: Ancient Sabean inscription, Timna, Yemen

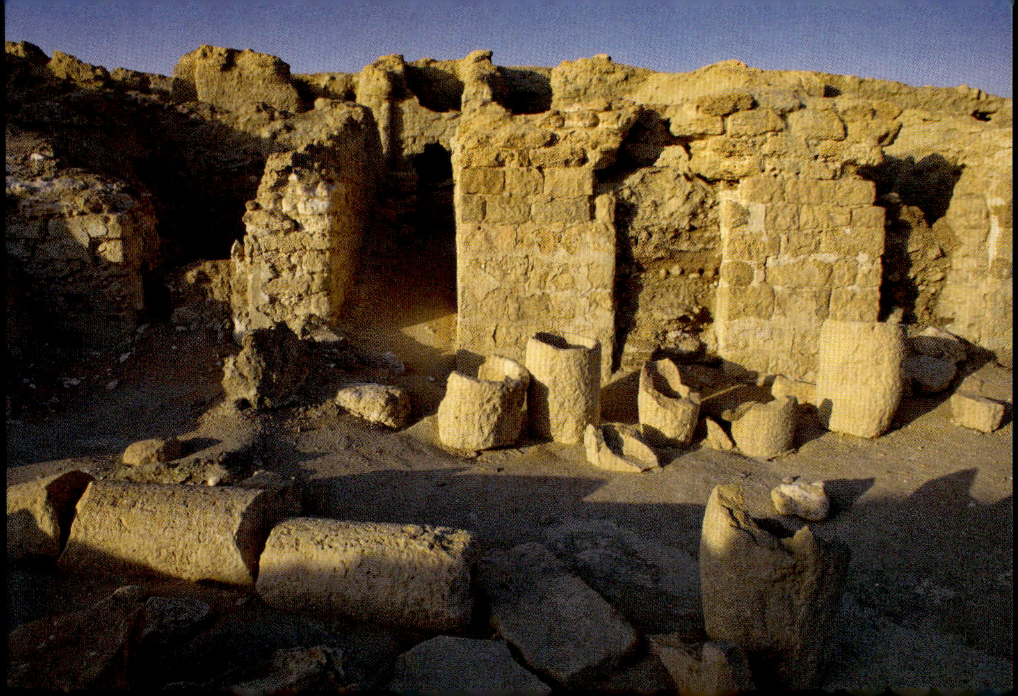

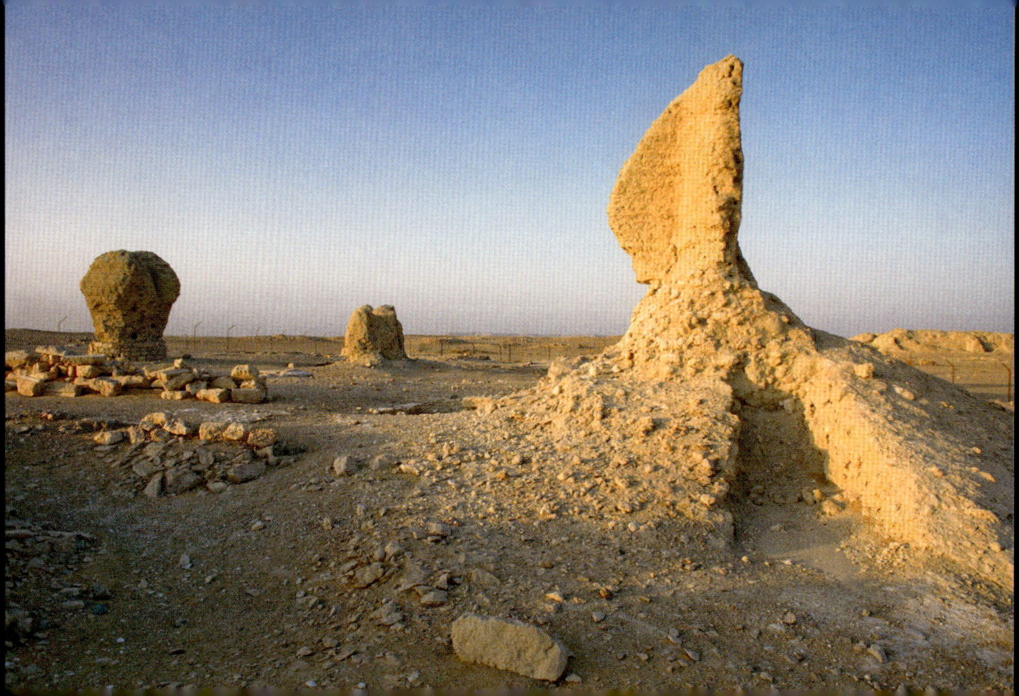

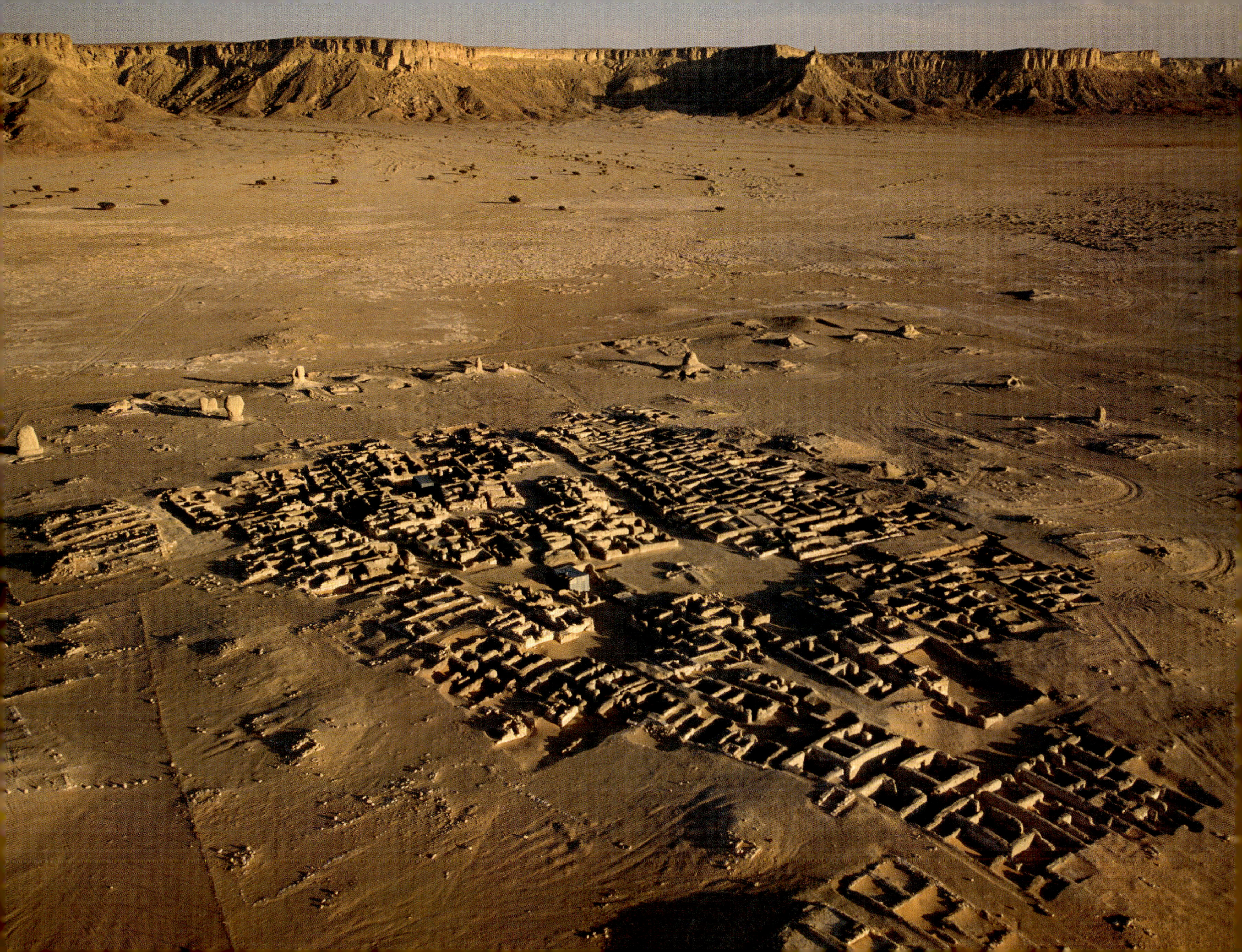

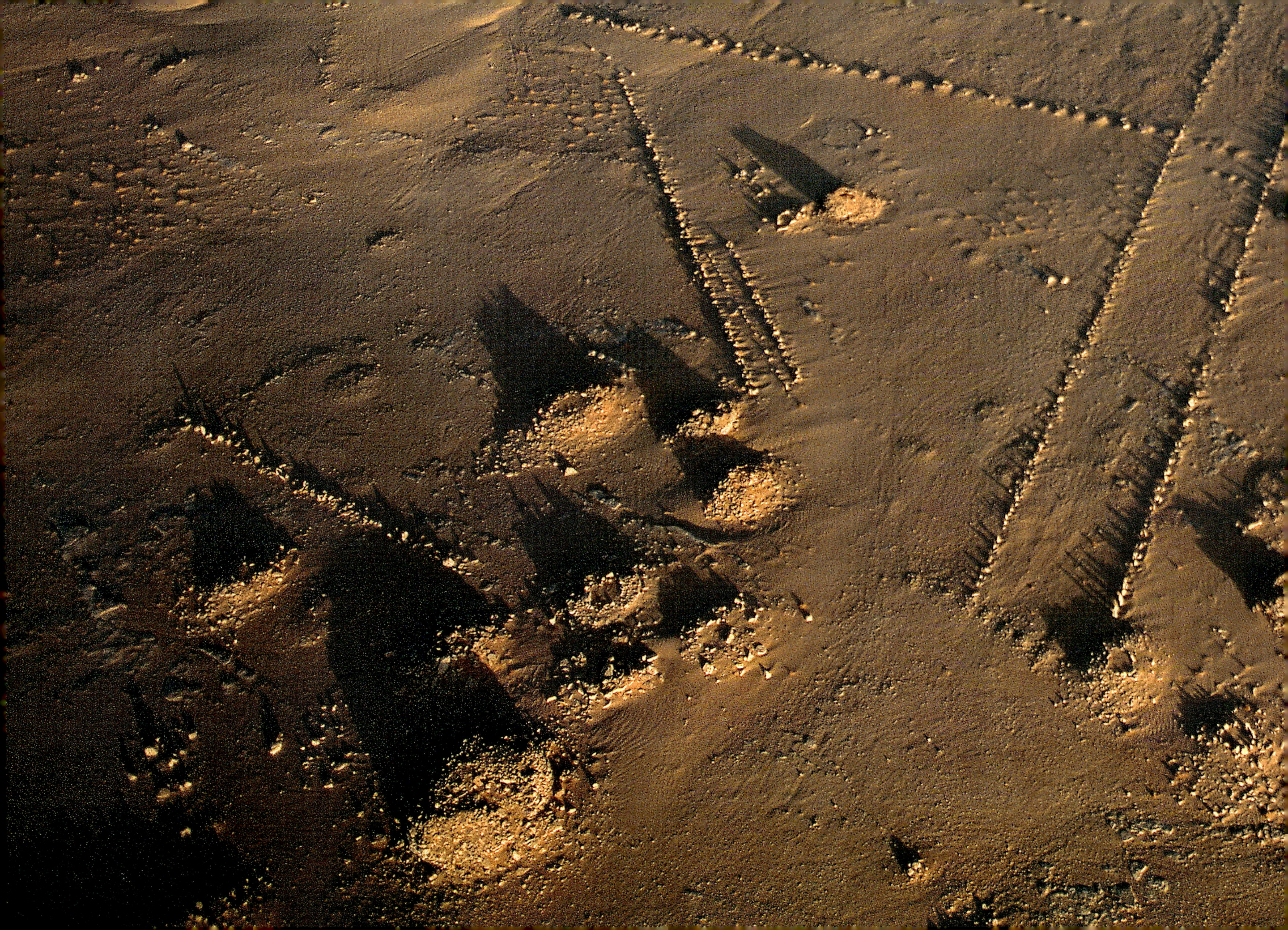

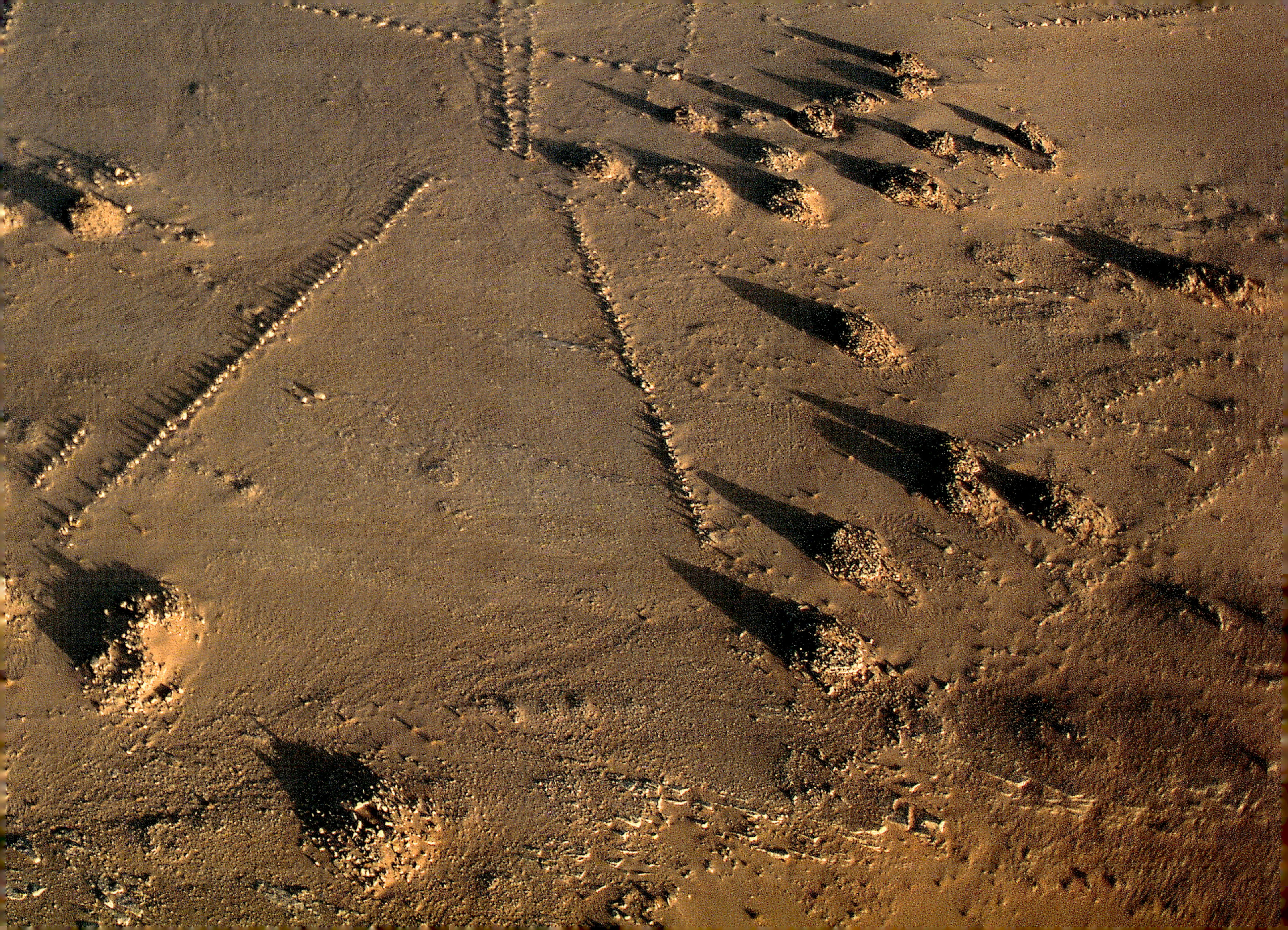

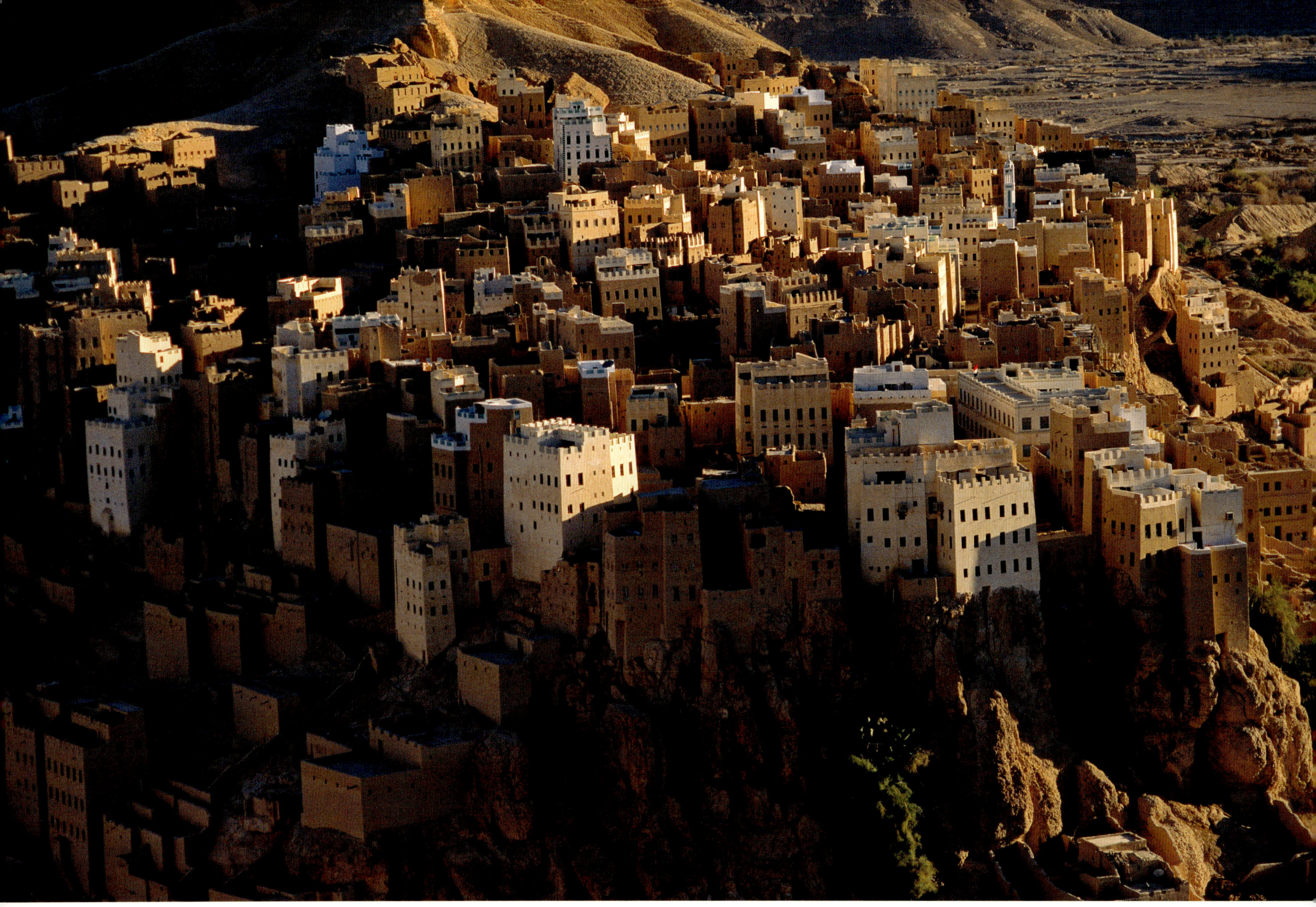

Naturally fortified city of Al Hajarayn, Yemen

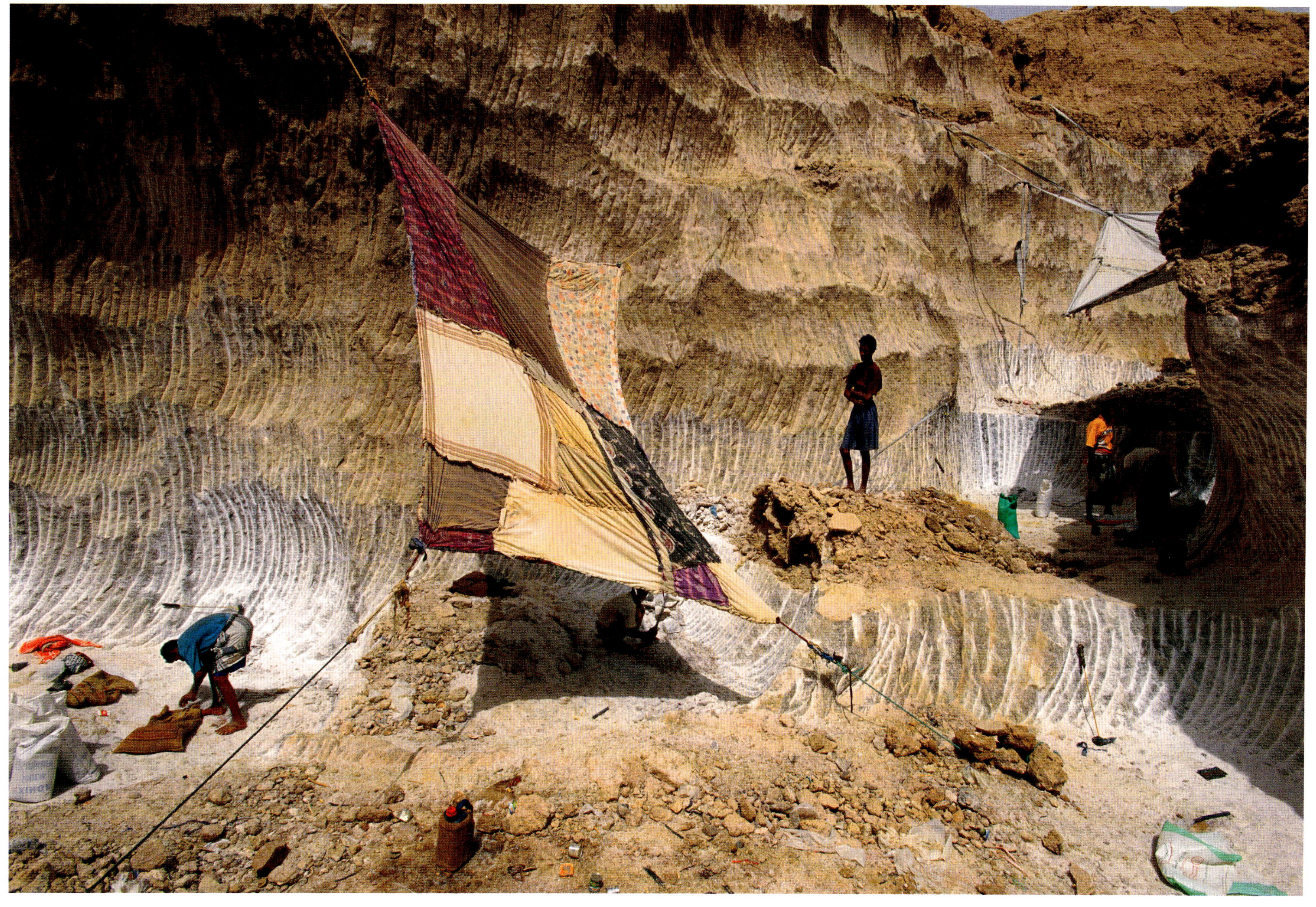

Salt mine, Ayad, Yemen

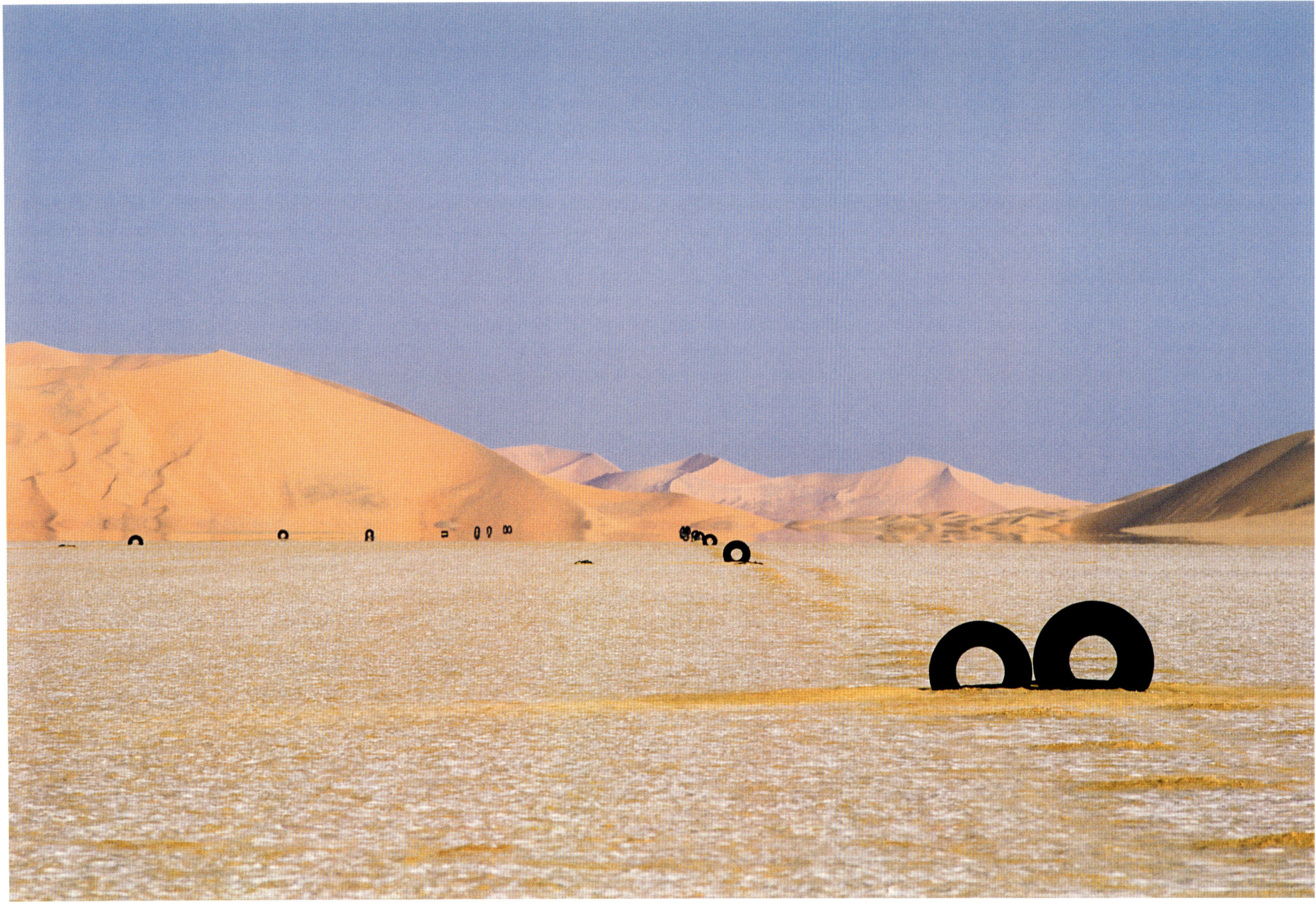

  Airfield of abandoned oil exploration camp, 'Uruq al Mutaridah, Saudi Arabia

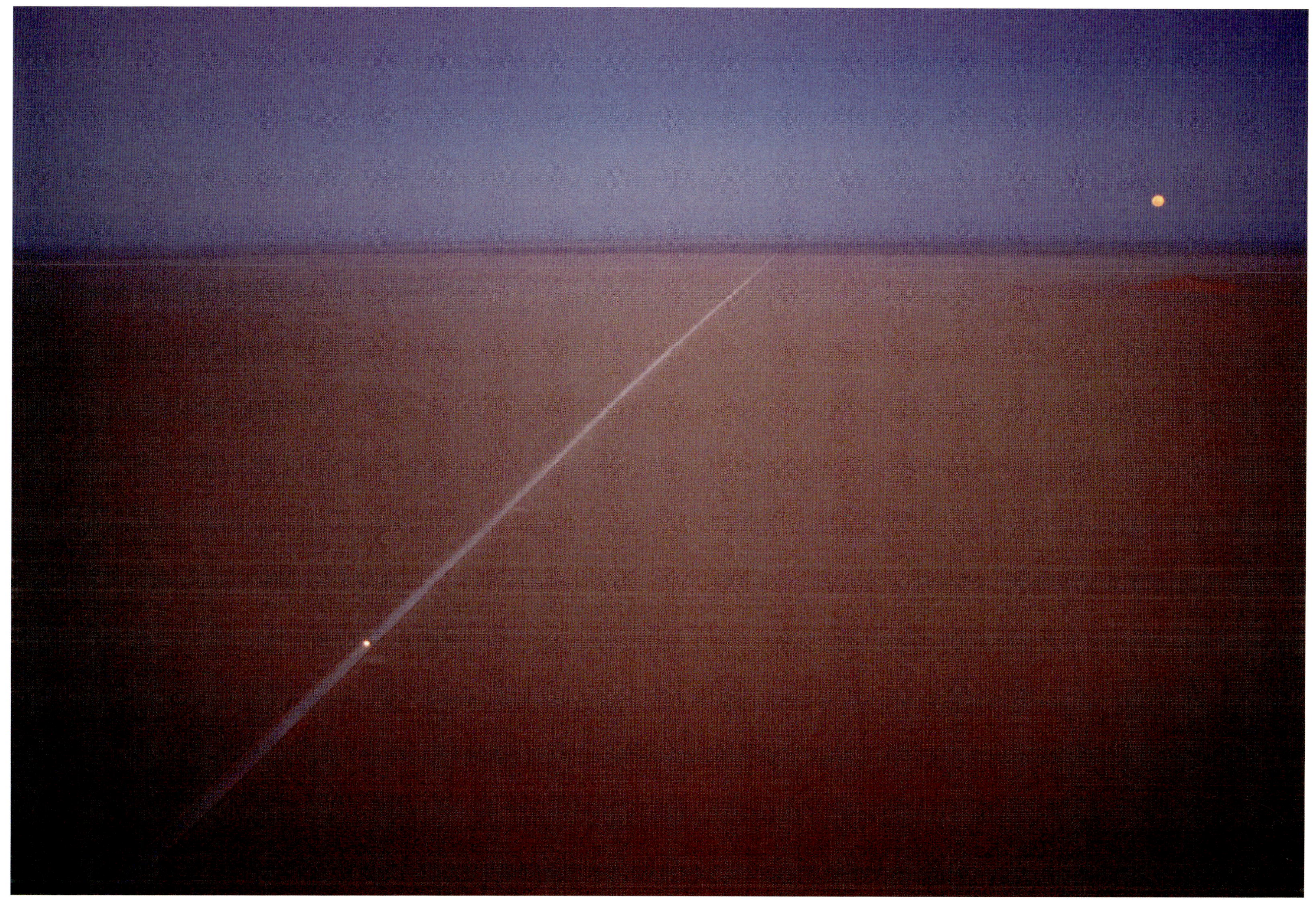

Full moon rising, Umm as-Samim (Mother of Poisons), Oman

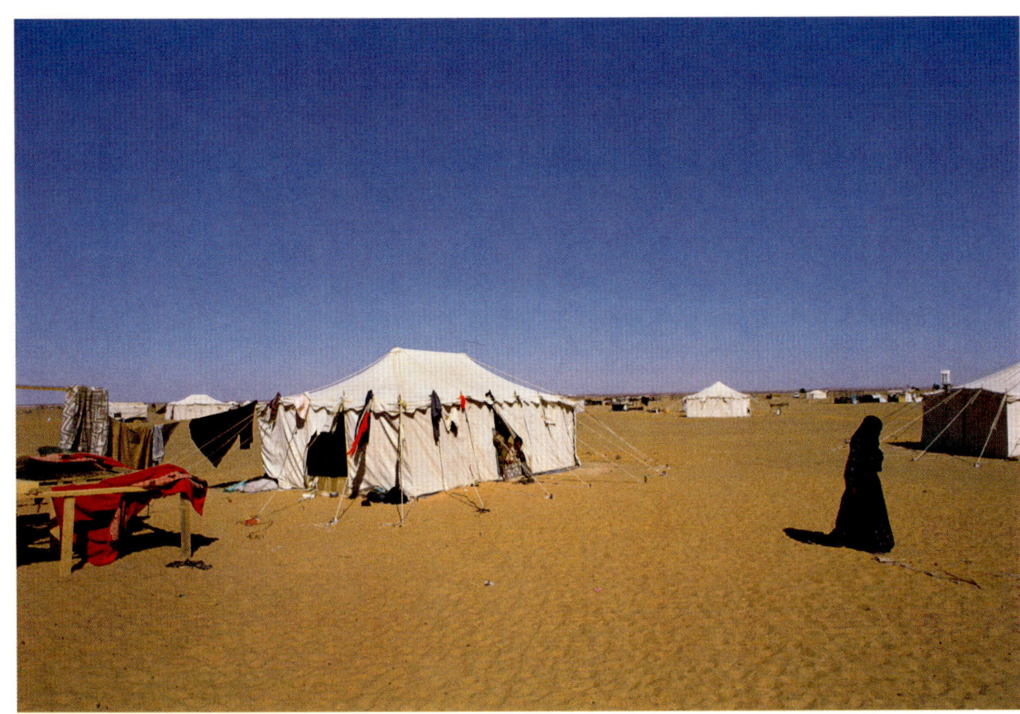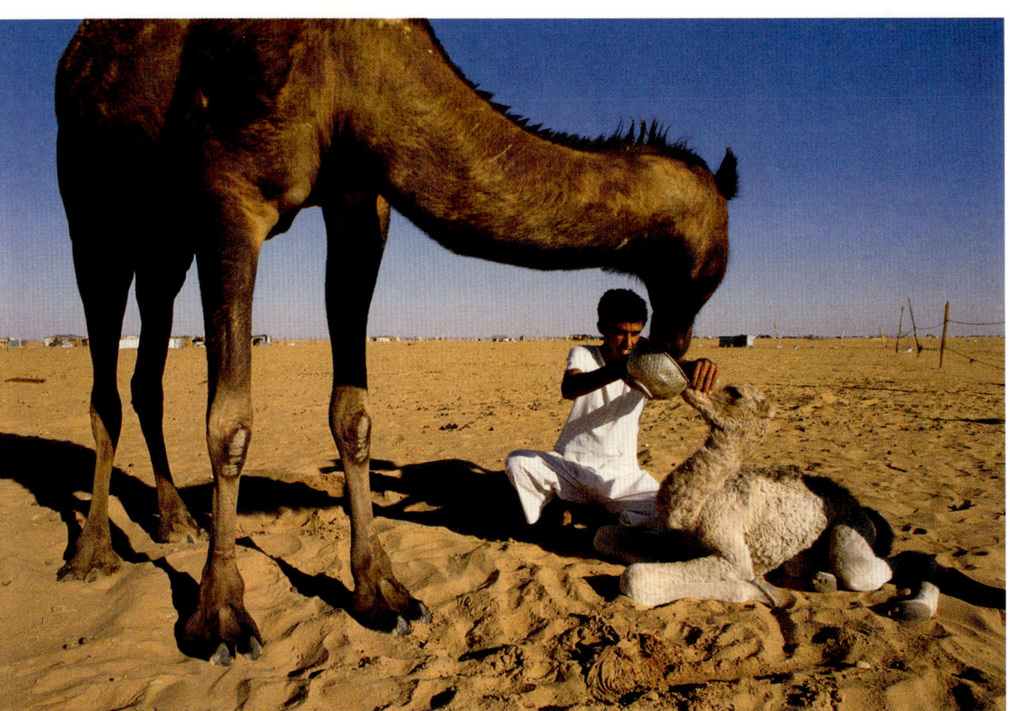

ABOVE LEFT: Bedouin camp, Wuday'ah, Yemen
ABOVE RIGHT: Newborn camel, Wuday'ah, Yemen

Bedouin camp, 'Uruq Bani Ma'arid, Saudi Arabia

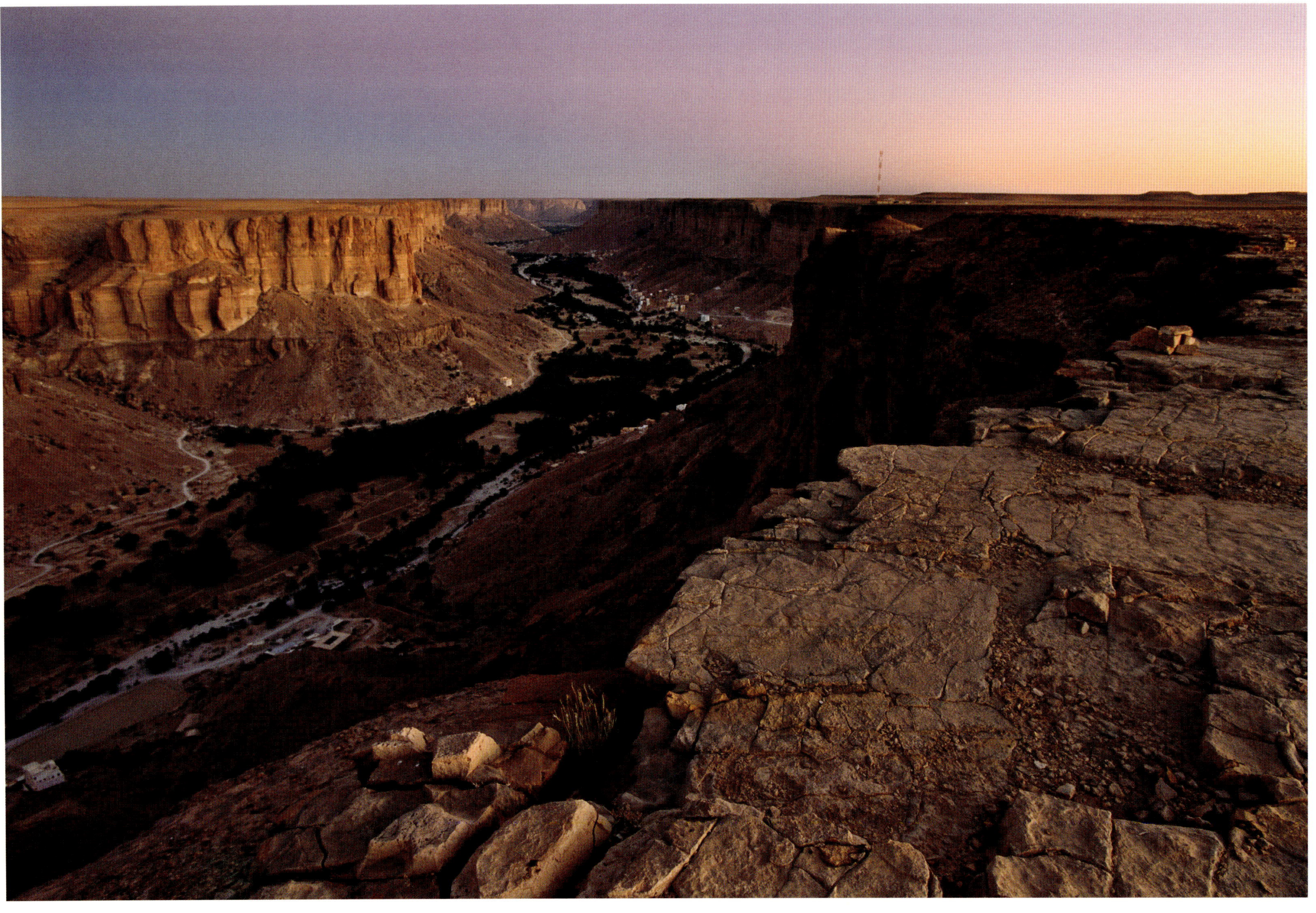

Tributary of Wadi Hajarayn, Yemen

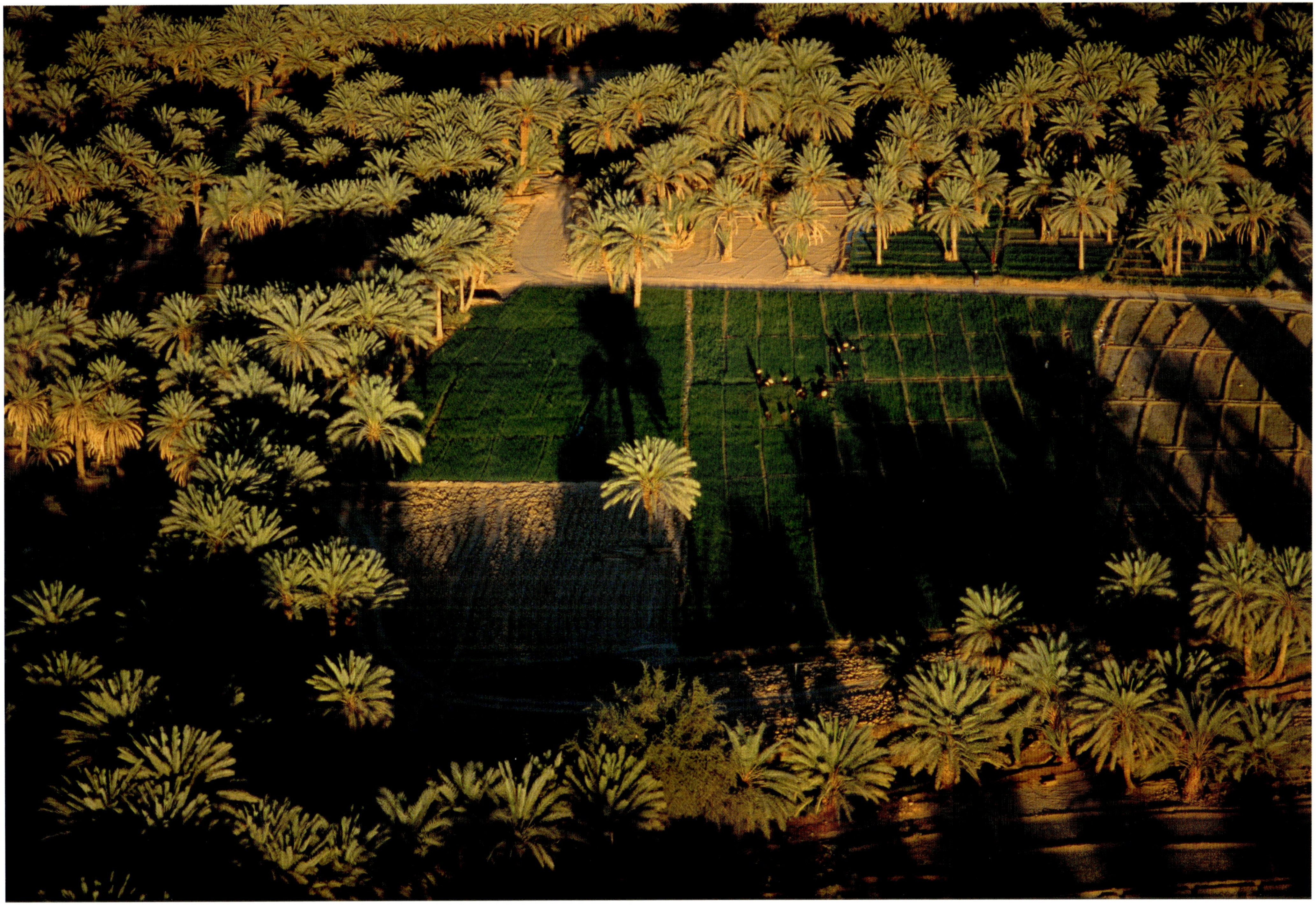

Palm groves, Wadi Hadramawt, Yemen

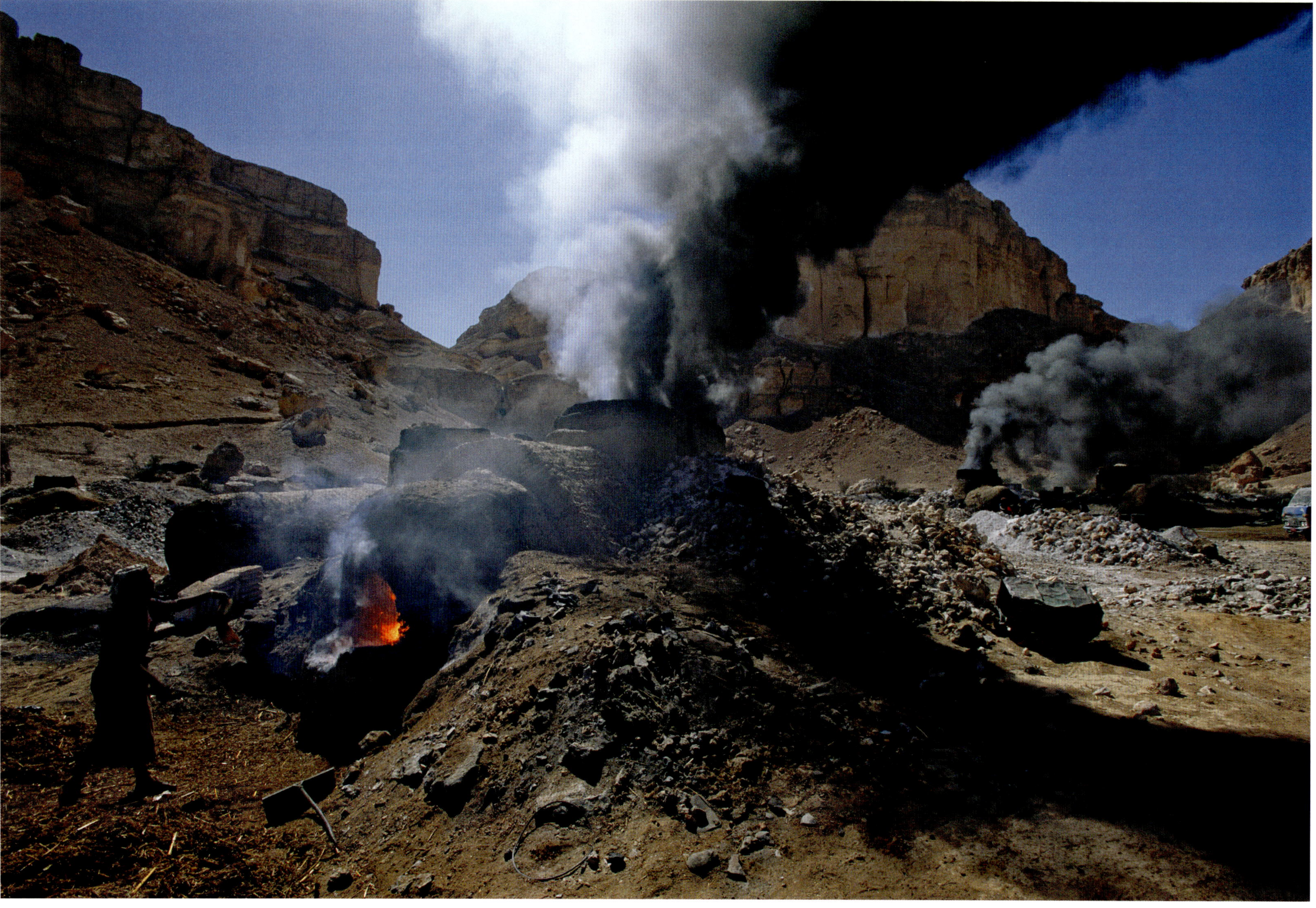

    Baking limestone to make plaster for roofs, Wadi Hadramawt, Yemen

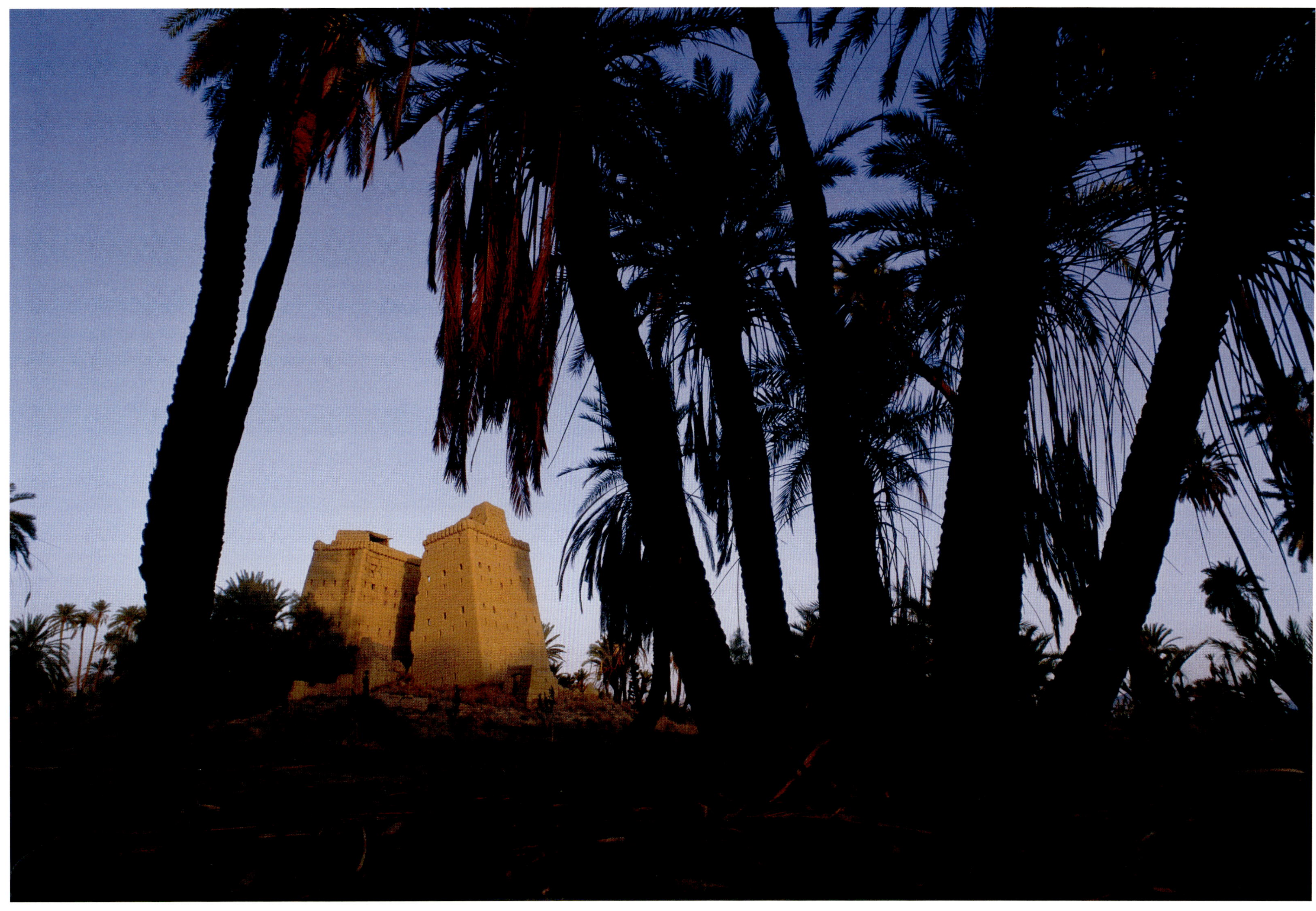

Abandoned tower homes, Najran, Saudi Arabia

"My companions had been accustomed to this life
since birth, but I had been racked by the weariness
of long marches through wind-whipped dunes, or
across plains where monotony was emphasized
by the mirages shimmering through the heat."

Wilfred Thesiger, *Arabian Sands*

  OPPOSITE: Camel caravan, Wadi Mitan, Oman

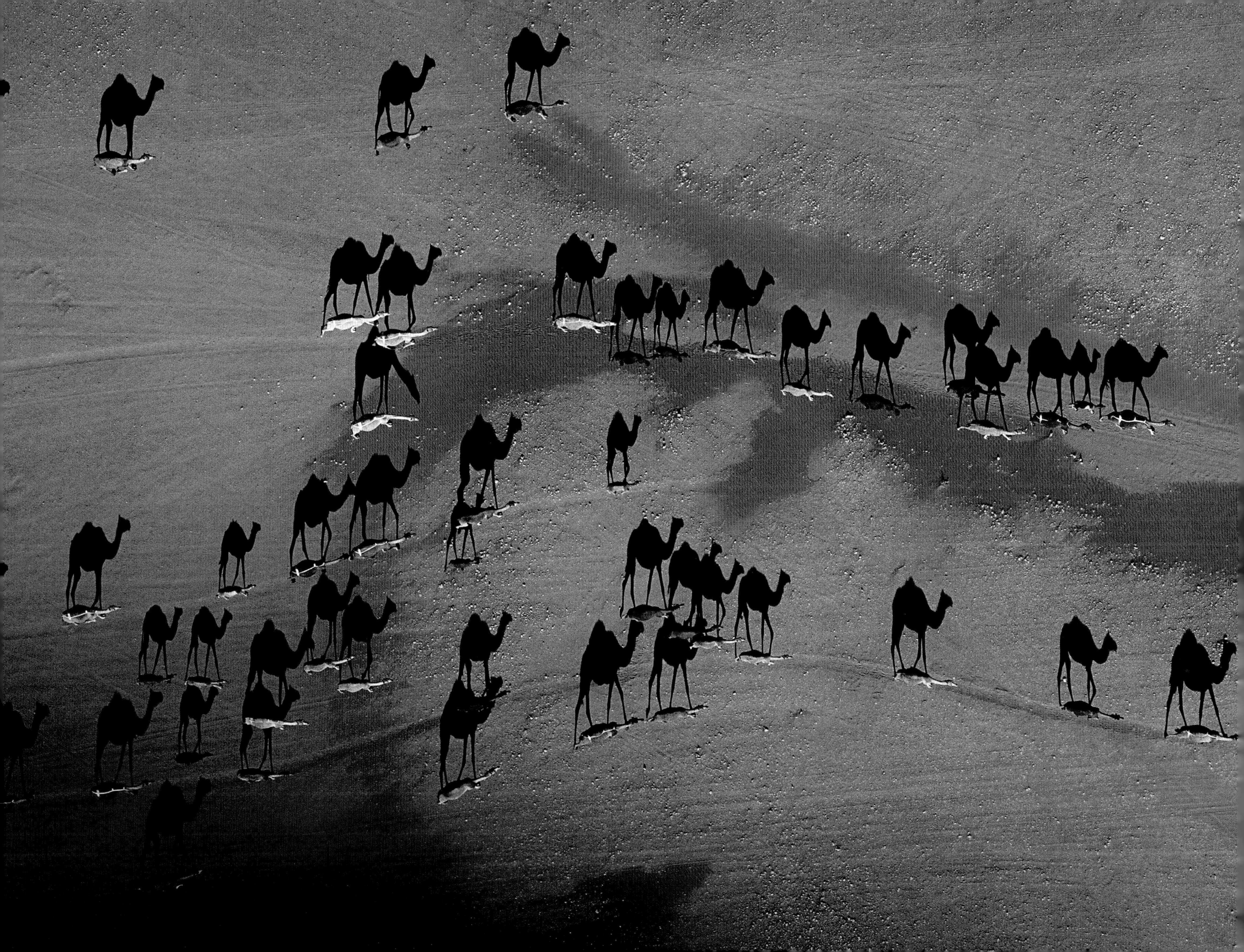

They appeared like a mirage. Thirteen Arabian oryx, the largest and most elegant animals in the Empty Quarter, were among the rarest of sights. Viewed in profile, it is easy to see how oryx inspired the ancient myth of unicorns. Traditionally hunted by Bedouin, wild Arabian oryx were pushed to the brink of extinction in the early 1970s, with the introduction of cars and modern rifles. Eric Bedin, a wildlife biologist with the Saudi National Wildlife Research Centre, was kind enough to escort me around the newly created ‘Uruq Bani Ma’arid Reserve. This herd was the largest grouping of oryx Eric had ever seen, and we approached very slowly in his jeep. It was an early winter morning, and their normally white coats looked strangely gray. Eric explained that this was one of their many adaptations to this extreme climate. In cold weather, oryx extend their fur straight out to increase insulation and capture more warmth by revealing their dark skin to the early morning sun. Eric carefully maneuvered us to within a hundred feet, which is not easy to do in the wild with such skittish animals. Oryx are one of the few desert creatures that don’t need to drink, sometimes for periods exceeding several years. They are superb conservators of water, getting what little they need from moisture contained in

plants and occasionally dew. When the heat of the Rub‘ al-Khali reaches over 115°F in the summer, oryx minimize their movement and take shelter in the meager shade, where they let their body temperature slowly increase to 100–106°F, storing the heat before dissipating it passively during the cool night. Such temperature swings limit the water losses oryx would inevitably incur if they maintained a constant body temperature. They have large footpads that leave characteristic and very visible footprints in the sand.

In 1962, with few Arabian oryx left in the wild, a breeding herd was established at the Phoenix Zoo in Arizona from a mixture of captured wild oryx and captive pairs from the private collections of Arab royal families. The first reintroduction into the wild took place in 1982 in Oman, followed by one in ‘Uruq Bani Ma’arid in 1995. When I visited ‘Uruq Bani Ma’arid, the area hosted the world’s only viable herd of Arabian oryx to roam free without protective fences or artificial supports of food or water. It was a privilege to see them thriving in an area that receives less than two inches of rain per year.

Six years later I went to visit a new reserve in the southernmost corner of the U.A.E., near the point where the U.A.E.,

Oman, and Saudi Arabia come together. The Abu Dhabi Environment Agency was in the early phases of reintroducing oryx and sand gazelles to their native range on the opposite side of the sands from ‘Uruq Bani Ma’arid. Here the wildlife was slowly adjusting to their natural habitat, with a safety net of feeding and watering stations scattered over a large area of spectacular orange dunes. It was unclear how well this population would do without such a safety net, because new border fences cut them off from their natural migration to the gravel plains of Oman or out into the Saudi part of the sands. To survive in such an unforgiving environment, oryx are able to smell rain and fresh grazing across tens and tens of miles and require enormous, unrestricted areas to travel wherever there is plant life to support them.

I made my last flight over the Empty Quarter here, and caught the most amazing sight: a herd of wild Arabian oryx as they galloped over huge dunes of brick-orange sands. I didn’t want to disturb these rare creatures, but it was hard to leave such a magnificent sight. It gave hope that perhaps man and nature can coexist and survive even in the severest of environments.

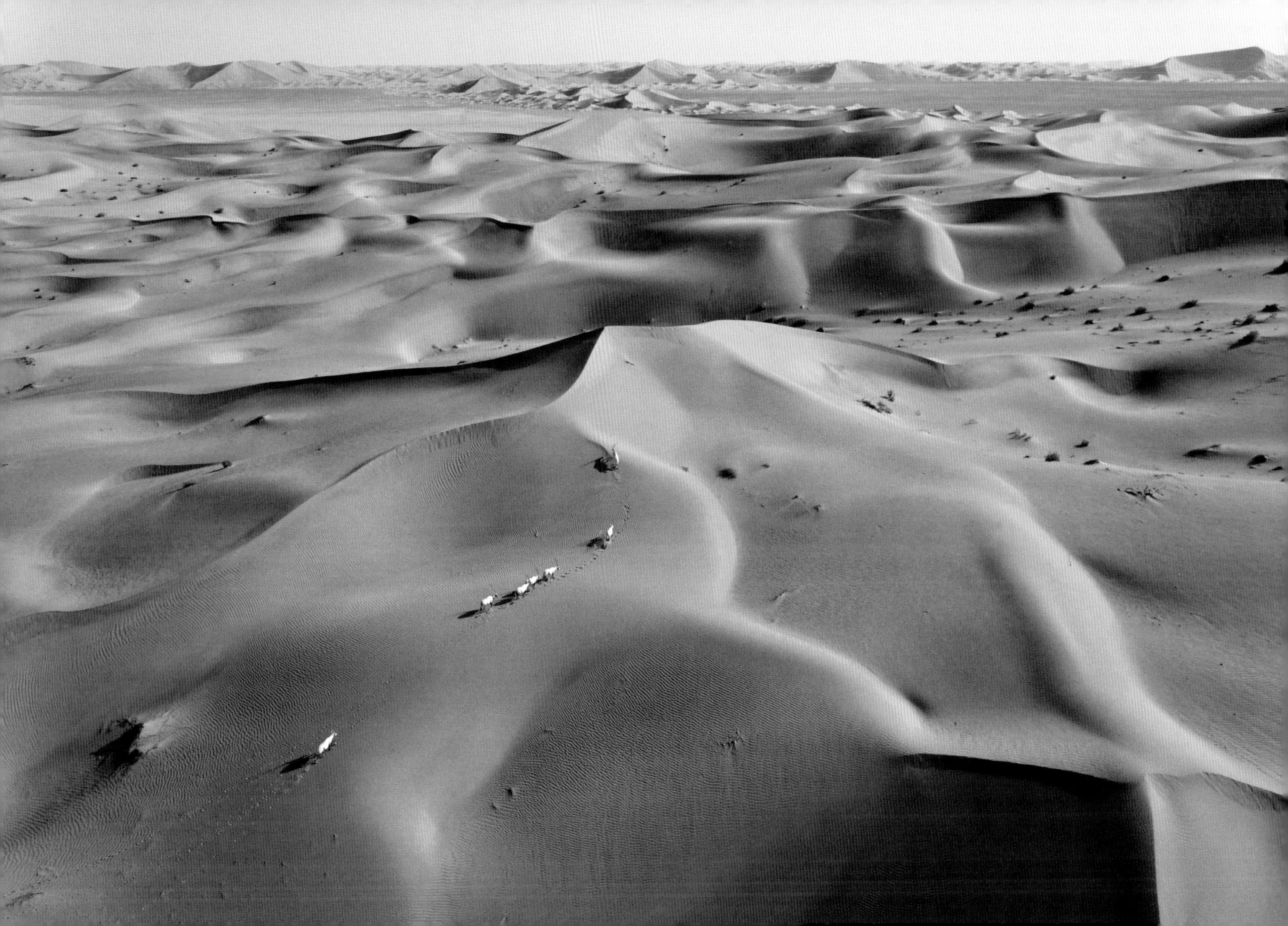

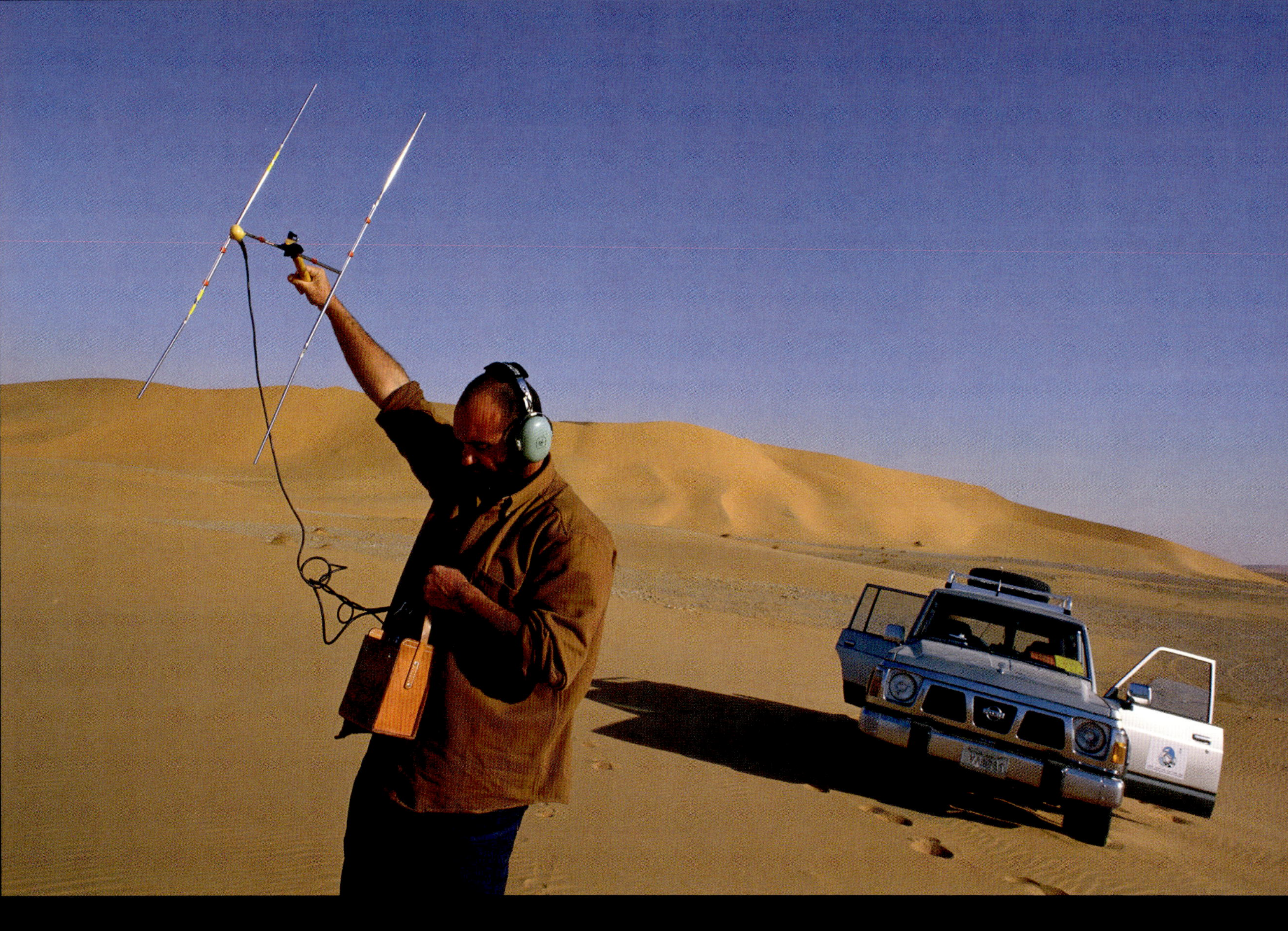

Eric Bedin searching for radio-collared oryx, 'Uruq Bani Ma'arid Reserve, Saudi Arabia

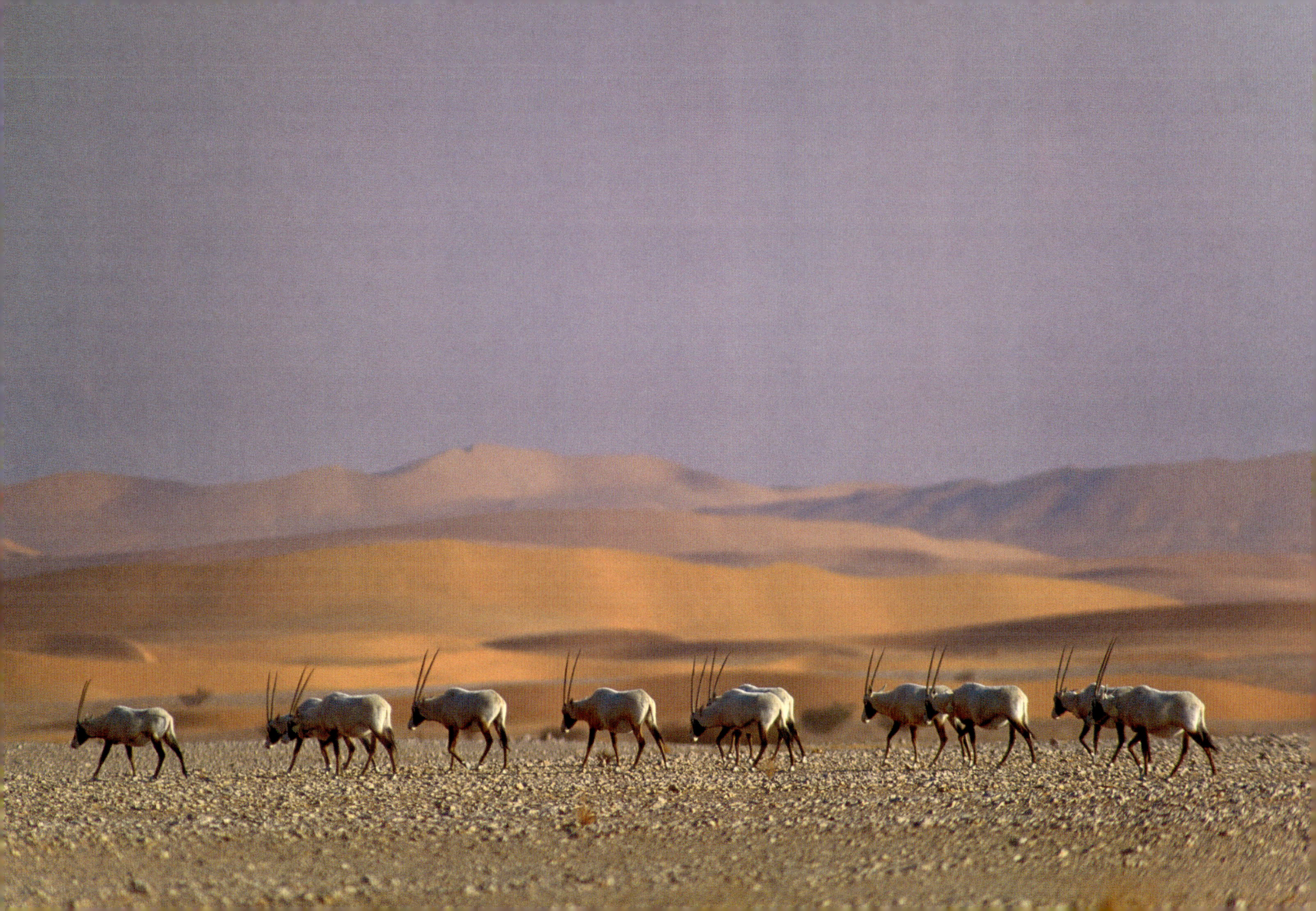

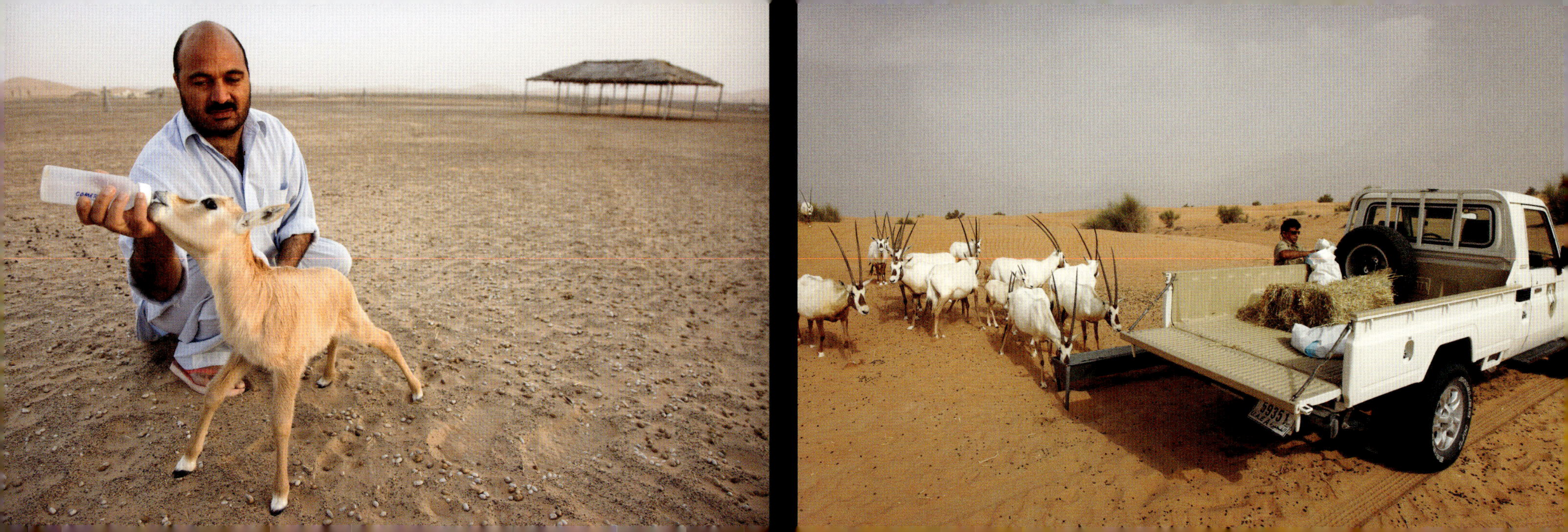

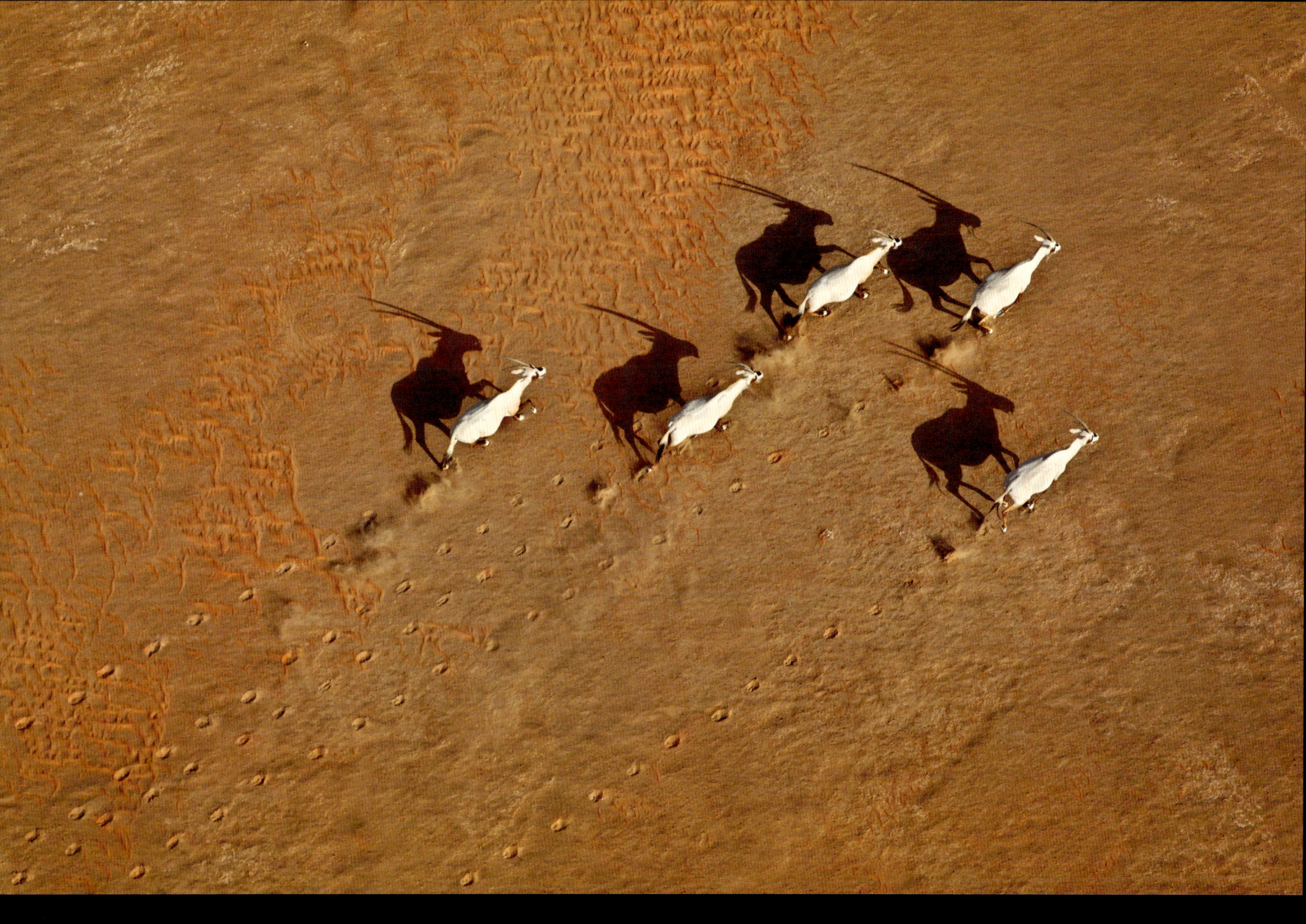

Wild oryx on the plains of Umm az-Zamul, U.A.E.
OVERLEAF: Wild herd of rheem gazelles, Umm az-Zamul, U.A.E.

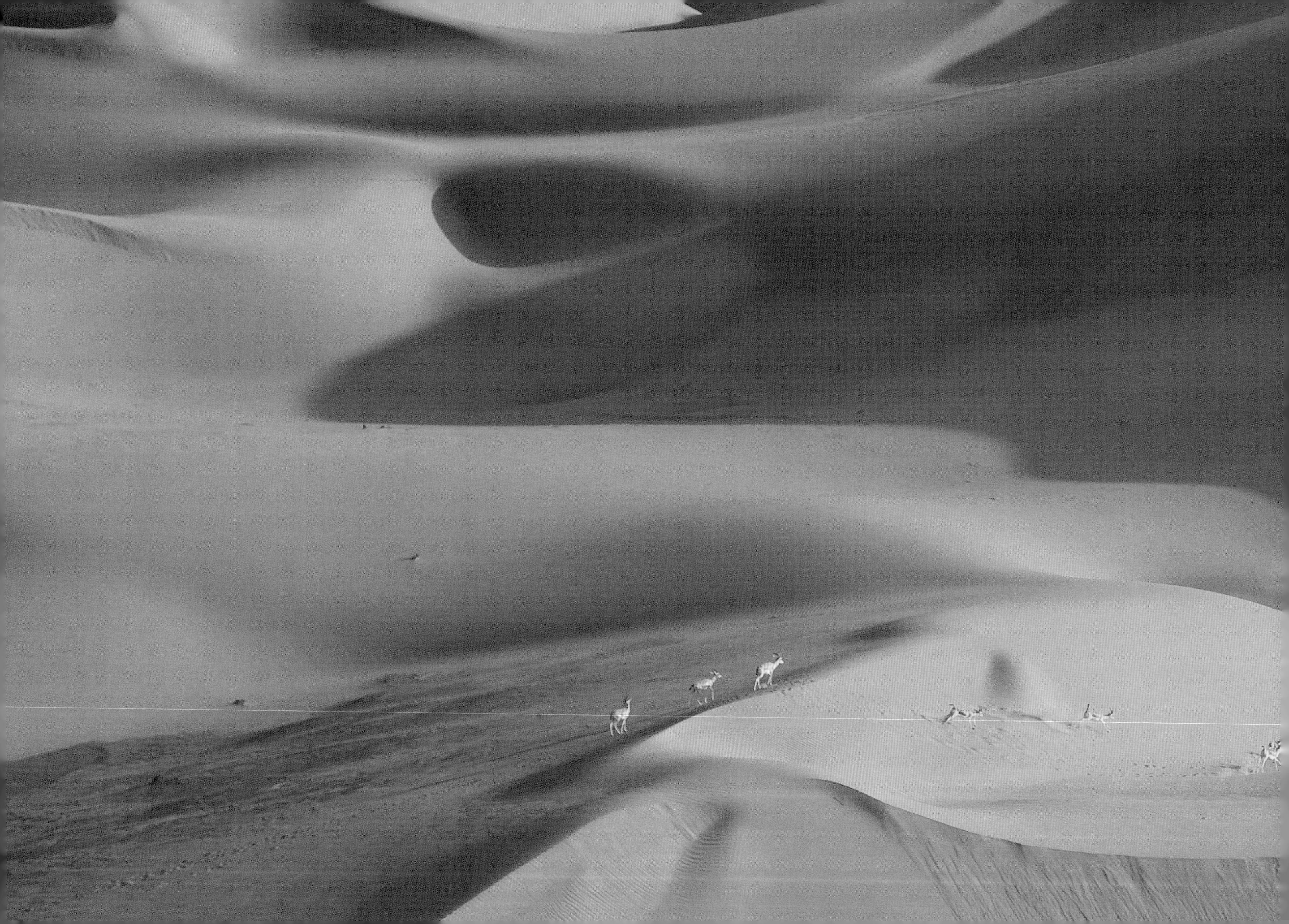

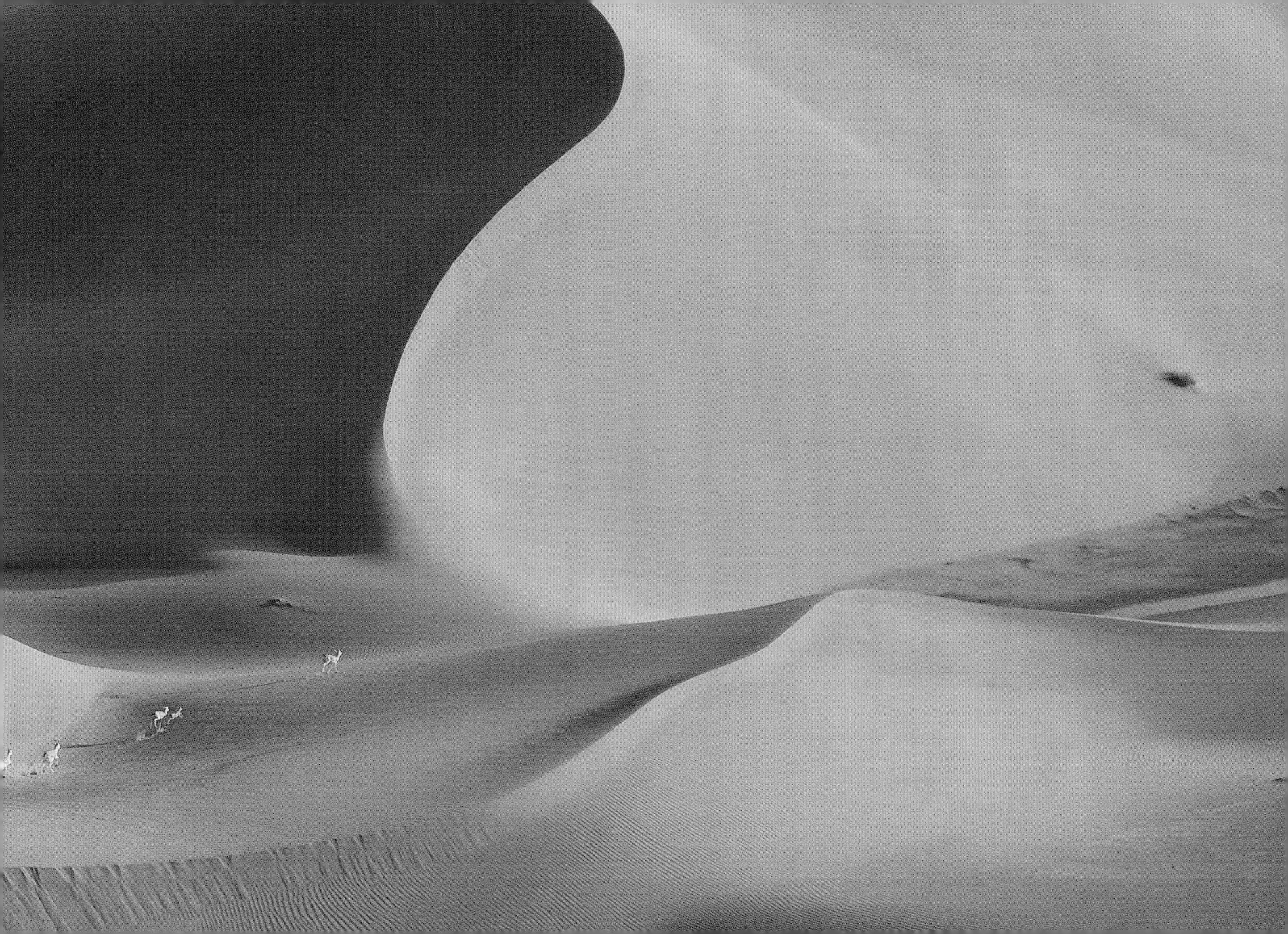

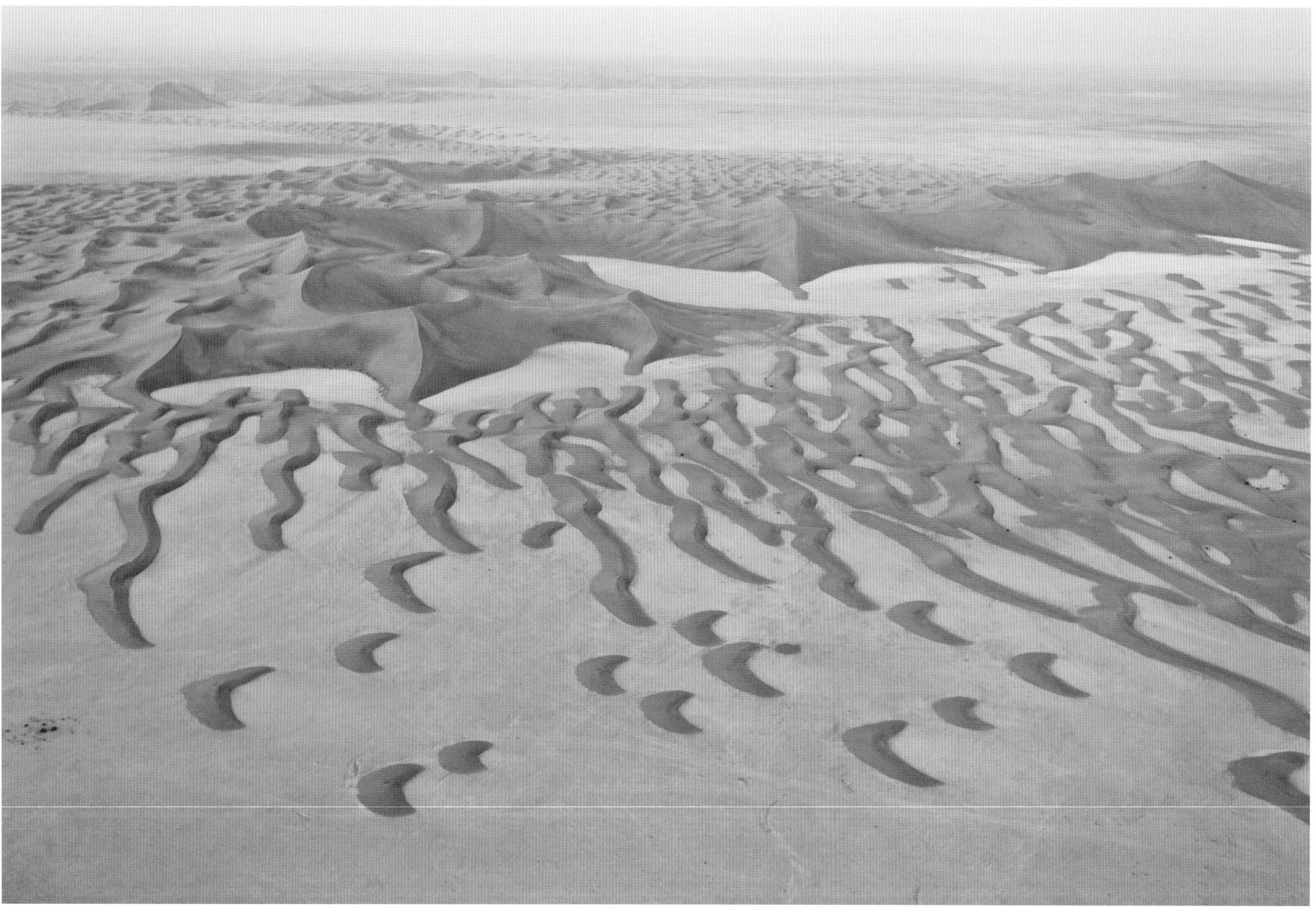

 ABOVE AND OPPOSITE: Umm az-Zamul, U.A.E.

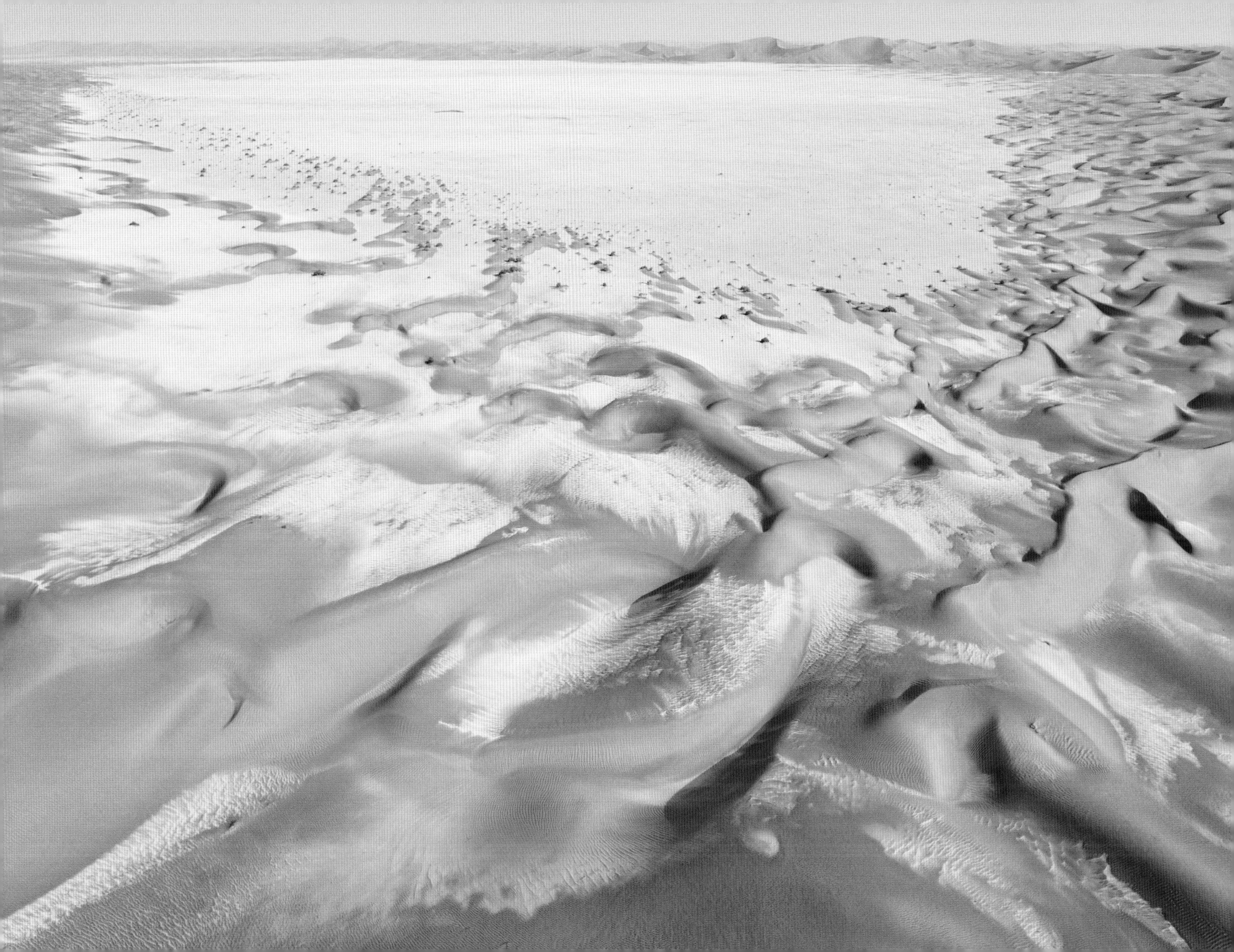

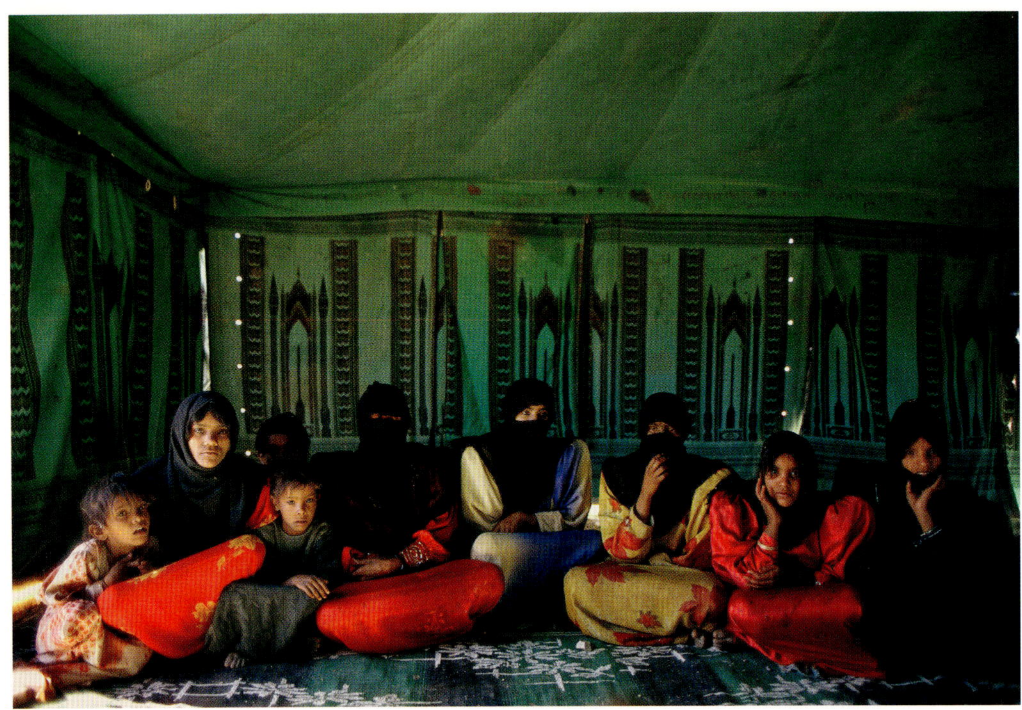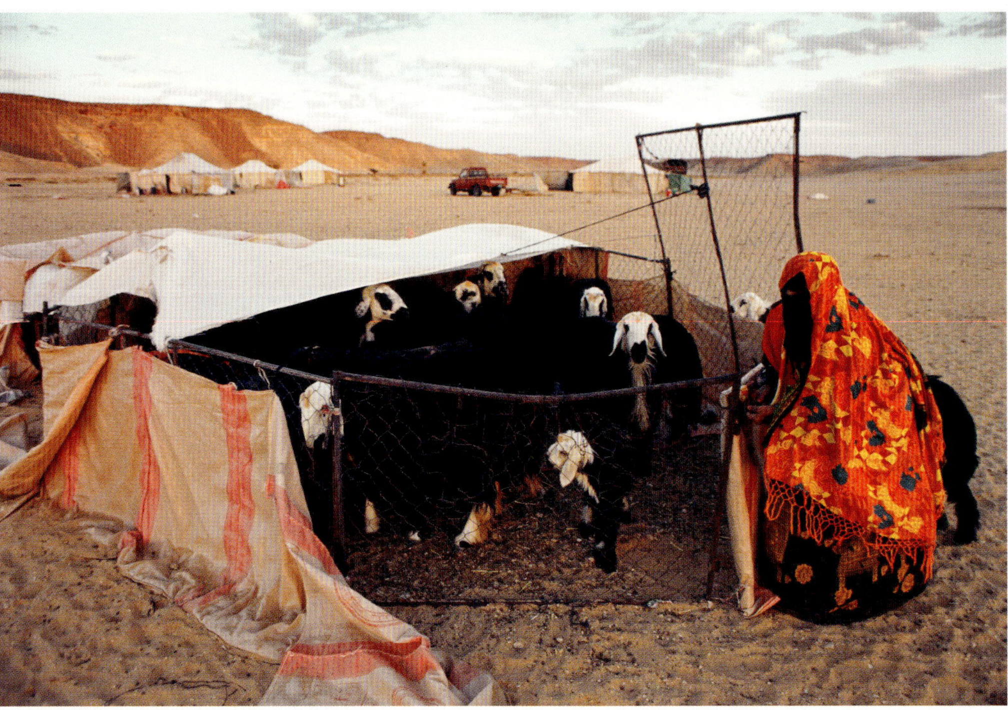

ABOVE LEFT: Al Mahra-speaking Bedouin camp near Sanaw, Yemen
ABOVE RIGHT: Bedouin camp, 'Uruq Bani Ma'arid, Saudi Arabia

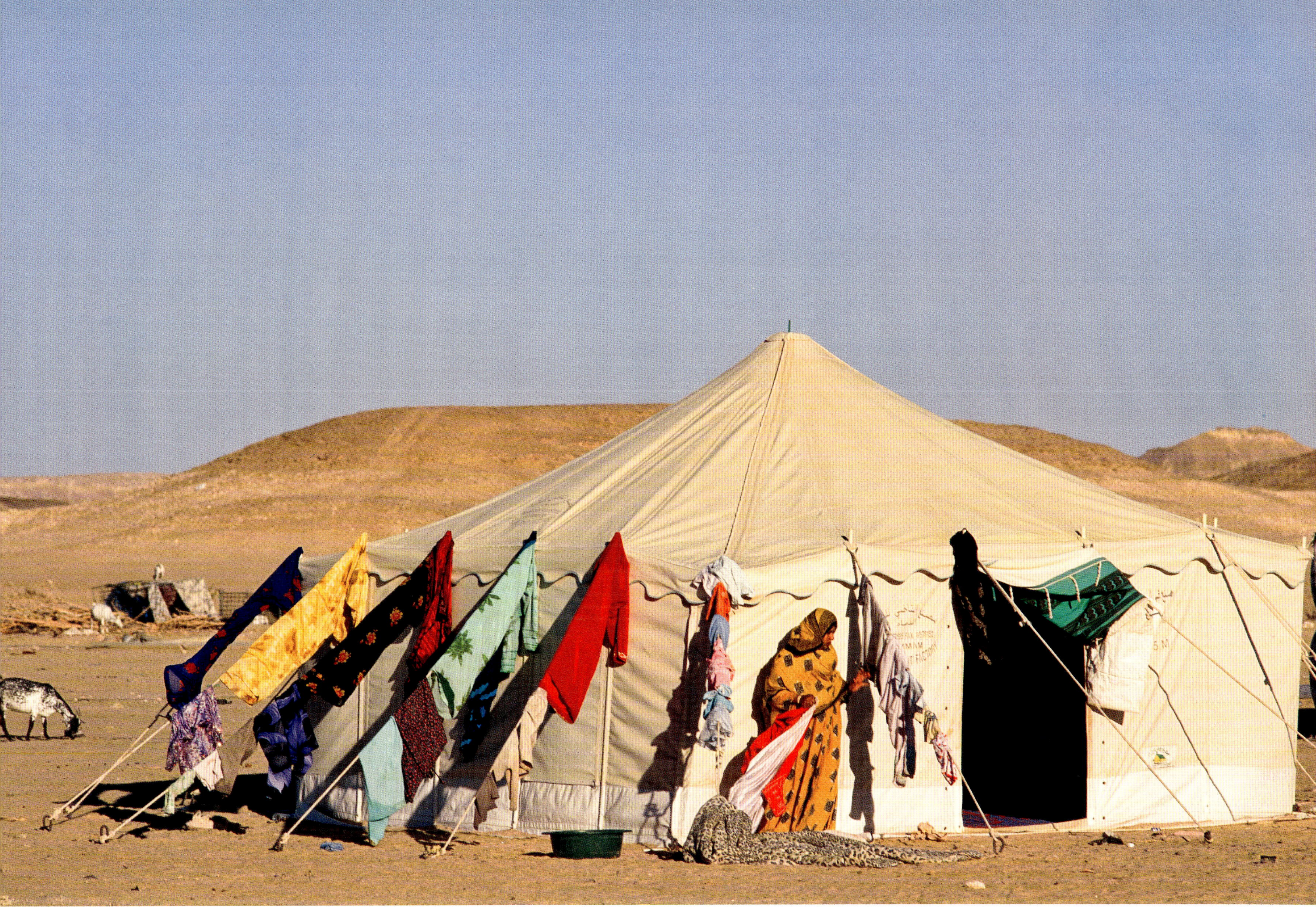

Laundry day, Bedouin camp, Rumah, Yemen

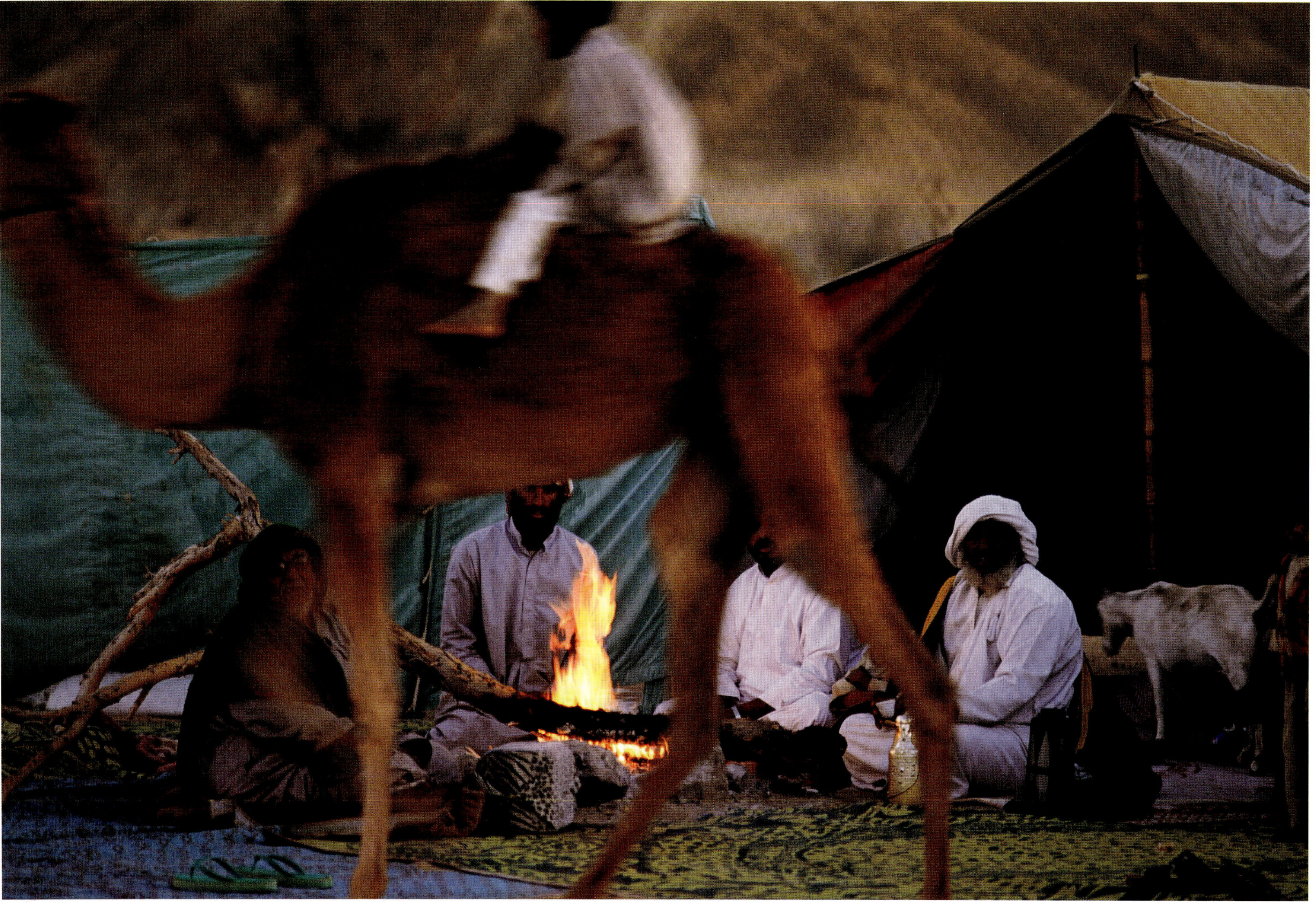

   Dusk in Bedouin camp, Rumah, Yemen

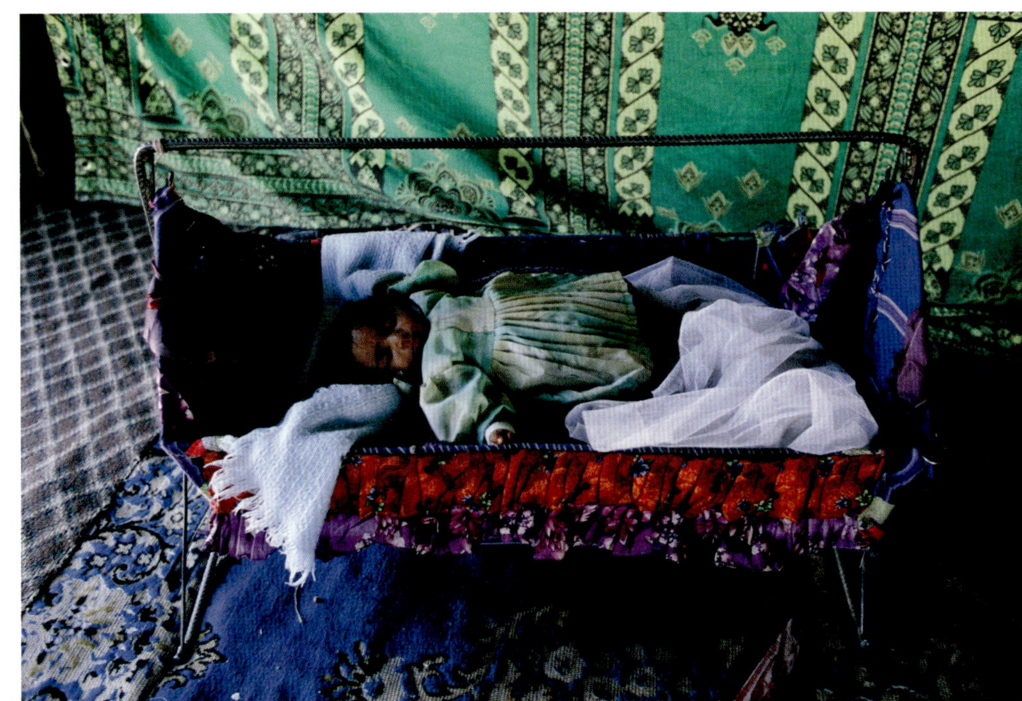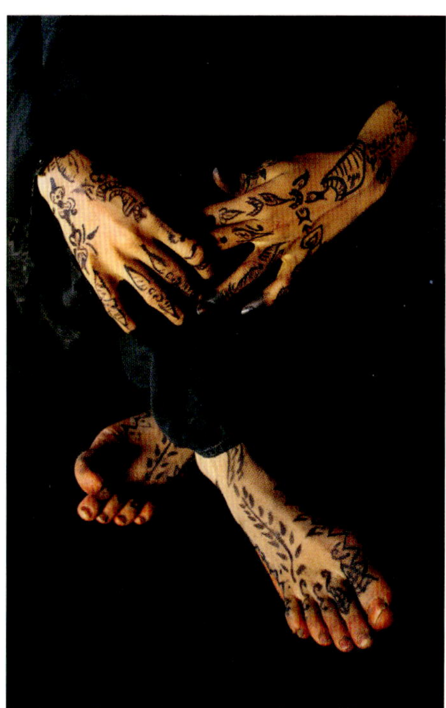

ABOVE LEFT: Bedouin camp, Shabwa, Yemen
ABOVE RIGHT: Henna tattoos, Marib, Yemen

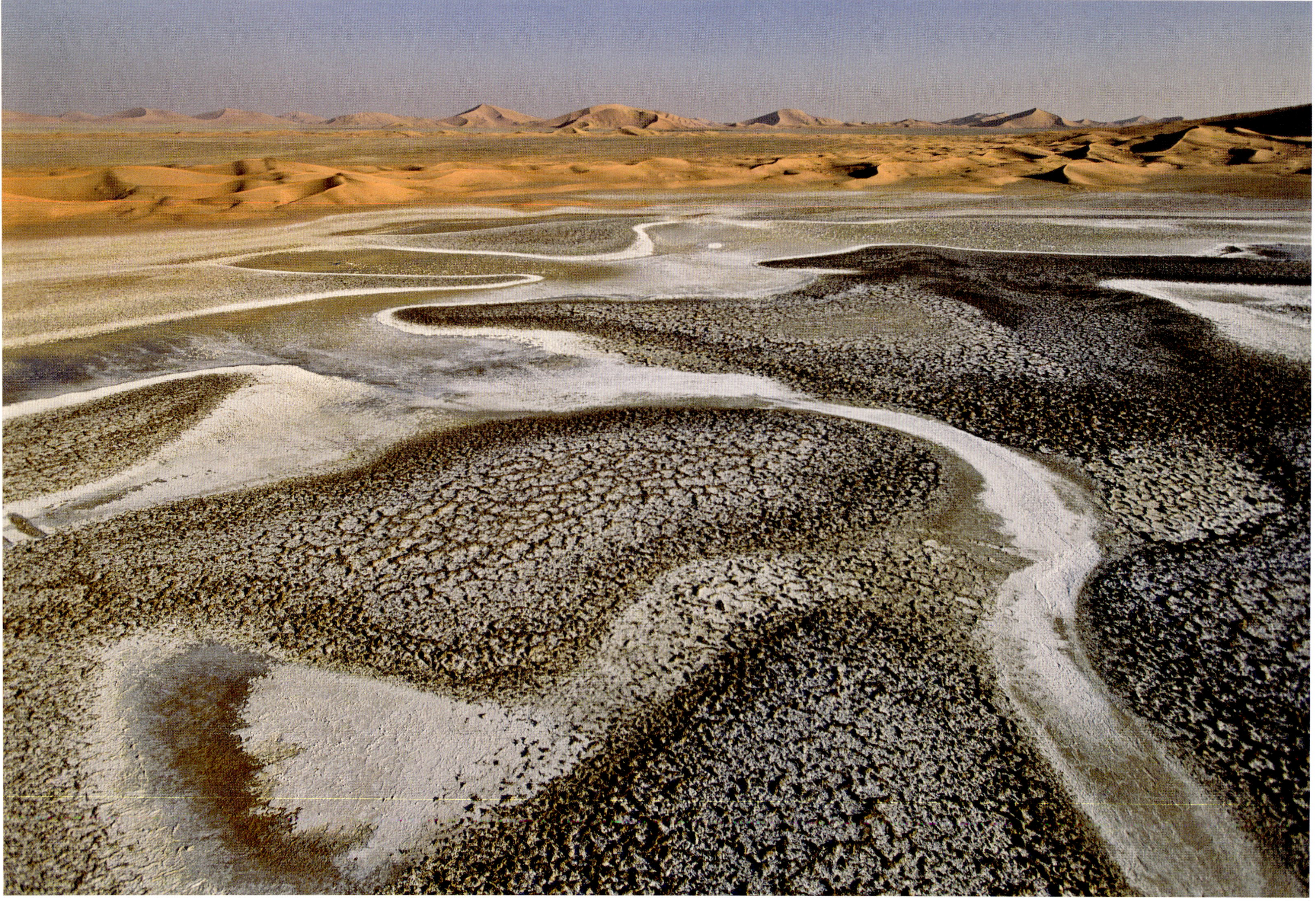

    Salt flats of Khawr Hamidan, Saudi Arabia

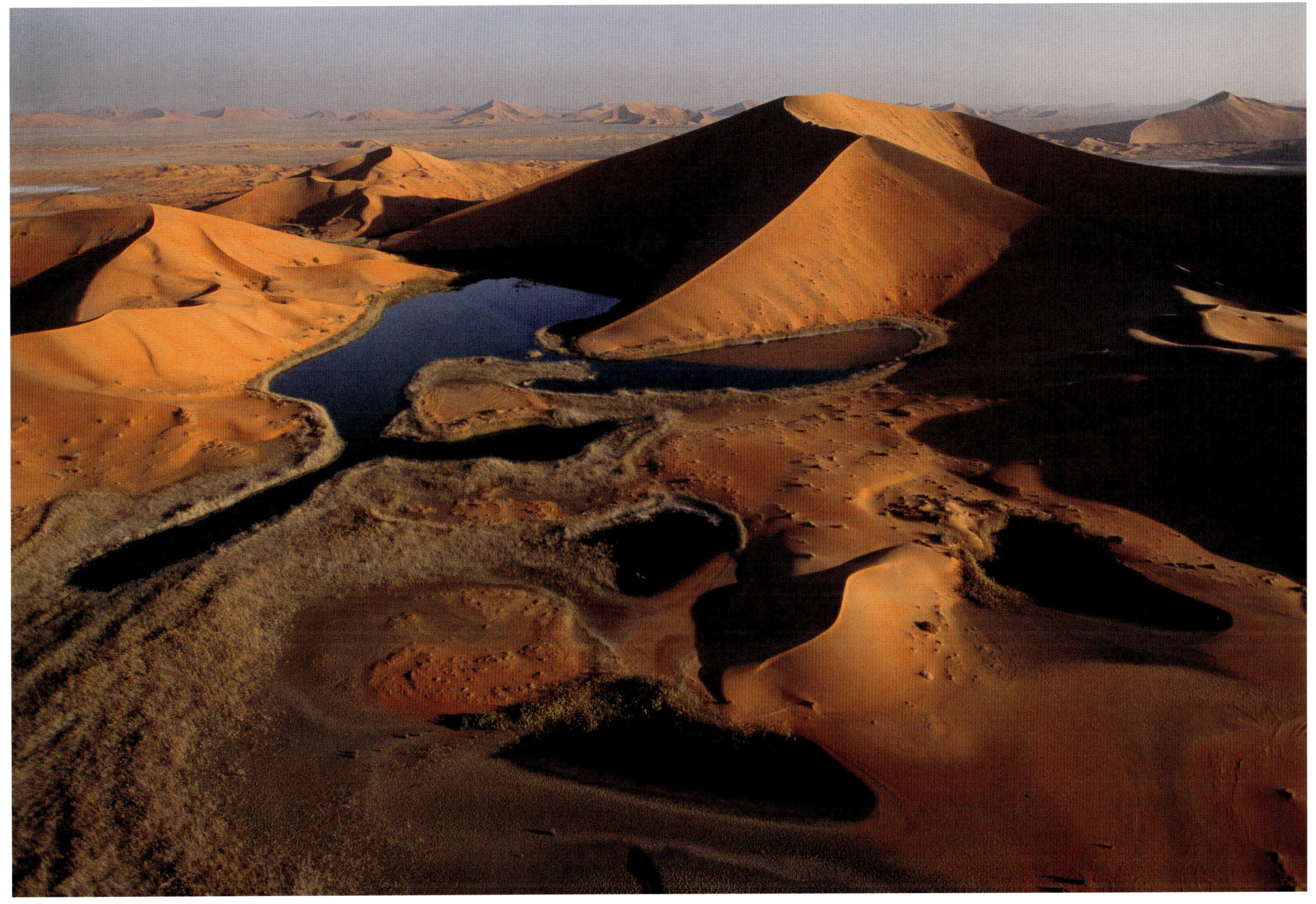

Freshwater lakes of Khawr Hamidan, Saudi Arabia

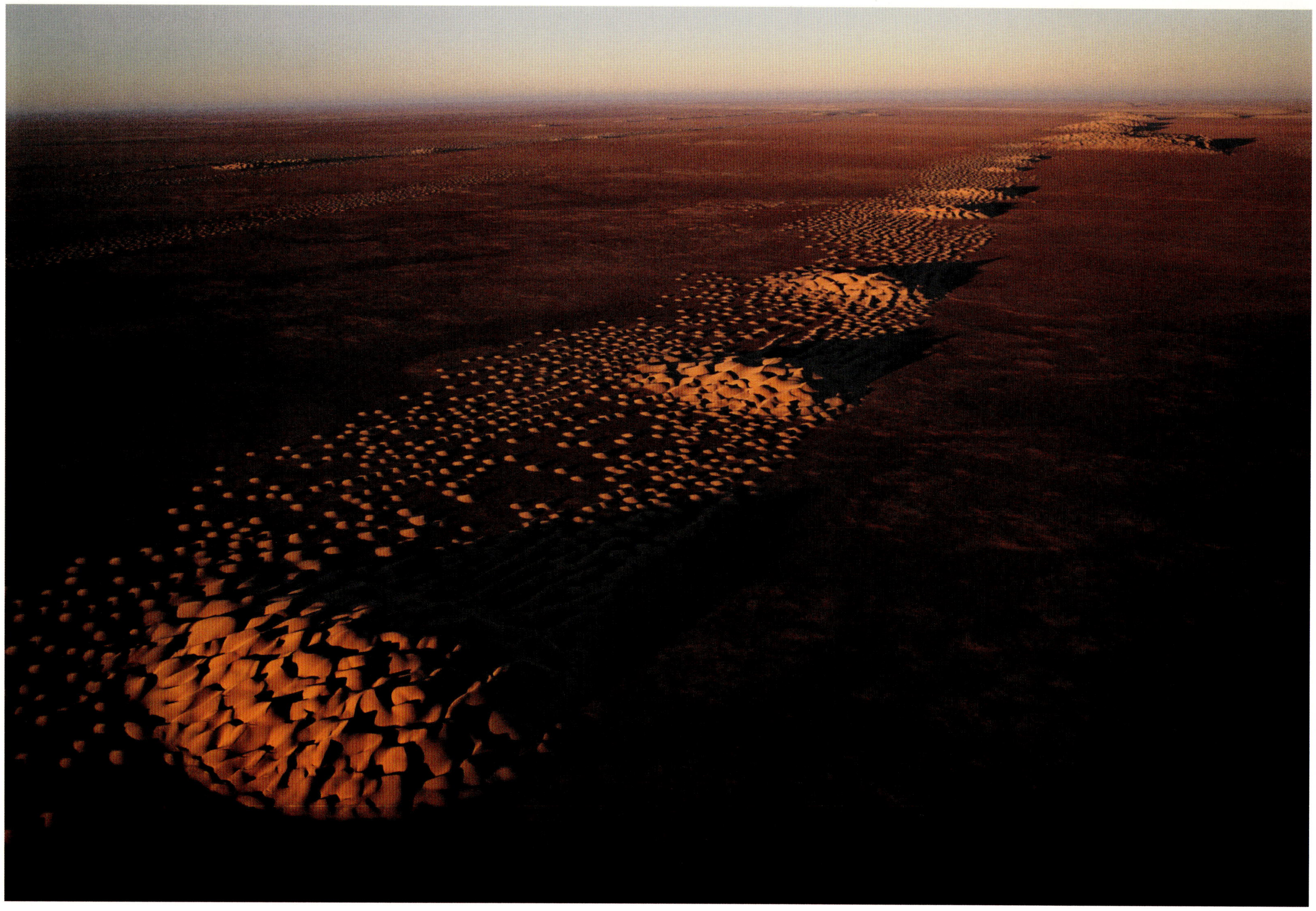

   Migrating barchan dunes, Ramlat Hazar, Yemen

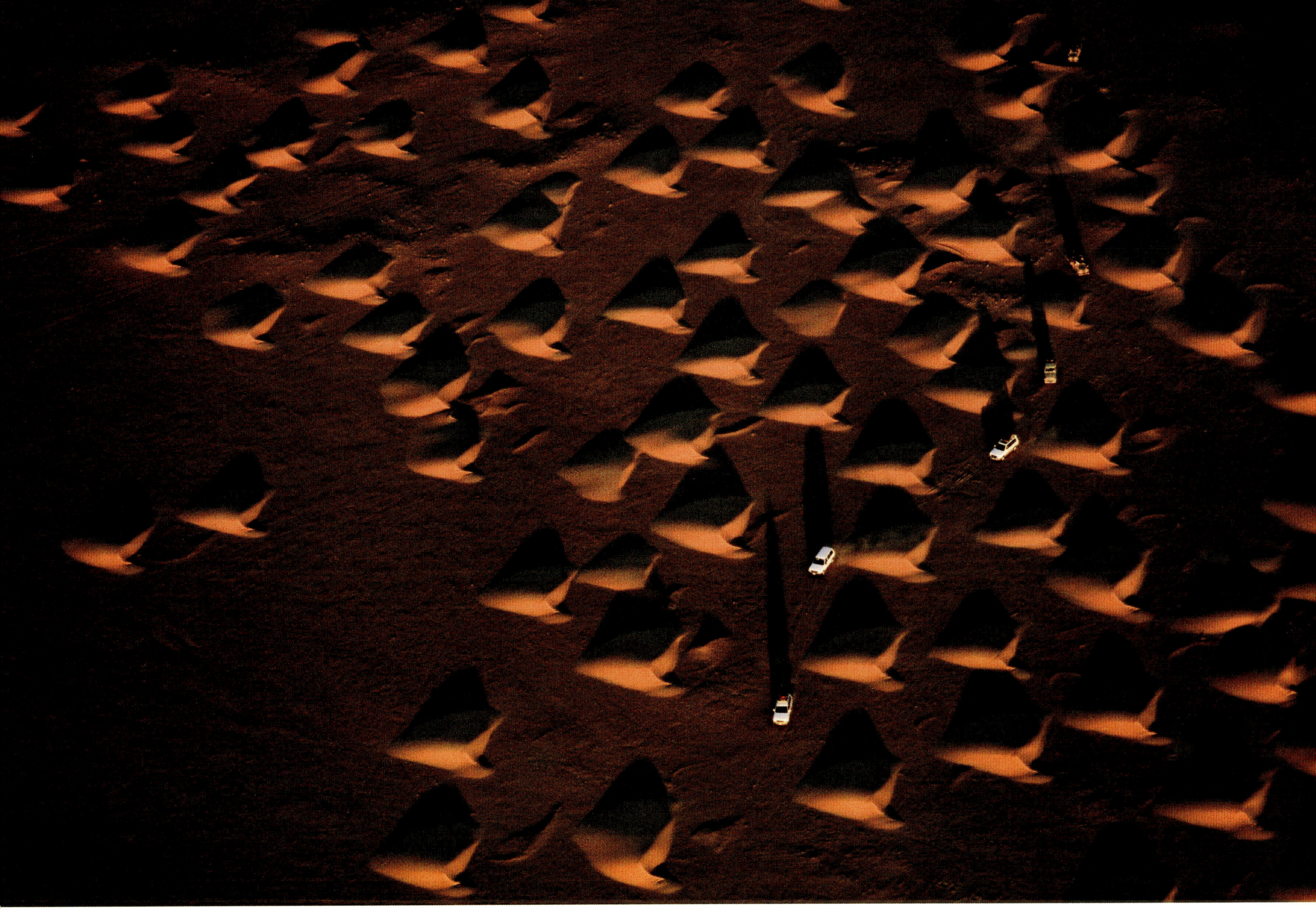

Crossing barchan field of Ramlat Mitan, Oman

"So far the sands we had passed on this journey
had been dreary and uninteresting. Now for the
first time the dunes were a lovely golden-red
and, although I was tired, hungry, and thirsty,
their shapes gave me great pleasure."

Wilfred Thesiger, *Arabian Sands*

OPPOSITE: Ramlat Butabul, Oman

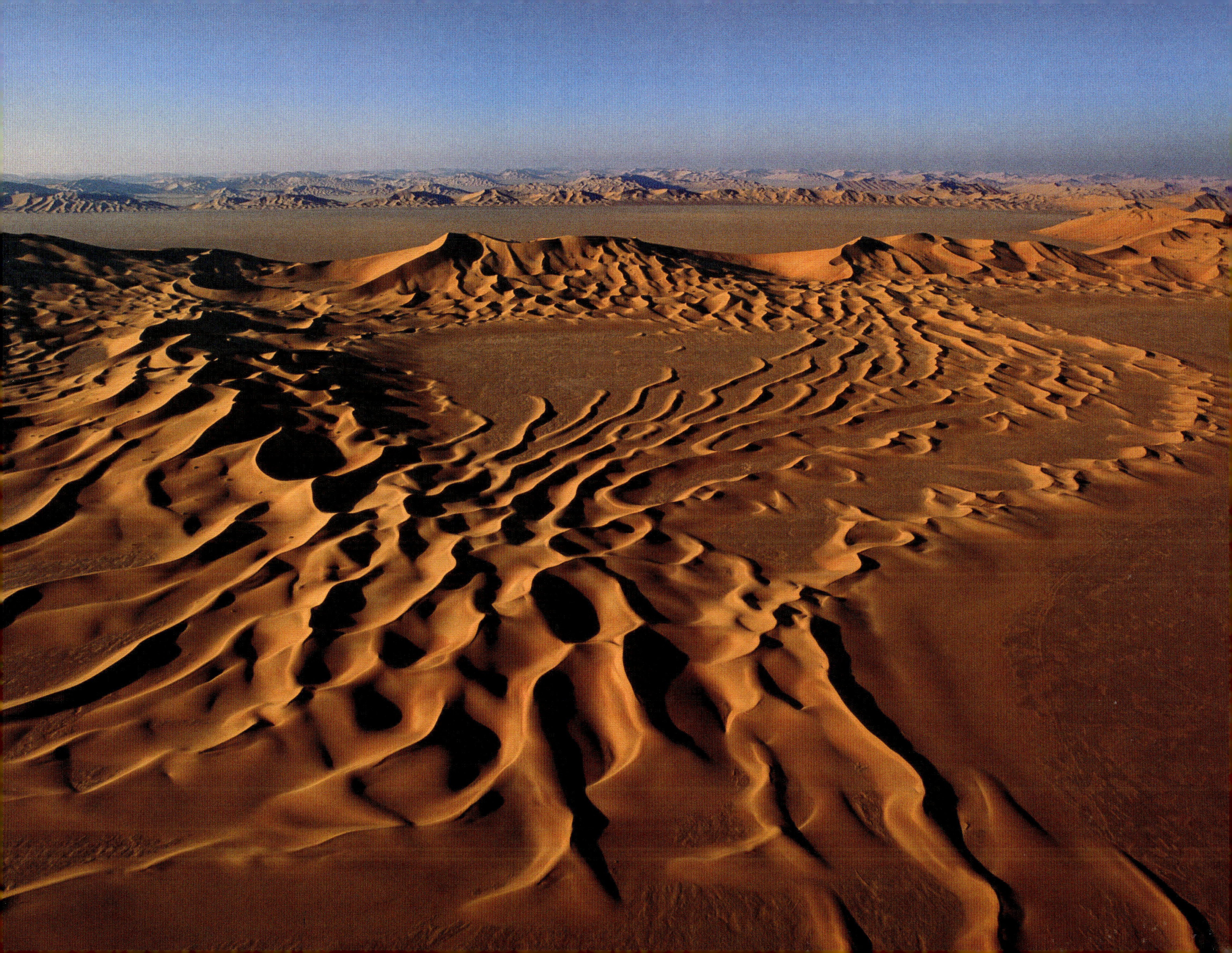

SHIBAM

Observed from above, Shibam looks like a small bed of ceramic nails. Sometimes referred to as the "medieval Manhattan of Arabia," it's made up of the tallest collection of mud buildings in the world. It's also the last surviving representative of an urban architectural style that once dominated the Yemeni part of the Empty Quarter. Sitting on a low mound on the south side of the Hadramawt Valley, its five hundred narrow tower homes rise six to eight stories into the sky. With no concrete or reinforcement, it's a marvel of traditional engineering.

Walking through its canyon-like streets, the town can seem deceptively quiet and deserted. Inside the city walls, this dusty maze of narrow passageways once kept intruders vulnerable to attack from above, for looming over the streets are screened windows where inhabitants can observe without being seen and drain flumes protrude out of the walls from kitchens and toilets on the upper floors, as if ready to discharge their contents onto the unsuspecting below. The tall buildings create deep chasms, keeping the town cool by protecting the walls of neighboring façades from intense sunlight.

Sitting directly on a stone foundation, the walls are made of unfired bricks and are canted inwards on all sides as they slowly taper upwards. While each tower home is unique, they all follow a basic plan. The ground floor is used for dry goods, and the first floor for small animals such as goats and chickens. The second floor is for receiving male guests, the third and fourth floors are for women and children, and the uppermost floors are for the younger members of the family as they come of age. At one point I was invited to the upper story of a tower home and felt the floor, made of plaster, mud, and palm trunks, flex under foot, as if I was walking through a piece of fragile antique cabinetry. Many of these buildings are capped with private rooftop patios for drying laundry and sleeping on hot summer nights. To survive the rare but intense monsoonal downpours, the roofs and exteriors are coated in lime-based plaster mixed with ash and require constant maintenance.

There is evidence that the town was built as early as the second century BCE, but it was so frequently sacked in wars and damaged by floods that most of the buildings that one sees here today are about five hundred years old. The town almost died from neglect thirty years ago, as most enterprising men of the Hadramawt had gone to the oil-rich countries in the Arabian Gulf to find work. It was during one such prolonged absence that some of the mud homes in Shibam were partially dissolved due to leaky plumbing in upper-floor bathrooms. In 1982 Shibam was declared a UNESCO World Heritage Site. Starting in 2000, a Yemeni-German cooperation program has been working to preserve the houses and upgrade the infrastructure, bringing the city slowly to its former glory while retaining its original inhabitants.

On my first flight over Shibam I spent an hour trying to capture its beauty and structure from just the right angle and even ventured over the city center. Donovan Webster, the writer who was accompanying me for *National Geographic,* was in Shibam at the time and described the chaos as an excited tide of children ran from one side of town to another trying to catch a glimpse of my hot-pink paraglider from the bottom of the narrow streets. From four hundred feet up in the sky I was totally unaware of this, as I was preoccupied with where I would land if my motor cut out. When we got back to our lodgings that night I was told that the Shibam police were looking for me, and that they were upset by all the excitement and confusion, even though I had warned them I'd be flying overhead (though I didn't specify exactly when that would occur). It seemed that Bertram Thomas was right once again: It's a lot easier to receive forgiveness than to obtain permission, but sometimes even permission is not enough. ▤

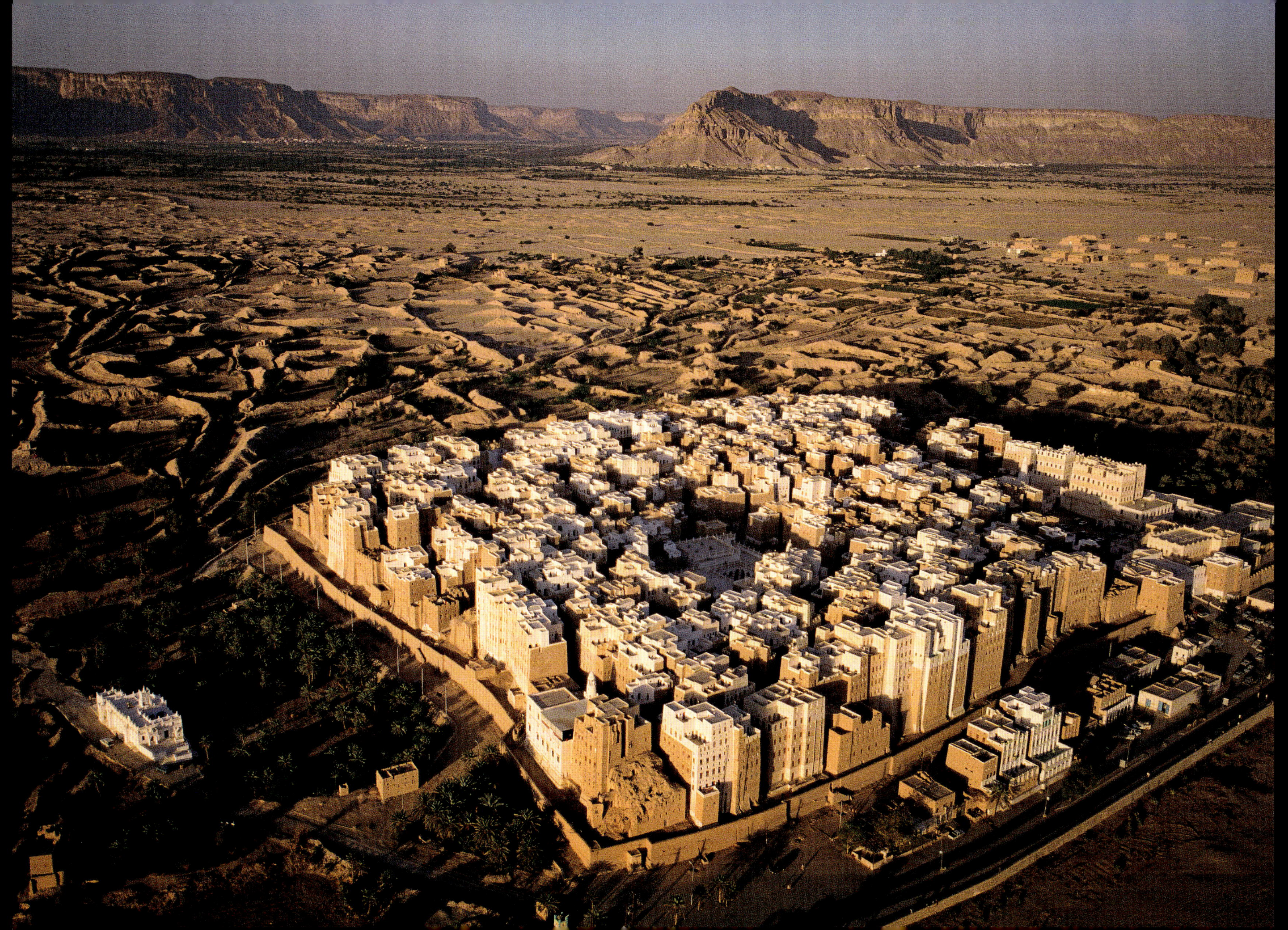

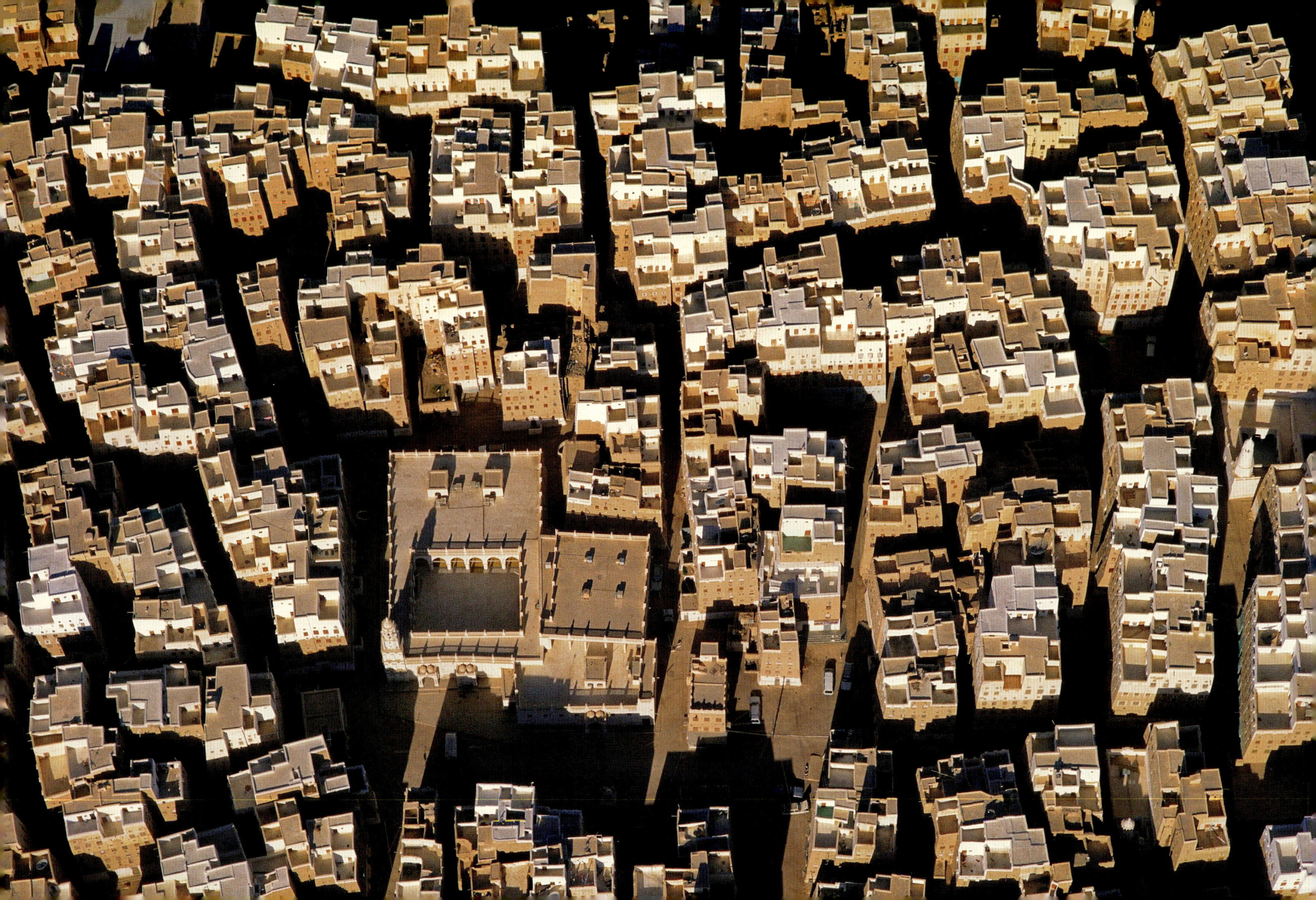

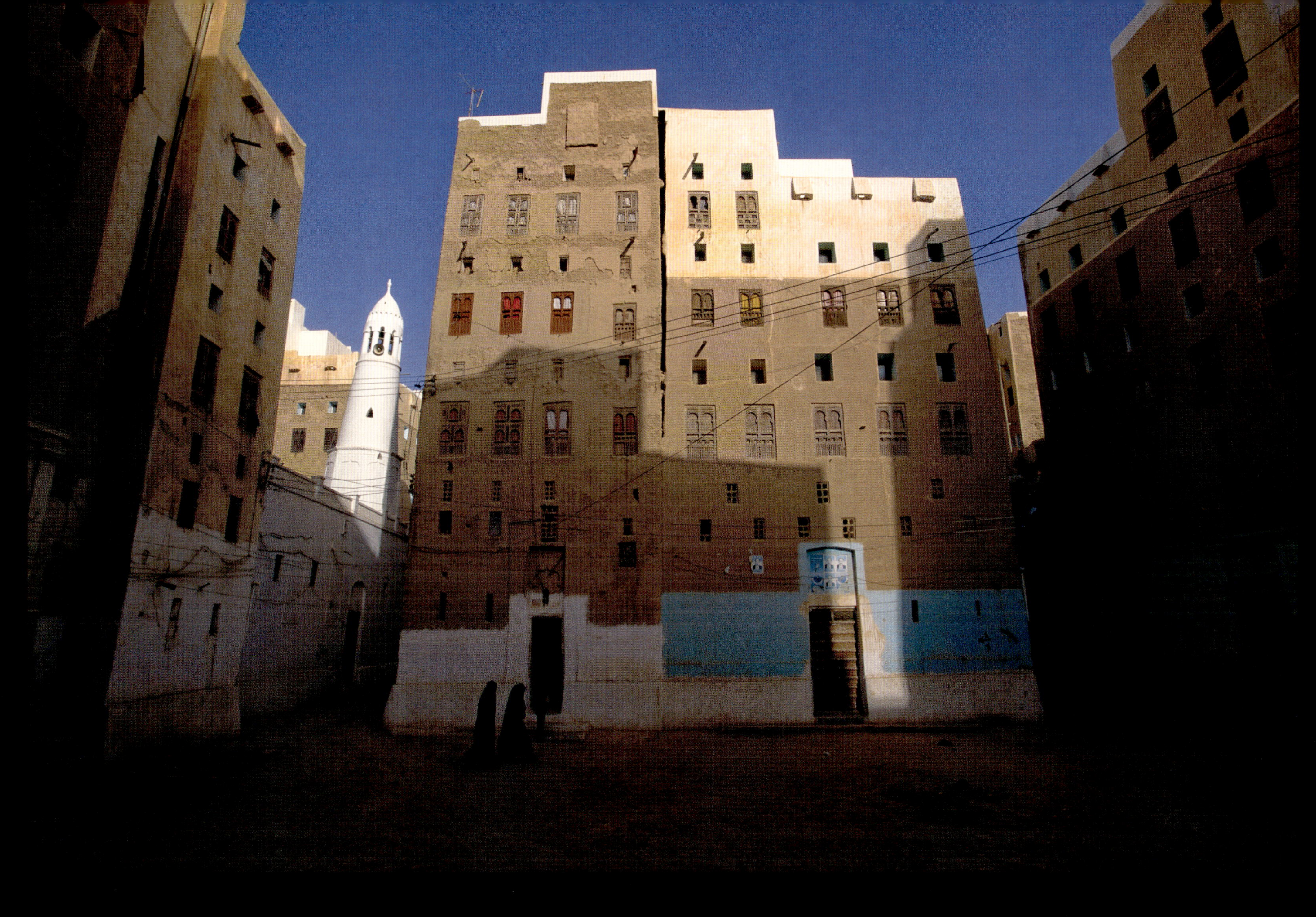

Residential square, Shibam, Yemen

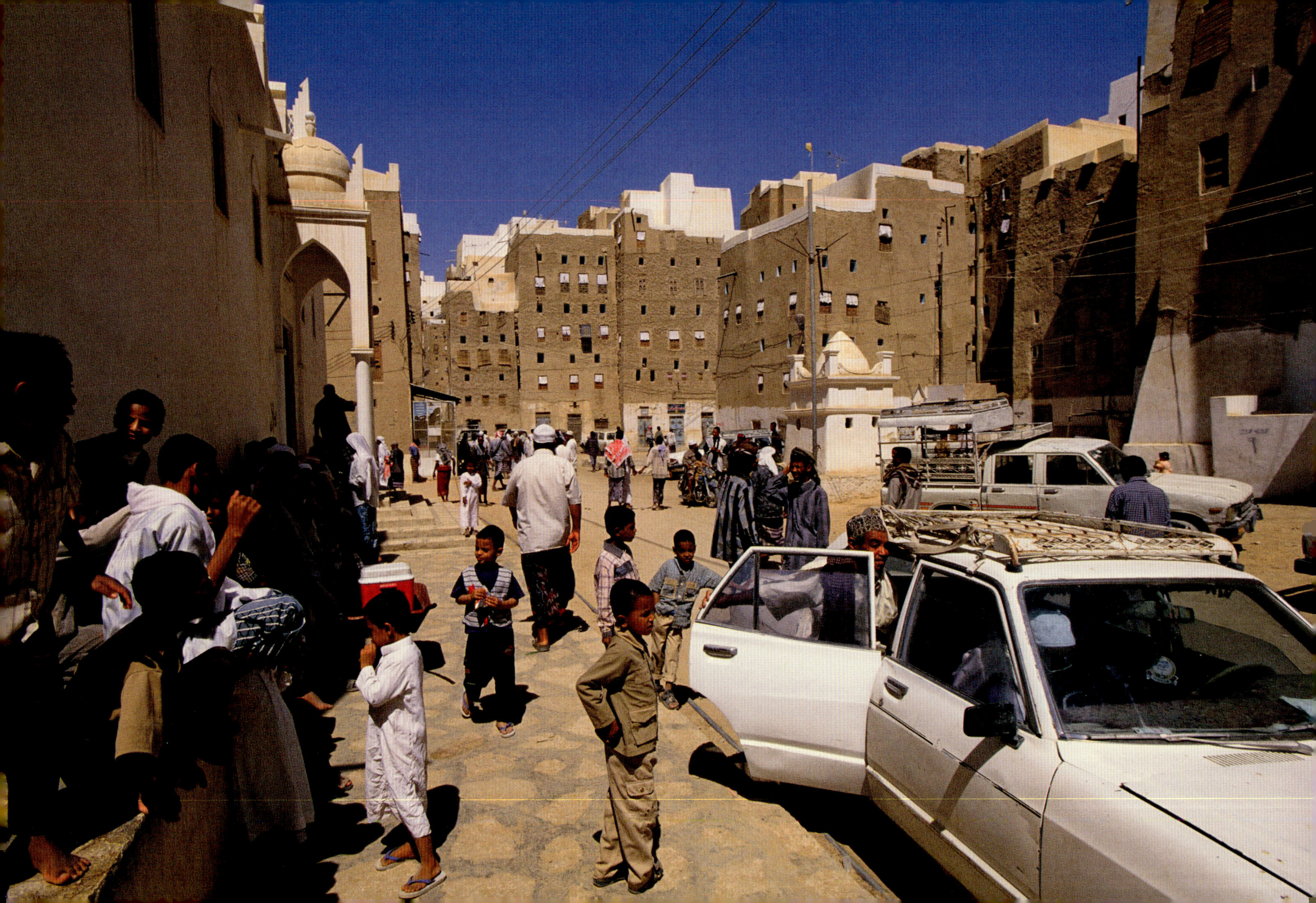

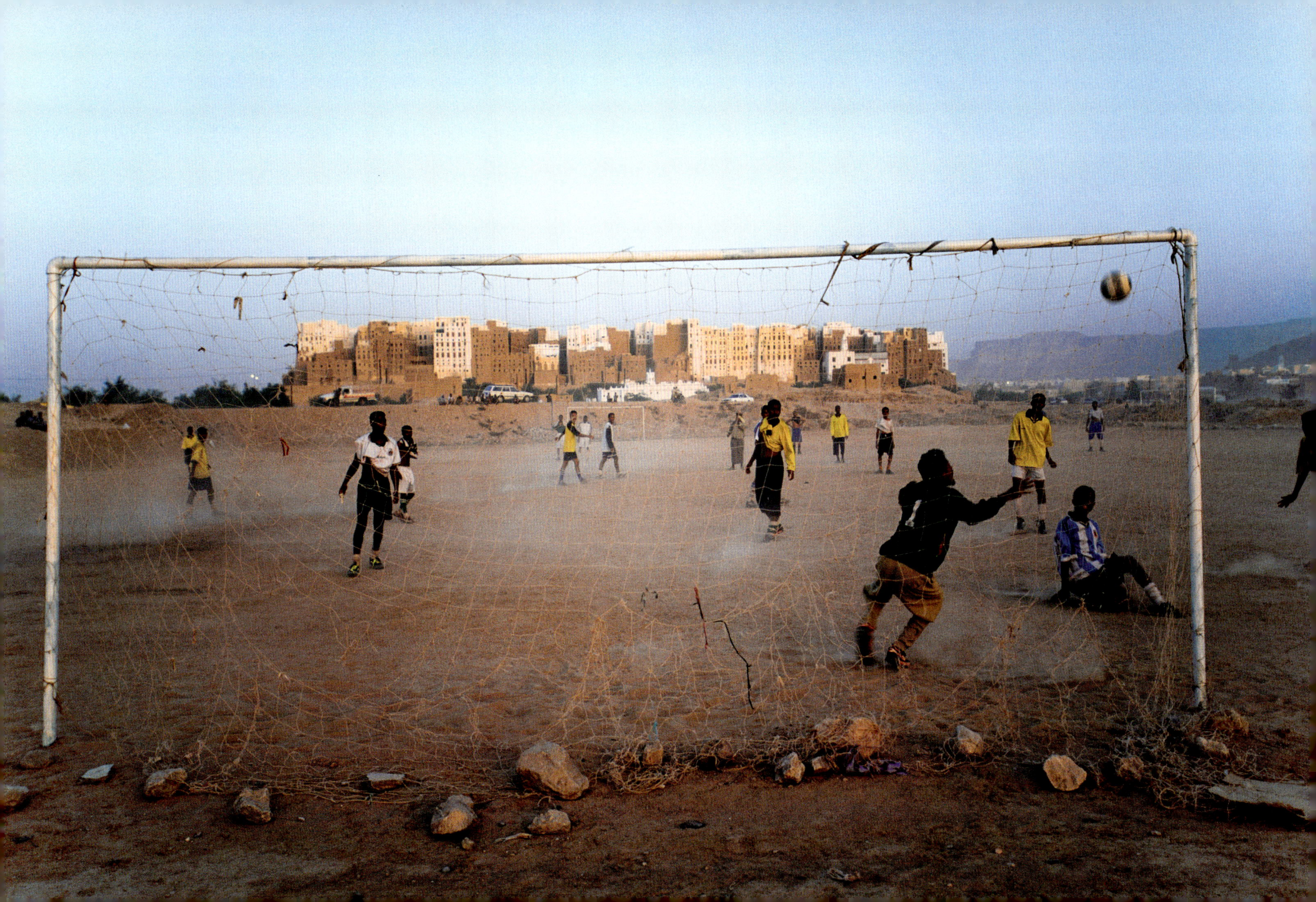

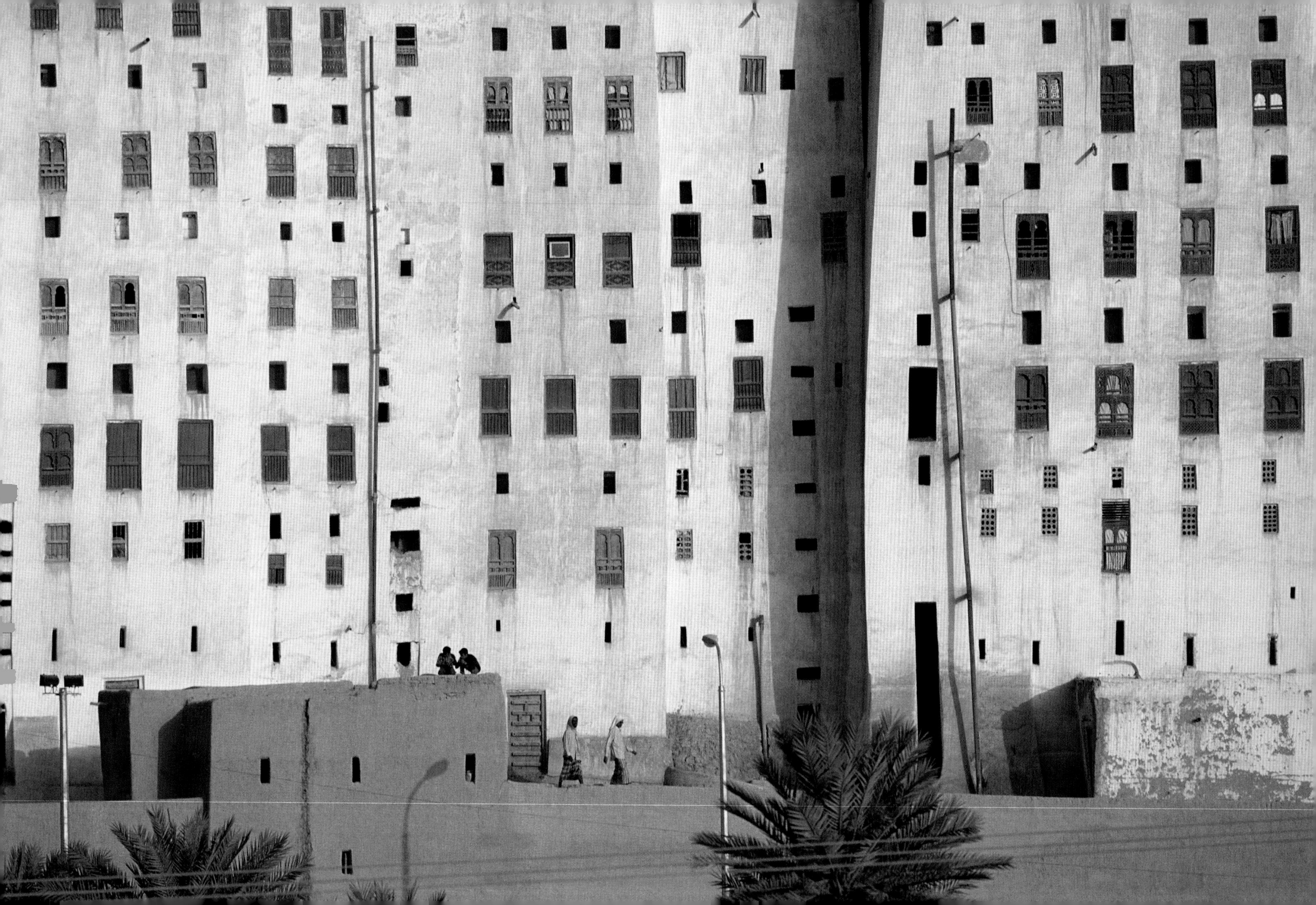

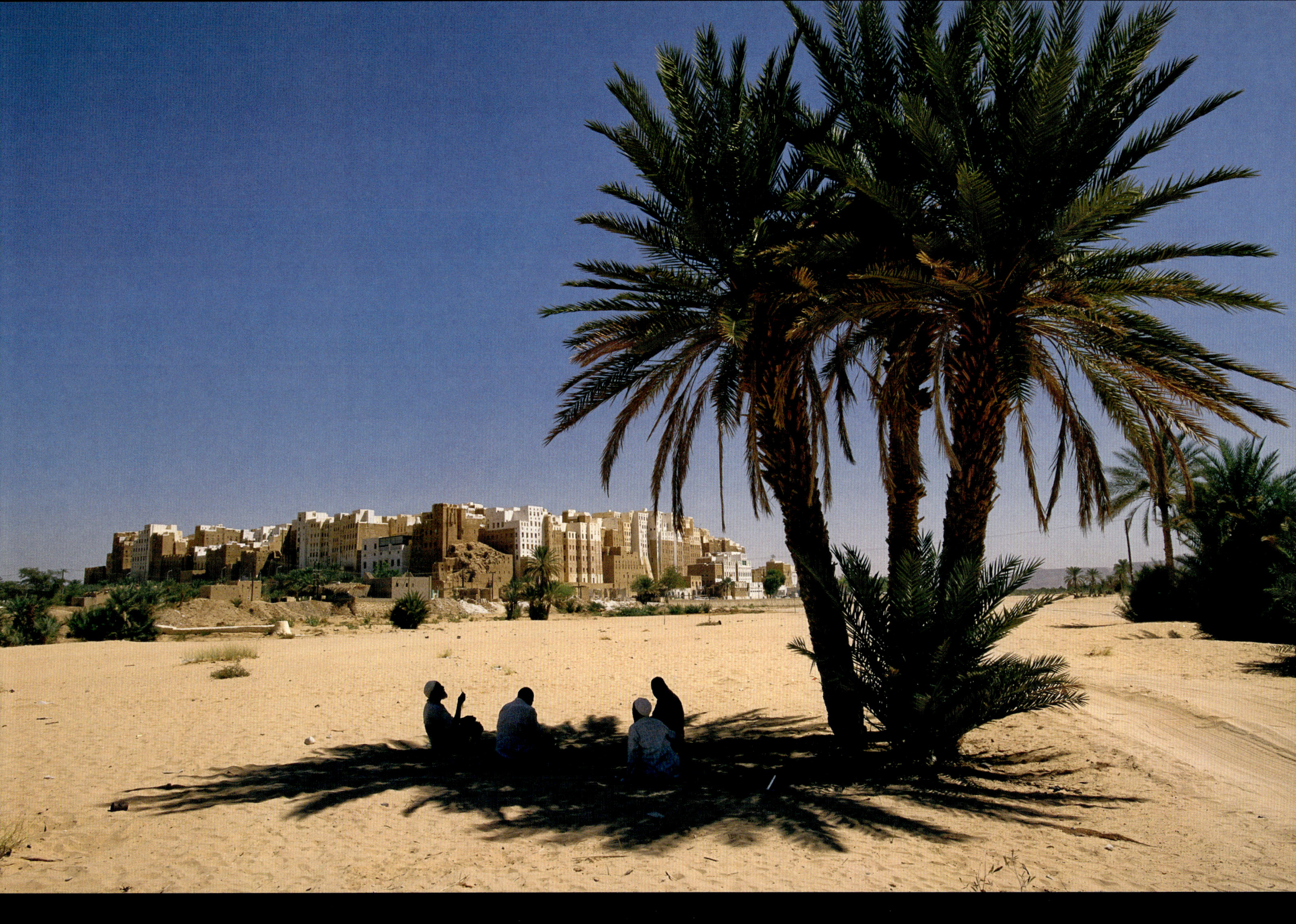
ABOVE: Old men gather under palms, Shibam, Yemen
OVERLEAF: Women harvesting fields of Wadi Hadramawt, Shibam, Yemen

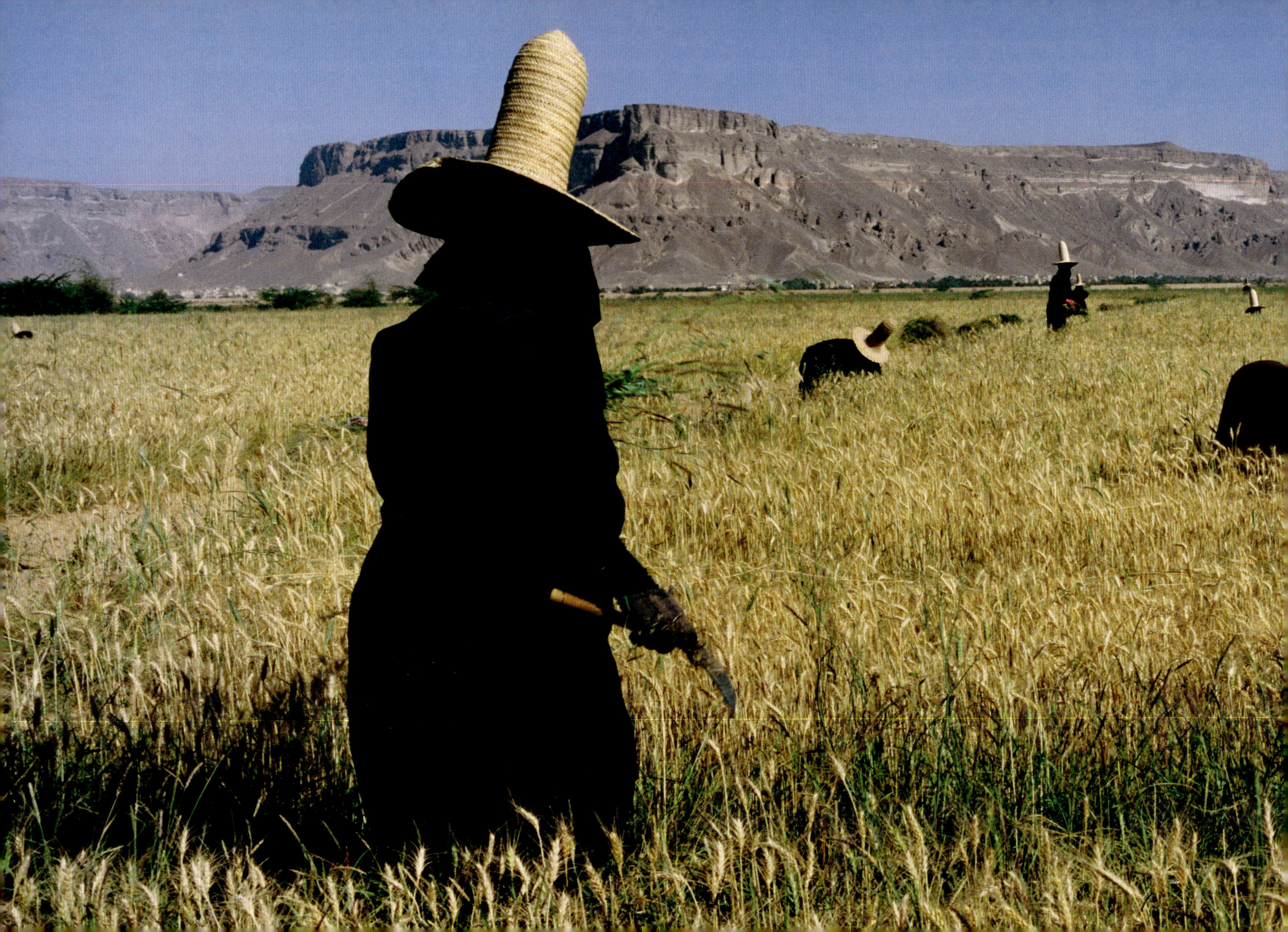

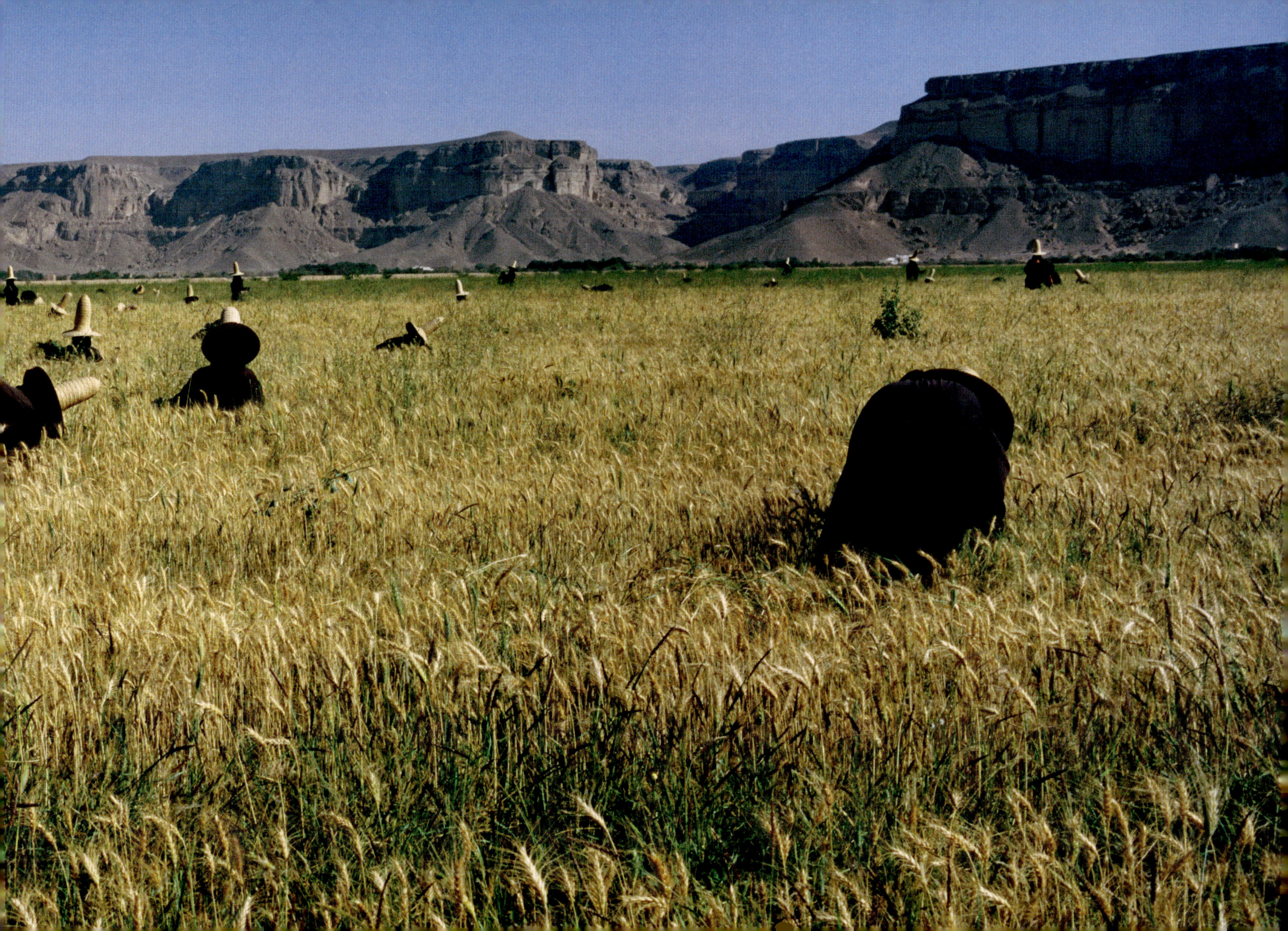

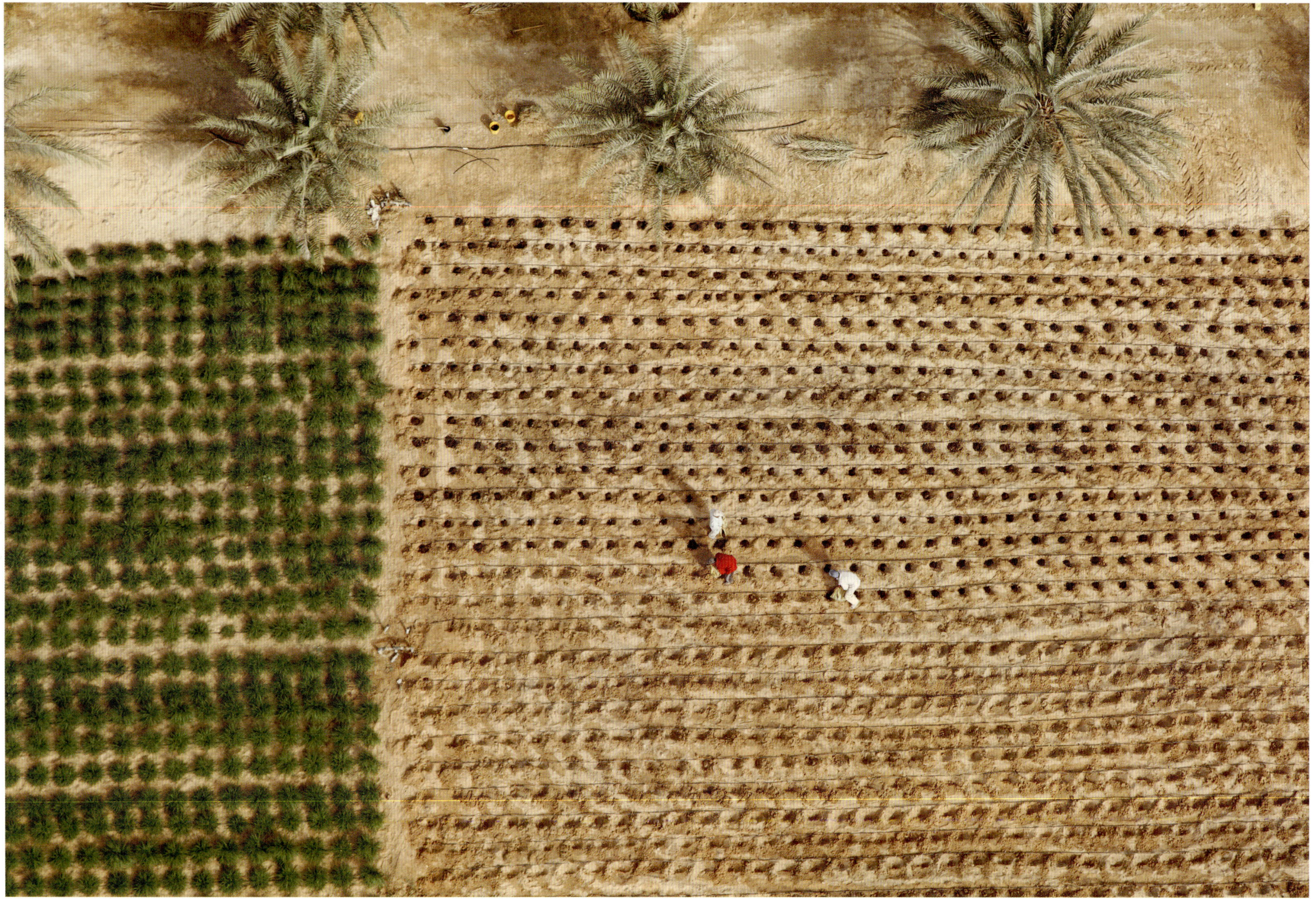

   Drip irrigation, Liwa, U.A.E.

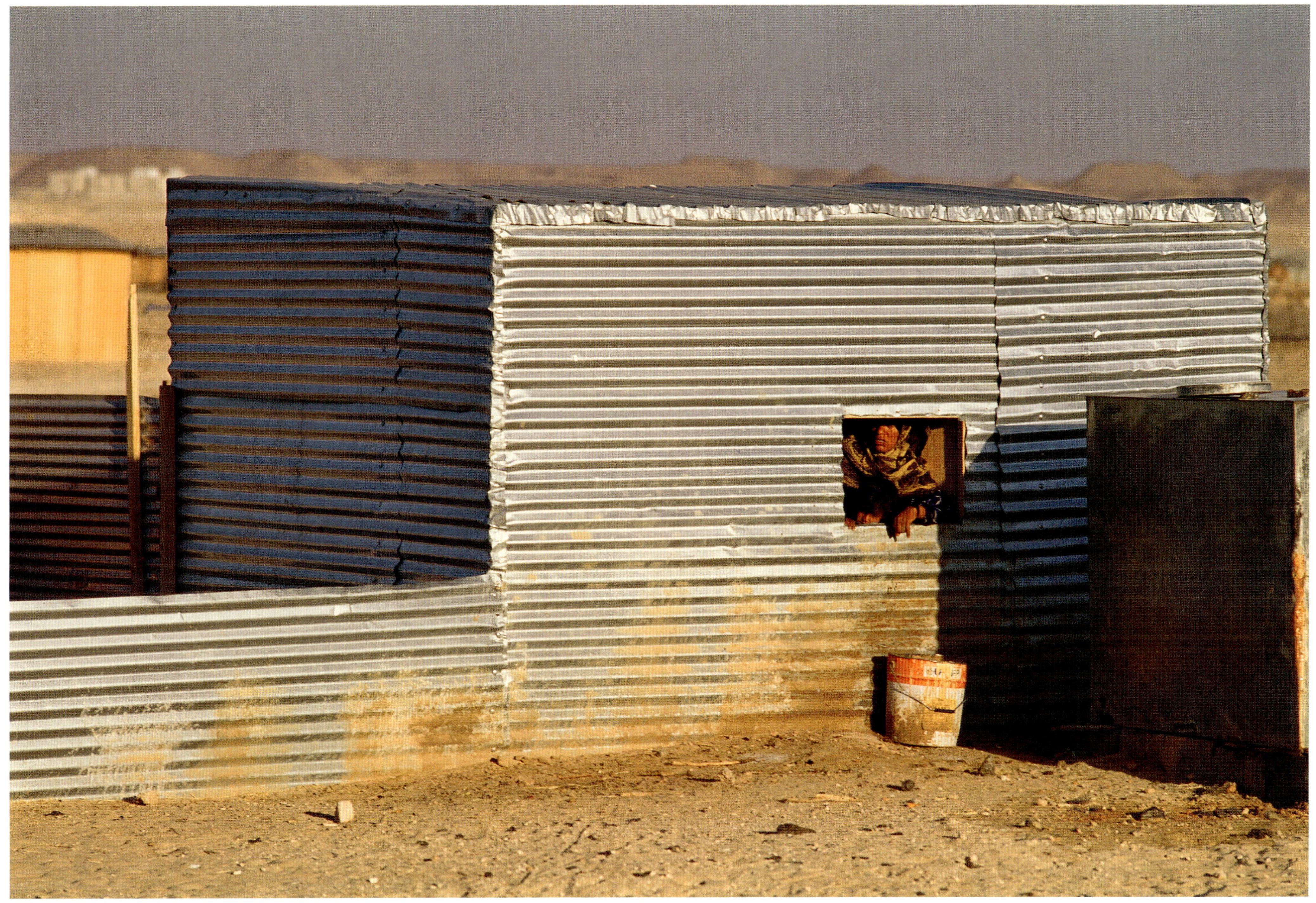

Vernacular architecture, Wadi Shihan, Oman

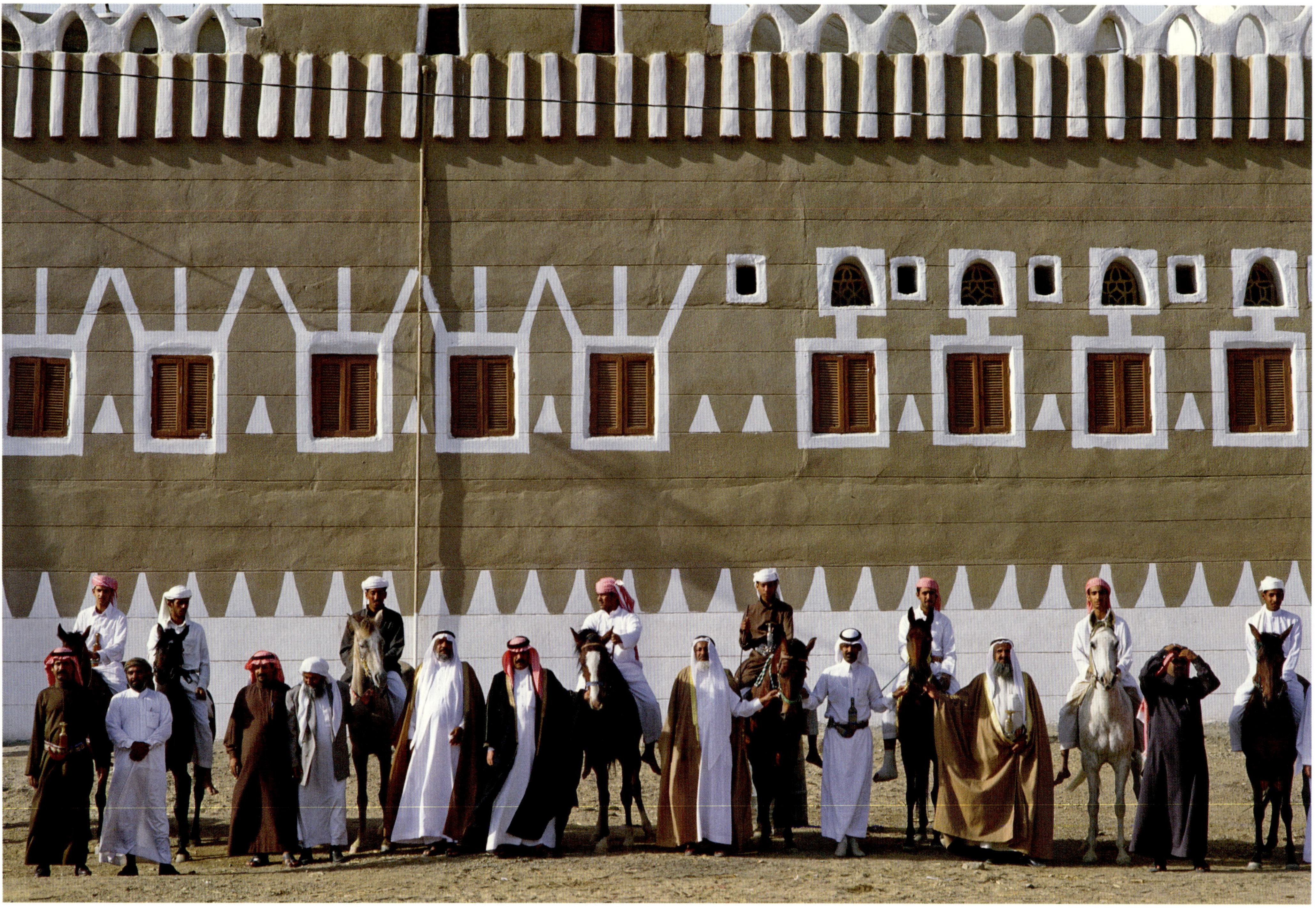

     Arabian horses of al-Haider clan, Najran, Saudi Arabia

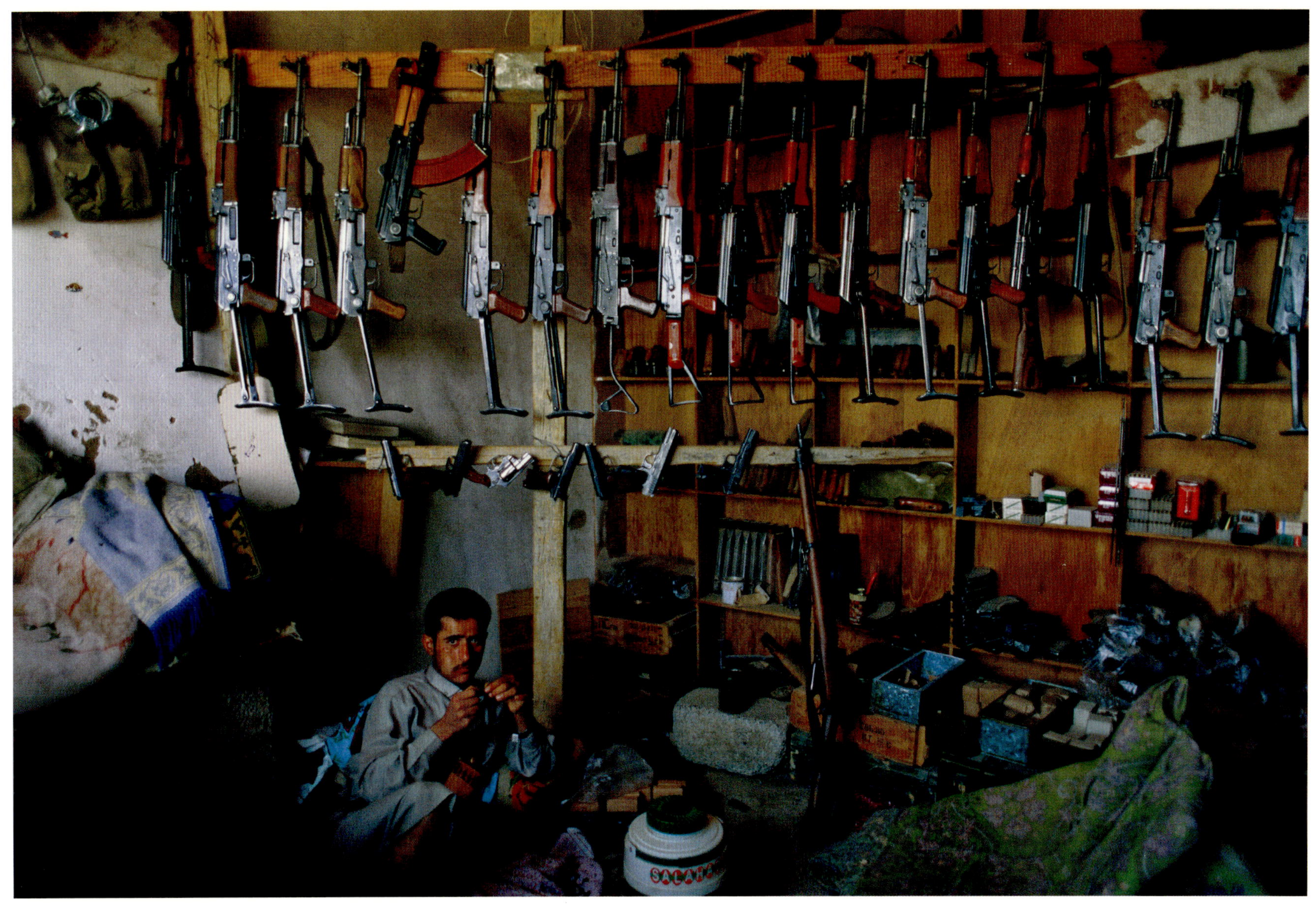

Gun shop, Marib, Yemen

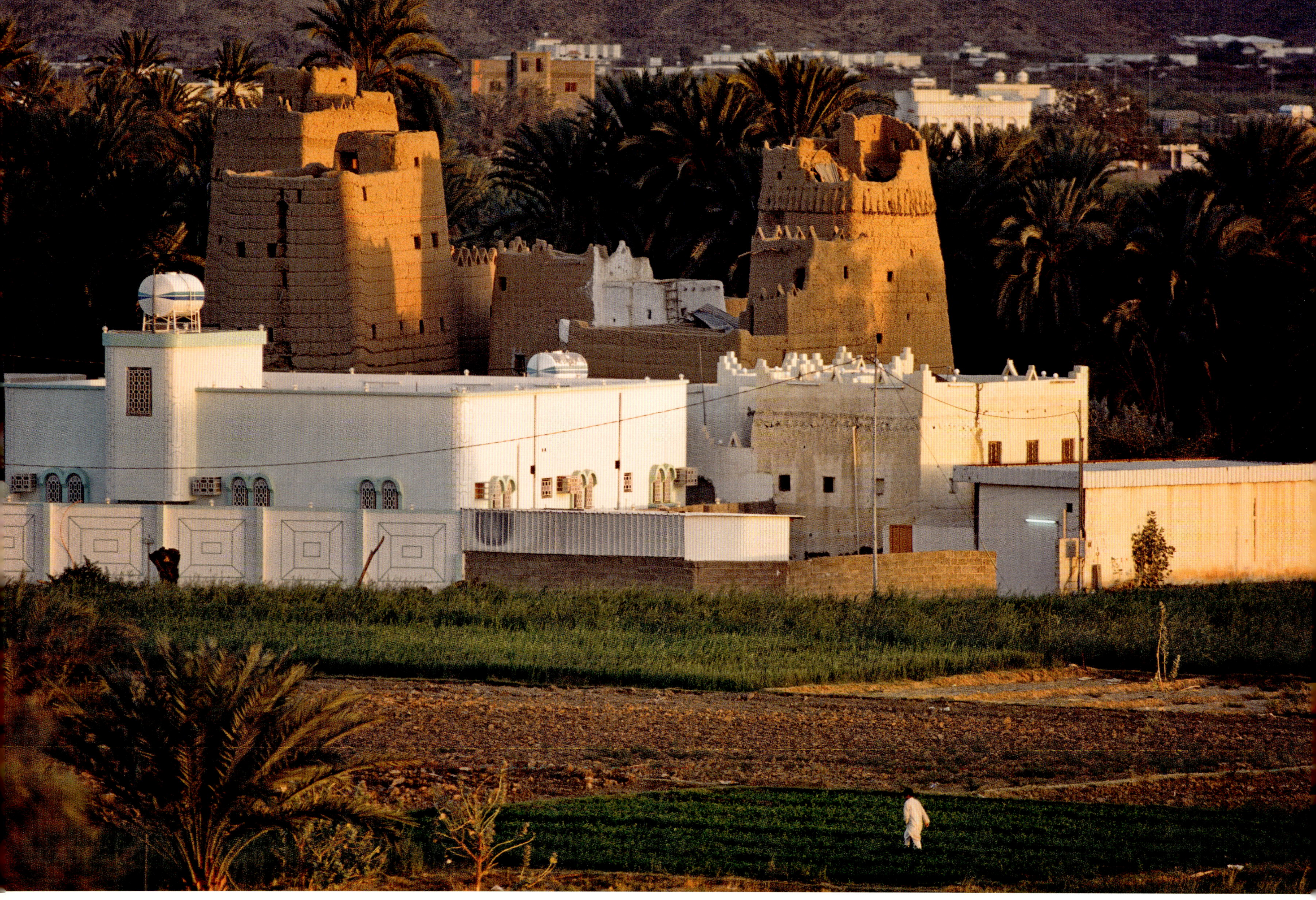

  Modern family complex, Najran, Saudi Arabia

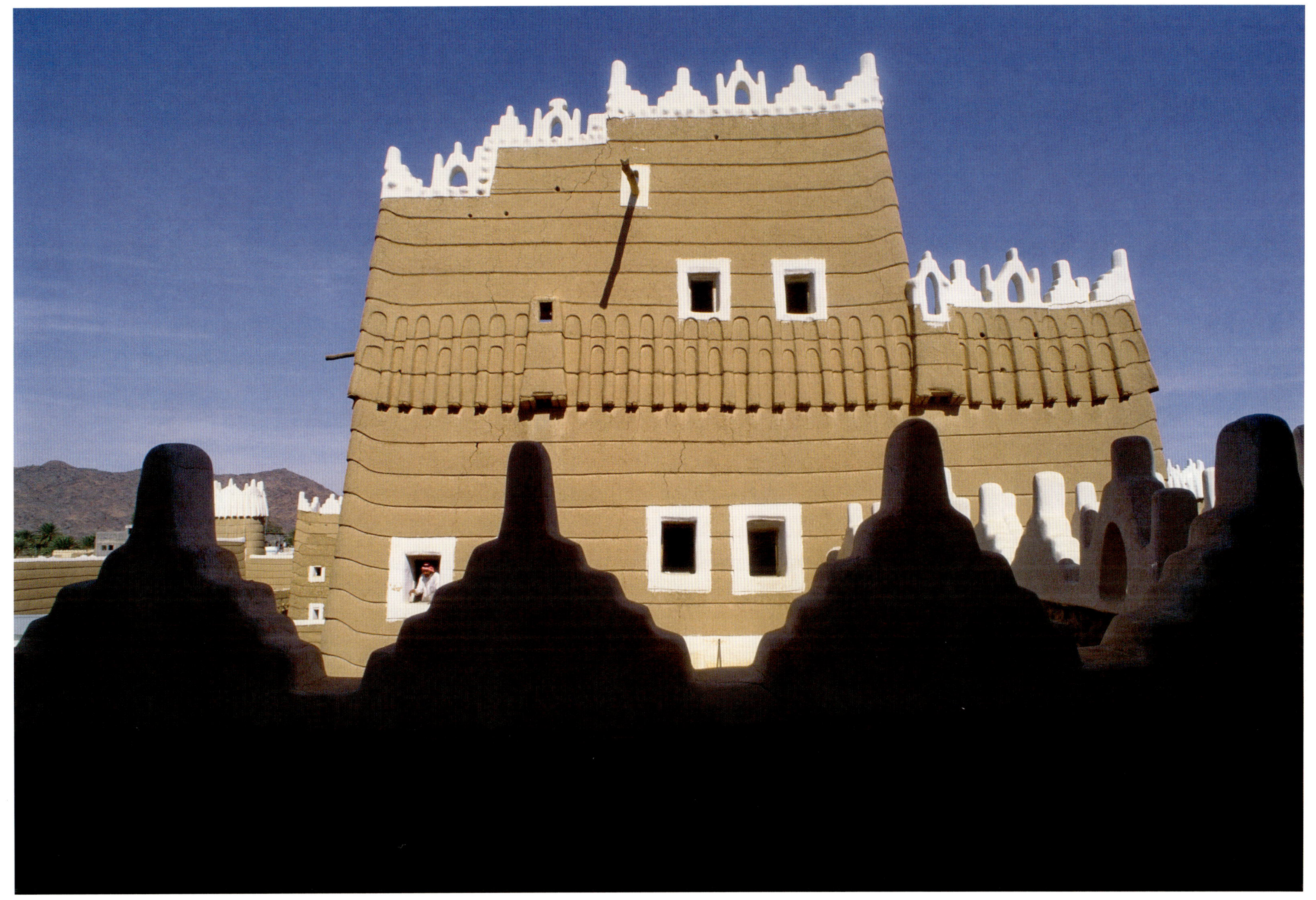

Emara Palace, Najran, Saudi Arabia

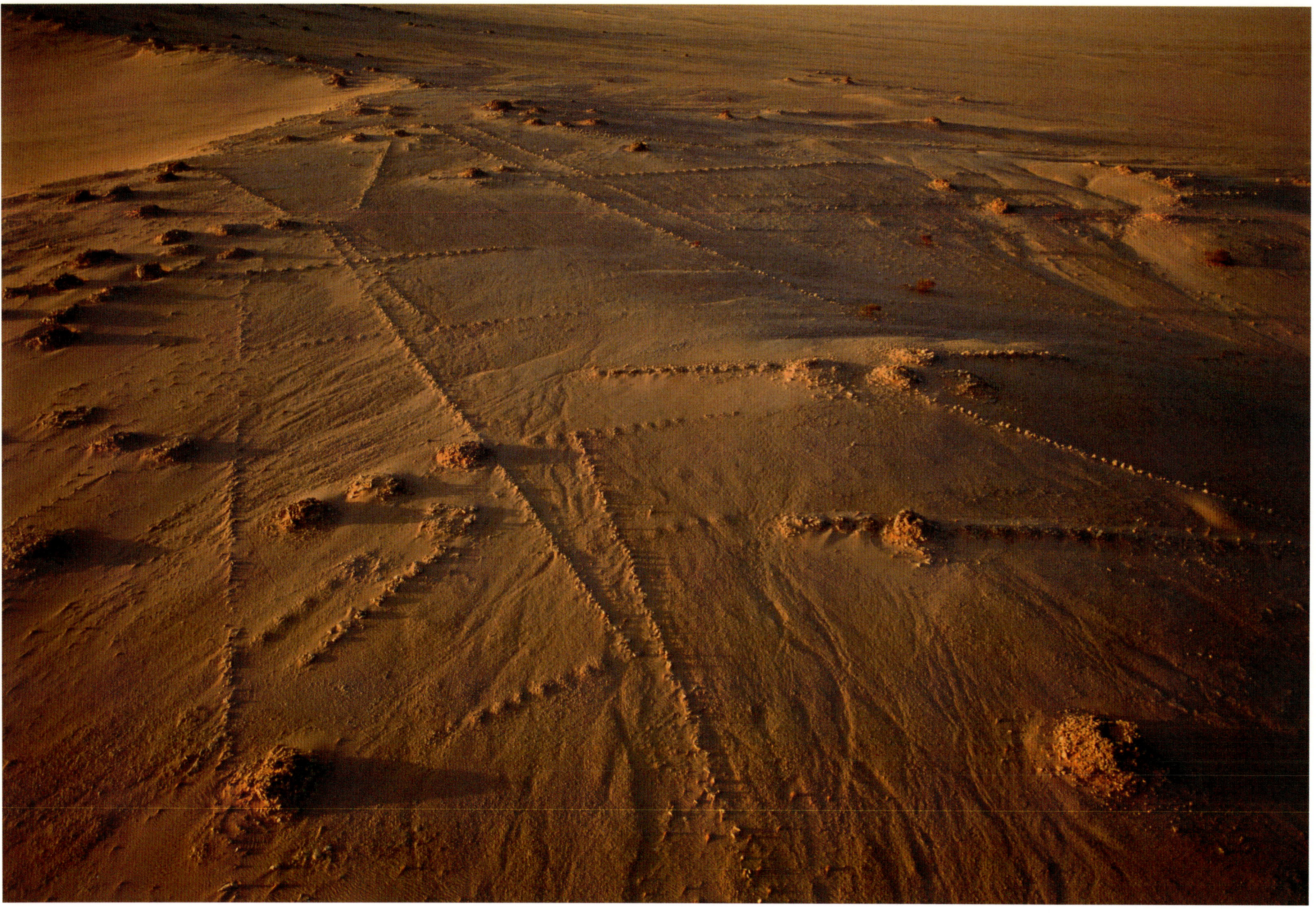

    Bronze Age necropolis, Alam al-Abyad, Yemen

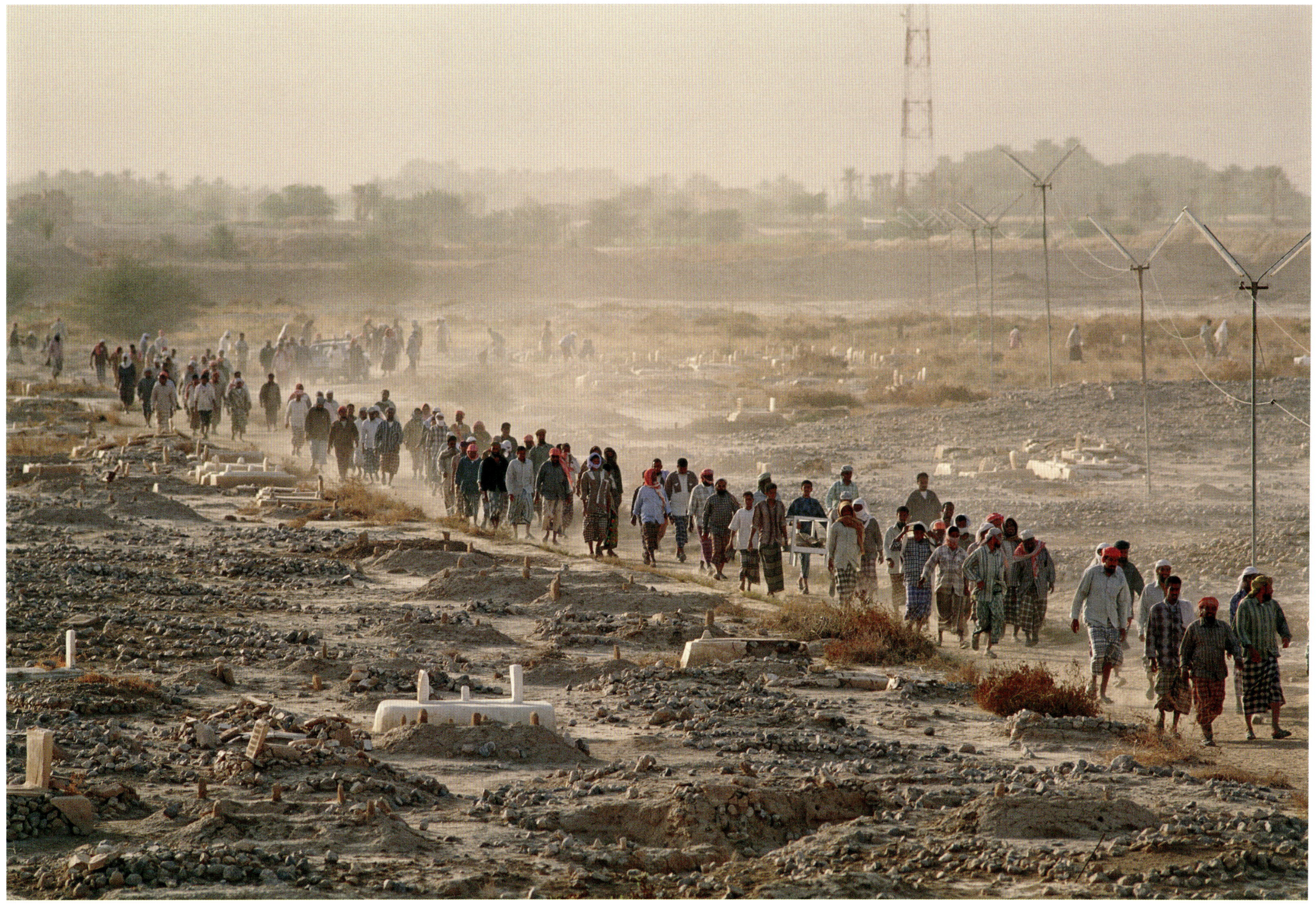

Returning from a funeral, Shibam, Yemen

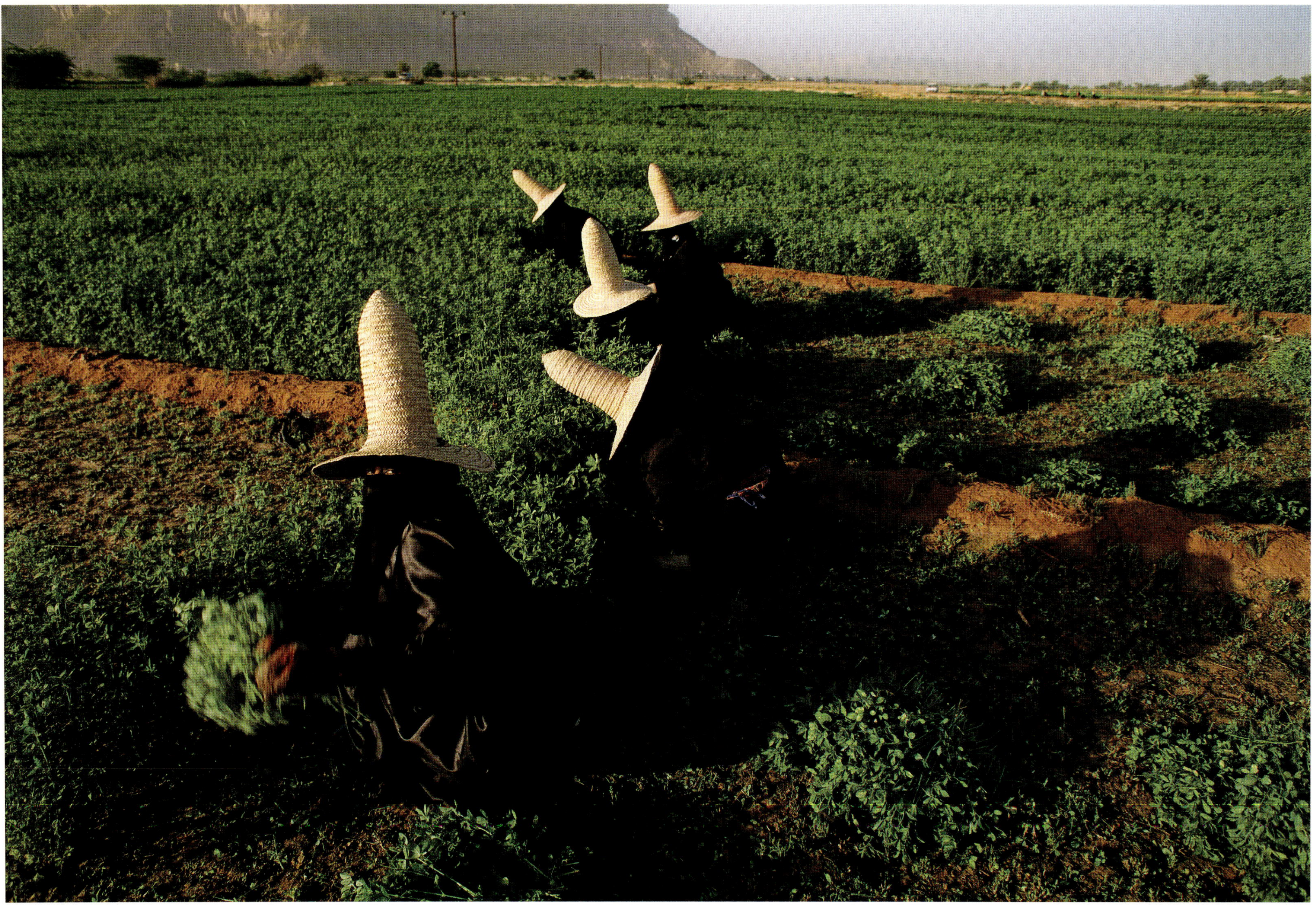

    Women harvesting fodder, Wadi Hadramawt, Yemen

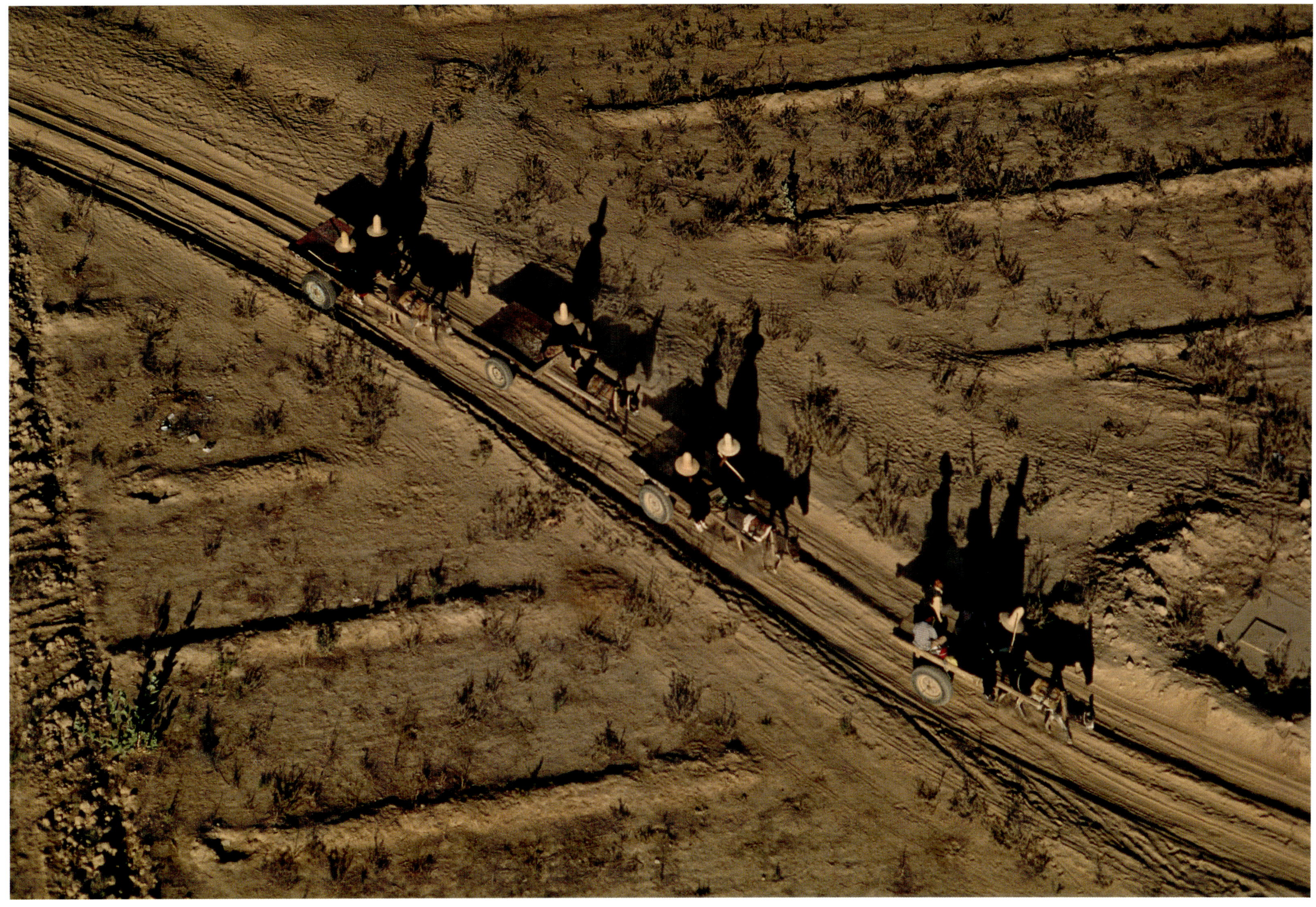

Women heading to the fields, Wadi Hadramawt, Yemen

"Also there seems to be something indelicate
in the intrusion of Western machines into
these virgin silences; a feeling not to be
confused with the thrill of the unknown...."

Bertram Thomas, *Arabia Felix*

     OPPOSITE: New road with wind breaks, near Al Qua'a, U.A.E.

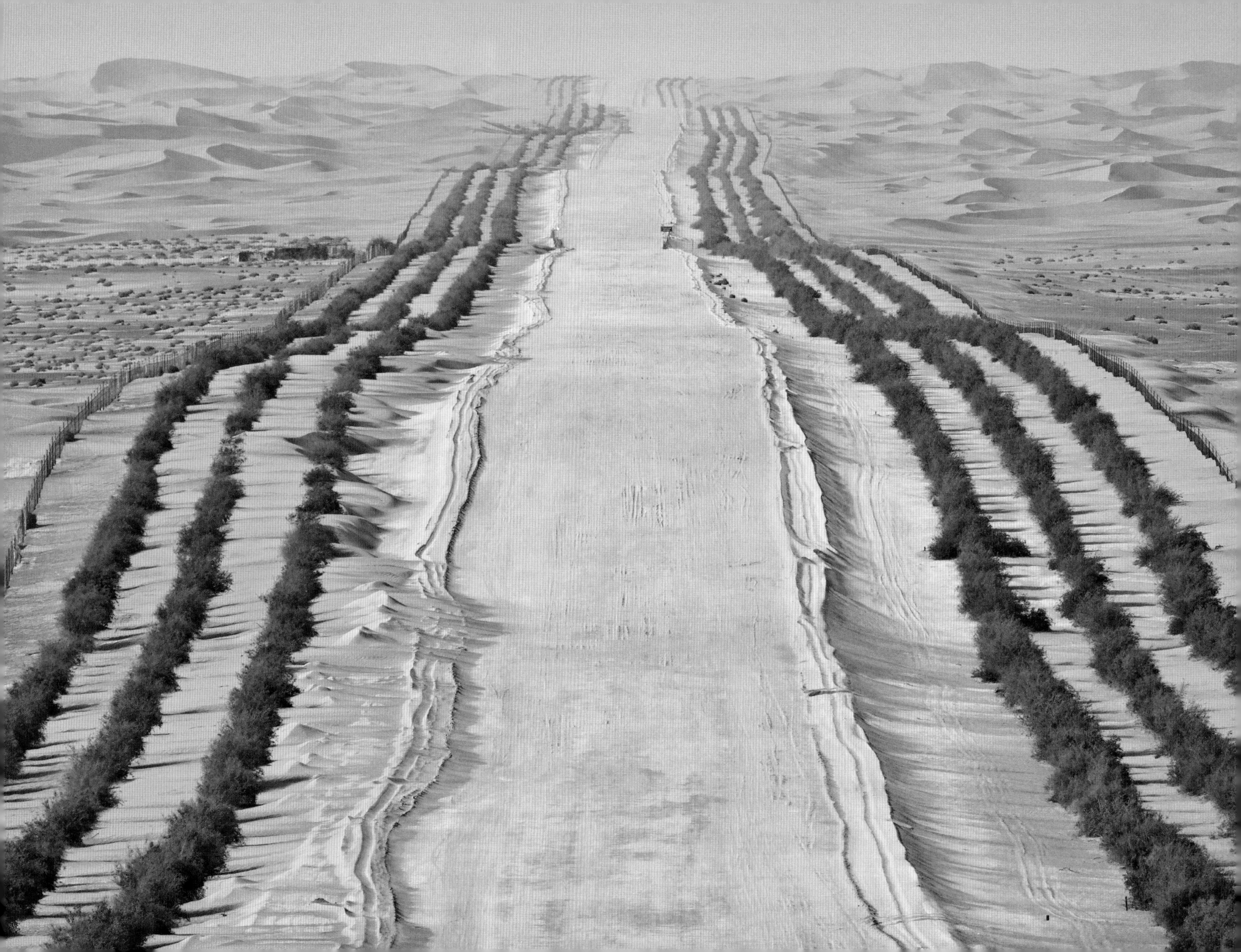

CAMEL BEAUTY

We had met Sayed about an hour north of the Liwa oasis, in the posh viewing stands of Abu Dhabi's first annual camel beauty contest. It was the Arab version of a horse show and a chance for urbanites to reconnect with their roots and get a little sand in their sandals. For me it was an opportunity to explore the ties between modern Arabia and its nomadic past. Some ten thousand camels were registered to participate. To draw a crowd, Abu Dhabi's ruling family was giving away 150 new Land Cruisers and Range Rovers to first and second place winners, plus thirty-five million dirhams ($9.5 million) in prize money. Sayed quickly became our informal guide, as he was the only person we met among the several hundred spectators who spoke English and we were the only ones not wearing flowing white robes. My friend François and I lamented that every hotel for a hundred miles was full, so Sayed graciously invited us to his camp for dinner. He pointed toward a collection of tents off to the south, and two hours later, we were racing across the dunes in the gathering darkness, heading toward the brightest lit tent in the area.

As we got out of the car, we entered what looked like a used car lot of gold-accented Toyota Land Cruisers with a big red carpet and a fire pit in its center. We were greeted warmly by Sheikh Khaled bin Ternaf Al-Minhali, a small, charismatic man who approached quickly across his red-carpeted realm with a customized crutch to compensate for an atrophied right leg.

Nobody there knew Sayed, and we had clearly arrived at the wrong tent, but the irresistible charm of Sheikh Khaled drew us in. Everyone there was from the Bani Yas clan, which for centuries had eked out a simple living during the winter in the oasis of Liwa on the edge of the Empty Quarter and spent summers pearl diving in the waters of the Arabian Gulf. It was a tough existence until oil was discovered in 1958. Now all were dressed identically in crisp white robes, red-checked ghutras, and simple sandals and watching TV under an outdoor canopy of electric lights. Sheikh Khaled owned one of the biggest Toyota dealerships in Abu Dhabi and had extensive trucking and real estate holdings as well. The week earlier Sheikh Khaled had had one of the larger dunes near the parade grounds bulldozed flat for his camp and brought in three mobile-home trailers to support his entourage, along with two enormous tents, one for shade and another for dining, plus a diesel-powered generator for evening entertainment. Numerous guests came and went while we were there, but as the only foreigners at the camel festival, François and I seemed to be the center of attention. After rounds of tea, green coffee, and the passing of a large bowl of foaming fresh camel milk, I explained that François and I had come to Abu Dhabi to photograph their part of the Empty Quarter. I asked if they would like to see some photos of the sands from my previous travels in Oman, Yemen, and Saudi Arabia. Taking photos in the Arab world is often greeted with suspicion, but here I found that showing them was quite a different matter. Soon some twenty men were crowded around my laptop, excitedly peppering me with questions and exclaiming in recognition. I was impressed by their breadth of firsthand knowledge of the Empty Quarter's most obscure regions, even those that lay in other countries. They became particularly excited by photos of Bedouin women, especially those without veils, a rare sight in this part of Arabia.

Soon we were invited into the dining tent where two baby camels had been cooked whole and laid out on enormous platters of rice. Over a dozen men clustered around the largest platter on the carpeted floor and proceeded to devour the camels with their bare right hands. A long knife was protruding from the roasted camel hump, and one of our hosts used it to cut out the choicest pieces of camel meat for François and me. After dinner there were rounds of dancing, with young men twirling in circles surrounded by their clan, which chanted and clapped in accompaniment. Sometime after midnight we rolled our sleeping bags out for a little sleep inside the tent reserved for daytime meetings.

The following morning we were given a tour of Sheikh Khaled's livestock enclosure and invited to watch his herd mating and nursing, and we saw a new camel as it was born in the

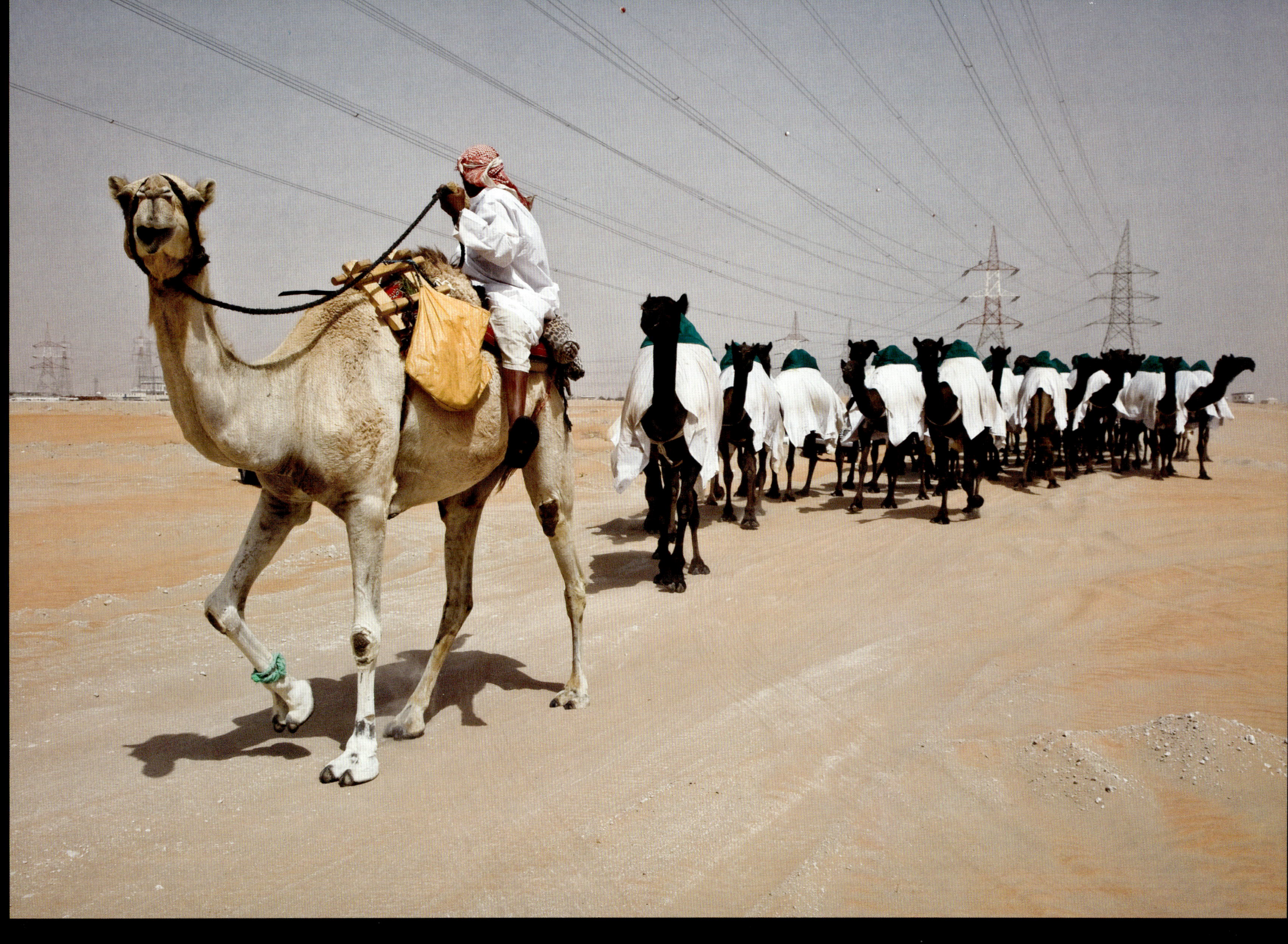

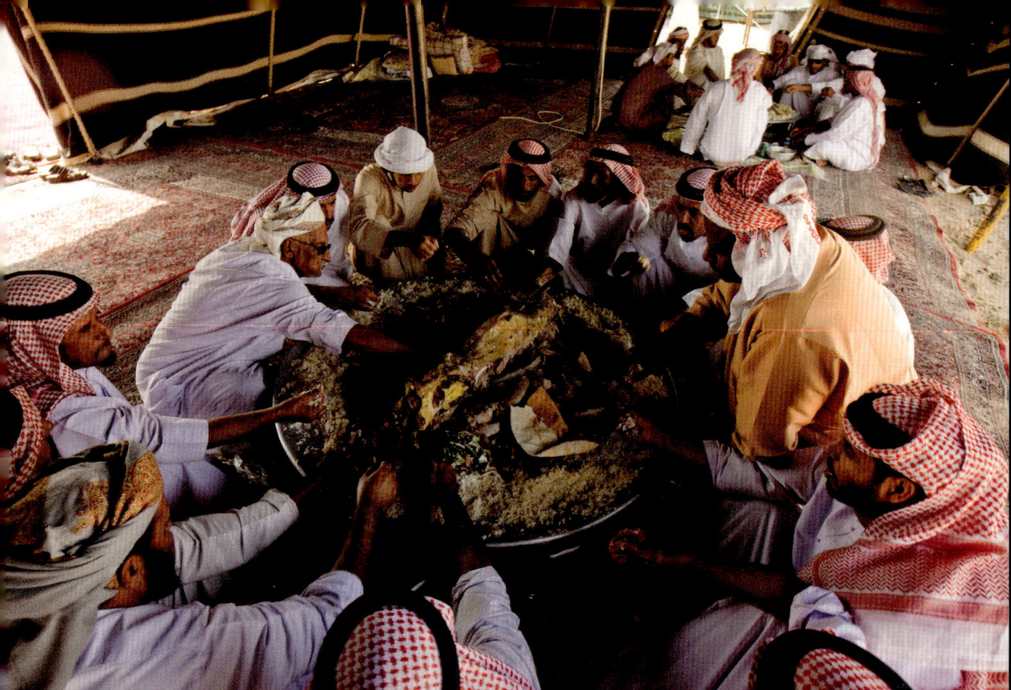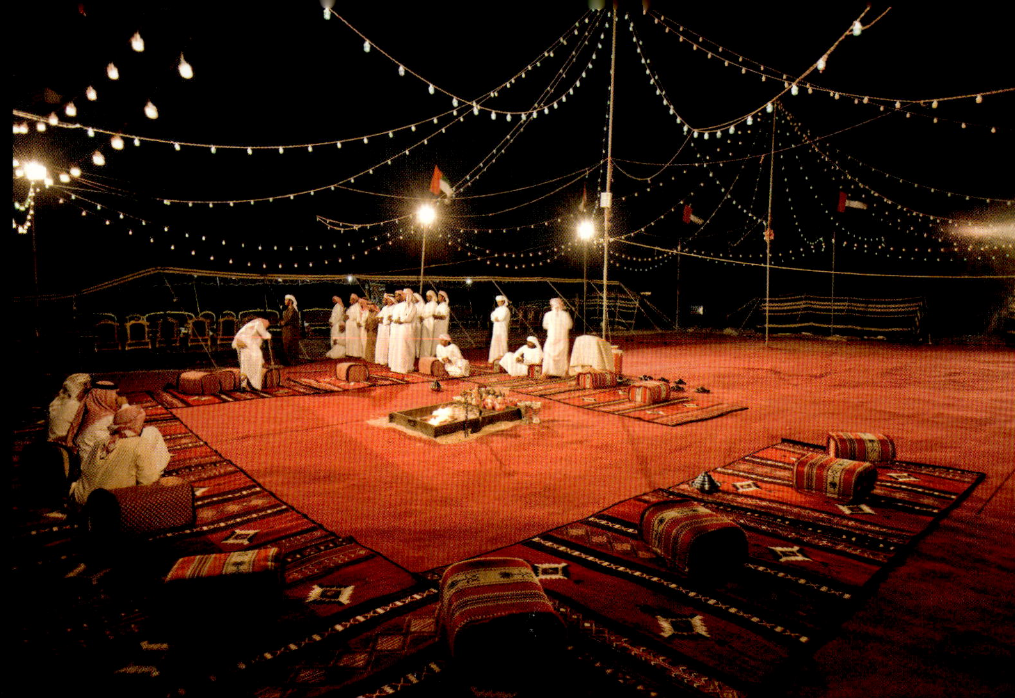

shade of his water truck. Sheikh Khaled proudly told us how the previous day he had been offered $1.3 million for one of his camels and had refused. Camels have long been a measure of a man's wealth in the Arab world, and Sheikh Khaled was a successful businessman in Abu Dhabi, which was floating on a rising tide of oil money at the time as the price of crude had just passed $110 a barrel. In 2008, the U.A.E., with only 900,000 citizens, produced 2.6 million barrels of oil per day, while Saudi Arabia, with twenty-two million citizens, produced 9.2 million barrels of oil per day. The result is that the U.A.E. had roughly seven times the oil income per capita of Saudi Arabia.

That afternoon we returned to the festival, which was admittedly difficult for a non-Arabic speaker to understand or appreciate. The spectators were ensconced in faux Louis XIV chairs, with red velvet upholstery and gilded wood, and gazed out at the camels, which were partly obscured by the forty-inch flat-screen TV monitors with "NO SIGNAL" flashing on them. The camels were brought out for judging a half dozen at a time and evaluated for how well they displayed the characteristics of their particular breed, the fullness of their hump, the shape of their face, and the droop of their lip. The crowd seemed a bit list-less, until the final round when winners were announced, and then it went wild with singing and dancing. I looked around for Sheikh Khaled, but he was not in the stands, and I suspected that the beauty contest for him was only a sideshow. It was a bit like having his own corporate hospitality tent at the Kentucky Derby, and with such a red-hot economy, there was lot of business to do. ⌂

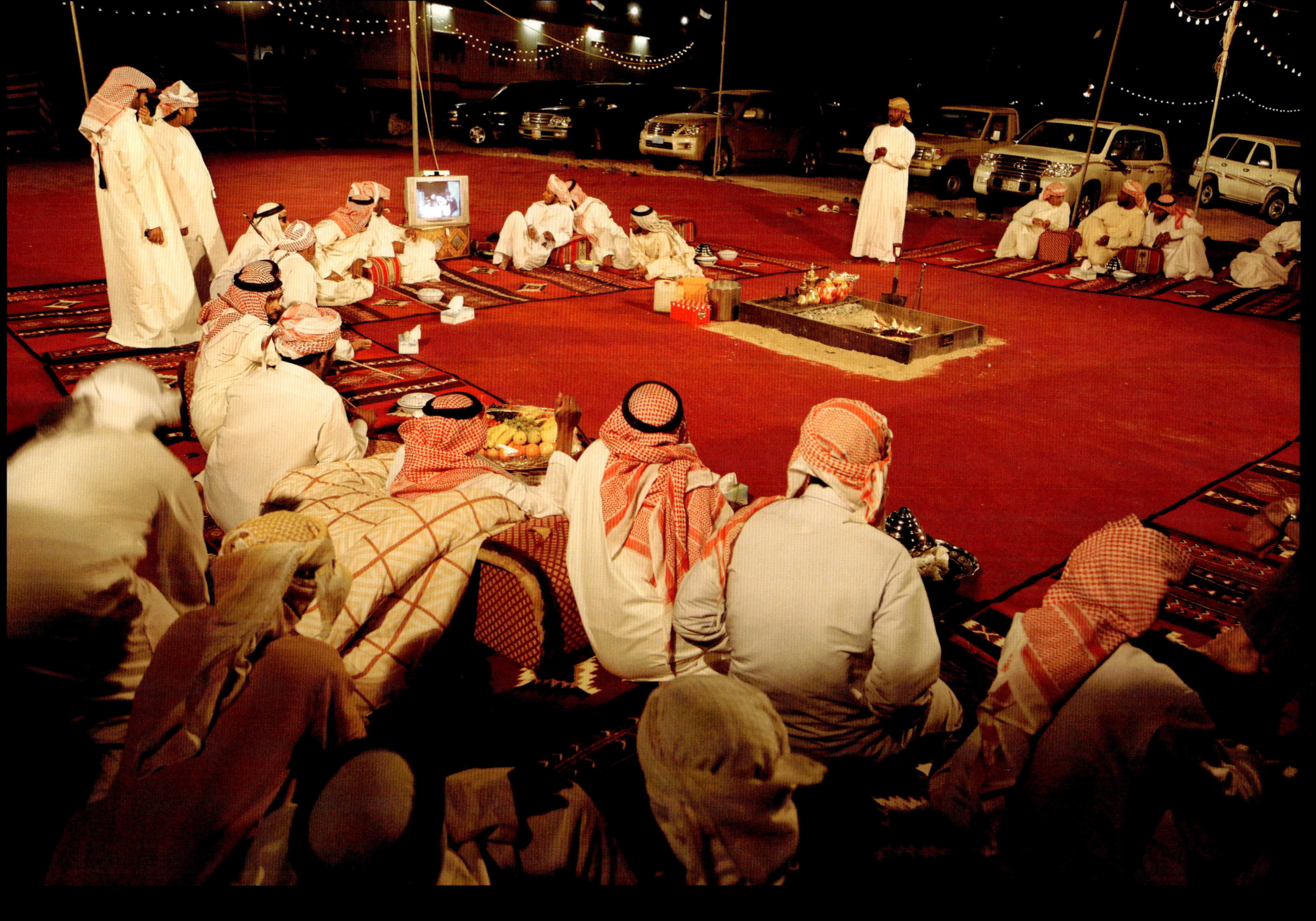

Waiting for dinner, Sheikh Khaled's camp, Madinat Zayed, U.A.E.

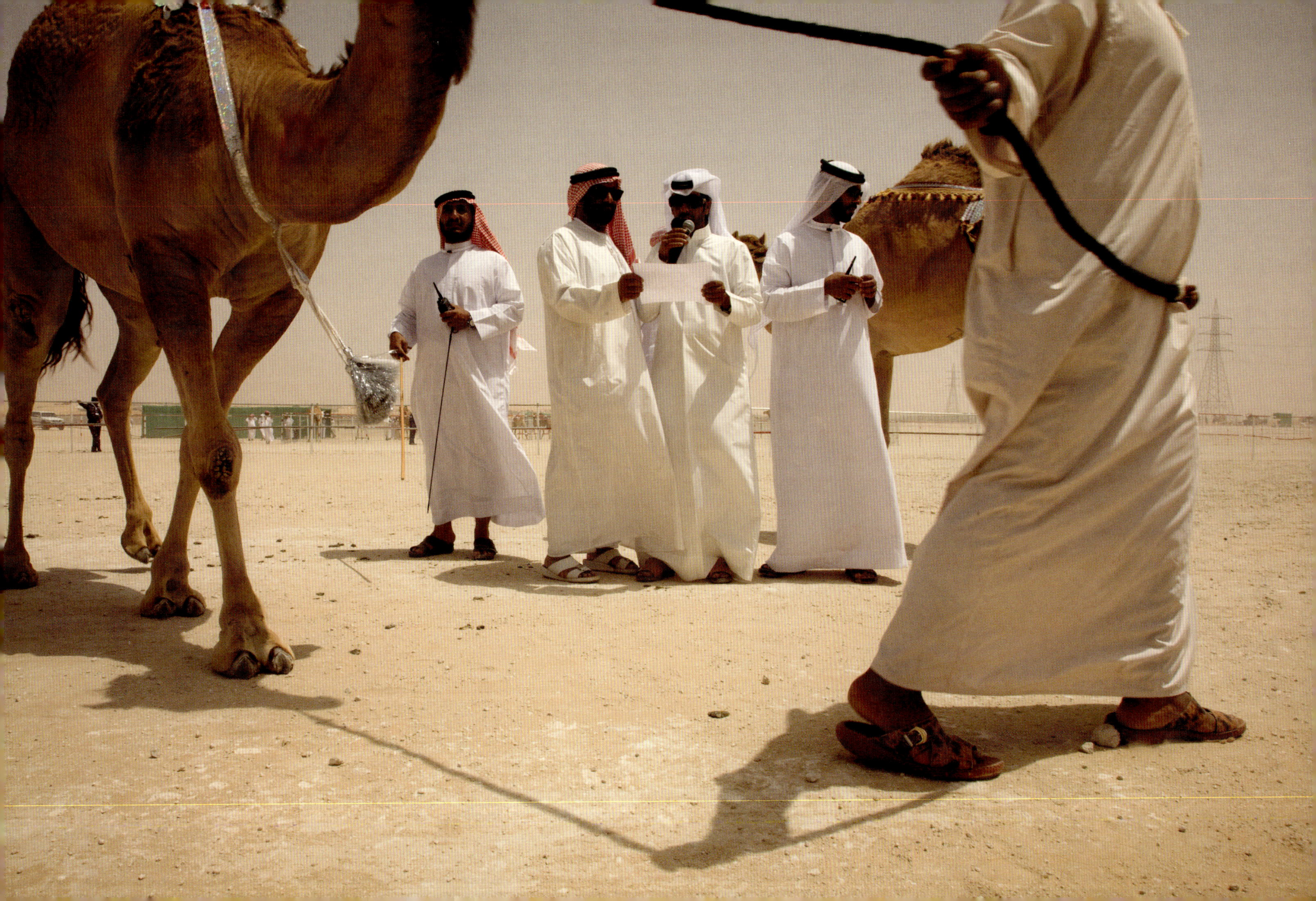

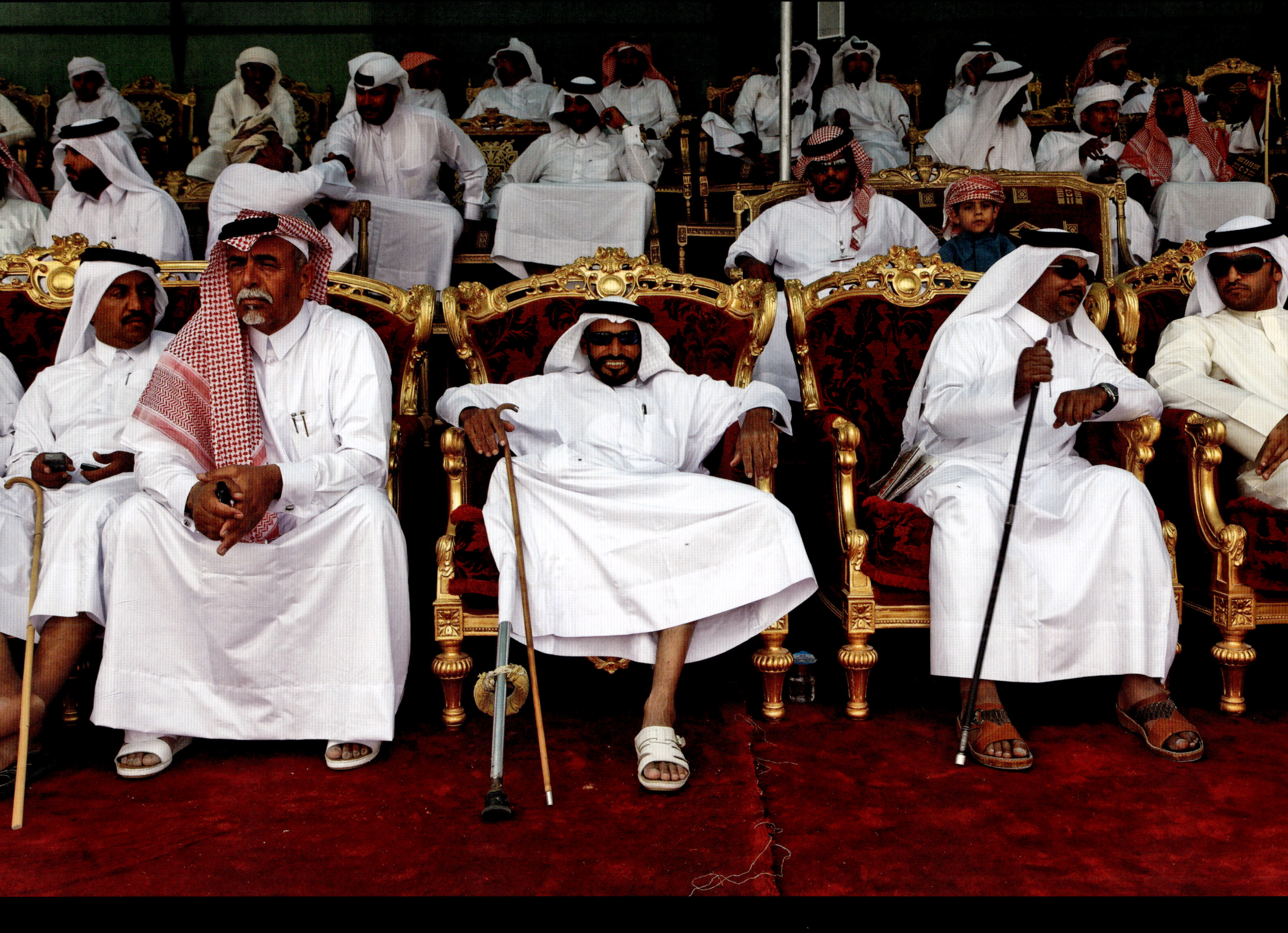

Sheikh Khaled bin Ternaf Al-Minhali (center) in reviewing stand, Madinat Zayed, U.A.E.

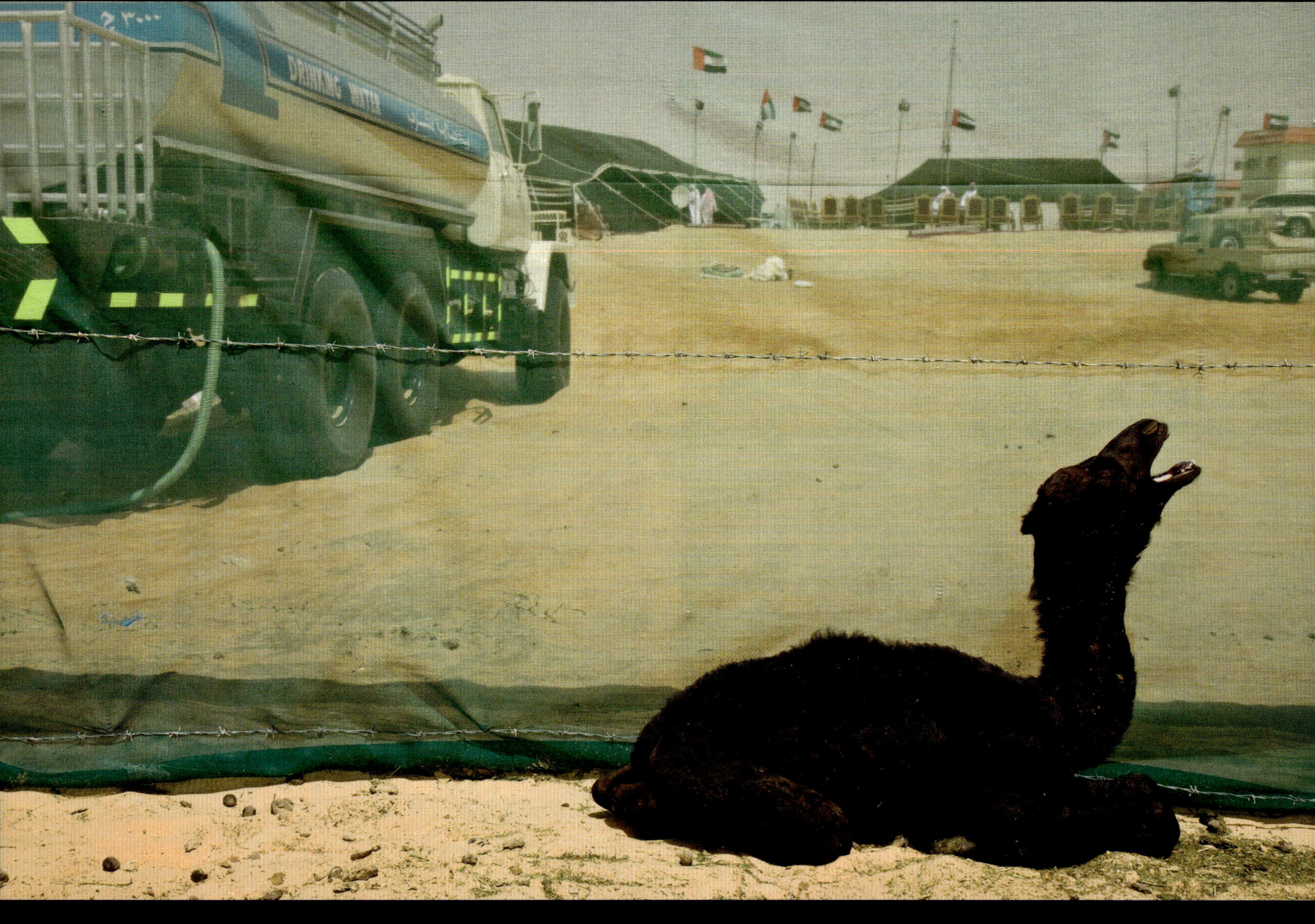

ABOVE: Baby camel in Sheikh Khaled's livestock enclosure, Madinat Zayed, U.A.E.
OPPOSITE: Encampment of participants at camel beauty contest, Madinat Zayed, U.A.E.
OVERLEAF: Camels from the U.A.E. grazing, Shaybah, Saudi Arabia

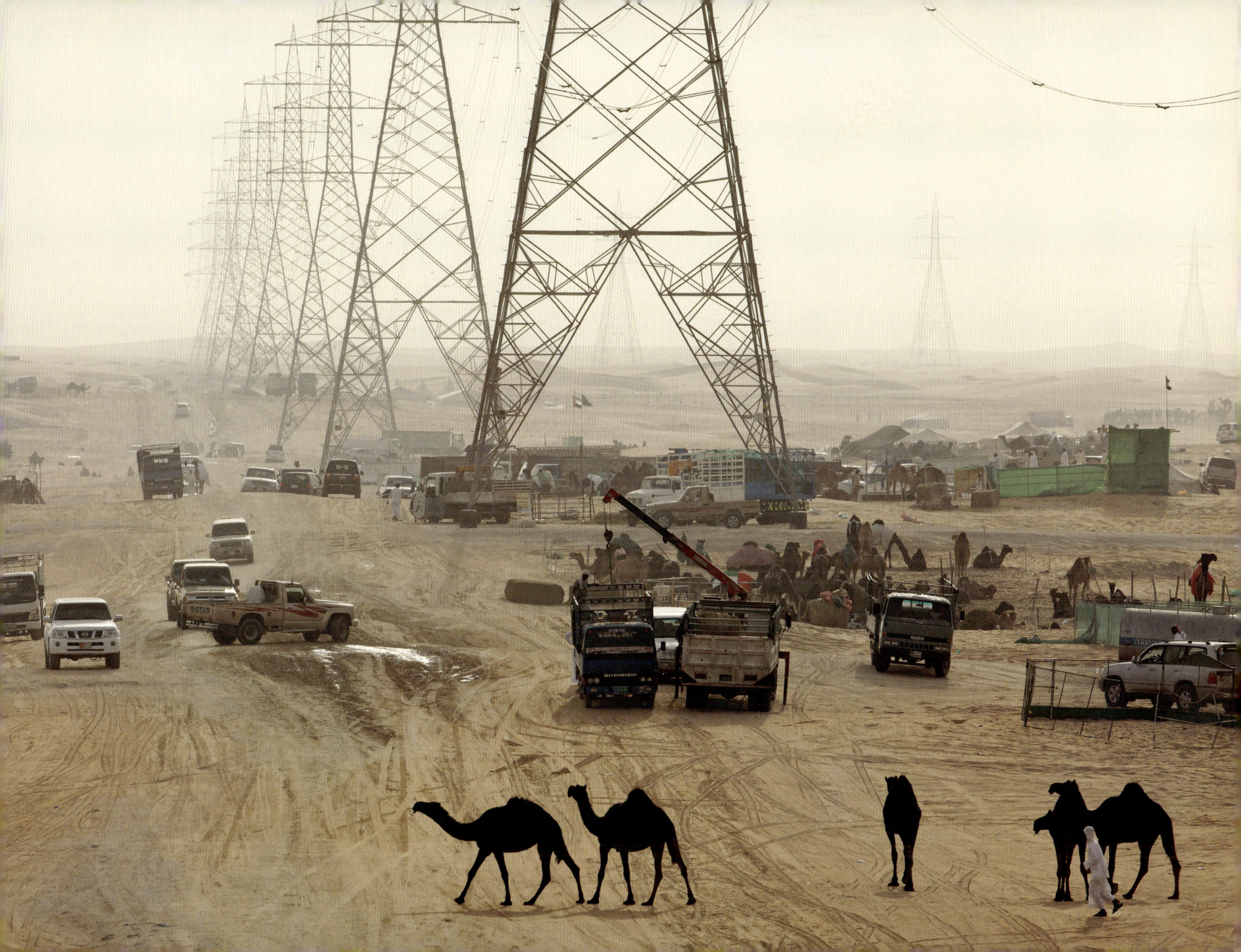

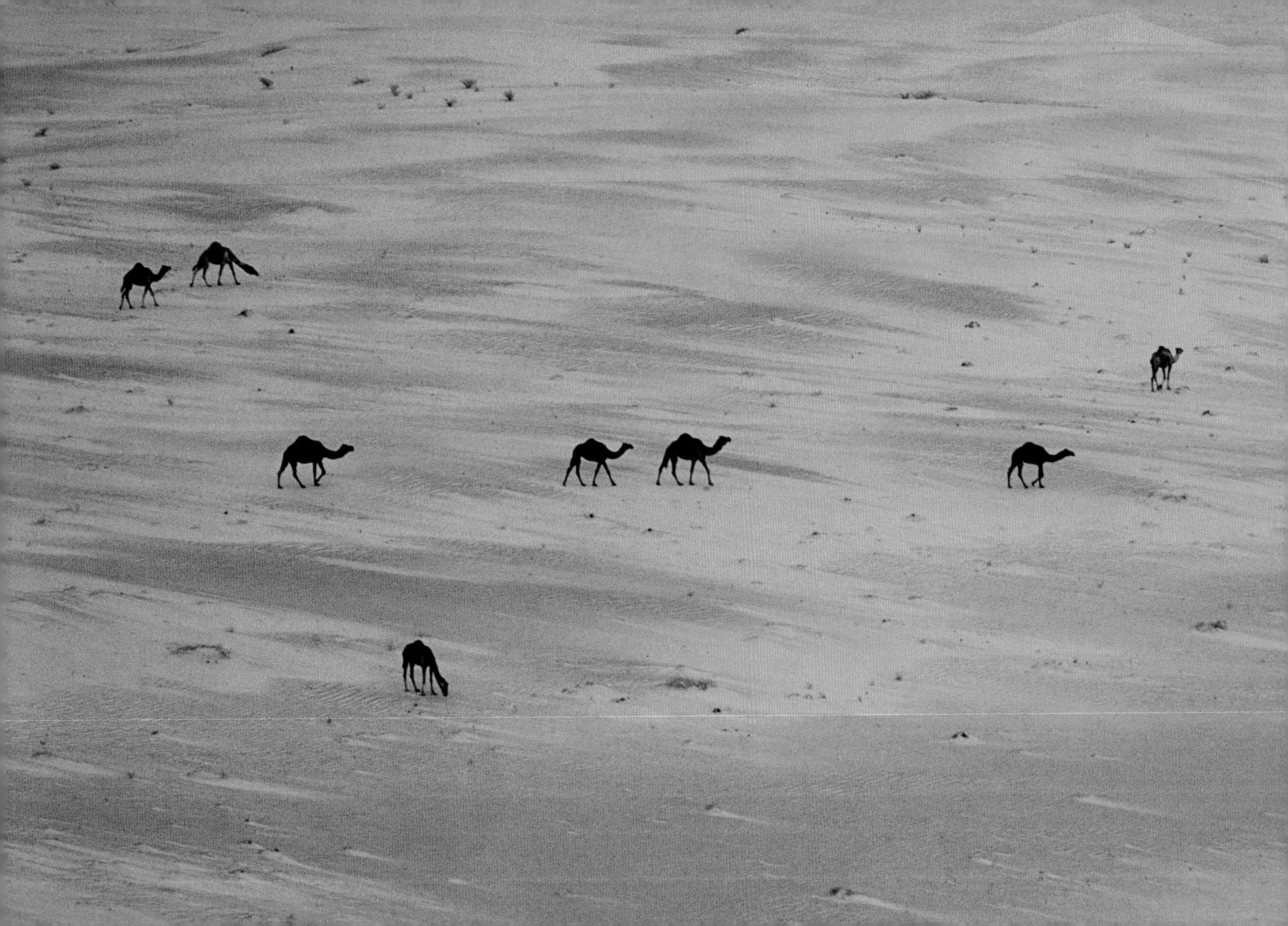

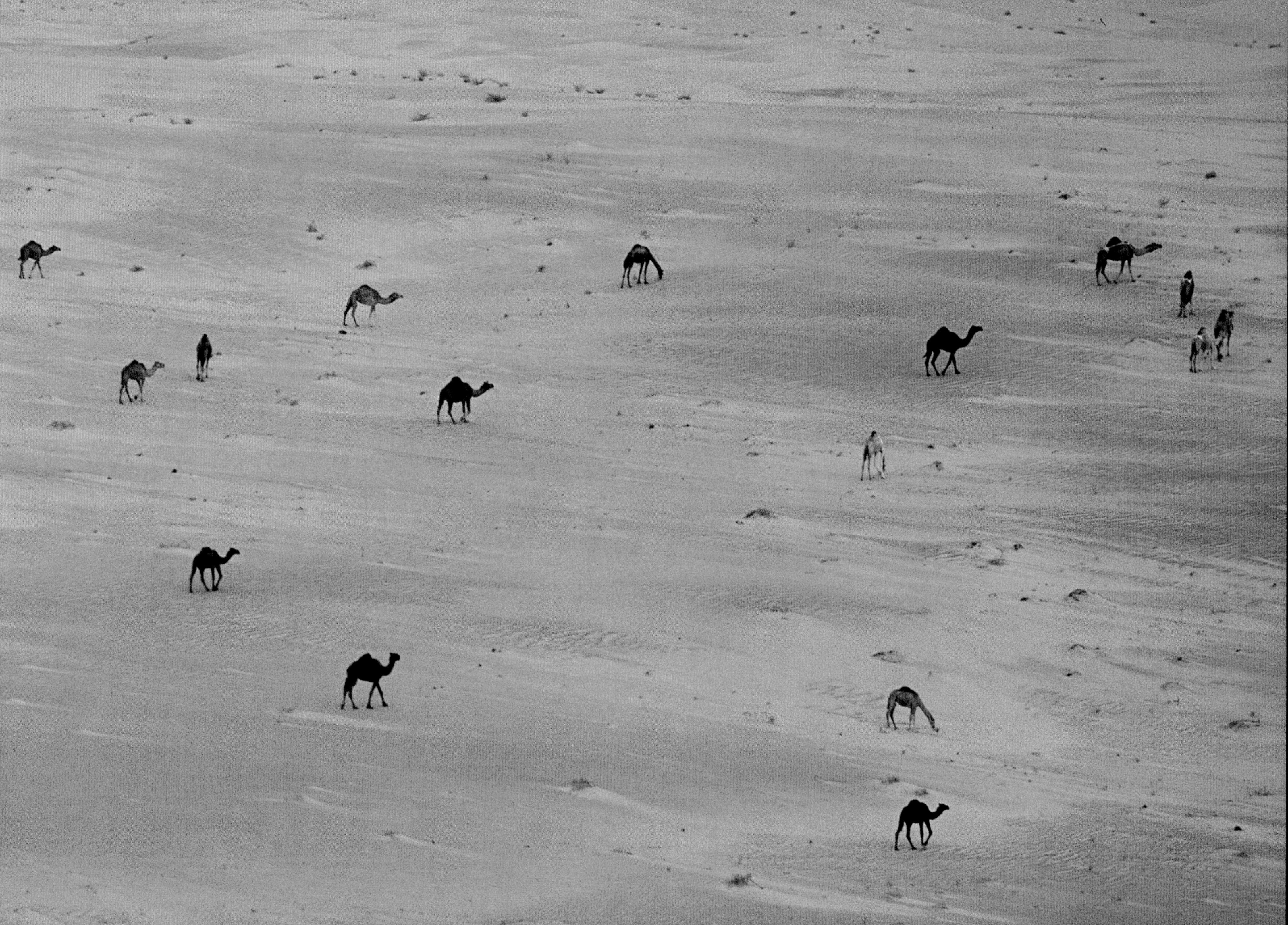

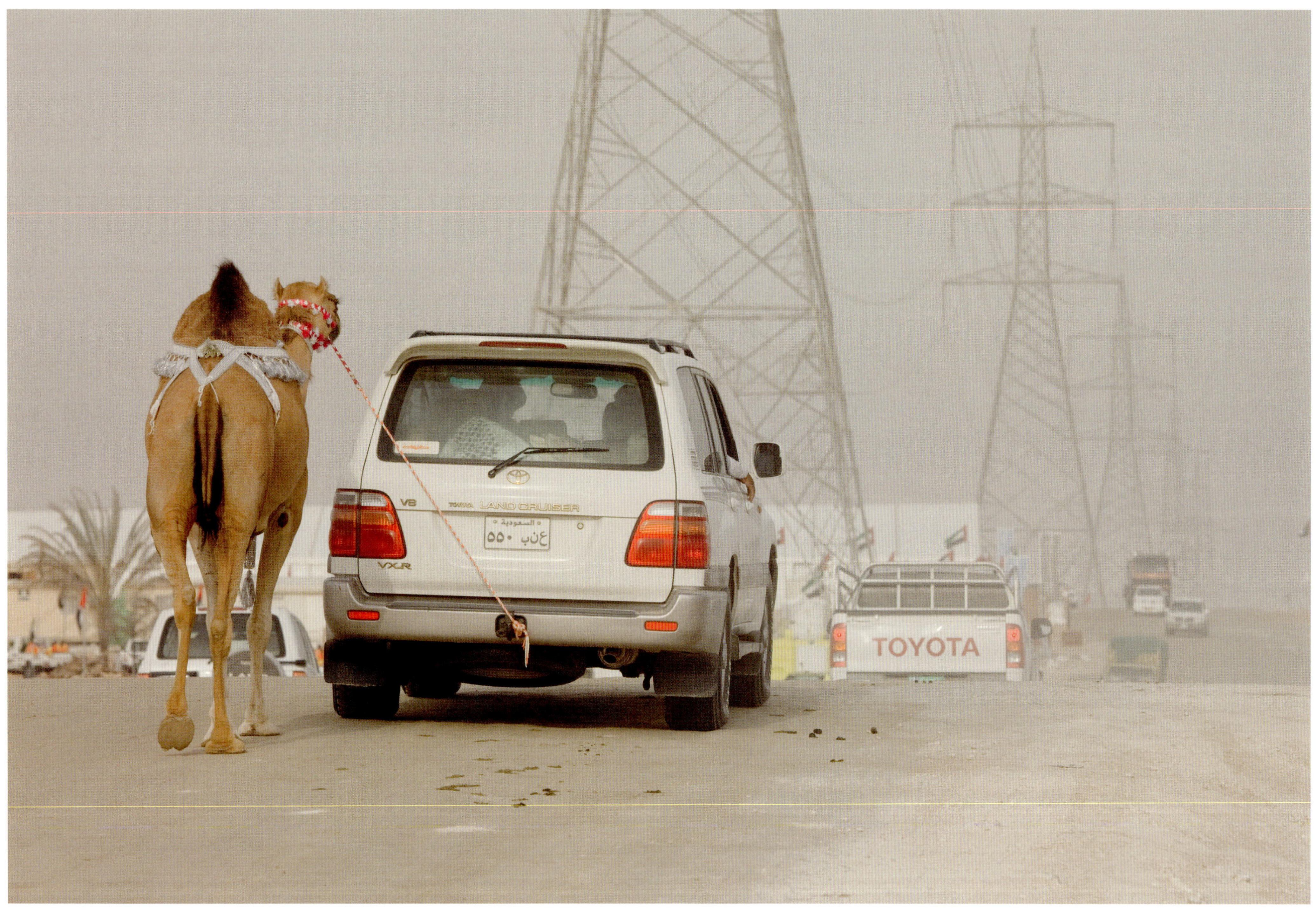

    Leaving camel beauty contest, Madinat Zayed, U.A.E.

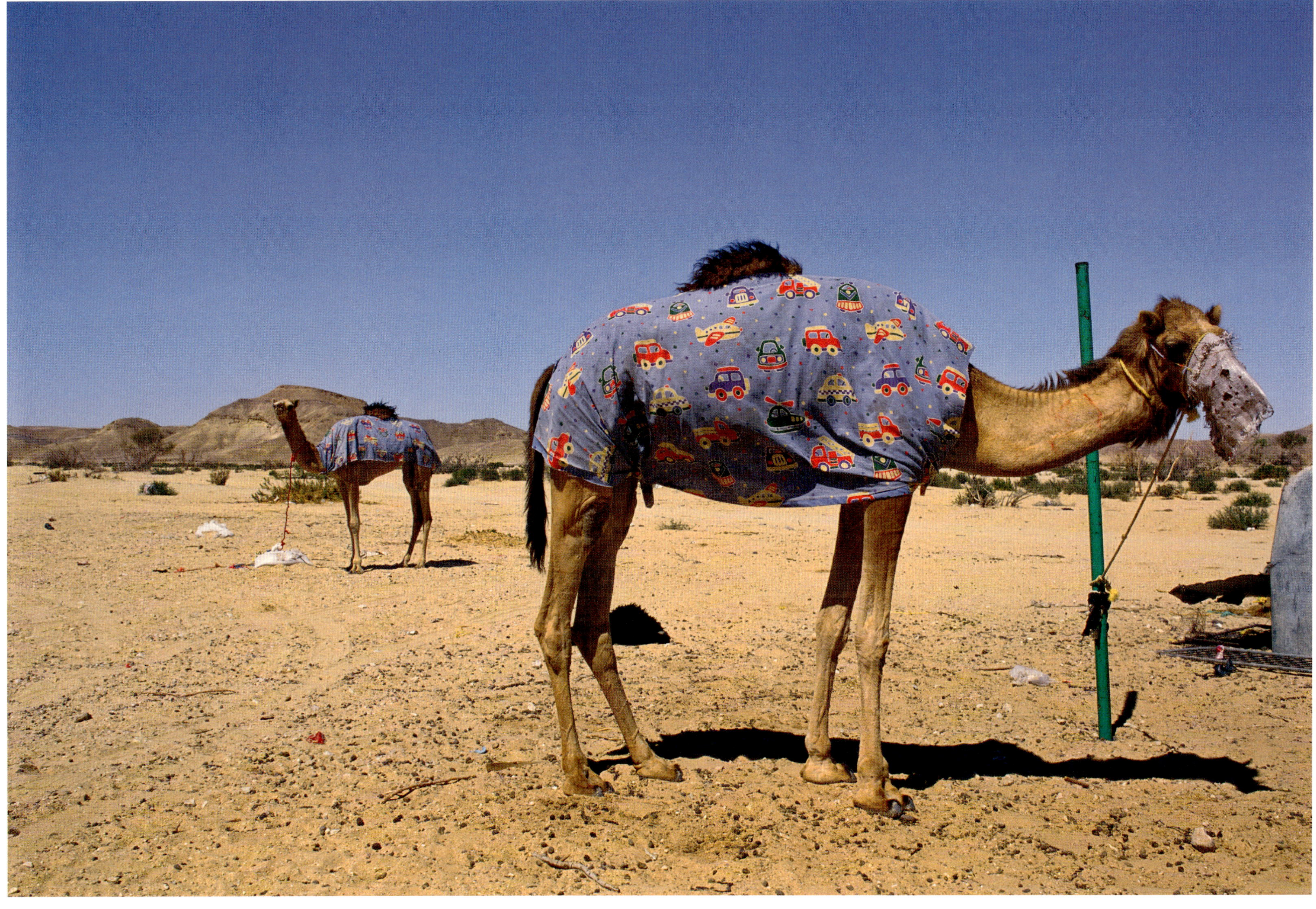

Wadi Shihan, Yemen

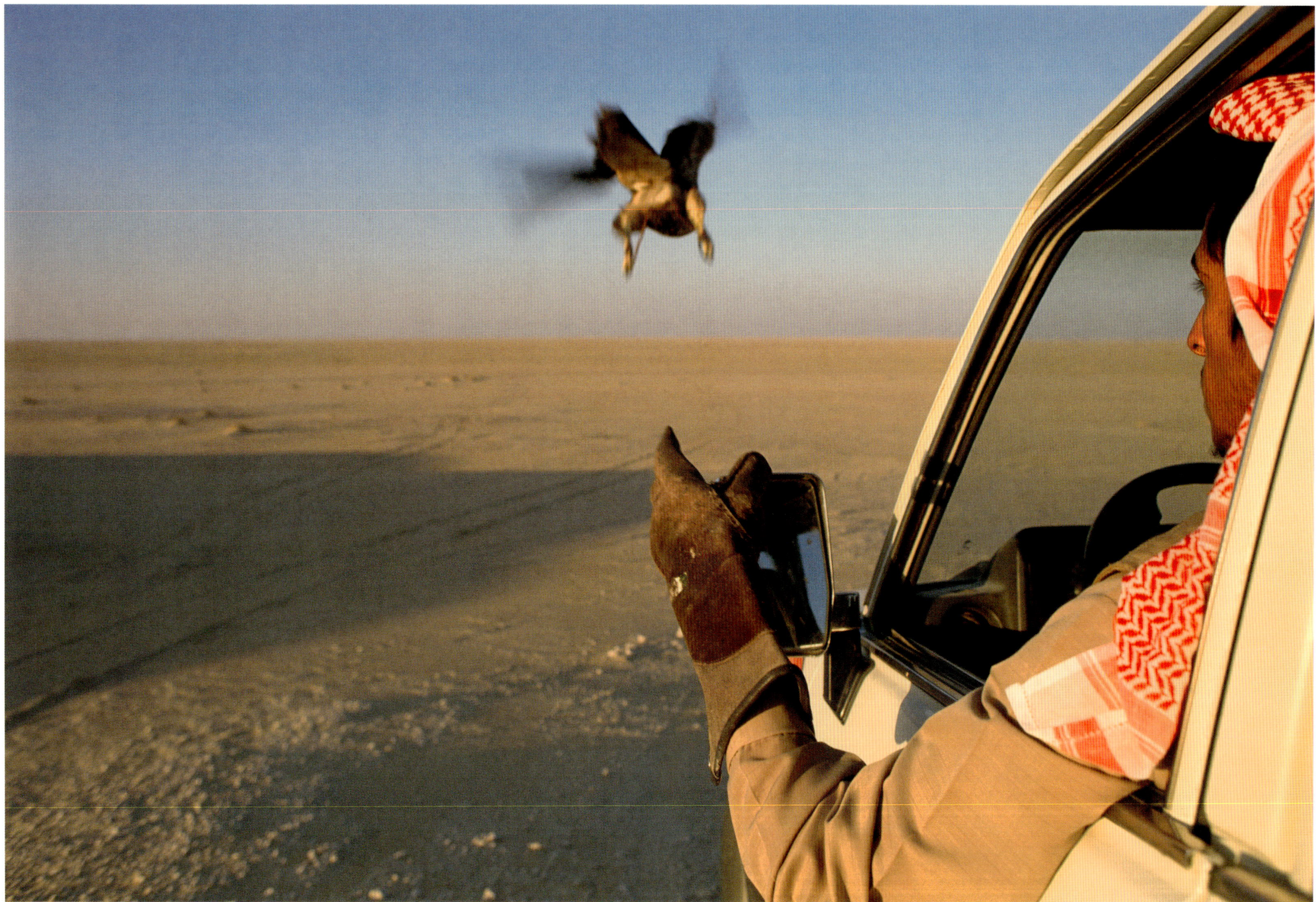

   Mohammed Hamad Al-Mari training his falcon, Yabrin, Saudi Arabia

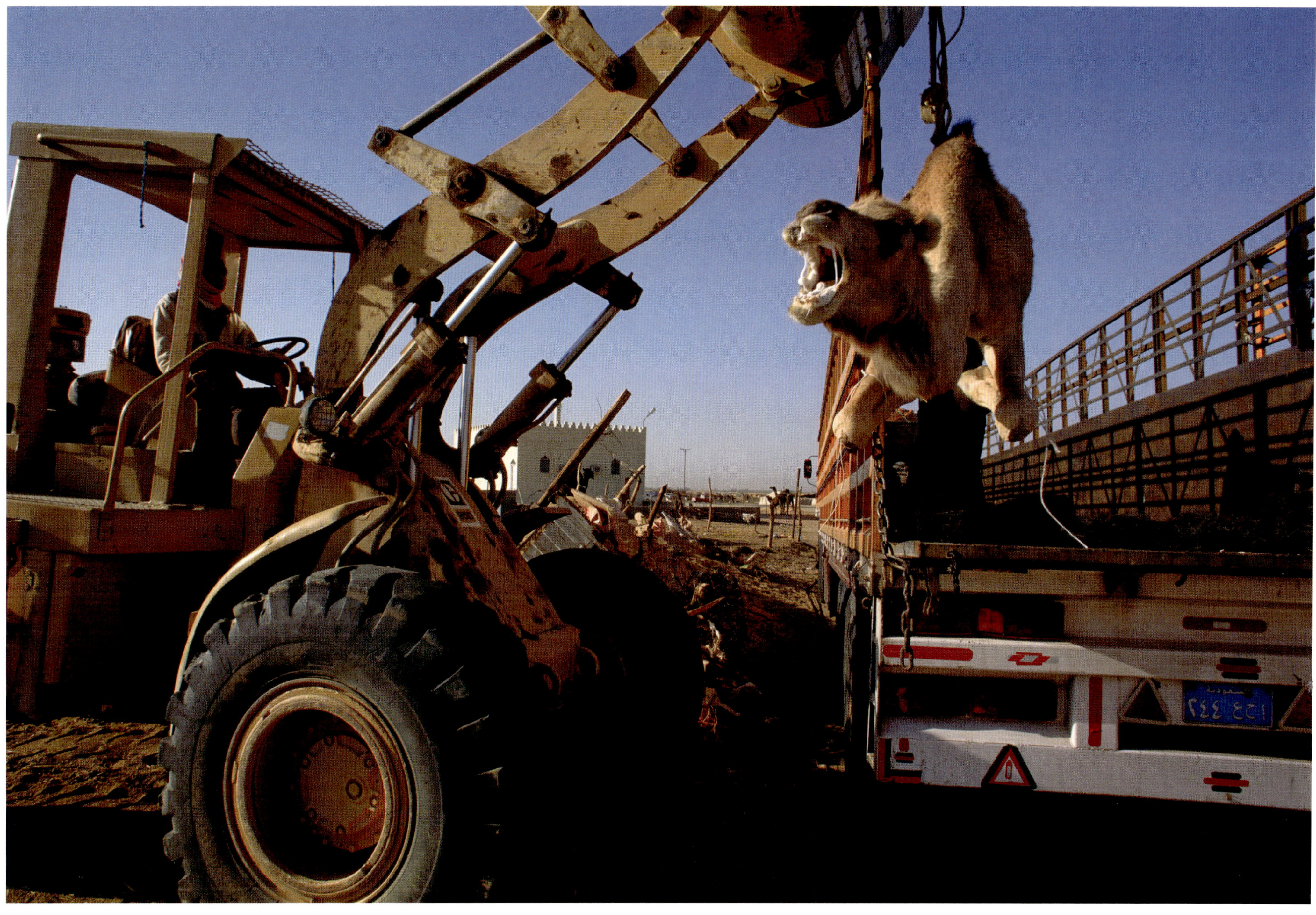

Camel being loaded for slaughter, Al-Khamasin, Saudi Arabia

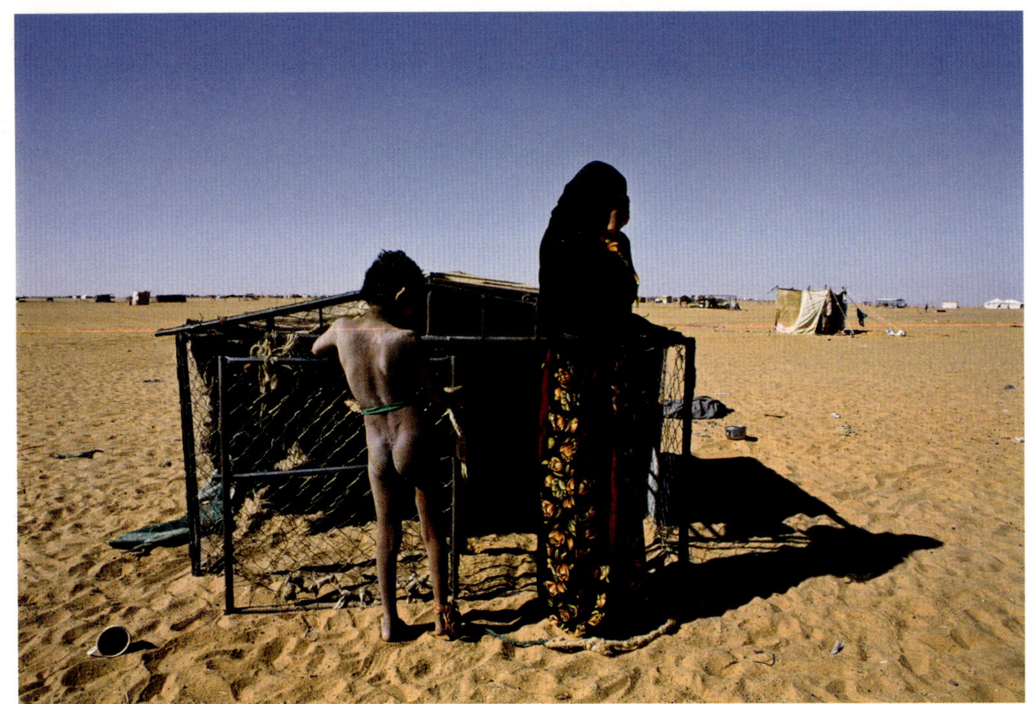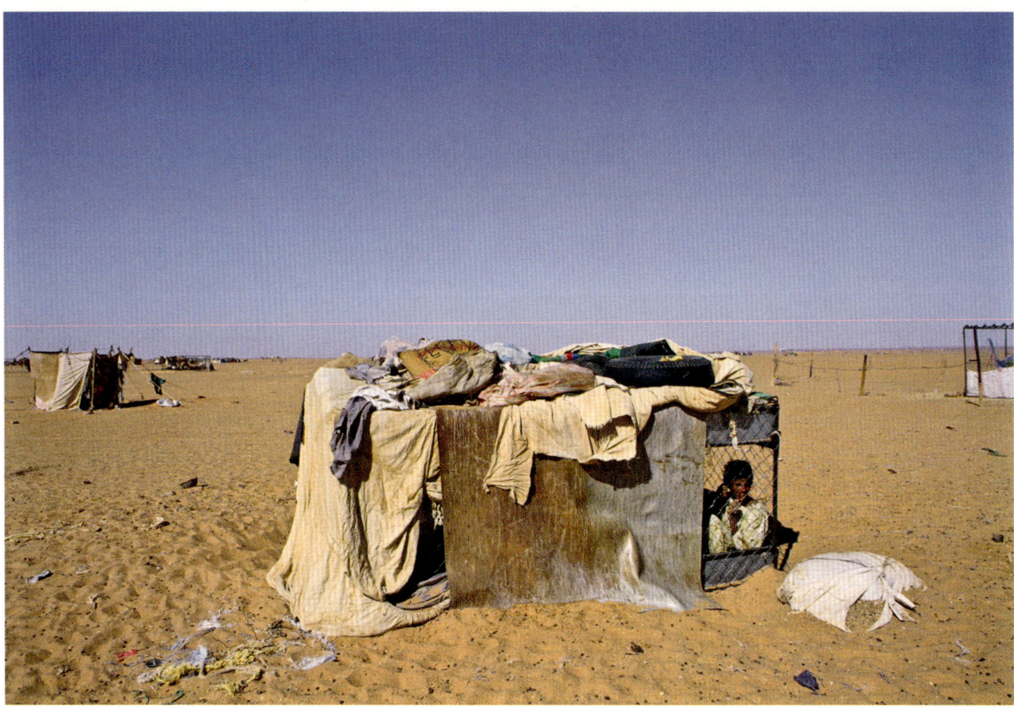

   ABOVE LEFT AND RIGHT: Handicapped children born to first cousins in Bedouin camp, Wuday'ah, Saudi Arabia

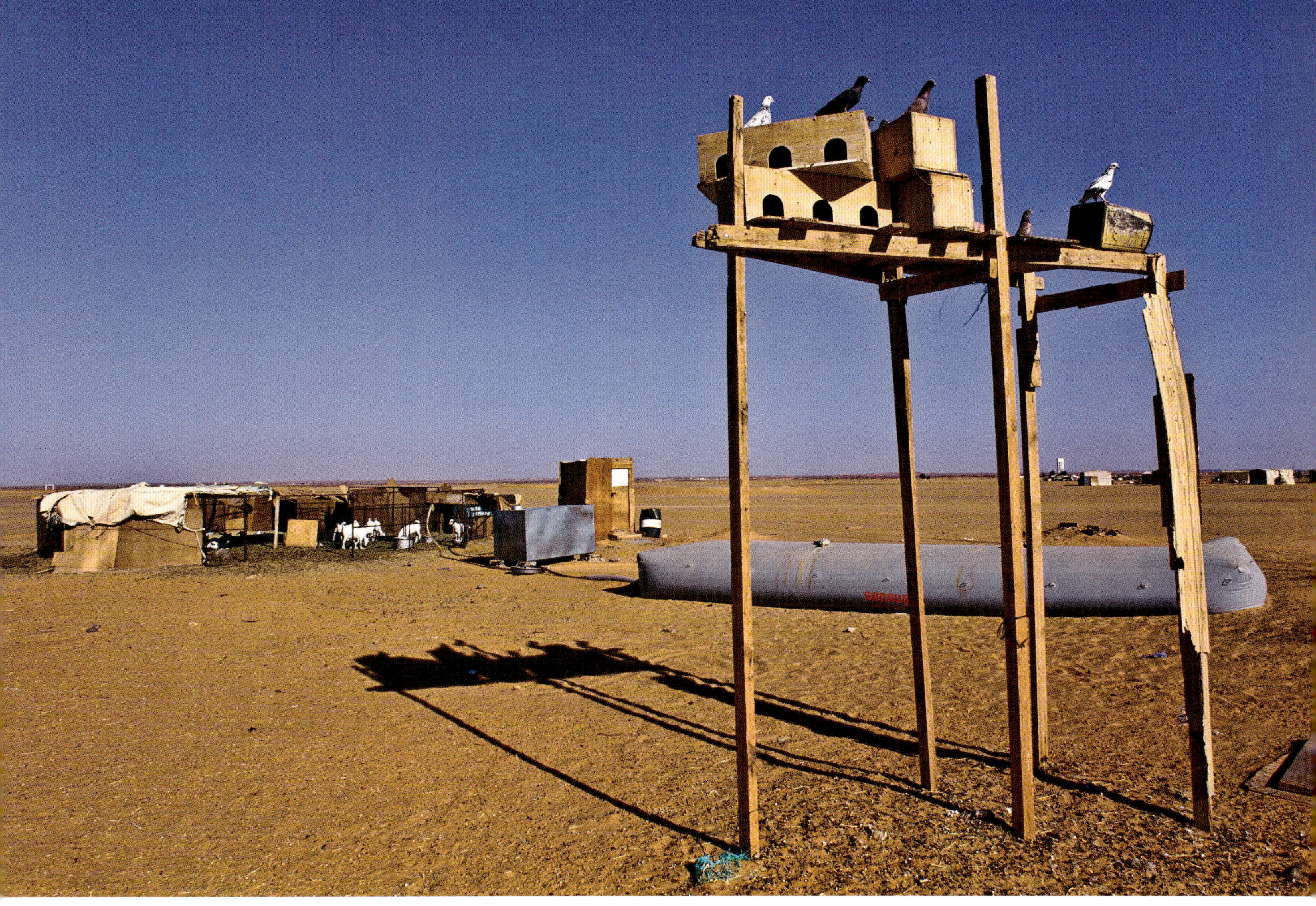

Pigeons in Bedouin camp, Wuday'ah, Saudi Arabia

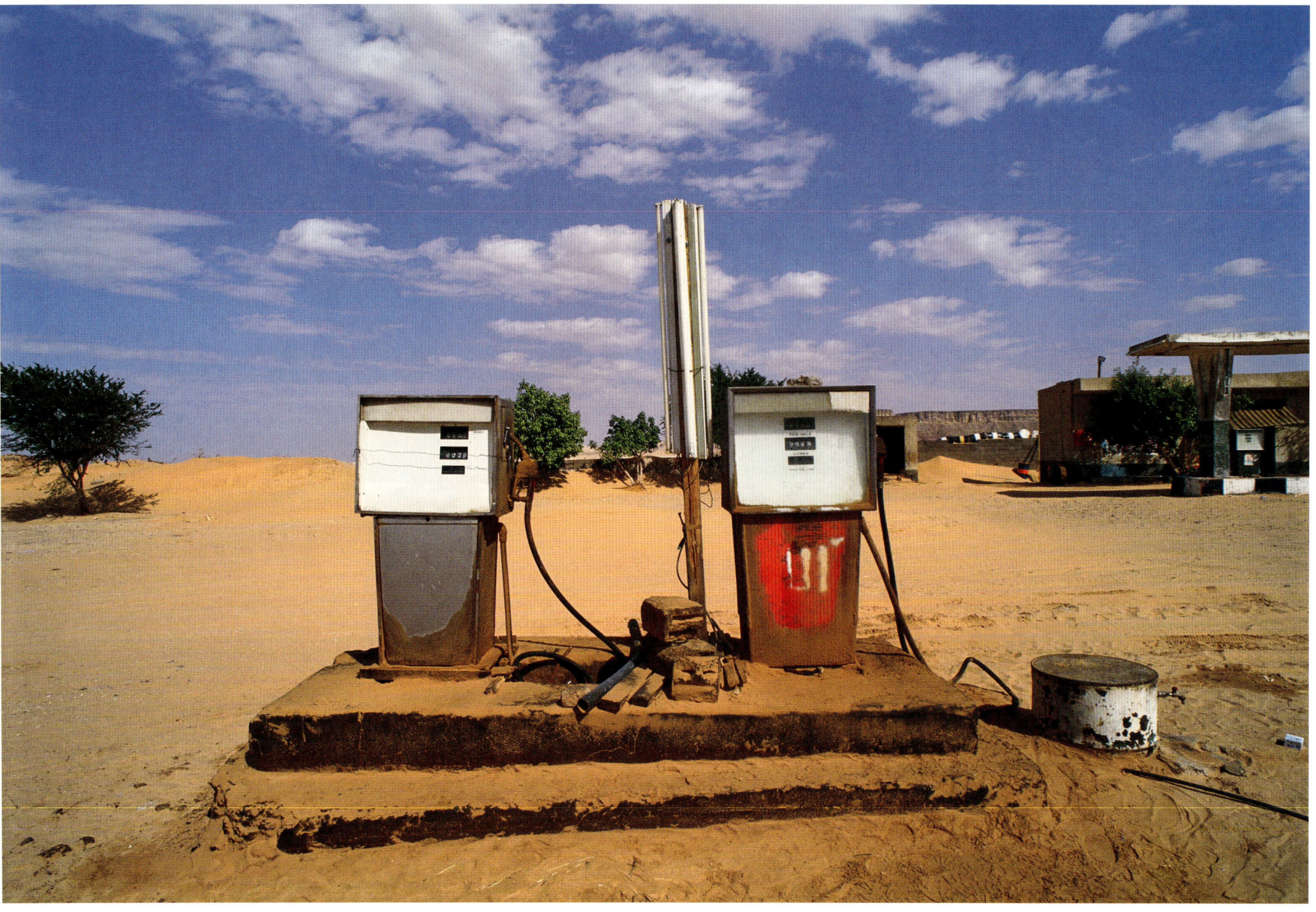

Broken fuel pumps, Qaryat al-Fau, Saudi Arabia

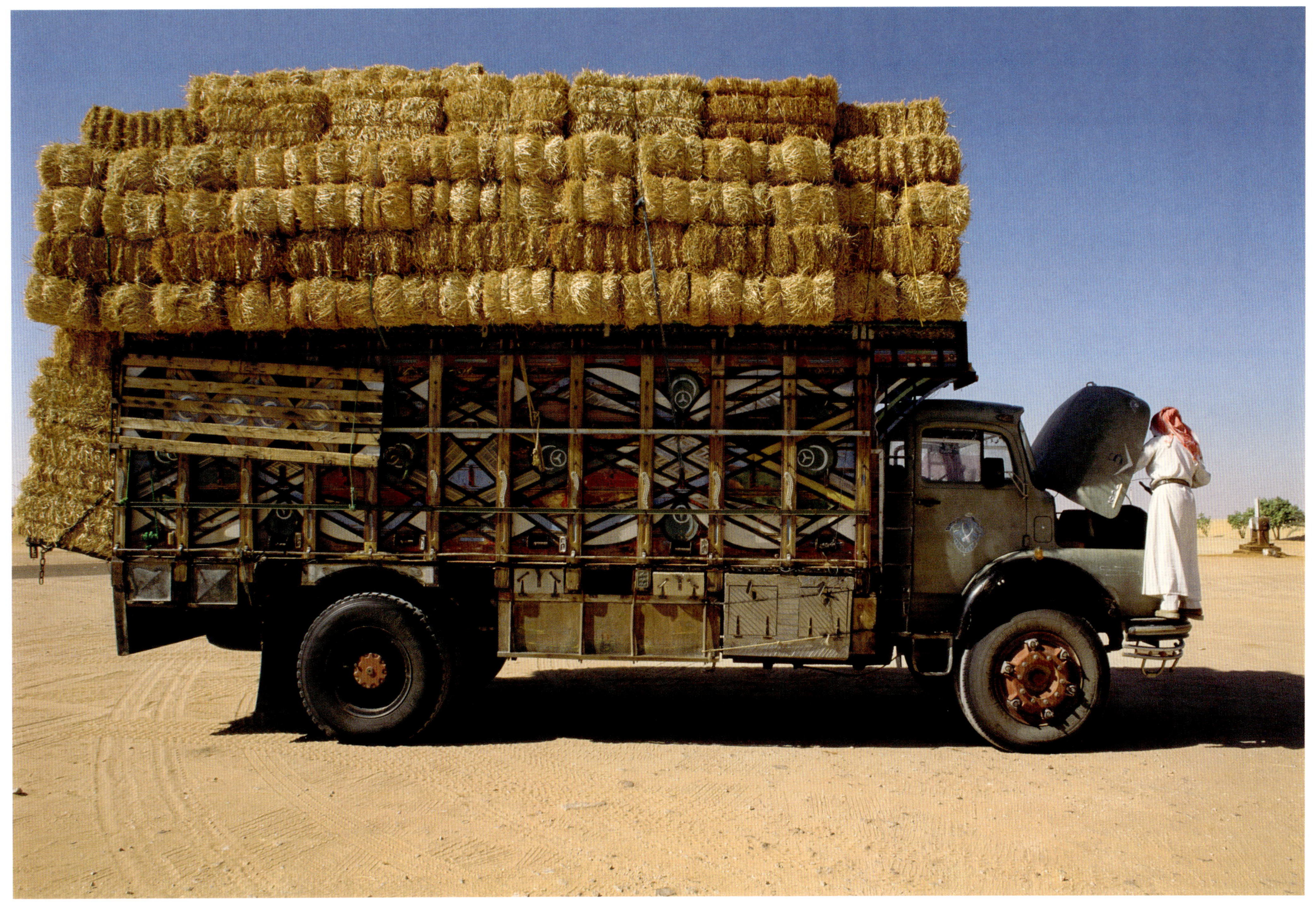

Fodder truck at fuel station, Qaryat al-Fau, Saudi Arabia

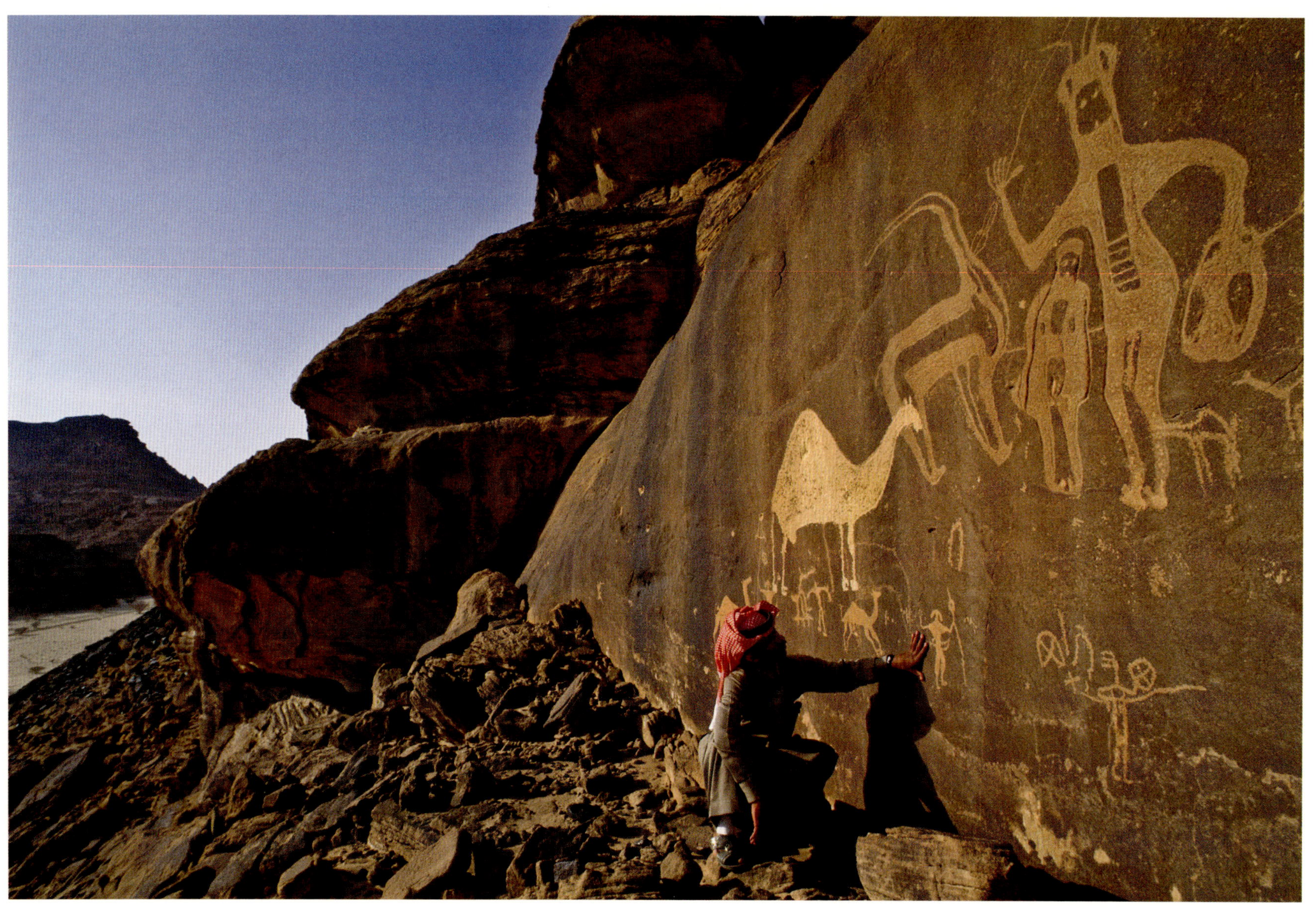

ABOVE: Bir Hima rock art, Saudi Arabia
OPPOSITE: Dot-formed barchan dunes, Ramlat Hazar, Yemen
OVERLEAF: Alain Arnoux after landing in seif dunes, Ramlat Butabul, Oman

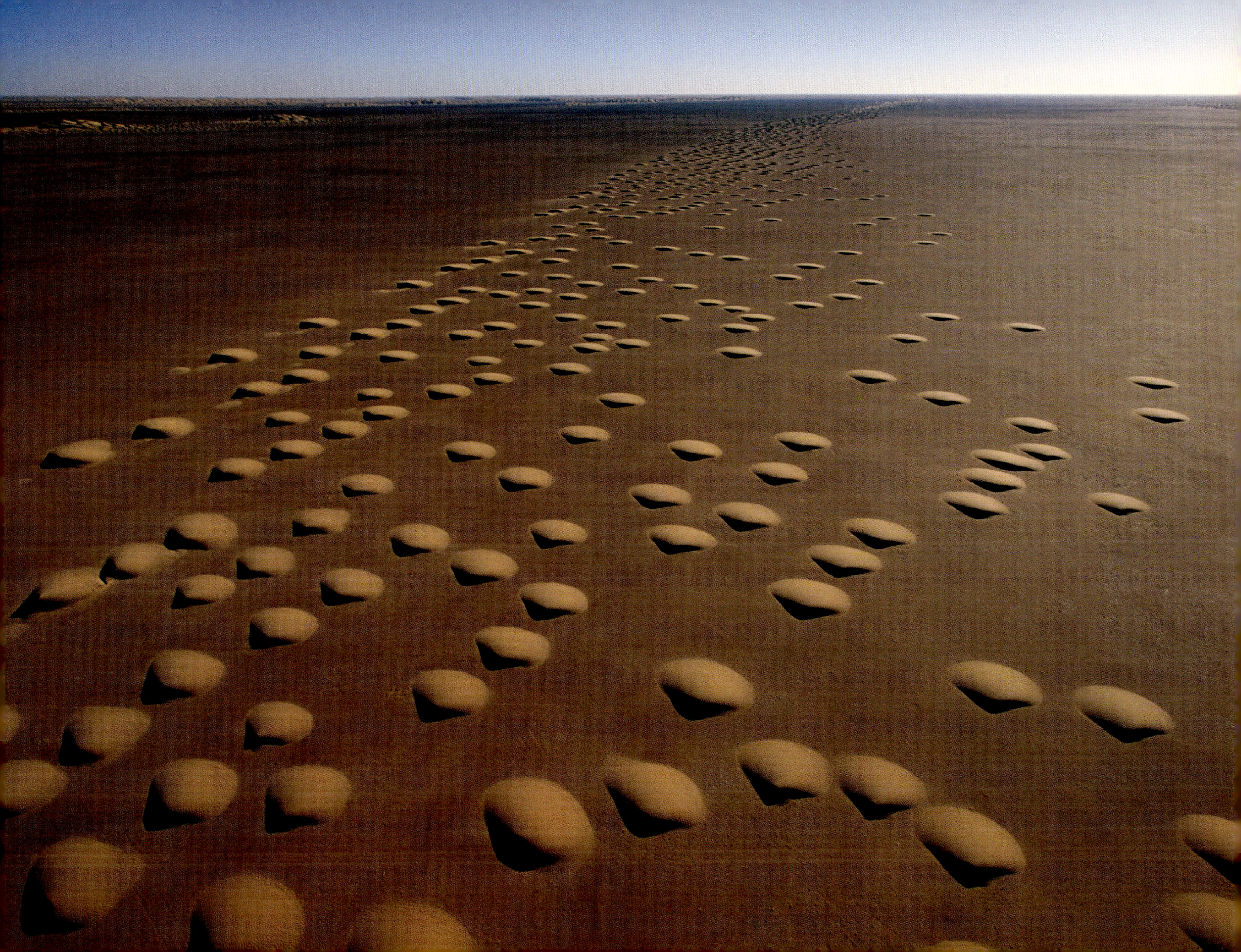

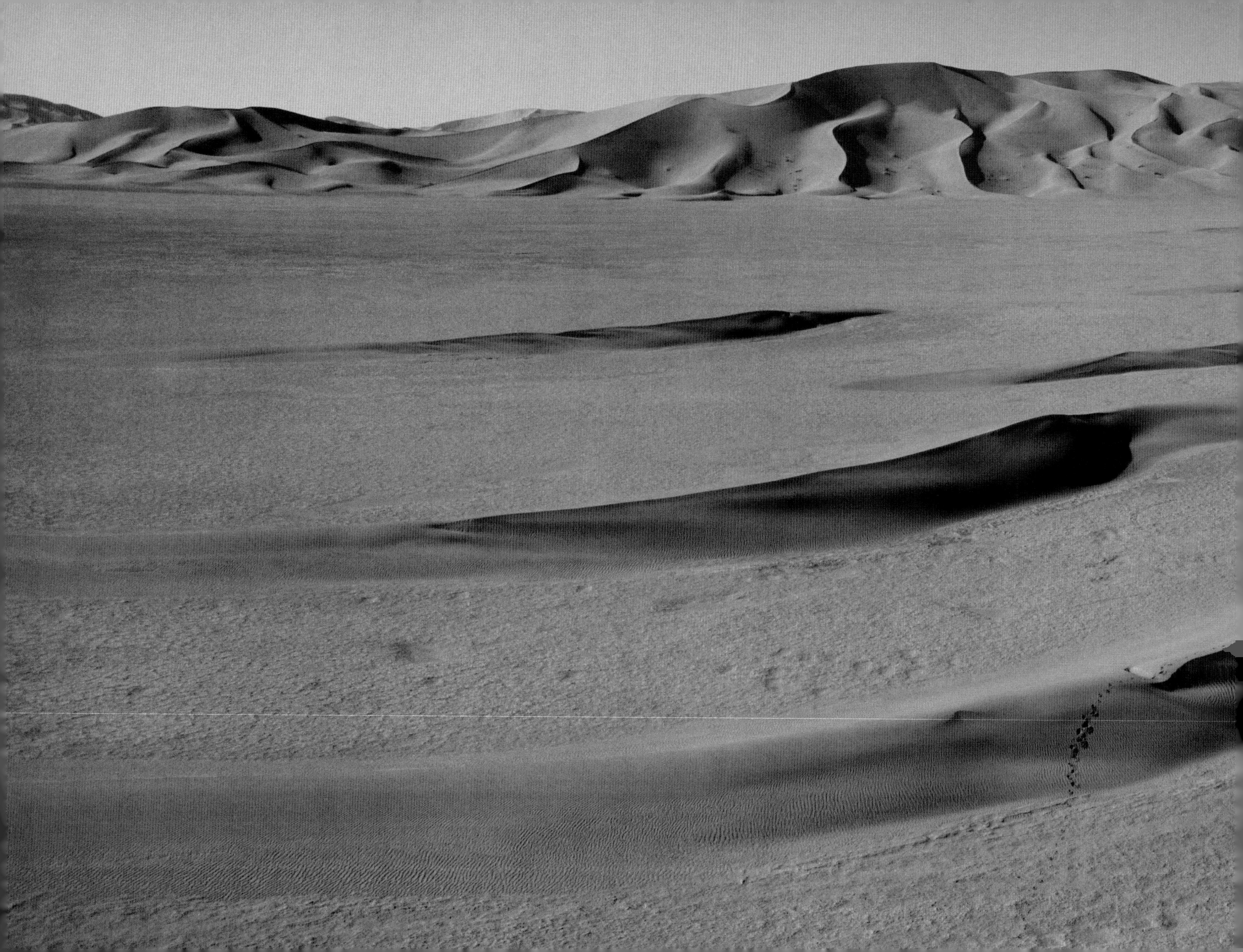

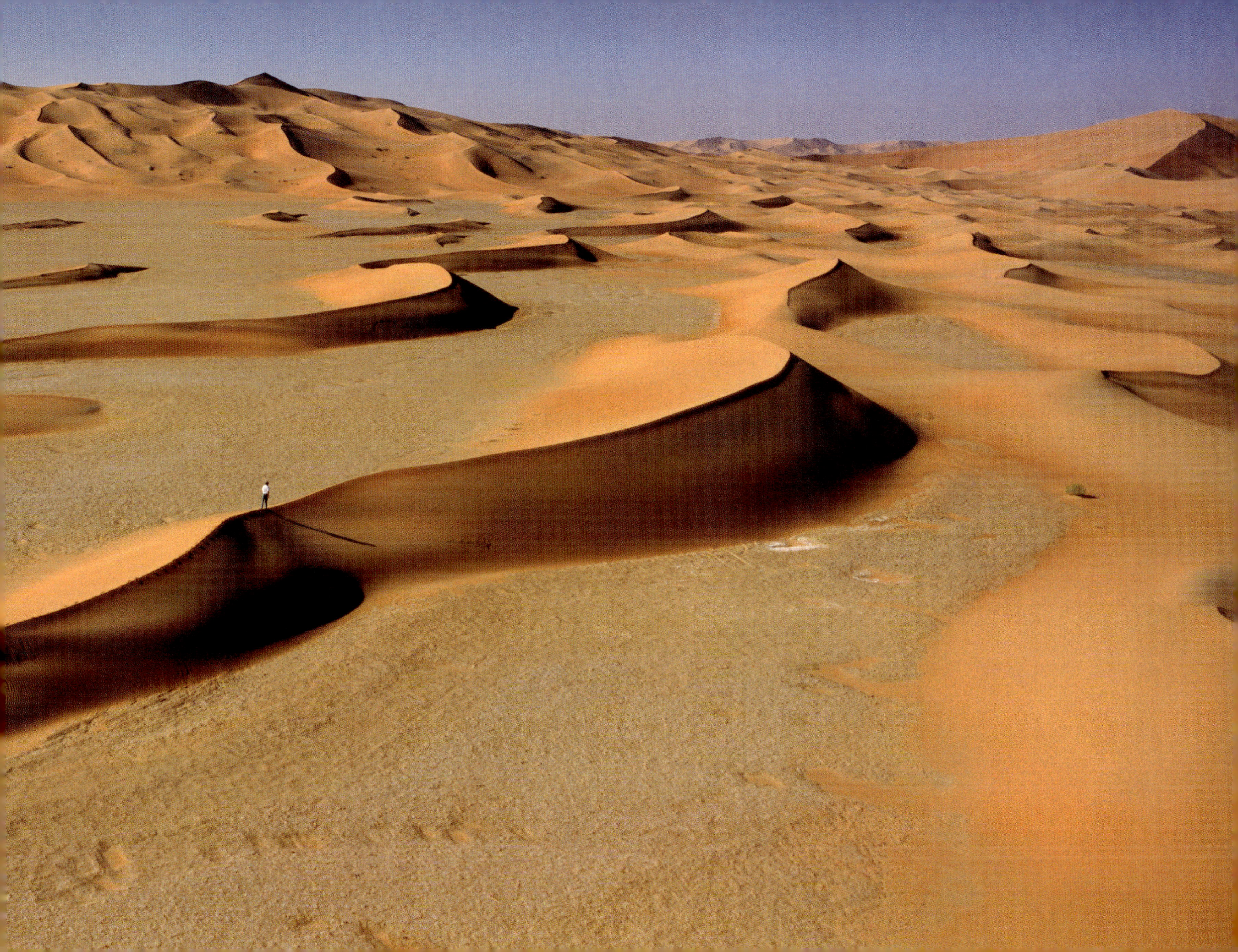

While preparing for my explorations of the Empty Quarter, I was particularly interested in what parts of the sands would be most spectacular to photograph from the air. In my research I had read about an effort in 1990 to discover the lost city of Ubar, the so-called Atlantis of the Sands, in what is now Oman. Ubar was a highland area that separated the Empty Quarter from the coast, and it was the world's primary source of frankincense from 2800 BCE to 300 CE. During that era, camel caravans took the aromatic tree sap all the way to Persia and Rome, where it was worth its weight in gold. According to the Koran, God destroyed Ubar in a mysterious and cataclysmic event, and archaeologists had spent decades searching for its trading centers. Ron Blom, a scientist working at NASA's Jet Propulsion Laboratory in California, had analyzed satellite imagery to find these ancient caravan routes, with the idea that the trails would converge on the missing cities of Ubar.

The Landsat Thematic Mapper data that Ron preferred to use in his research was a bit old, gathered in 1984, with a resolution of only one pixel per square measuring one hundred by one hundred feet, but it had recorded both visible and thermal infrared bands of radiation that were ignored by subsequent satellite systems with much higher resolution. The key advantage of the Landsat data is that the image information is collected in the reflective infrared, a slightly longer wavelength of light just beyond the visible, in which rocks and soils appear in sharper relief. To overcome the limited resolution, Landsat data was combined with the thirty-by-thirty-foot-resolution data from the French SPOT satellites. With such processing, Ron and his colleague Bob Crippen were able to find the tracks of camel caravans that plied the edges of the Empty Quarter over two thousand years ago. As Ron explained, "Your eye is tuned to finding the difference between blood and leaves, and the Landsat data is used for differentiating between rocks and soils." Ron assigned artificial colors to the varying wavelengths of light gathered by Landsat for the entire southeast edge of the sands, which had been traversed by the frankincense trade along caravan routes. The patterns he revealed were both beautiful and fascinating, but it was unclear how they would translate into reality on the ground or how they would look from the air in my paraglider. This was the most revealing method of surveying the remote sections of the Empty Quarter. Reds represent limestone, gypsum, or vegetation, yellow is usually sand, and blue indicates oxidized iron minerals (rust) or soils of abandoned agricultural areas.

The dune patterns that Ron's analysis revealed were magnificent, and showed me where to find the most unique forms. Late at night I would methodically scroll through these enormously large data files on my computer, as if crawling across a large carpet with a magnifying glass, looking for interesting landscapes. Before leaving for Saudi Arabia I made printouts of the most interesting sections, annotating areas of interest with latitude and longitude. When I got out into the field I was then able to compare the false colors of the satellite images with what I found on the ground, and they lead me to some amazing discoveries.

One of the biggest disappointments was the huge delta of Wadi Fasad near Shisur in Oman. On Ron's satellite images it looked like one of the larger rivers coming out of the Omani coastal mountains had created a string of emerald lakes scattered between the dunes. But two full days of driving revealed nothing but old clay flats covered in dreary sheets of khaki sand. But a week later, while exploring the delta of Wadi Hazar in Yemen, I noticed chains of small dot-shaped dunes with strange little tails. They were very finely detailed, and hard to make out with only one pixel per one-hundred-by-one-hundred-foot square. We arrived out on the plains in the dark with low expectations, but when I took off at sunrise I discovered chains of the most surreal dot-shaped barchan dunes that looked like they were the spawning emissaries of enormous jellyfish dunes. I have never seen anything like it before or since.

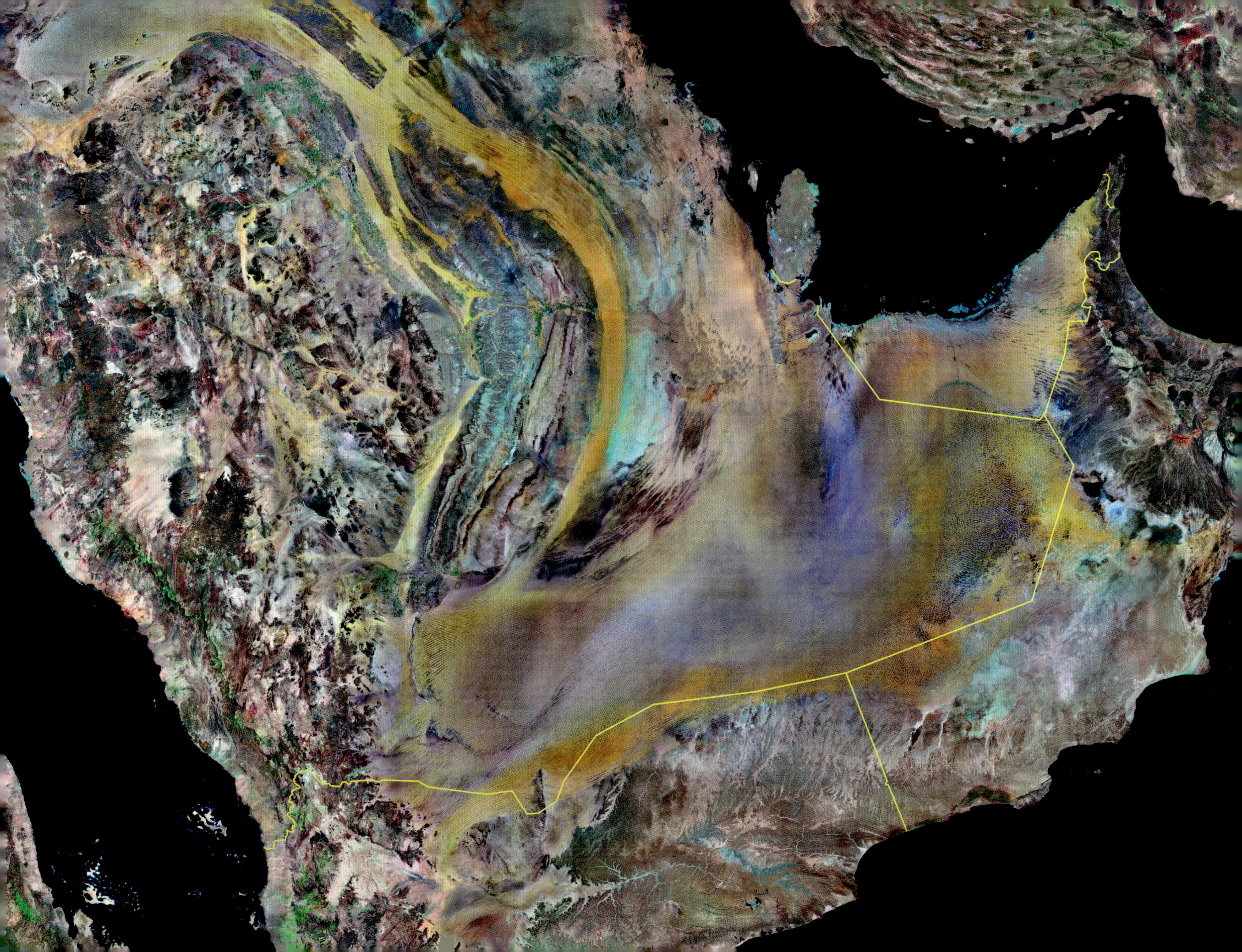

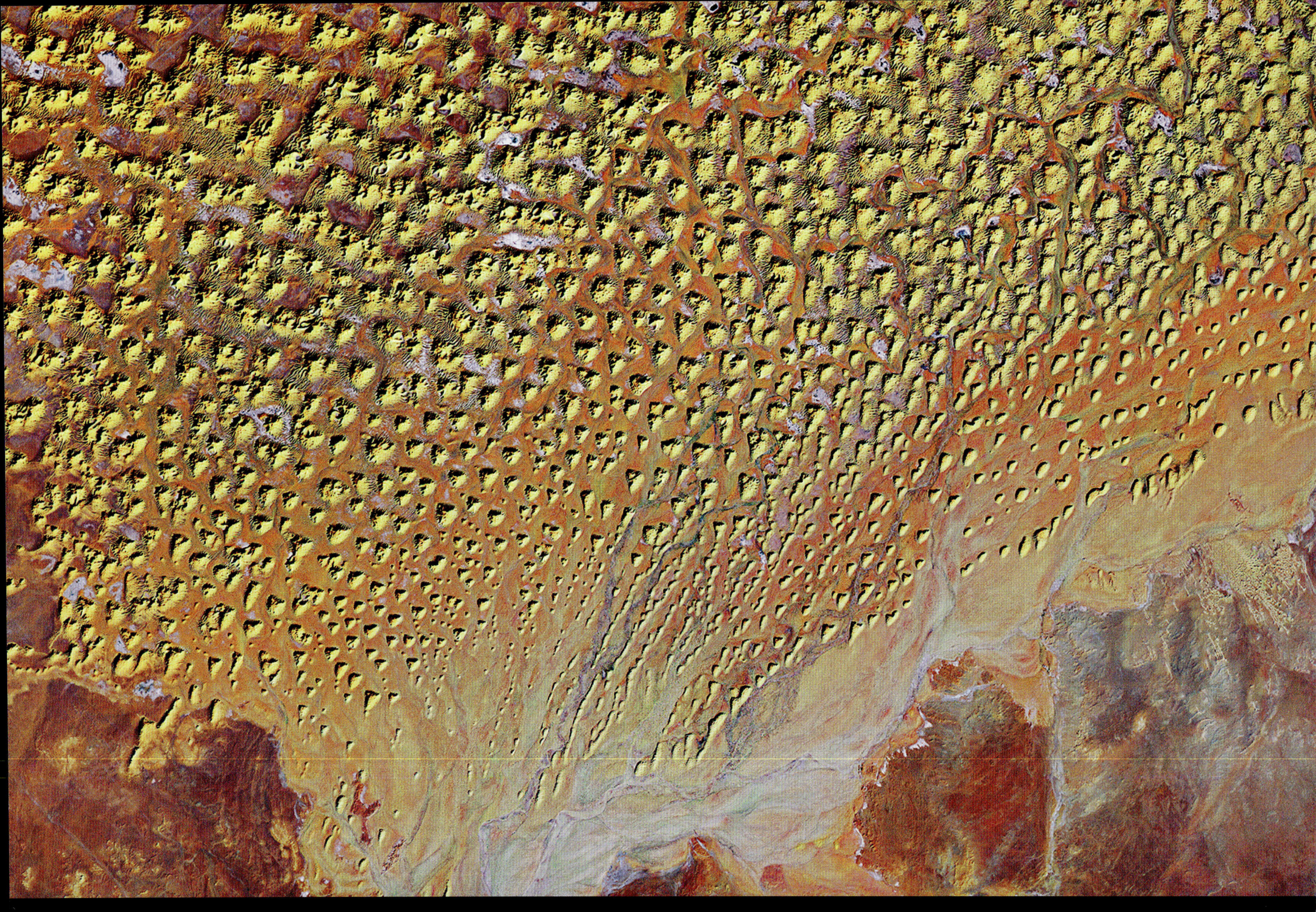

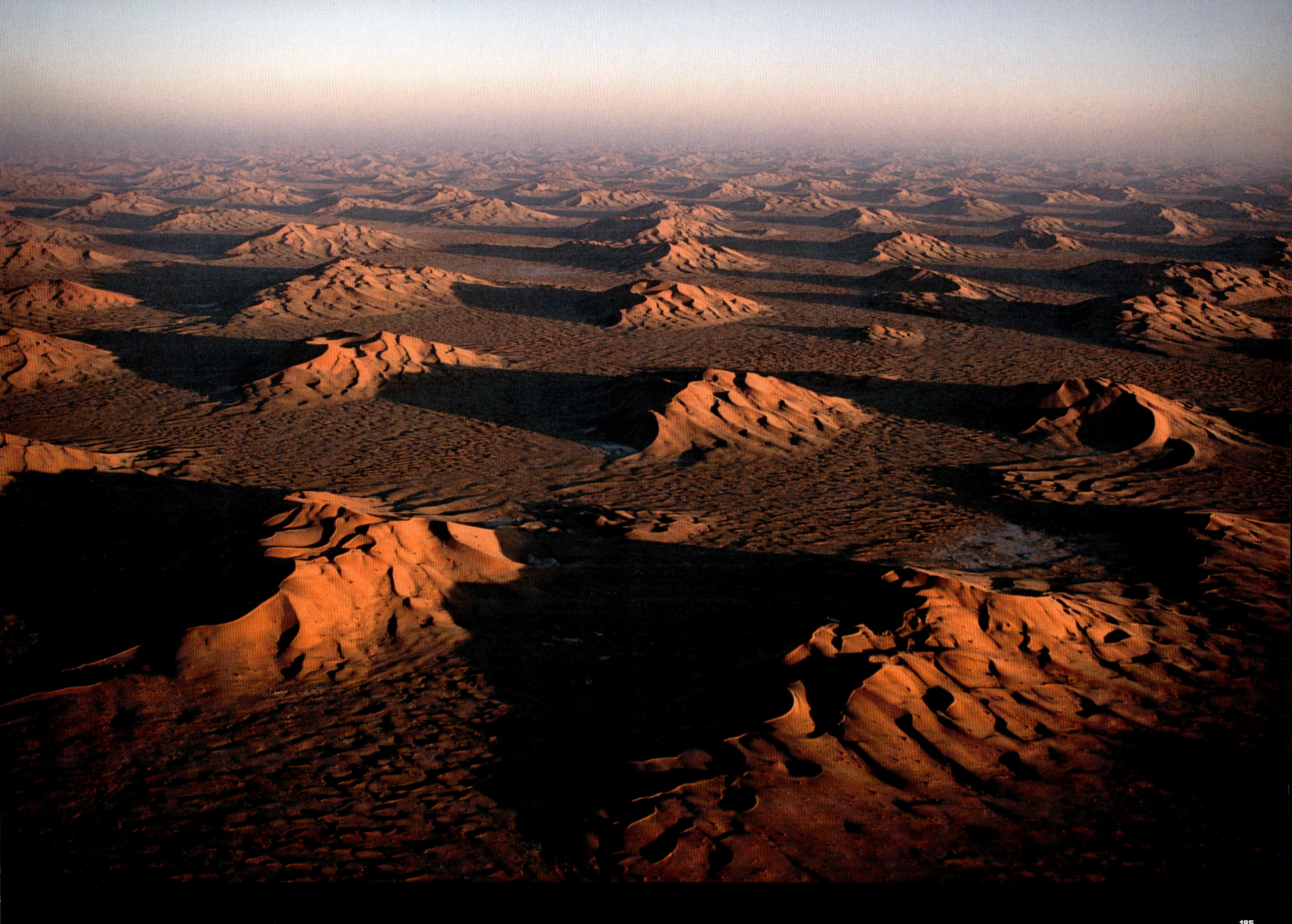

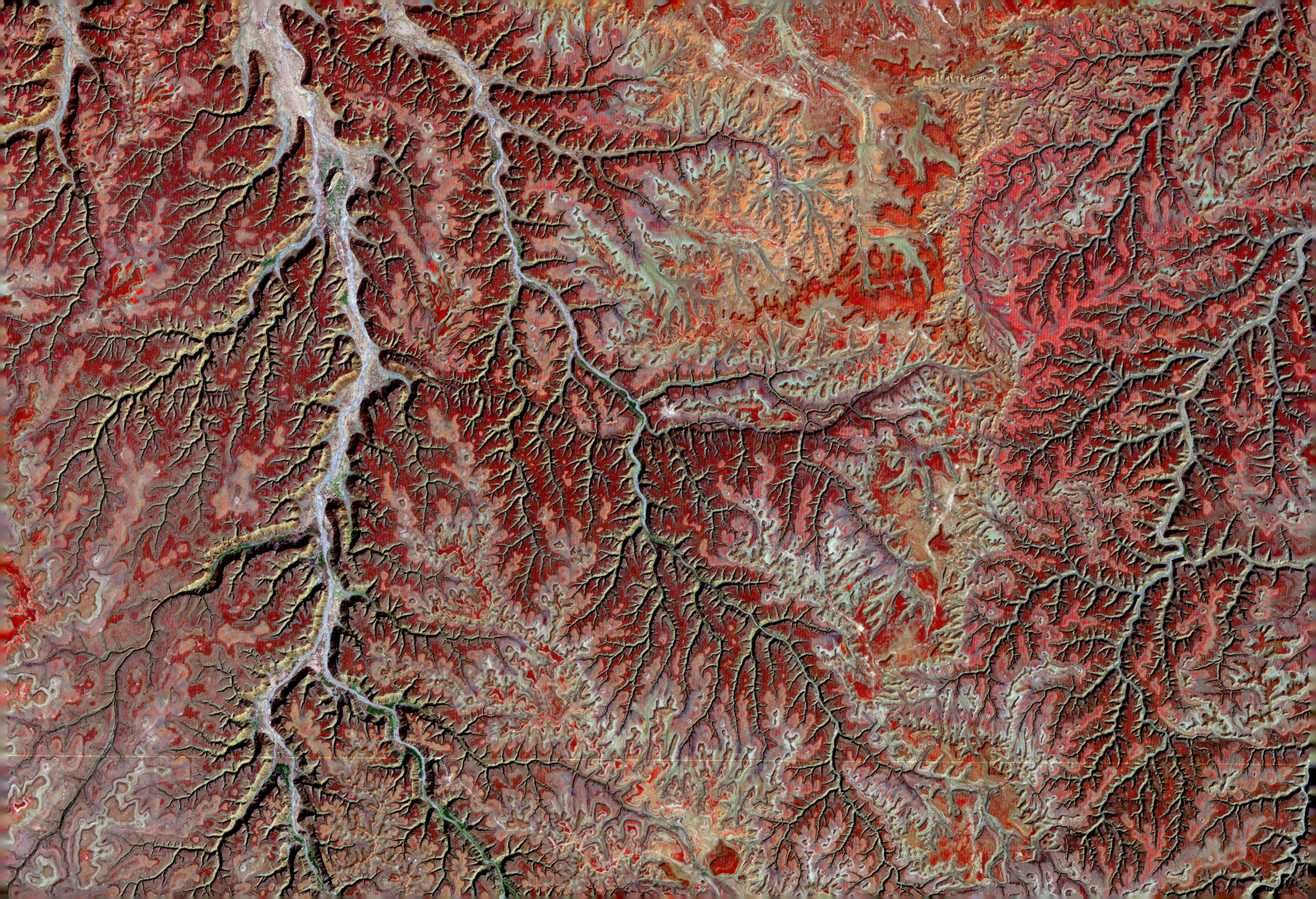

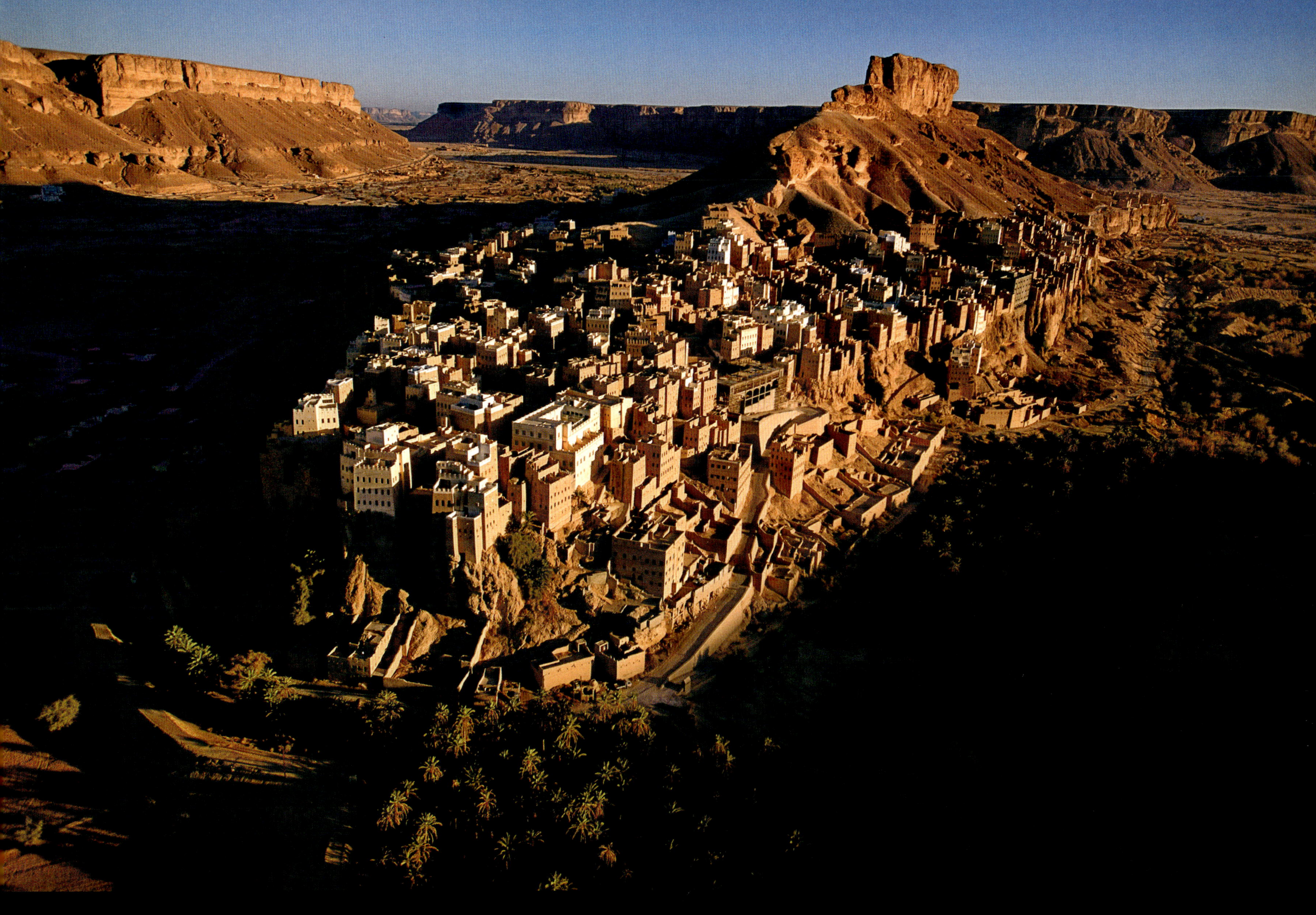

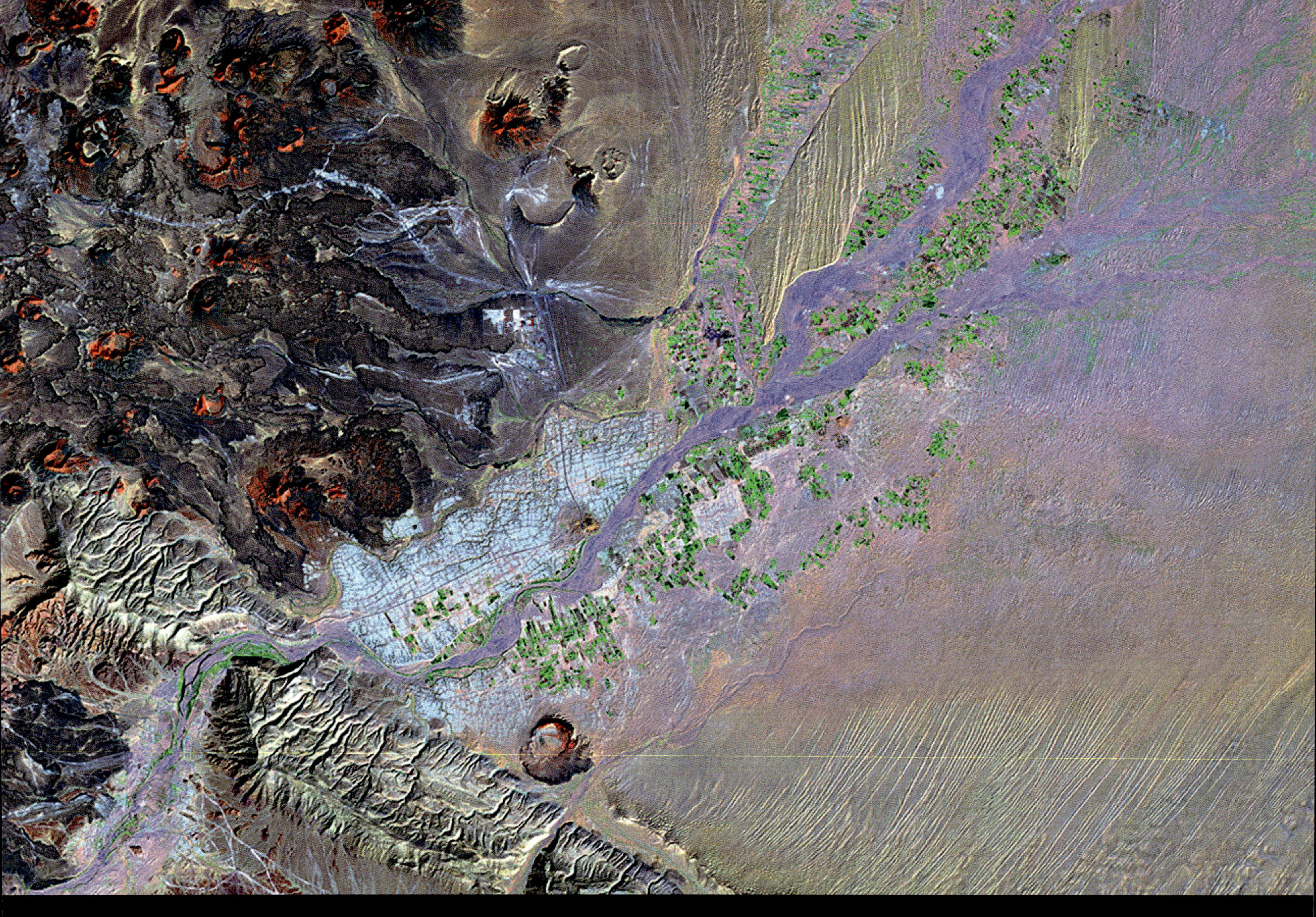

ABOVE AND OPPOSITE: Marib, Yemen

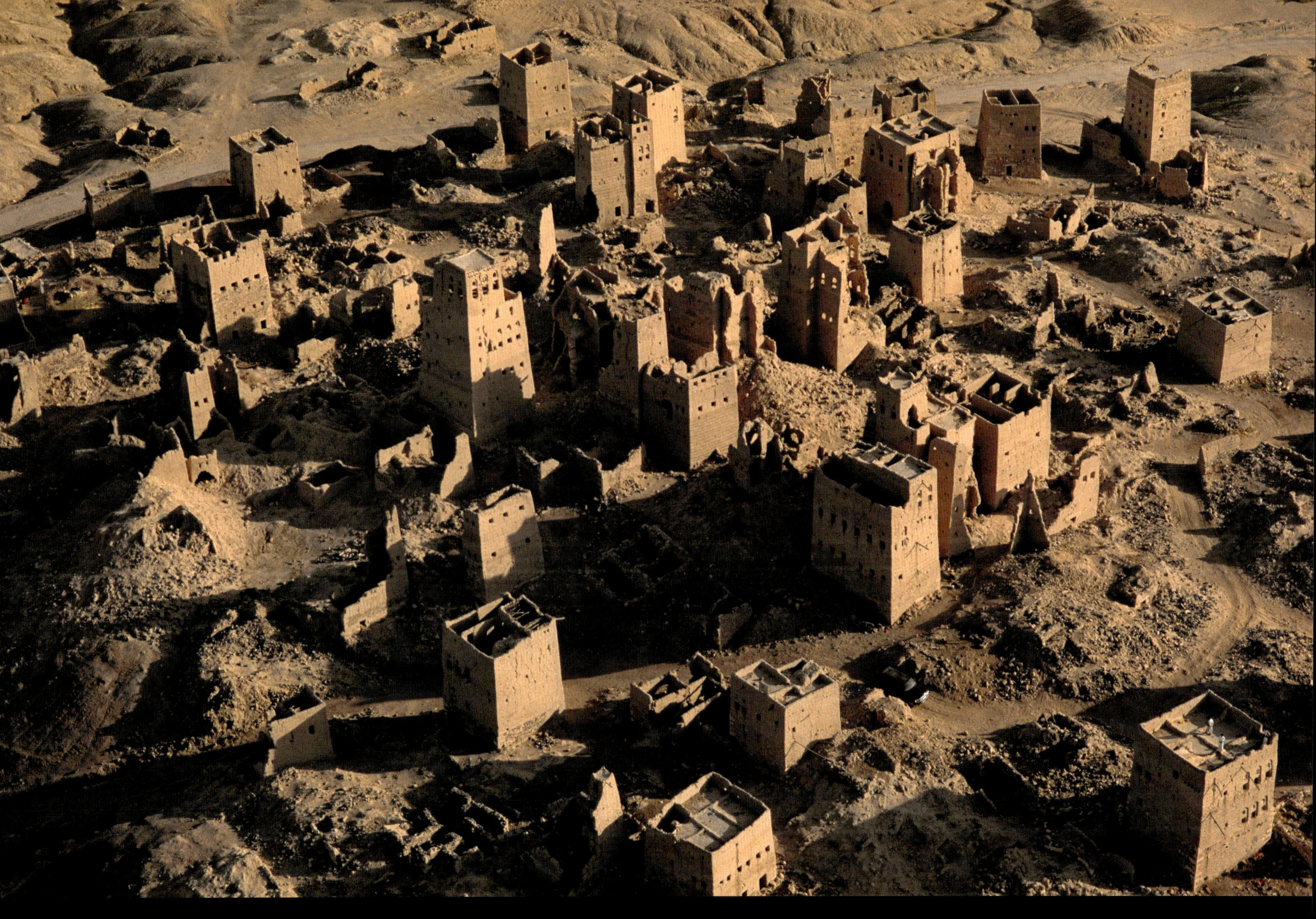

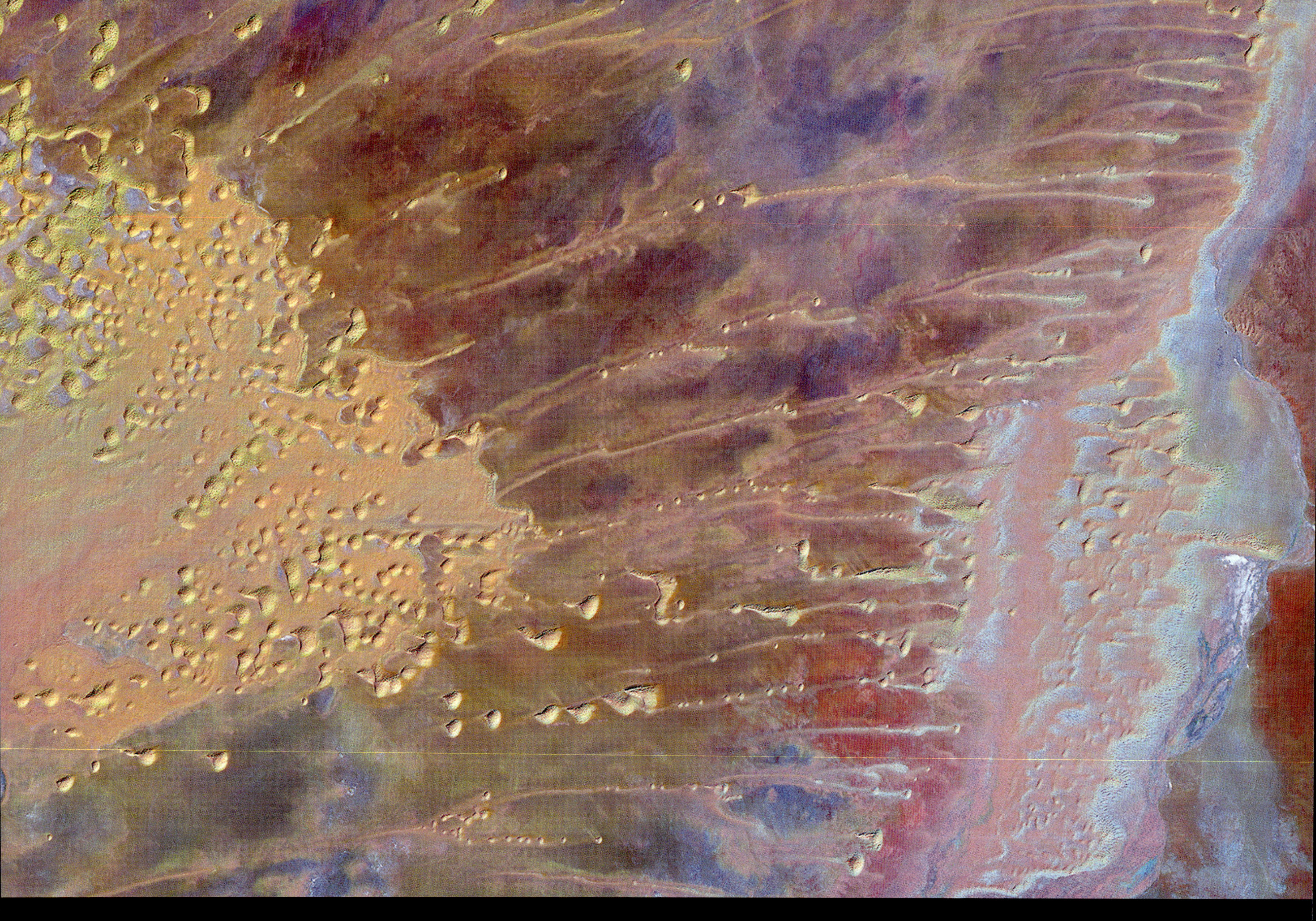

 ABOVE AND OPPOSITE: Barchan dunes of Ramlat Hazar, Yemen

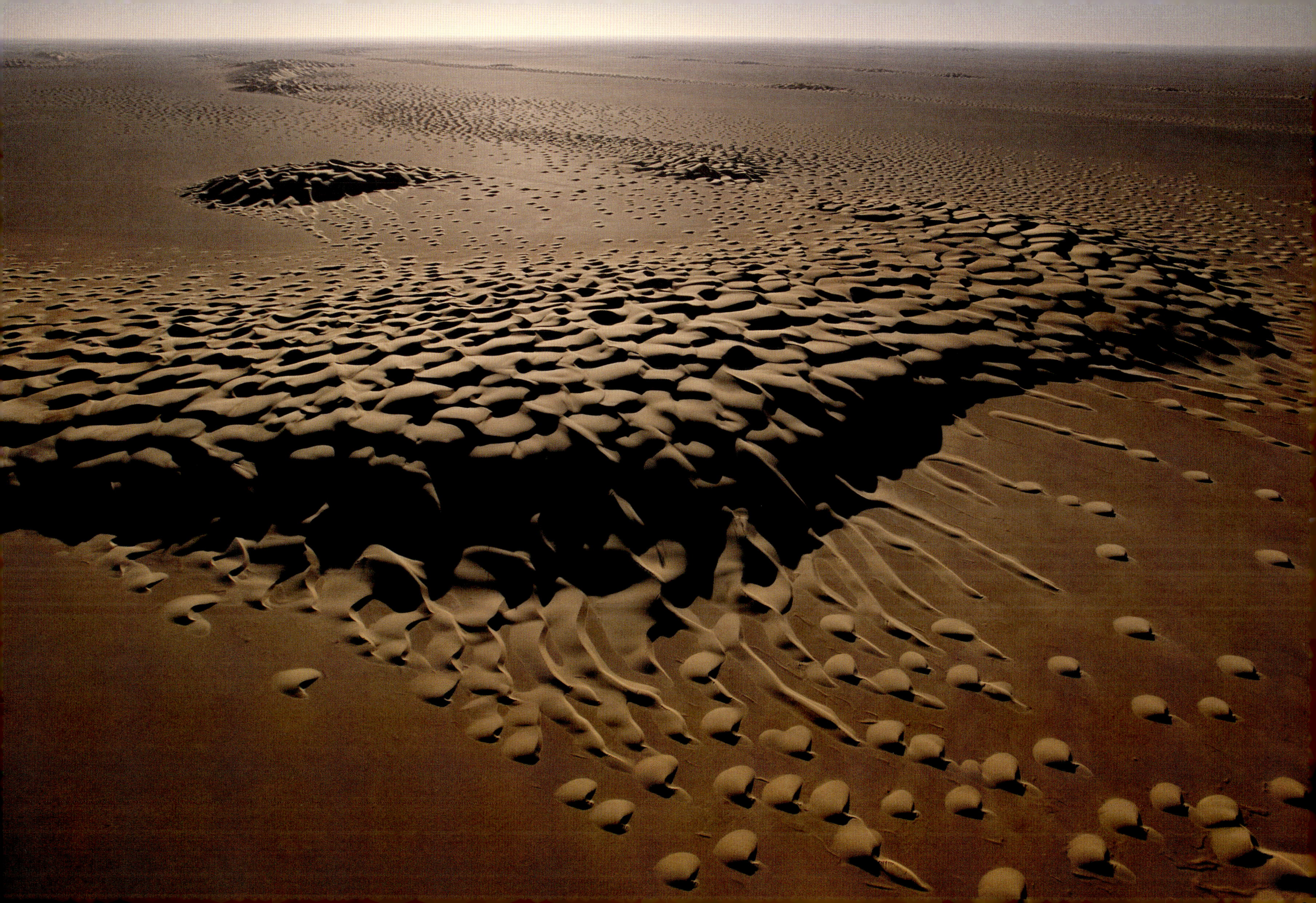

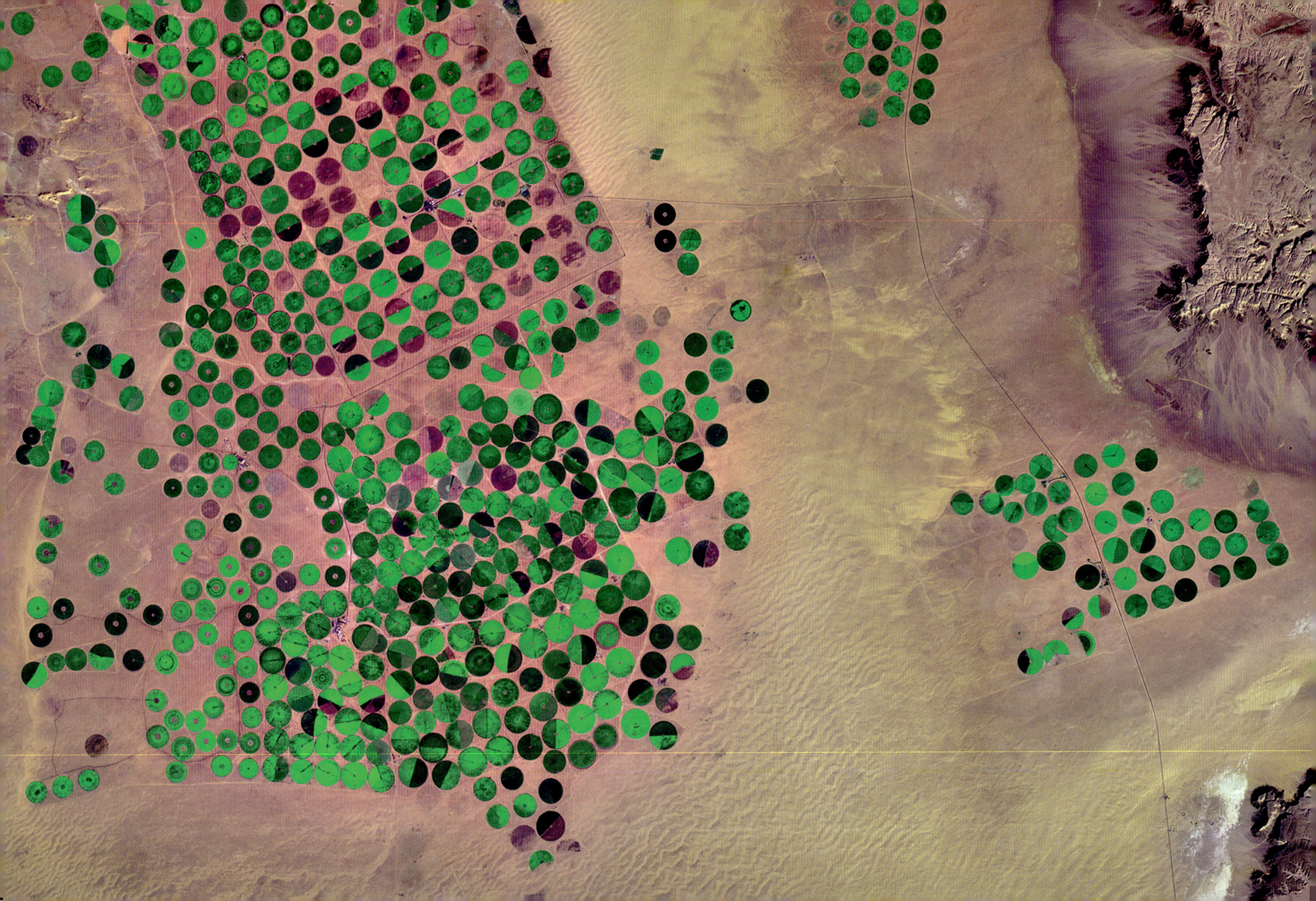

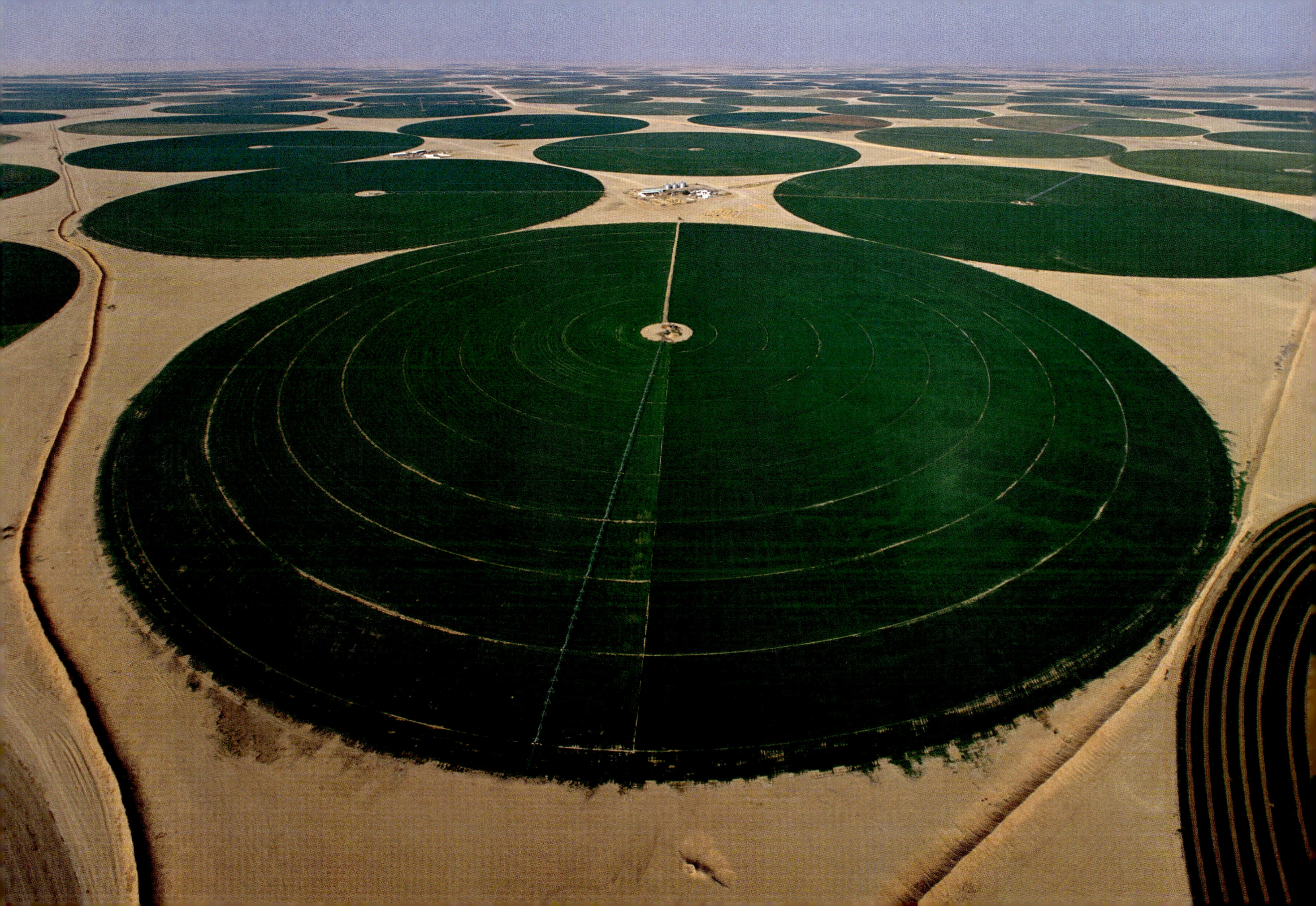

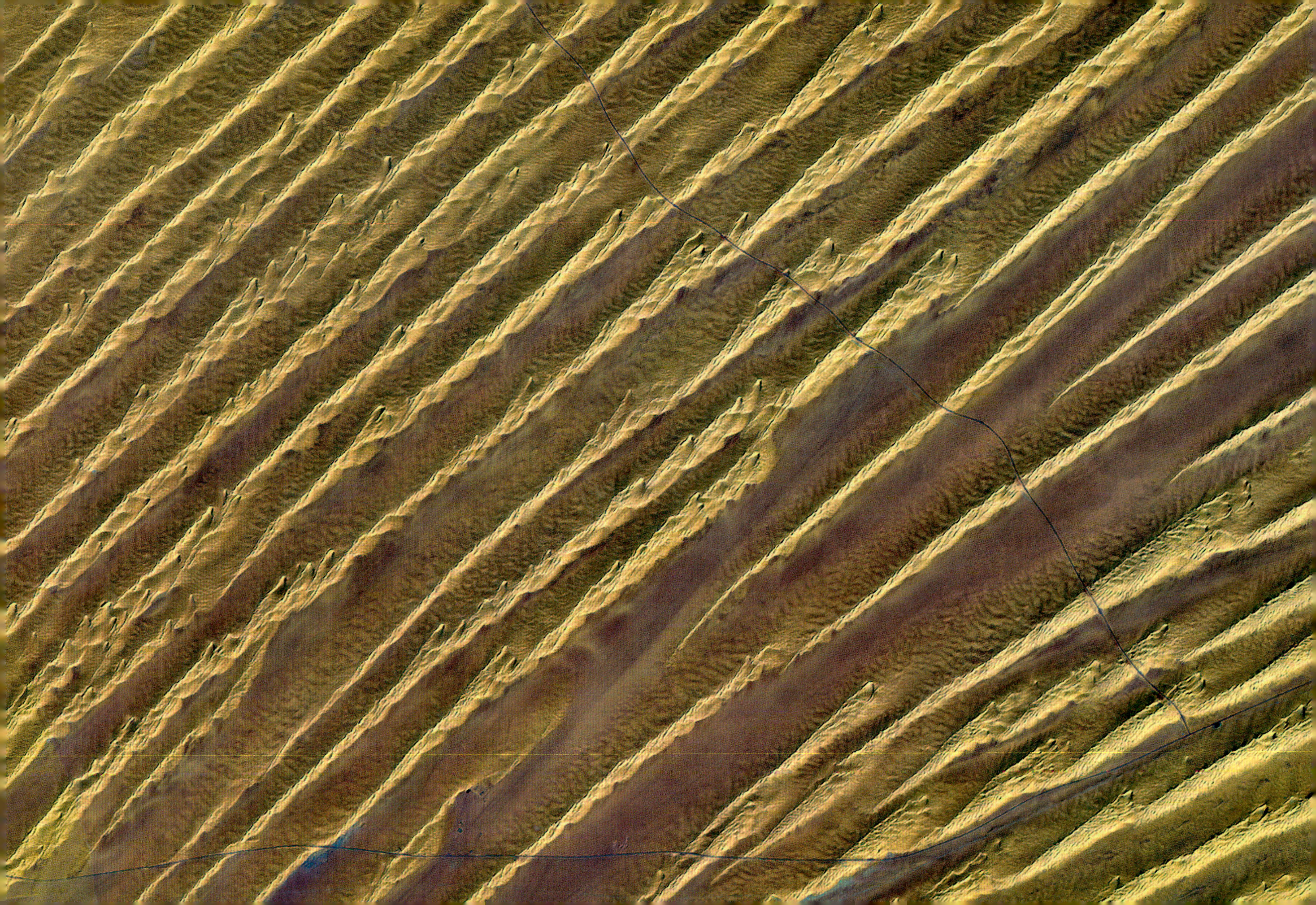

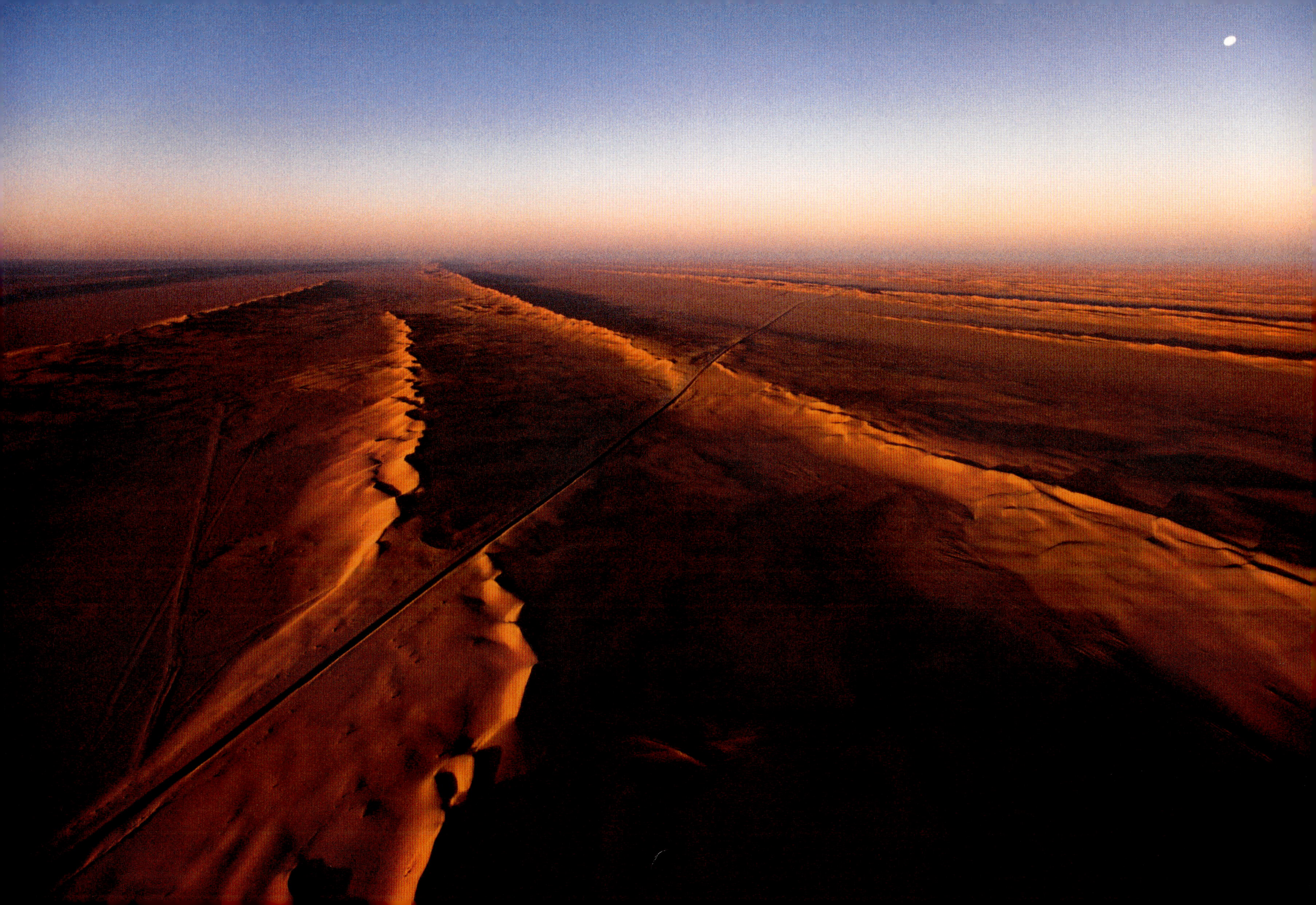

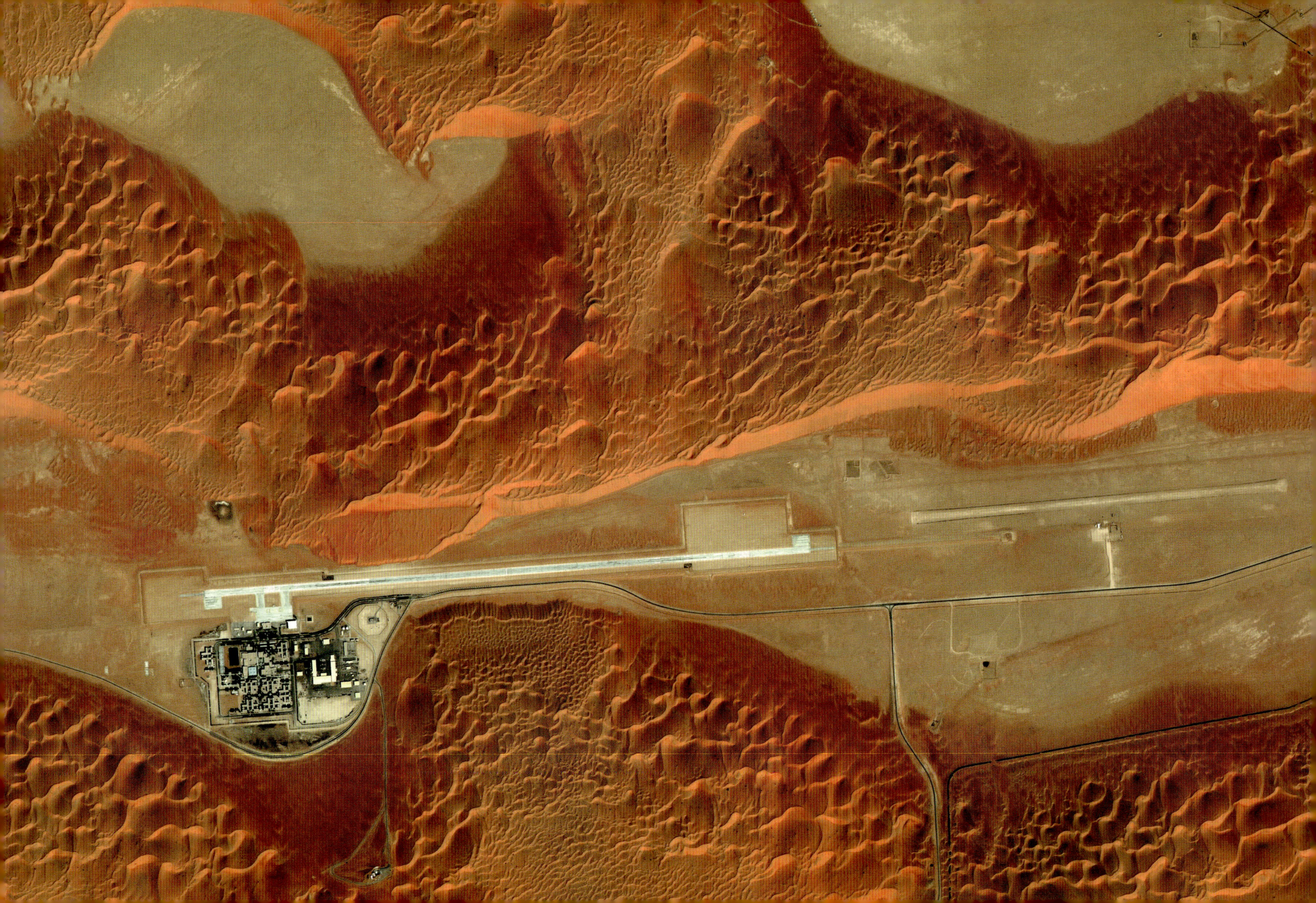

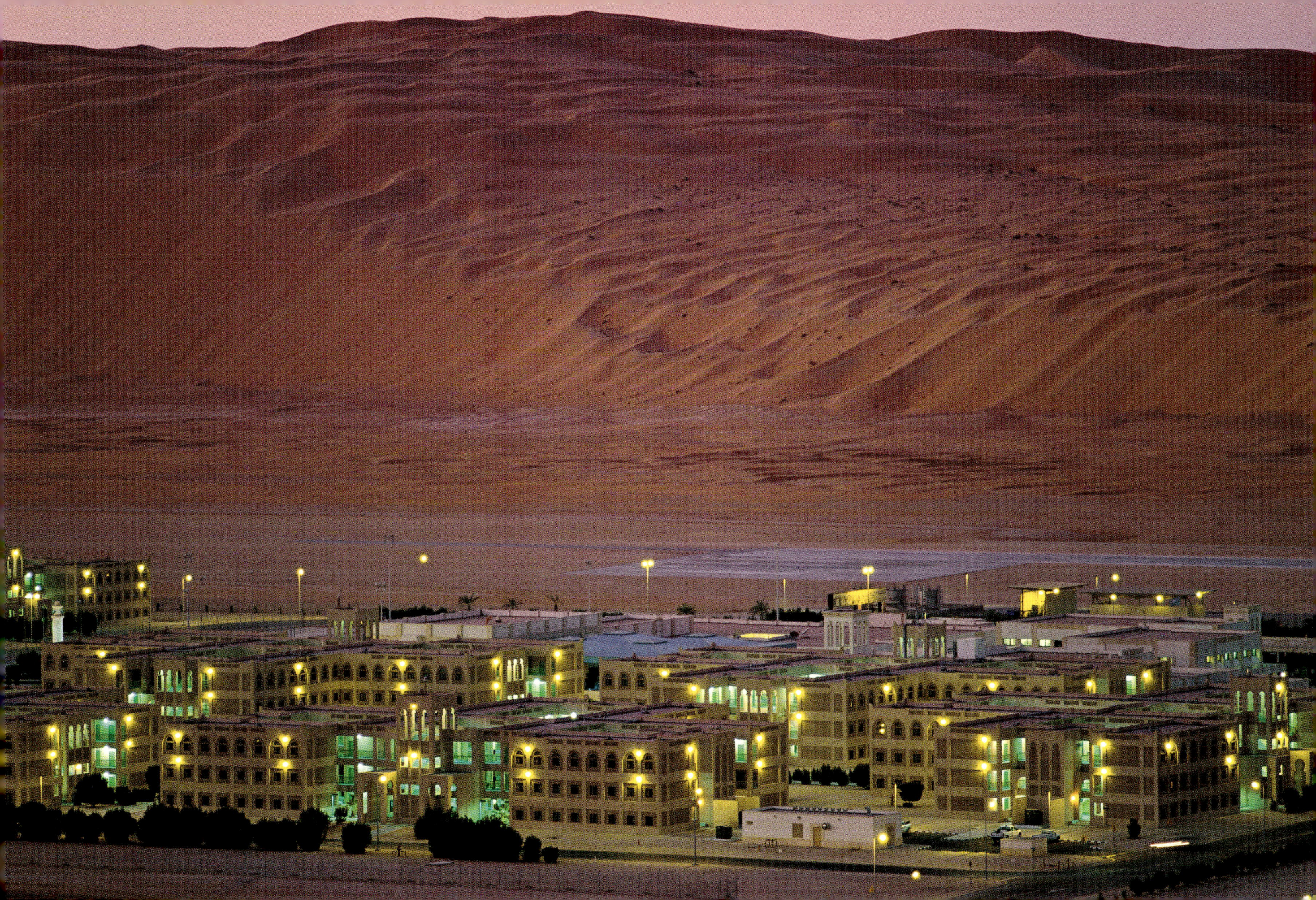

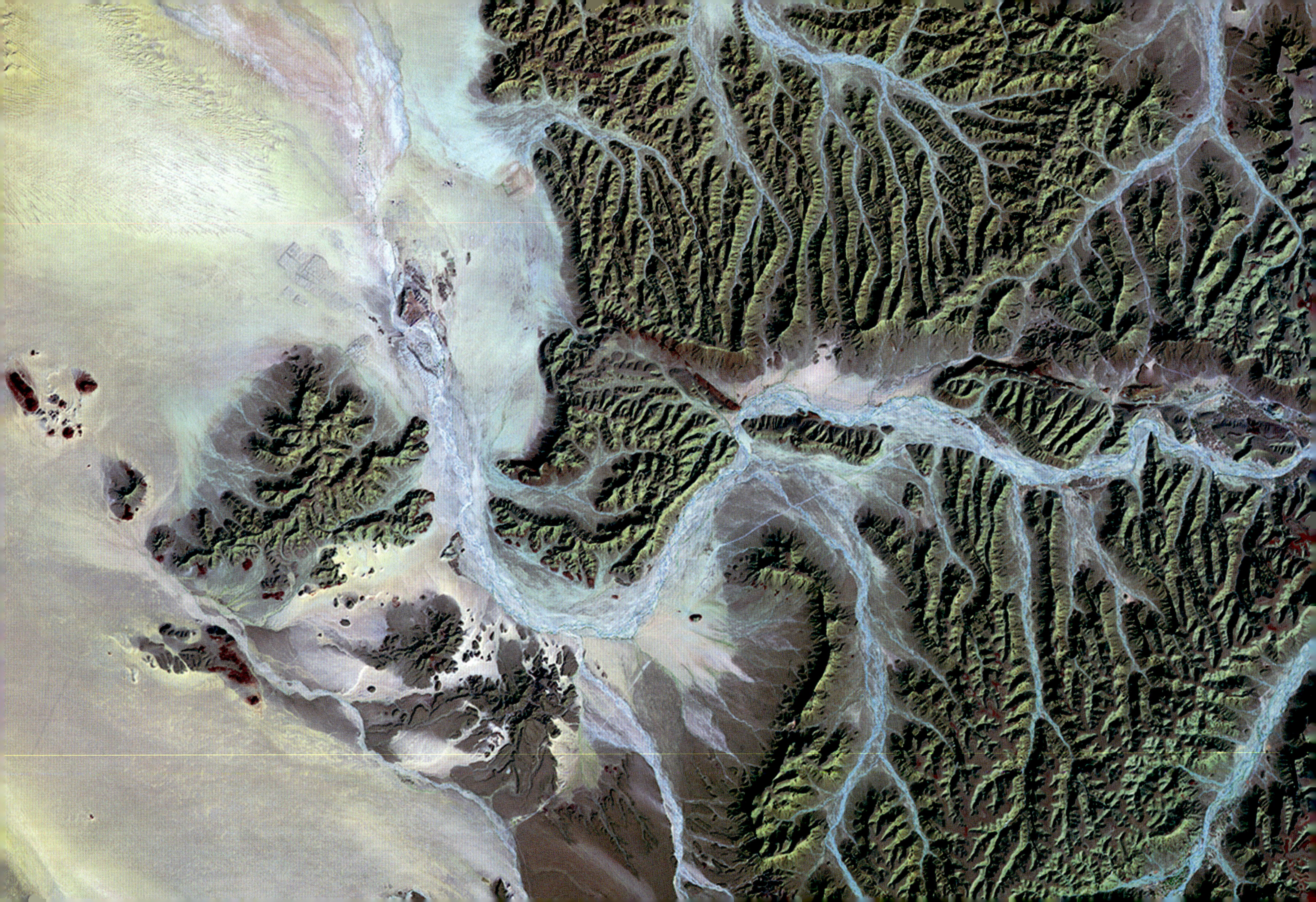

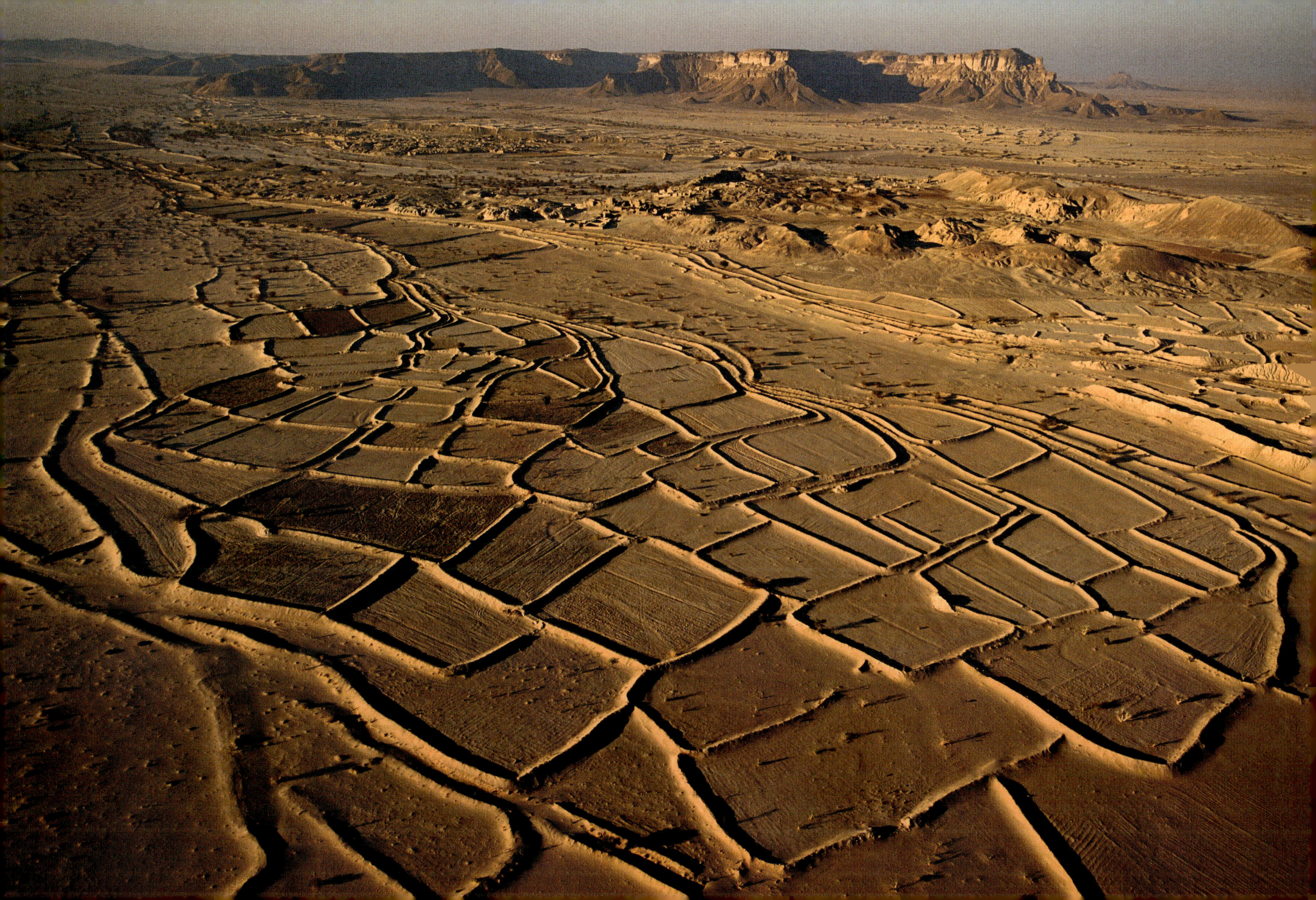

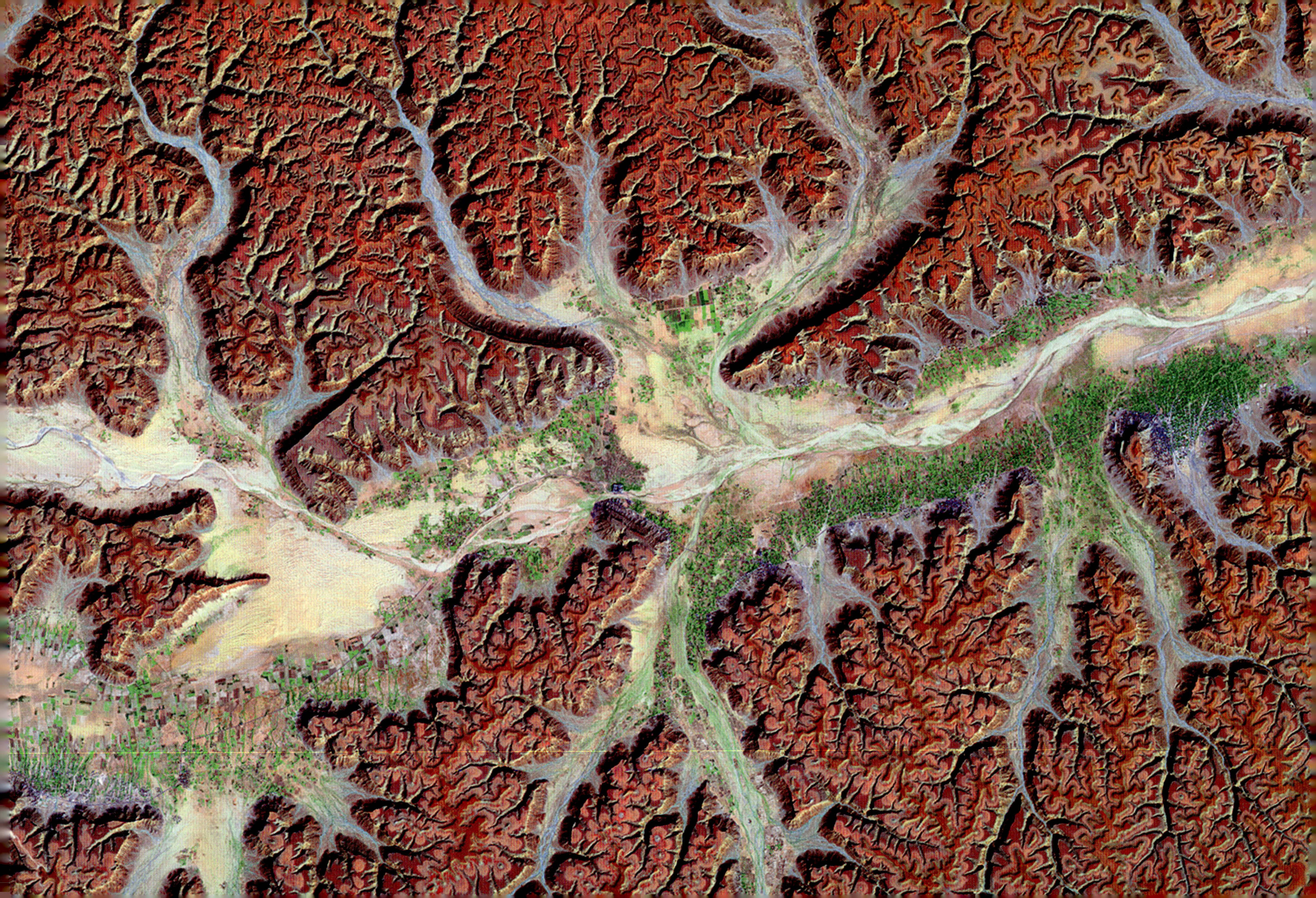

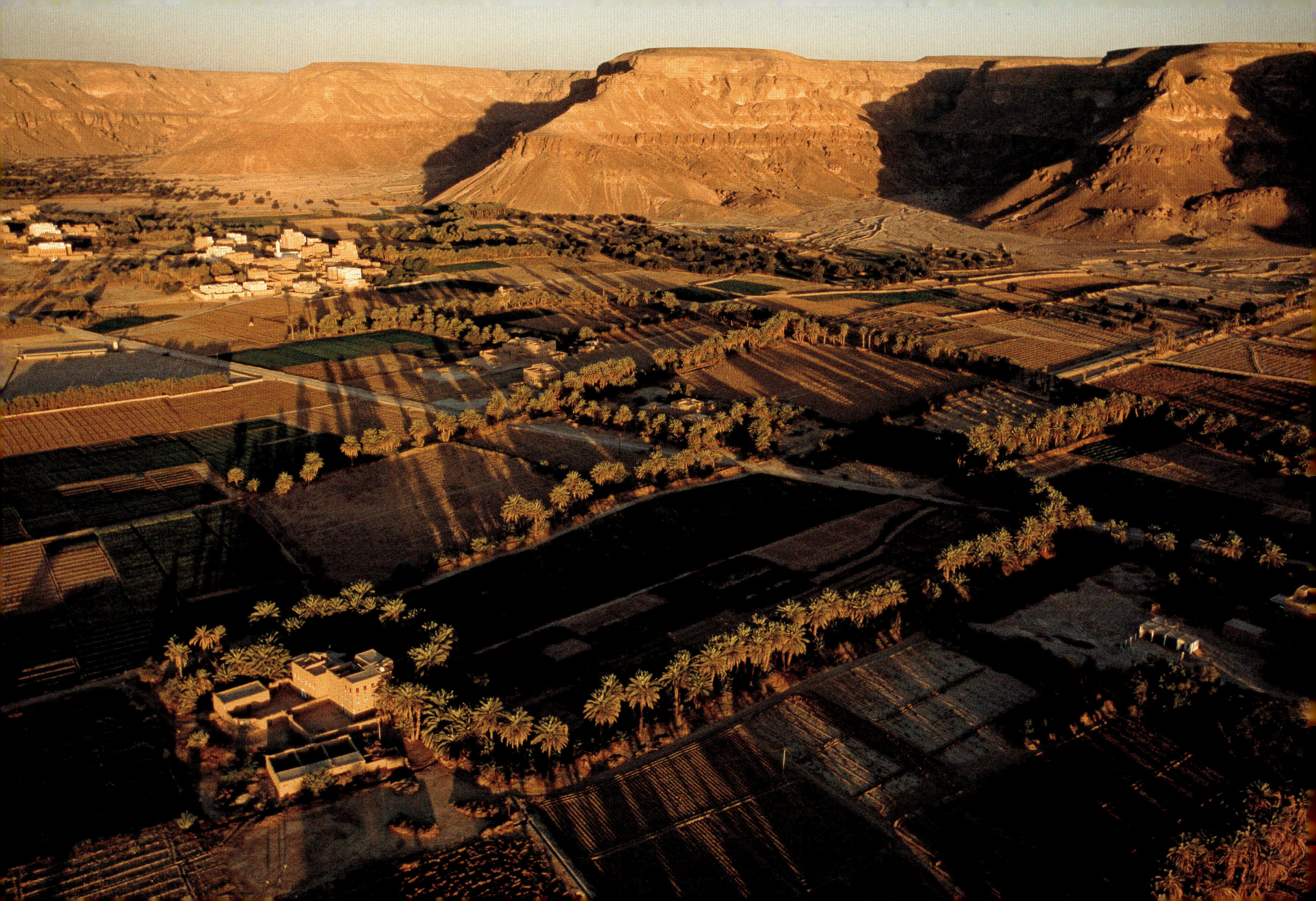

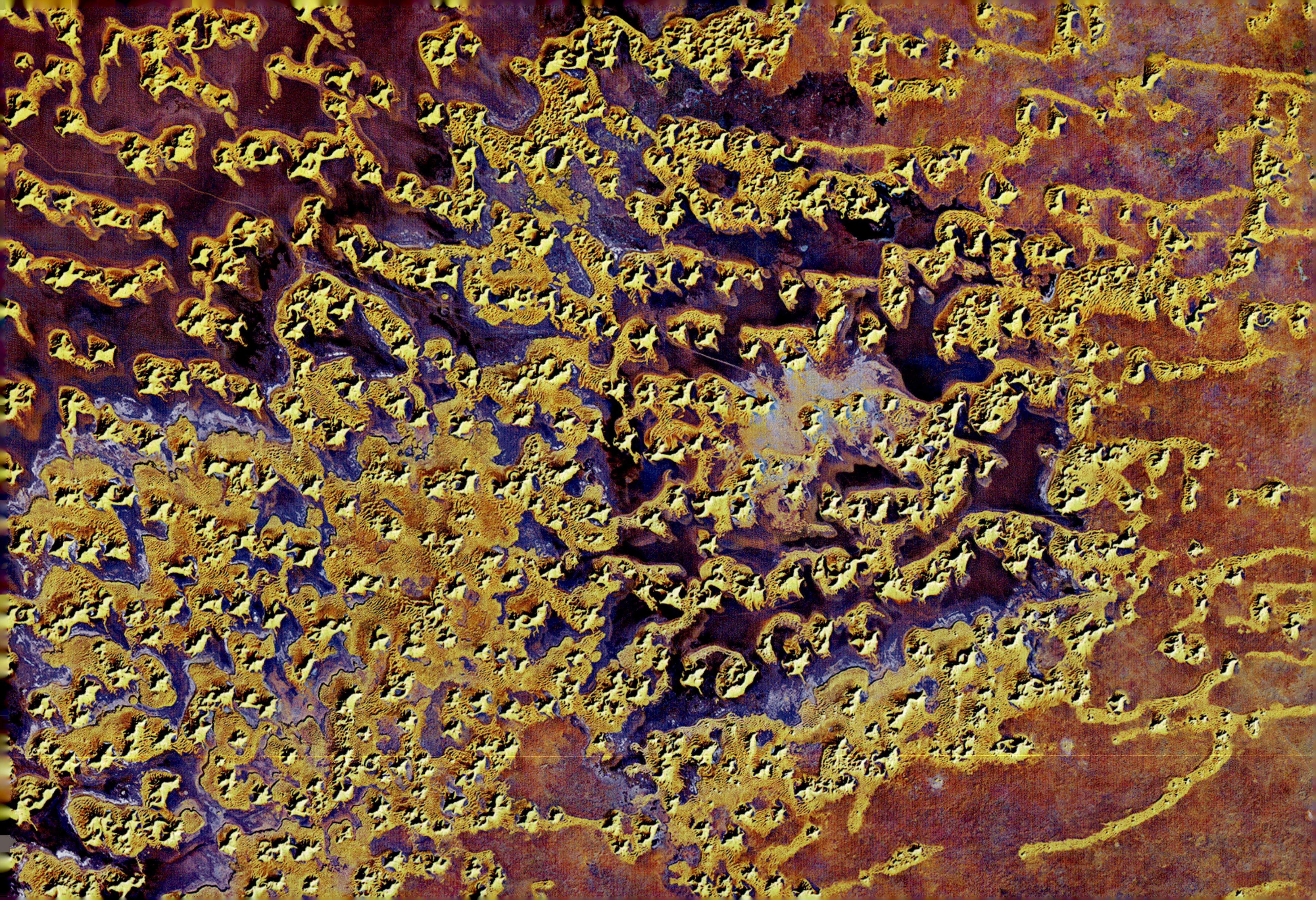

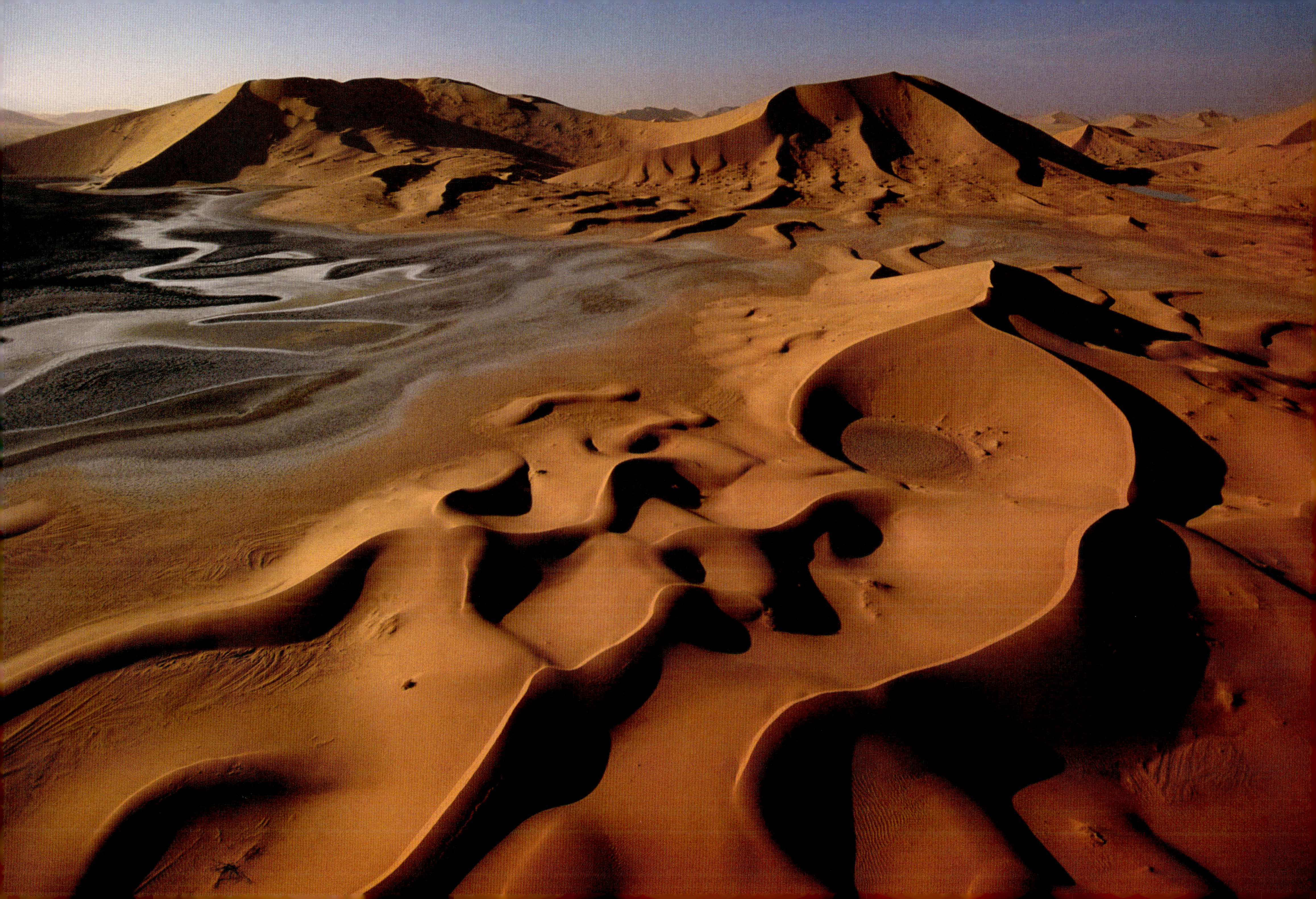

MOSAIC OF THE ARABIAN PENINSULA FROM LANDSAT 7

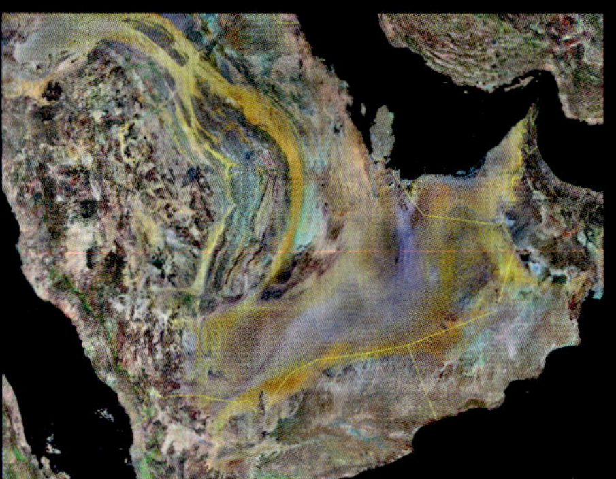

A mosaic of satellite images from the newest generation of Landsat 7 ETM+ data shows the sand flow of the Arabian Peninsula in false color. The Empty Quarter is shaped by strong seasonal Shamal winds that transport sand from the north via the Ad Dahna sand belt and directly off the coast of the Arabian Gulf. On the southern side of the Empty Quarter, these clockwise winds produce some of the longest dune ridges in the world, and where they blow up onto the mountainous plains of Oman and Yemen, they create a massive labyrinth of barchan and star dunes.

MARIB, YEMEN

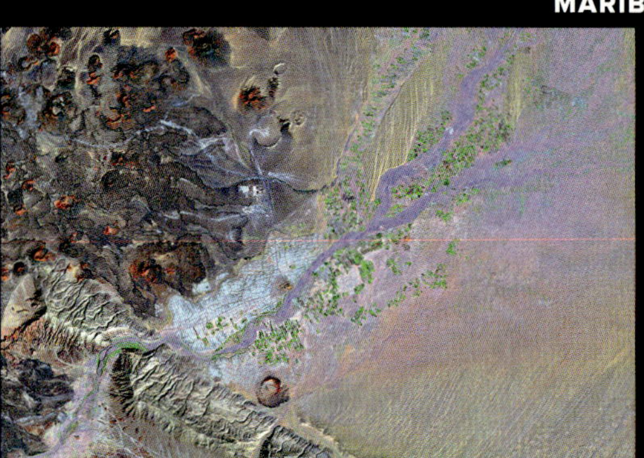

The town of old Marib, now in ruins, appears as a small orange bump in the center of the satellite image alongside the purple-colored silt channel of Wadi Dahna. In the lower left corner of the satellite image is the area where the wadi was dammed in the eighth century BCE. This revolutionary irrigation project gave rise to one of the great early civilizations of Arabia—Saba, the land of the legendary Queen of Sheba. The blue areas of the satellite image are the paleo-soils that were once irrigated by the dam's canals. The dam was breached and repaired on many occasions, but significant damage occurred in the sixth century CE, leading to abandonment and dispersal of the inhabitants of the region. Areas of modern irrigation appear green in this image.

DOT DUNES OF RAMLAT FASAD, OMAN

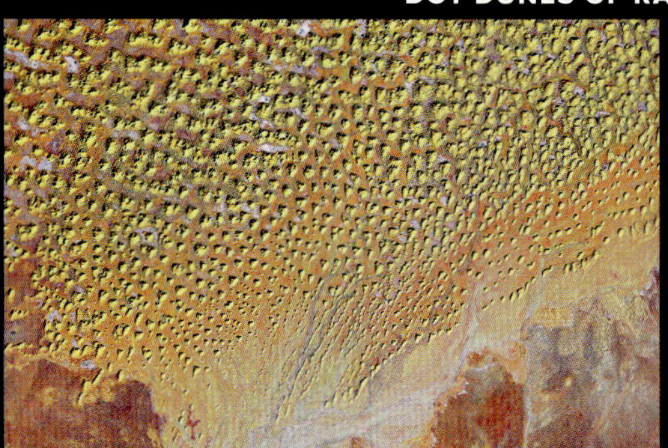

Winds from multiple directions have created a field of star dunes in Ramlat Fasad near the southern edge of the Empty Quarter in Oman. This dune field lies at the end of a delta that occasionally floods after heavy monsoon rains in the coastal mountains. In the satellite image, the star dunes appear yellow, and the fine-grained silty sands appear orange, with the underlying mineralized clay appearing in white and blue.

BARCHAN DUNES OF RAMLAT HAZAR, YEMEN

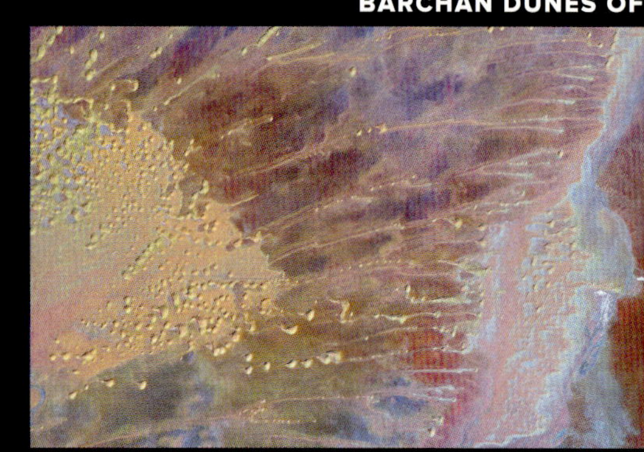

Barchan dunes usually take on a crescent form, but the barchans of Ramlat Hazar are subject to strong shifting winds, which blow their twined tails away as they migrate across the sandy plain of eastern Yemen. Strong winds have blown sand off the summit of the mother dunes and sent a spawn of smaller, dot-shaped barchans off to the west. The dunes appear yellow in the satellite image, and the sabkhas (salt-encrusted mud flats) are light blue.

WADI DO'AN, YEMEN

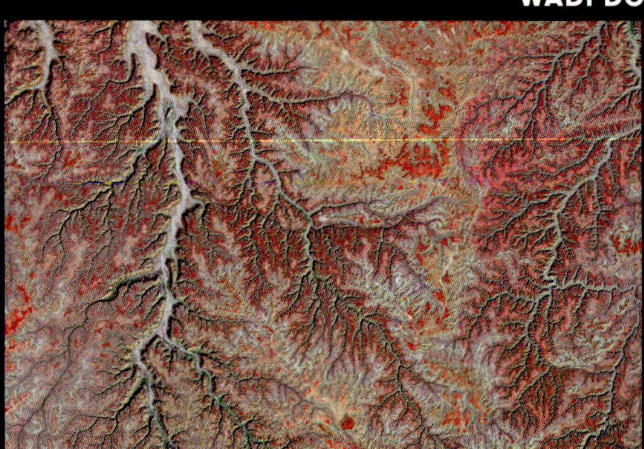

Al Hajjarayn (upper left center of satellite image) clings to an island of sandstone in the middle of Wadi Do'an, a tributary of Wadi Hadramawt (wadi means "dry riverbed"). The area is dominated by a plateau of hard marine limestone and sandstone that has been cut by monsoon rains. The canyon bottoms are fertile, spring-fed gardens, and villages perch up on the hillsides as a defense against both attack and flood and to allow the fertile areas to be utilized for agriculture. The gravel-strewn sandstone plateau appears red in the satellite image, while the clays of the fertile bottoms are colored light blue and the gardens light green. This wadi yields some of the world's finest honey, much of it from the wild 'ilb tree, which is used

CENTER-PIVOT IRRIGATION CIRCLES OF WADI DAWASIR, SAUDI ARABIA

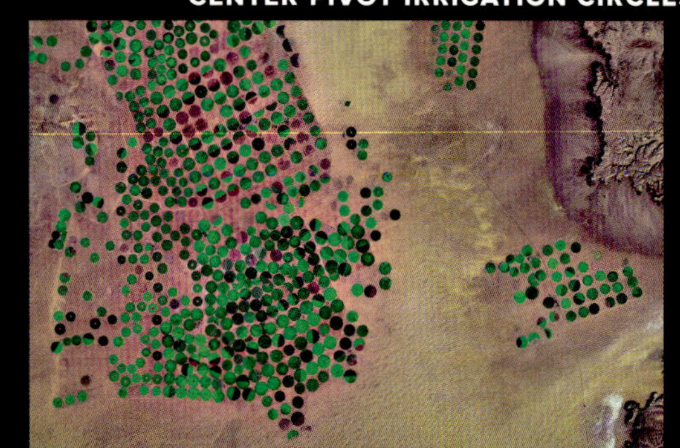

Kilometer-wide green circles of alfalfa are irrigated from centrally located wells that tap into fossil waters from the last ice age, when the Empty Quarter was a grassland with a scattering of ephemeral lakes and abundant wildlife. At the current rate of irrigation (twenty-eight gallons per square foot), these disks of green will last only twenty years or so before the fossil water is exhausted. This intensive groundwater withdrawal creates sinkholes and cave-ins, which crush subterranean rock cavities and compress pores in the rock, ensuring that these aquifers will never be recharged again. The ancient trading center of Qaryat al-Fau is located at the lower right, adjacent to the white-colored dry lakebeds at the foot of the Tuwayq

'URUQ DUNES OF SHAQQAT AL KHARITAH, SAUDI ARABIA

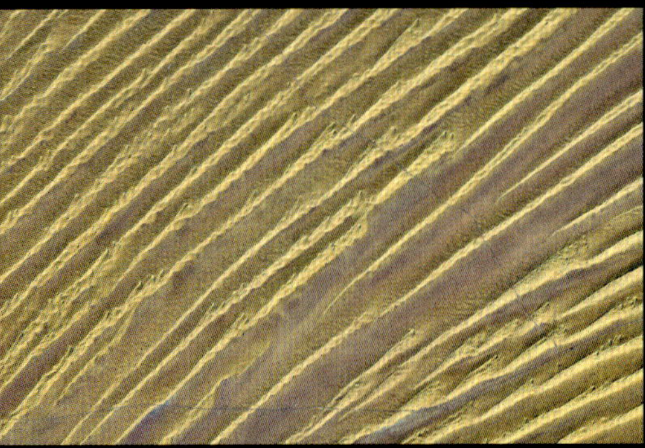

'Uruq, or "vein," dunes stretch individually for hundreds of miles across the southwest corner of the Empty Quarter. They are built by strong winds with a slight seasonal variation and appear as if a giant comb has raked the sands. Saudi Arabia built the paved road snaking its way across the dunes to supply a military post at Sharurah and assure Saudi control over this remote corner of the Kingdom. The road requires constant maintenance by crews of foreign workers with brooms and shovels to keep it clear of sand.

HADRAMAWT VALLEY, YEMEN

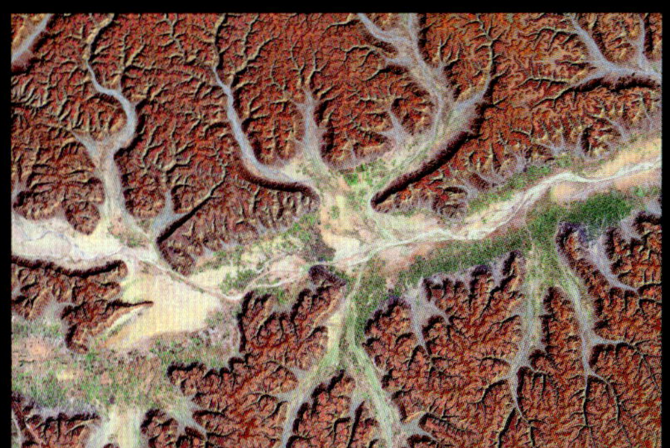

The hard limestone and sandstone gravel plateau of southern Yemen appears deep red in the satellite image, while the area's thousand-foot-deep valleys are a patchwork of sand and agriculture colored yellow and green in false color. This area has been one of the most fertile in the Arabian Desert for millennia. This region has been subjected to severe flooding and erosion from monsoonal rains that have carved out a dramatic landscape that resembles the red-rock country of the American Southwest. In the Hadramawt Valley bottom are lush groves of palm trees and other crops.

SHAYBAH AIRFIELD AND RESIDENTIAL COMPLEX, SAUDI ARABIA

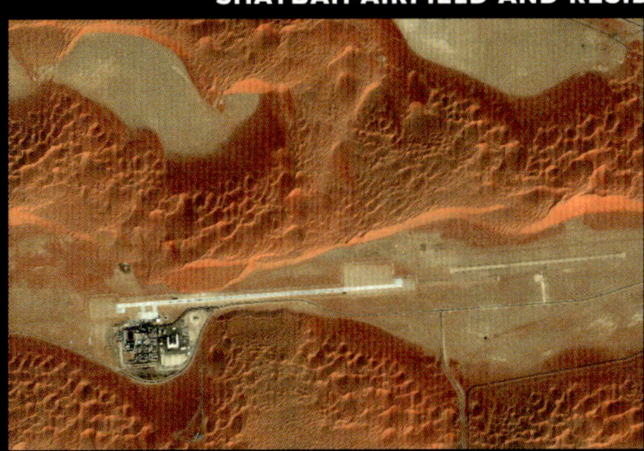

Shaybah, Saudi Arabia's showcase oil field, is located in the most beautiful and extreme part of the Empty Quarter. The oil field was discovered in 1968 but was not exploited for another thirty years until development in directional drilling made it more economical. Two hundred miles from the nearest Saudi town, the facility includes a modern residential complex, a two-mile-long jet airfield, and three oil separation plants. All was completed in less than three years at a cost of approximately $2.5 billion, in order to tap reserves of some nineteen billion barrels of oil. Since Ron Blom's Landsat data was gathered before Shaybah was developed, this satellite image was generated from new data gathered from visible wavelengths of light. This new data from DigitalGlobe has higher spatial resolution to reveal more detailed features.

KHAWR HAMIDAN, SAUDI ARABIA

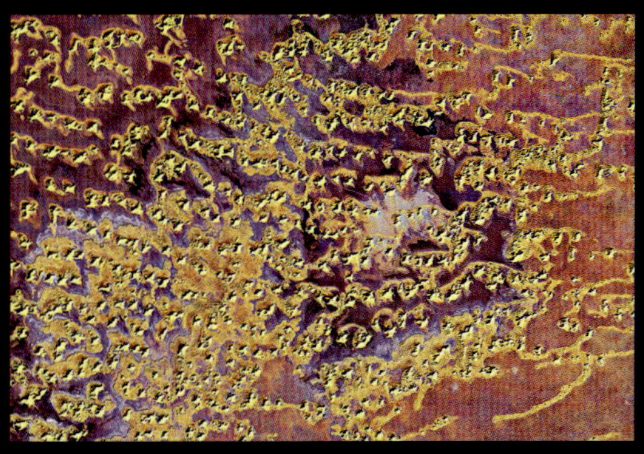

The five-hundred-foot-tall star dunes and drifting sands appear yellow and the sabkha is purple in this false-color satellite image of the 'Uruq al Mutaridah. The patch of light blue surrounded by purple in the center-right area of the satellite image marks the natural spring known as Khawr Hamidan—the only naturally occurring potable source of water I found in the Empty Quarter. The spring is visible in the upper right corner of the aerial photograph. The light color of the ground surrounding the spring in the satellite image correlates to minerals evaporating from the spring water in the intense heat of what is the hottest region on Earth.

IRRIGATED FIELDS, SHABWA, YEMEN

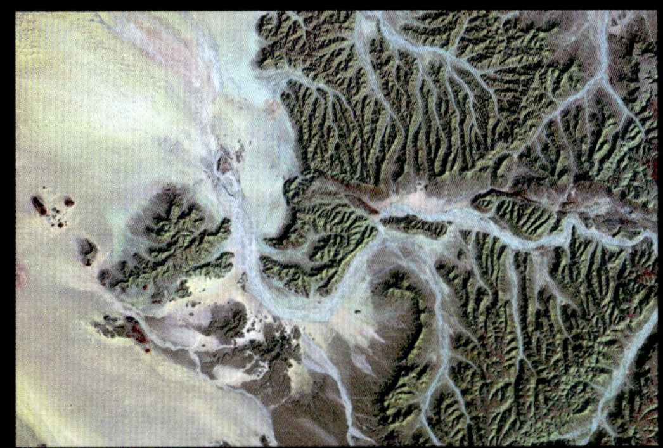

Shabwa was once the capital of the Yemeni section of the Empty Quarter, and it thrived from the passing camel caravans of the frankincense trade. Like Marib, its prosperity depended on harnessing seasonal floodwaters to irrigate desert fields, but most of Shabwa's fields have not been used in two thousand years. On the Landsat imagery, the gypsum-laden paleo-soils appear pale blue, and the ruins of the ancient city are a gray trapezoid in the upper left center of the satellite image. Irrigation with mineral-laden water over the centuries made the soil increasingly infertile and ruined productivity. The raised edges of the fields are from scraping the surface salt away for fresh plantings.

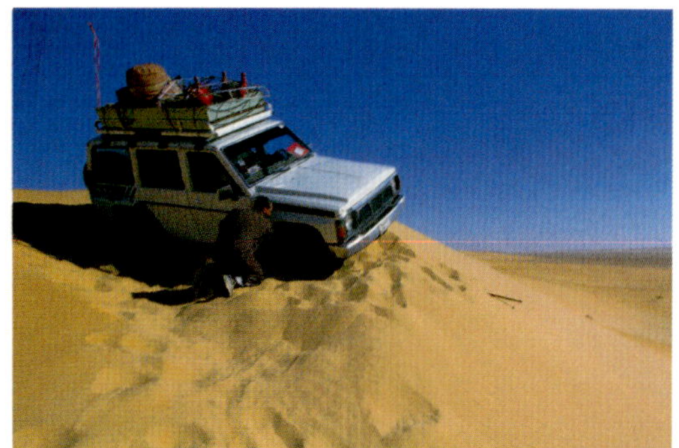

Mohammed Banounah

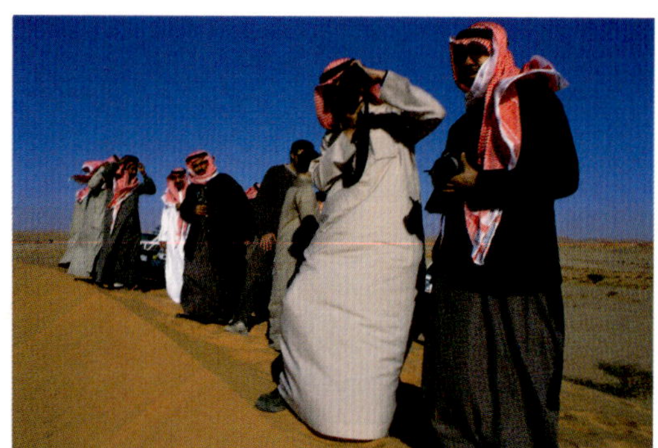

Prince Sultan bin Salman and Tariq Alireza

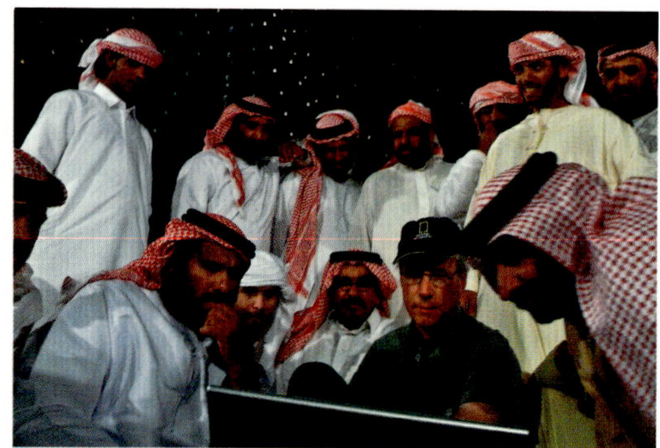

Sharing photos in Sheikh Khaled's camp

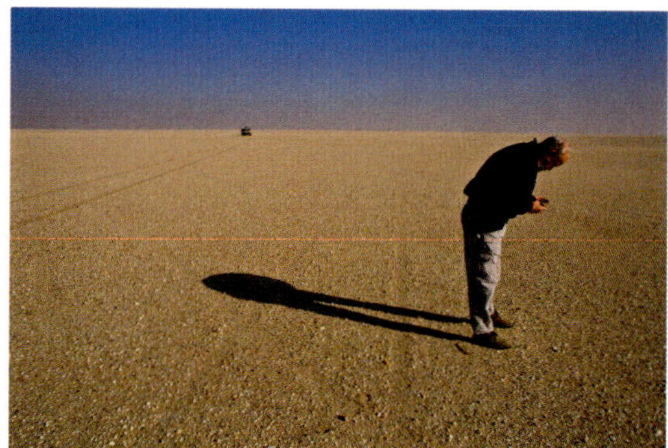

Uwe George looking for meteorite fragments

My explorations of the Empty Quarter would not have been possible without the extraordinary support of *GEO* and *National Geographic.* At the outset it was not clear what I might find in this incredibly remote area, let alone whether I could actually get there and back, and making trips like this is not cheap. These two magazines stood by me through it all.

Ruth Eichhorn and Peter-Matthias Gaede at German *GEO* and Sylvie Rebbot and Jean-Luc Marty at French *GEO* agreed to finance my first trip into the Empty Quarter at a most uncertain time, just after the terrorist attacks of September 11, 2001. Uwe George accompanied me on this first trip and endured innumerable hardships with me as we covered more terrain than was humanly reasonable; Venita Kaleps at *GEO* helped with editing my pictures. My travels on this first journey would not have been possible without the generous assistance of Prince Sultan bin Salman bin Abdul Aziz Al-Saud, the former astronaut and current

Secretary General of the Supreme Commission on Tourism in Saudi Arabia. Prince Sultan organized the unusual permits required for my two flying trips in the Kingdom; Iyad Alzaru took on the challenge of finalizing those permits, organizing the ground team and vehicles, and introduced me to a most extraordinary man, Colonel (now retired Brigadier General) Mohammed Banounah. Banounah guided me across the sands and kindly endured the countless cultural gaffes that an American inevitably makes in the Arab world. He cheerfully put up with the hardships of the field and the near total destruction of his personal Nissan Patrol as we covered thousands of miles of sand in four weeks of nonstop travel. I am also indebted to Ali Al-Mari, who flawlessly drove one of our vehicles on two trips across the sands and opened up his heart and his extended family to three determined men from distant lands. Abdallah Dajani graciously acted as our interpreter on both crossings of the Empty Quarter, as if doing it once

was not enough. Geologist Jeff Wynn and Bill Chasteen, veterans of multiple Hummer crossings of the sands, gave me GPS points, insight, and all kinds of practical advice for my first crossing of the Empty Quarter. Dick Doughty at *Saudi Aramco World* magazine offered invaluable advice and helped open the doors of Saudi Aramco. At Saudi Aramco, I owe heartfelt thanks to Robert Lebling, Rick Snedeker, and Jamal Kheiry. Marianne Alireza kindly lent me the out-of-print maps that were key to navigating the sands, and her son, Tariq Alireza, gave many helpful suggestions as well. Also instrumental in making the first trip a success was Peter Voll.

My second crossing of the sands was made possible with the generous support of *National Geographic.* Bill Allen, who was then editor-in-chief, gave unwavering support to this project, as did the magazine's current editor-in-chief, Chris Johns. My picture editor, Elizabeth Krist, was also a constant supporter who helped get

me released from house arrest in Yemen after my flights in Marib raised the suspicions of the Yemeni military. However, her efforts would have had little impact without the assistance of Mr. Yahya Alshawakani at the Yemeni Embassy in Washington, D.C. While planning the trip to Yemen, I received help from Christopher Edens at the American Institute of Yemeni Studies, and Faris Sanabani, the media advisor to the President of Yemen. Marco Livadiotti at Universal Touring Company expertly organized all ground arrangements in Yemen with Ahmed Halim as our interpreter, Emad Bamatraf as guide, and drivers Mohammed Nasser al-Baidani, Mansour Raggas, and Abdulkarim. Abdul-Aziz bin Mohammed al-Rowas and Salim Almahruqi at Oman's ministry of Cultural Affairs made my entry into Oman possible and organized a military escort for my entire time in the Sultanate. George Hedges and Juris Zarins gave me extensive information about the archaeology and geography of the Omani and

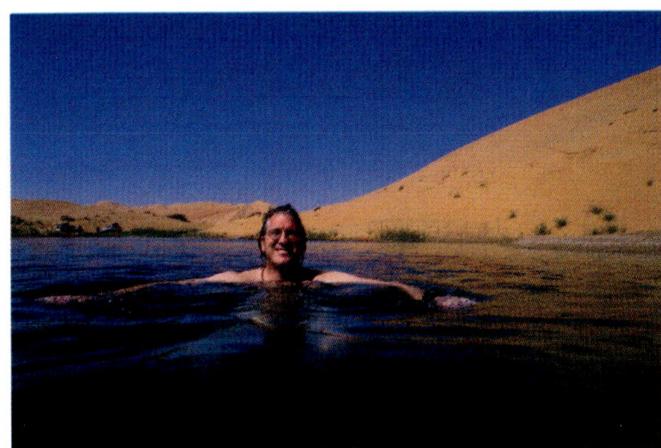

Donovan Webster in Khawr Hamidan

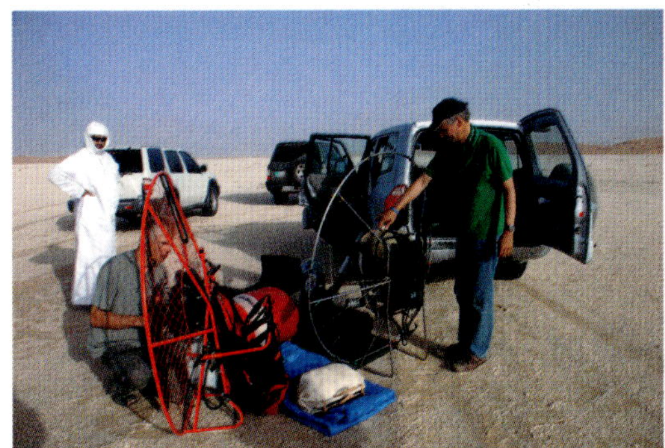

François Lagarde checking his motor

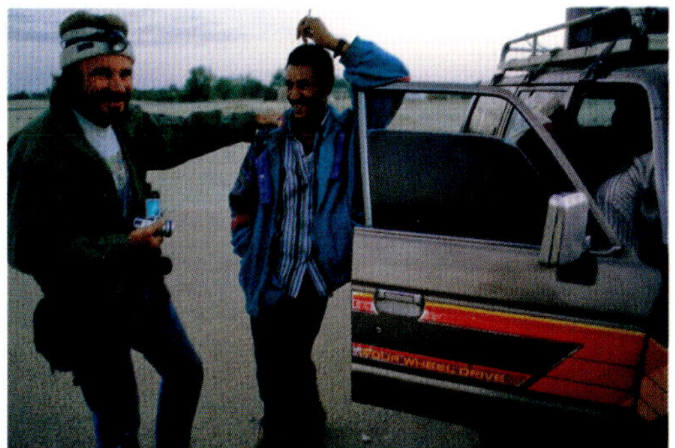

Alain Arnoux and Emad Bamatraf

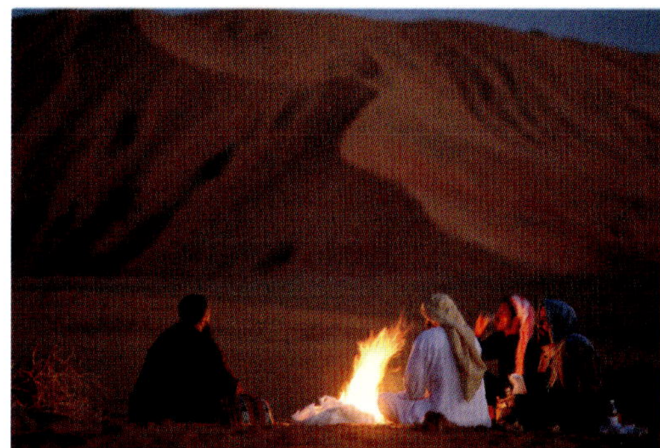

A camp in the 'Uruq al Mutaridah

Yemeni sections of the Empty Quarter. I would also like to thank Emad Khaled, who drove our second car across the sands from Riyadh to Oman and back and survived Abdallah rolling that car with both of them in it. I am indebted to Merilyn Phillips Hodgson, head of the American Foundation for the Study of Man, and Abdu Ghaleb of GOAM for making it possible for me to photograph Mahram Bilqis. Donovan Webster was my most patient friend and confidant on this trip while writing an insightful text for *National Geographic*.

My third trip into the sands was made possible through the endless generosity of Dr. Mark Beech of the Abu Dhabi Authority for Culture and Heritage, and Laila Al-Hassan and Majid Al-Mansouri of the Abu Dhabi Wildlife Department, who made it possible for me to visit the ambitious wildlife repopulation program at Umm az-Zamul.

Ron Blom at NASA/JPL was extraordinarily kind enough to lend me satellite data for my fieldwork and generously contributed his time to help me with the satellite section of this book.

Alain Arnoux, a world champion of motorized paragliding, accompanied me on my first two grueling trips through the the Empty Quarter. I don't know if I would have had much success (or survived) without his wonderful generosity and talents. And François Lagarde, who taught me how to fly, agreed to come on my last trip to the sands, in the U.A.E., with his only reward being the adventure of it all.

Kathy Moran donated vacation time from her day job at *National Geographic* magazine to help edit the pictures for this book, and my office manager, Jessica Licciardello, has been the hands of my photographic vision in making these pictures come to life on the printed page. And Andrea Danese, my editor at Abrams in New York, carefully made a photographer's words read like those of a talented writer. Nathalie Bec at Editions de La Martinière in Paris was untiringly patient with all the delays and complications of this book, which would not have been possible at all without the extraordinary commitment of the gentle emir of illustrated books, Hervé de La Martinière. I am also indebted to Marine Gille, who added grace and elegance to the design as it went through many revisions.

Many experts in the various fields of Arabian studies helped me with fact checking: Mohammed Maraqten and Abdul Rahman Al-Ansary, among others already mentioned above. I am also indebted to my dear friends and fellow photographers Ed Kashi, Gerd Ludwig, and Nick Nichols, who have been seemingly infinite sources of inspiration and advice for twenty-five years.

But most of all, I thank my wife, Lisa Bannon, who endured my long absences while I took considerable risks in faraway lands but who always welcomed me home with loving arms. It was she who collected my random thoughts and molded them into a manuscript for this book. My first trip across the sands occurred only a few months after our twin sons were born; I think I must have slept better in sandstorms than she did caring for our young family.

My travels in Arabia would simply not have been possible without the hospitality of the Arab people. Nowhere on earth have I experienced the level of generosity that they extended toward me, a perfect stranger in their world. Whether prince or barefoot Bedouin, the Arabs cared for me in a way that was humbling, to say the least. I've often wondered what would befall a Bedouin wandering down my street in suburban New Jersey in his native garb—I cringe at the probable outcome. Many of my countrymen are surprised that I enjoy traveling in a world that seems hostile to Americans, but in my experience, the guest of any Arab is treated like a brother, only better.

Book design by Marine Gille

For the English-language edition:
Andrea Danese, Editor
Shawn Dahl, Designer
Jules Thomson, Production Manager

All of the photographs in this book are by George Steinmetz, with the exception of the following:

© Bertram Thomas Archives, with the permission of the family: p. 17 (4th photo), p. 18 (1st, 2nd, and 3rd photos), taken from the Bertram Thomas book *Arabia Felix* (1932).
© Alain Arnoux, p. 21 (2nd photo), p. 23 (2nd photo).
© Courtesy of USGS, photograph by Elwood Friesen, p. 17 (2nd photo).
© Department of the Interior United States Geological Survey, Kingdom of Saudi Arabia Ministry of Petroleum and Mineral Resources, Miscellaneous Geologic Investigations Map I-215A, p. 29 (1st photo).
© DigitalGlobe / Terraserver, p. 196, p. 205.
© Glasgow Herald, p. 17 (3rd photo).
© Landsat Images™, Ronald G. Blom and Robert E. Crippen for the Mahra Archaeology Project, pp. 184, 186, 188, 190, 192, 194, 198, 200, 202, 204–205.
© Landsat-7 ETM+NASA 1999–2000. Compiled by Angela C. King / NASA Landsat, p. 183.
© Mark Beech, p. 35 (2nd photo).
© Middle East Centre Archive, St Antony's College, Oxford. Philby Collection: Album 21 RGS 100a p. 18 (4th photo); Album 4 no. 768 p. 19 (1st photo).
© Pitt Rivers Museum, University of Oxford, for the photographs of Wilfred Thesiger: p. 16 (2nd photo PRM 2004.130.17285.1); p. 19 (2nd photo PRM 2004.130.12884.1), (3rd photo PRM 2004.130.25553.1), (4th photo PRM 2004.130.12990.1); p. 20 (1st photo PRM 2004.130.3022.1), (2nd photo PRM 2004.130.17062.1), (3rd photo PRM 2004.130.22188.1), (4th photo PRM2004.130.25545.1) ; p. 34 (4th photo PRM 2004.130.22024.1).
For Michelin map 954, p. 14.: authorization no. 0905736.
© Michelin, 2009. 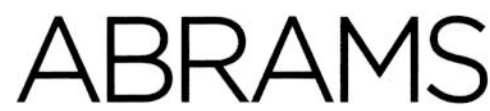

For more information go to www.GeorgeSteinmetz.com

Library of Congress Cataloging-in-Publication Data

Steinmetz, George, 1957–
    Empty Quarter : a photographic journey to the heart of the Arabian desert / by George Steinmetz.
        p. cm.
    ISBN 978-0-8109-8381-6
    1. Rub' al-Khali—Description and travel. 2. Rub' al-Khali—Aerial photography. 3. Landscape photography—Rub' al-Khali. I. Title.
    DS247.R82S74 2009
    915.38--dc22

                              2009019156

Copyright © 2009 Éditions de la Martinière, an imprint of La Martinière Groupe, Paris

English edition © 2009 Abrams, New York
Photographs and text copyright © 2009 George Steinmetz

Published in 2009 by Abrams, an imprint of ABRAMS. All rights reserved. No portion of this book may be reproduced, stored in a retrieval system, or transmitted in any form or by any means, mechanical, electronic, photocopying, recording, or otherwise, without written permission from the publisher.

Printed and bound in Malaysia
10 9 8 7 6 5 4 3 2 1

Abrams books are available at special discounts when purchased in quantity for premiums and promotions as well as fundraising or educational use. Special editions can also be created to specification. For details, contact specialmarkets@abramsbooks.com or the address below.

ABRAMS
THE ART OF BOOKS SINCE 1949

115 West 18th Street
New York, NY 10011
www.abramsbooks.com